Humana Festival '94
The Complete Plays

Humana Inc. is one of the nation's largest
managed health care companies
with more than 1.6 million members in its health care plans.

The Humana Foundation was established in 1981
to support the educational, social, medical and cultural development
of communities in ways that reflect
Humana's commitment to social responsibility
and an improved quality of life.

Humana Festival '94

The Complete Plays

Edited by Marisa Smith

Contemporary Playwrights Series

SK
A Smith and Kraus Book

A Smith and Kraus Book
Published by Smith and Kraus, Inc.

Copyright © 1994 by Smith and Kraus, Inc.
All rights reserved

Manufactured in the United States of America

First Edition: September 1994
10 9 8 7 6 5 4 3 2 1

Library of Congress Cataloguing-in-Publication Data

Humana Festival '94 : the complete plays / edited by Marisa Smith. --1st ed.
    p. cm. -- (Contemporary playwrights series)
    A collection of plays first produced at the Actor's Theatre of Louisville's Humana Festival in the 1994 season.

    Contents: The last time we saw her / Jane Anderson -- Julie Johnson / Wendy Hammond -- Betty the yeti / Jon Klein -- Slavs! / Tony Kushner -- 1969 / Tina Landau -- Shotgun / Romulus Linney -- The survivor / Jon Lipsky -- Stones and bones / Marion McClinton -- My left breast / Susan Miller -- Trip's cinch / Phyllis Nagy.

    ISBN: 1-880399-56-3 : $16.95
    1. American drama--20th century. I. Smith, Marisa. II. Humana Festival '94 (1994 : Louisville, Ky.) III. Actors Theatre of Louisville. IV. Series.

PS634.H86   1994   94-19395
812'.5408--dc20   CIP

Contents

INTRODUCTION *Jon Jory* vii

THE LAST TIME WE SAW HER *Jane Anderson* 1

JULIE JOHNSON *Wendy Hammond* 13

BETTY THE YETI *Jon Klein* 69

SLAVS! THINKING ABOUT THE LONGSTANDING PROBLEMS

OF VIRTUE AND HAPPINESS *Tony Kushner* 131

1969 *Tina Landau* 179

SHOTGUN *Romulus Linney* 221

THE SURVIVOR: A CAMBODIAN ODYSSEY *Jon Lipsky* 243

STONES AND BONES *Marion McClinton* 301

MY LEFT BREAST *Susan Miller* 311

TRIP'S CINCH *Phyllis Nagy* 341

Introduction

Okay, what have we got here?

Well, these plays got selected from a couple of thousand submissions for what has become America's leading New Play Festival, Humana.

Are they any different from plays in the '80s? Sure. Those were compelling, angst-ridden dramas of identity crisis and self-actualization, and these plays deal with self in relationship to larger social units: family, friends, work, society/nation and the planet. They, among other things, have an eye cocked on social consequences. Or, as my mother used to say, "Keep on doing that and you're going to get it!" These are plays about actions and reactions.

What else does the 1994 Humana Festival tell us? The American theatre is currently a stylistic circus. It used to be living rooms and kitchens, remember? It used to be revelations in Act III (whatever happened to Act III?). Now it's a series of time bends, space warps, emblematic objects, dance theatre, psychological gesture, expressionist impulse, lyrical naturalism, and God knows what-all in the service of a redefinition of American style. The implied message is: Get on board, the train's leaving.

These are also plays about loss. The theatre is losing friends and lovers, losing funds, losing audiences, losing Broadway, and what survives and prospers won't look like those other decades. Each play in this volume explores loss for its pain, its humour and its social and human instruction. Landau looks at the loss of youth. Kushner looks at the loss of ideals. Lipsky examines loss of love and country. Miller deals with loss of self-image, Klein with loss of innocence, Hammond with loss of limitations, Linney with loss of a marriage, Nagy with loss of credibility, and Anderson and McClinton with loss of trust. In the midst of this widely defined loss, the playwrights test tactics, spiritual and practical, for going on.

Tolstoy and Kushner ask, "What is to be done?" Everybody here takes a shot at it.

—*Jon Jory*
Producing Director
Actors Theatre of Louisville

Humana Festival '94
The Complete Plays

The Last Time We Saw Her

by Jane Anderson

For Tess, my heart and my courage

THE LAST TIME WE SAW HER was directed by Frazier W. Marsh with the following cast (in order of appearance) :

HUNTER . . . . Fred Major
FRAN . . . . Jennifer Hubbard

Scenic Designer . . . . Paul Owen
Costume Designer . . . . Hollis Jenkins-Evans
Lighting Designer . . . . Matthew Reinert
Sound Designer . . . . Casey L. Warren
Props Master . . . . Mark Bissonnette
Dramaturg . . . . Michael Bigelow Dixon
Casting . . . . Brett Goldstein

Ms. Anderson received an Emmy Award and Writer's Guild Award for her HBO movie, THE POSITIVELY TRUE ADVENTURES OF THE ALLEGED TEXAS CHEERLEADER–MURDERING MOM. Screenplays include the Tri Star release, IT COULD HAPPEN TO YOU.

Ms. Anderson's works have been widely produced off–Broadway and in major theatres around the country, including Long Wharf, the McCarter, Williamstown, Actors Theatre of Louisville, and Pasadena Playhouse. Her plays include: THE BABY DANCE, DEFYING GRAVITY (recipient of a W. Alton Jones grant), HOTEL OUBLIETTE (recipient of the Susan Smith Blackburn Prize), FOOD & SHELTER, THE PINK STUDIO, and SMART CHOICES FOR THE NEW CENTURY. LYNETTE AT 3 AM as well as THE LAST TIME WE SAW HER are both winners of the Heideman Award.

Ms. Anderson is a member of the Dramatists Guild.

Author's Note

In April of 1993 I took part in the Gay March on Washington. After ten years of being together, my spouse, Tess, and I finally learned what it's like to perform the simple act of holding hands in public. On the way back to L.A., we had to take separate planes because the airlines were over booked with marchers. Every person on the plane was gay except for perhaps the pilot, a few of the flight attendants and my seatmate. He was an older businessman, a Catholic and very polite. He wanted to know why people like me felt the need to march at all. And after he had several drinks, he wanted to know if I'd consider going to bed with him. I had the window seat. I couldn't leave. I shut my eyes and wrote a play instead.

—Jane Anderson

FOR CAUTION NOTICE SEE PAGE OPPOSITE TABLE OF CONTENTS.

THE LAST TIME WE SAW HER by Jane Anderson. ©1994 by Jane Anderson. Reprinted by permission of the author. All inquiries should be addressed to Martin Gage, The Gage Group, 9255 Sunset Blvd., #515, Los Angeles, CA 90069.

CHARACTERS

Hunter – an executive in his early 60's

Fran – a manager in her mid 40's

TIME:

Present

LOCATION:

An office, somewhere in Ohio

The Last Time We Saw Her

Lights up. We're in an executive office. Hunter, a well-bred man of logic in his early 60's is talking on the phone. Golf memorabilia and pictures of his family are displayed on a very organized desk. He tends to talk in thoughtful, measured tones.

Seated in front of the desk, waiting to talk to him, is Fran, mid-40's, an attractive woman wearing a tasteful middle-management business ensemble – skirt and jacket, comfortable heels, pearls and matching earrings. She's considered extremely competent and a good performer.

HUNTER: (*On the phone.*) ...uh-huh, well then I think we should have a meeting with management, find out what's going on down there. . . exactly, no I couldn't agree more . . . sooner than later, absolutely . . . all right . . . I appreciate it.

(*Hunter hangs up, makes a long note to himself while Fran stares at her nails. Hunter finally puts his pen down. Fran looks up, ready to talk.*)

Excuse me.

(*Hunter punches his intercom.*)

Nancy could you call Paul Christianson at the Columbus office and tell him we'd like to review his client records back through '86. And as soon as I'm done with this meeting, get Don Lillie on the phone for me. Thank you.

(*Hunter snaps the intercom off, moves his note pad to another part of his desk, and turns to Fran, indicating that she now has his complete attention.*)

Yes, Fran.

FRAN: Well, I'm not going to take up a lot of your time with this – or my time, for that matter, because, to be frank, I have quite a full morning ahead of me, as I'm sure you do and so I'll be very brief about this.

HUNTER: All right.

FRAN: As you know, I've made a long-term commitment to the company and I'd like to contribute as much as I can.

HUNTER: Well, Fran, as a matter of fact we're very happy with your performance and we'll certainly look into extending your opportunities.

FRAN: Oh. Well, thank you. I appreciate that, thank you very much.

HUNTER: So.

(*A beat.*)

Is there a problem?

FRAN: No, I wouldn't consider it a problem. It's just something I would like you to be aware of so I can continue here without spending unnecessary energy on this particular issue. My primary goal, really, is to remove any obstacles to my own efficiency level.

HUNTER: That sounds fine to me.

FRAN: And again, this is not something that needs to take up your time, or be a concern or whatever – but I happen to be gay, for whatever that's worth, and basically I wanted you to be aware of that so that I don't have to be concerned about you finding out from another source.

HUNTER: I see.

(*A beat.*)

Well, I don't have any opinion about this particular issue one way or the other.

FRAN: No, well, that's fine.

HUNTER: It's uh . . . well, in any case these things exist and as I see it, what you do in the privacy of your home is your business and I certainly respect that.

FRAN: Thank you. Normally I wouldn't have brought this to your attention because I believe that, uh, the work is primary, but certain things have become rather problematic for me, and as I said, in order for me to maintain my own efficiency level I'm going to let certain people in the office know about me and I didn't want that information to reach you without my talking to you first.

HUNTER: Well, I appreciate that.

(*A short beat.*)

FRAN: And that's really all I needed to say.

(*Another short beat.*)

HUNTER: Can I ask you why you feel you need to discuss this in your office?

FRAN: Well, it's the whole effort of secrecy that's becoming rather burdensome.

HUNTER: I see.

FRAN: For instance, my secretary who handles all of my personal calls – she's been talking to my companion, to Judith, for six years now, and she still thinks that Judith is my roommate. Frankly, I'm too old to have roommates.

HUNTER: Maybe you could tell your secretary that Judith is not your roommate but just a very good friend.

FRAN: But my secretary already knows that Judith lives with me . . .

HUNTER: Oh, I see, yes, that would still make her suspect.

FRAN: I think the whole point is that my secretary has probably guessed by now who Judith is and there's no point in lying about our relationship.

HUNTER: Then if you feel she knows, then why is there a need to discuss it with her?

FRAN: Because there's a certain discomfort when things are left unsaid, you see, it's like – well for instance, what if you couldn't tell your secretary that your wife was your wife. What if you had to make some story that, uh, your wife was your sister who was sharing the house with you until both of you could afford to live on your own?

HUNTER: Uh-huh.

FRAN: And your secretary knew that she was your wife but she treated her like your sister.

HUNTER: Well, in fact when my secretary does speak to my sister she treats her with as much courtesy as she does my wife. I expect her to treat everyone with courtesy.

FRAN: That was a bad example. It's not really about courtesy. My secretary is very polite.

HUNTER: Uh-huh.

FRAN: I just think that we waste a lot of time dancing around the subject.

HUNTER: No, I can understand that.

FRAN: And my relationship with Judith – it's put a very big strain between us. We've been together for eight years now. We own a house together. She's a successful marketing executive. She doesn't appreciate it when my secretary says, "Fran, your roommate is on the line."

HUNTER: Well, again, that's something you can correct with your secretary. You know, my secretary once referred to my wife as "The Mrs." – I don't know why she did that but I found it inappropriate and I told her to please always refer to my wife as either my wife or as Mrs. Hunter. So you might tell your secretary not to refer to Judith as your roommate but as Judith. Or you might even prefer that she only use her last name, which I feel is always more respectful.

FRAN: Yes, but I still think I need to discuss with my secretary who, exactly, Judith is.

HUNTER: Not necessarily, you're simply asking her not to use that particular reference.

FRAN: But you see it goes beyond that. Judith has reached a point where she doesn't want to be treated as something unmentionable any more.

HUNTER: Yes, but that's your personal business. If my wife and I have any kind of argument or personal problem to resolve, I leave it at home. I don't discuss it with my secretary or my partners – or anyone else.

FRAN: No, I absolutely agree with that. Please understand that I'm a very private person—

HUNTER: I think the same thing applies with expressing affection in public. For instance, my youngest daughter and her boyfriend are physically very expressive with each other and there are times when I find it inappropriate. I believe in discretion no matter what particular bent you are.

FRAN: I'm not disagreeing . . .

HUNTER: You know what it is, Fran? I think that people are losing their manners. And I mean that in a larger sense. For instance in business, it used to be, if there was a dispute, there was a protocol for sitting down and talking things over. But now, people just pick up the phone – and I'm not a prude, but when someone uses foul language with me it just puts me in the wrong frame of mind.

FRAN: Uh-huh.

HUNTER: And here's another example: my oldest daughter, Melissa, works for a law firm downtown. And at lunchtime she goes to a certain coffee shop and there are some individuals who work behind the counter who are consistently rude to her. Not just rude, mind you, but outright abusive, turning their backs on her when she tries to talk to them, giving her evil looks – and by the way my daughter is one of the nicest gals you could ever meet. Melissa calls me in tears and says, "Dad, I just don't understand it." And frankly, neither do I. These particular individuals happen to be black and I don't mean to sound prejudiced, in fact I've hired a lot of black individuals and some of them were very fine people – but I've noticed a general hostility coming from that particular group that's very disturbing. I want to sit down and say to them, "Look, if you really want things to change, then you're going to have to learn some manners." That kind of behavior is just plain counterproductive. Is that being racist?

FRAN: Uh, well . . .

HUNTER: Or maybe it's just being old-fashioned. I don't know. The world is going too fast for me. I wish my daughter could have grown up in a gentler time. There's no reason that she should have to fear for her life when she goes to lunch, absolutely no reason.

FRAN: (*Trying to be polite.*) No, I can understand that.

HUNTER: But my hunch is that it's perhaps different with the gays – that is the term you like to use?

FRAN: (*A beat.*) Yes.

HUNTER: I think that, as a whole, the gays are probably better educated and I'd say, quieter, more polite than the other groups. There's a young man who works over in accounting who's questionable, but he's sharp as a tack and works harder than anyone else over there. It'd be foolish for me to fire him. It'd just be plain bad business.

FRAN: Well. Yes it would.

HUNTER: (*A beat.*) So as we stand, you will be talking to your secretary and I assume this will be confidential?

FRAN: No, actually I was planning on telling everyone in my division.

HUNTER: I see. May I ask why?

FRAN: Well, because it will make things more comfortable.

HUNTER: For you or for them?

FRAN: For everyone, I hope.

HUNTER: Let me make a suggestion . . . let's recap the situation. You've been here for how long, six years?

FRAN: Yes.

HUNTER: And you're respected, well-liked, your division is extremely productive – so from a professional standpoint would you say that everything is working as it should?

FRAN: Fairly well, yes.

HUNTER: Well, not fairly well, Fran, I'd even say that your department is excelling.

FRAN: Oh, well, thank you.

HUNTER: So, if we were really to examine this situation, you'd have to say that whatever problem you're having is of a personal, not a professional, nature.

FRAN: But this does affect my professional relationships.

HUNTER: Ah, but now you're saying that you have a personal problem that may have a negative affect on those who you work with

FRAN: No, that's not what I'm saying.

HUNTER: Here's another example. We had a manager in a division over in Dayton who had an alcohol problem. It wasn't an overwhelming problem, he was never drunk when he came to work but his drinking habits were, in fact, affecting his home life. So finally, very quietly, he took two weeks off, got himself in to a program, and when he came back no one was the wiser. You see. It was no one's business that he had an alcohol problem, in fact, it would have undermined his authority if anyone knew. Do you see what I'm saying?

FRAN: I don't think this is really the same thing.

HUNTER: This is what I don't quite understand. Being that your situation is related to your sexual behavior, why would you think it appropriate to display that in the work place?

FRAN: I wouldn't be displaying any behavior—

HUNTER: It's not even appropriate for normal people to display their sexual feelings in the work place.

FRAN: I didn't say it was appropriate, that's not what I would do.

HUNTER: Then what, exactly, is it that you would want to do?

FRAN: I simply want to let people in my office know that I'm in a relationship with a woman and that for me it's a very normal part of my life.

HUNTER: And how exactly will that improve their work performance?
(*A beat.*)
Do you see what I'm saying now?

FRAN: Yes, but that wasn't my original point.

HUNTER: Yes, I believe that you said that you were concerned with maintaining the efficiency level in your department. Isn't that what you said?

FRAN: I don't think you understand my situation, Mr. Hunter. I eat lunch alone every day because I'm terrified that people will ask about my personal life. I sit with a sandwich and a Cup O' Soup at my desk reading old copies of Computer News. People think I'm strange. I'm beginning to think I'm strange. I don't show up to office parties. I don't show up to picnics. I don't have drinks with our clients. When I go away for a conference, after the seminars I go straight to my room and order room service. I don't have a personality any more. I have nothing to bring home to Judith. We eat dinner in silence. The only conversation is directed to the cat. This is not my idea of a life.

HUNTER: (*A beat.*) Fran, have you ever seen a play called *The Rainmaker*?

FRAN: Excuse me?

HUNTER: *The Rainmaker*, the movie had, ah, Burt Lancaster. Have you ever seen it? You know that scene when Lizzie says to Starbuck that she's always thought that she was plain? And Starbuck says, "Lizzie, that's all nonsense, it's all in your head. You can be the most beautiful woman in the world if you believe it." Remember that scene?

FRAN: I'm not sure what you're getting at.

HUNTER: Let me ask you, was there ever a time when you were attracted to men?

FRAN: Excuse me?

HUNTER: There was never a time when you were in love with a man or had a crush on some fellow?

FRAN: No, Mr. Hunter.

HUNTER: And perhaps you were disappointed or hurt?

FRAN: No, nothing like that ever occurred.

HUNTER: Have you sought counseling on this issue?

FRAN: I've been to a psychiatrist, if that's what you're asking.

HUNTER: (*Somewhat concerned.*) Oh, you have.

FRAN: But it was for a very brief period of time. I only went twice.

HUNTER: Uh-huh. And did you discuss the possibility of having sexual feelings towards men?

FRAN: Yes I did. And there didn't seem to be any feelings to discuss.

HUNTER: So if a man in your office, for instance, said, "Fran, I find you very attractive. Can I take you out to dinner," you wouldn't accept?

FRAN: Why would I do that? I live with Judith.

HUNTER: But what I don't quite understand is that, well, when a man and a woman are together, as opposed to a woman and a woman or a man and a man, the design of the male and female body is made in such a way that it's physically pleasurable for those of the opposite sex to be together. In other words, is the experience that you have, satisfying?

FRAN: Mr. Hunter, if you're asking me how I do it, it's none of your business.

HUNTER: But don't you think, Fran, that everyone in your office will be wondering the same thing?

FRAN: As I said, it's no one's business.

HUNTER: Bingo. And that's why you don't need to tell anyone.

FRAN: Mr. Hunter, I'm about to lose my life's companion. I swear to God, she's going to leave me.

HUNTER: Are you attracted to your secretary?

FRAN: Excuse me?

HUNTER: I'm wondering if you ever look at your secretary in a romantic way. It's a natural reaction. I certainly look at mine from time to time, not that I'd ever do anything about it. I've been married to my wife for twenty-six years and I've always been faithful to her. But it's a normal and healthy thing for a man to look at other women. I was just curious to know if you have the same impulse.

FRAN: Absolutely not.

HUNTER: Ah. Well, there you go. Perhaps you aren't attracted to women after all.

FRAN: She's not my type, Mr. Hunter.
(*Getting up.*)
I don't think we need to take any more time with this. Thank you for seeing me.

HUNTER: I'm sorry this has been such a problem for you, Fran. I wish we could find a solution to this. I'll put my thinking cap on it.
(*Fran ignores this, just wants to get out. Hunter takes Fran's hand and holds it in a fatherly fashion.*)
Believe in yourself, Franny. Don't be afraid to dream.

FRAN: (*To herself.*) Oh, Christ.
  (*Hunter, embarrassed, pats Fran's hand, lets it go.*)
HUNTER: In any case . . .
  (*He turns back to his desk, moves some of the items around.*)
  I'm glad you came in, Fran . . .
FRAN: God help your wife, God help your children, God help everyone you ever come in contact with.
  (*Fran leaves.*

  Hunter looks after her, smooths his tie to his chest. He frowns, rearranges the pictures of his family. His intercom buzzes. Hunter sits down in his chair, doesn't answer it. The intercom buzzes again. Hunter finally punches it.)
HUNTER: Nancy, I'm not ready for that call yet.
  (*Hunter stares out, slowly swivels in his chair from side to side, still deeply perplexed. Fade out.*)

END.

Julie Johnson

by Wendy Hammond

For Lily, Carolyn, Craig, Jennifer, Wilder and especially Jon.

JULIE JOHNSON was directed by Jon Jory with the following cast (in order of appearance) :

JULIE . . . . Lily Knight
LISA . . . . Jennifer Carpenter
FRANK . . . . Wilder Schwartz
CLAIRE . . . . Carolyn Swift
MR. MIRANDA . . . . V Craig Heidenreich

WENDY HAMMOND is making her ATL debut with JULIE JOHNSON. Her other plays include: JERSEY CITY, THE GHOSTMAN, and FAMILY LIFE: 3 BRUTAL COMEDIES produced at Second Stage Theatre, Long Wharf Theatre, Soho Repertory and HOME for Contemporary Theatre and Art, as well as in theatres in London and Germany. She regularly performs her one-woman show, WENDY IN THE WACKO WARD. Currently, she is working on a new play MORMONS IN MALIBU. This year, Hammond was chosen as one of the Chesterfield Film Project writers. She holds an MFA from New York University's Dramatic Writing Program and has taught playwriting courses at several universities, the Sewanee Writers Conference, and in the prison ward of Bellevue Hospital. Hammond is the recipient of an NEA grant, a New York Foundation Arts Grant, a McKnight Fellowship, and a Drama League Award. She has twice been invited to Sundance Institute and is a member of New Dramatists.

Author's Note

People ask me all the time, "Did you write JULIE JOHNSON because you're gay?"

The first time someone asked me this I was on a panel introducing the Humana plays to the staff of ATL. A young man with a pony tail waved his hand at me. "Is your play anti-male and are you gay?"

"I don't mean my play to be anti-male at all, "I said, "and I'm...." I couldn't go on. I looked out at all those unfamiliar faces and I could not announce to them the way I make love. "I don't wanna answer," I mumbled, then took the next question.

Later, I called my friend Max. "You tell people you're gay," I said. "Don't you feel violated, trotting out in public something as private as your sexual preference?"

"Of course I feel violated," he said. "But how else are gays going to gain acceptance?"

"So the politics of this is so important to you, you sacrifice your privacy."

"Yes," he said.

Pretty soon people began to take for granted I was gay. An actor in another play said to me, "You're beautiful and sexy, and you're GAY!" I didn't know how to respond. Back in Los Angeles I had meetings with executives who had read or seen JULIE. Subtly, in the way they put words together was the assumption that I was gay. They treated me as an alien, special. They seemed proud of themselves for asking me to their offices. Sometimes the women flirted with me and then talked about their husbands.

I called Max again. "I'm in a rotten mood," he said. "It's my kids." Max is a brilliant teacher of at-risk teenagers in New Haven, CT. "One of my kids wrote a play about a gay boy dying of AIDS, but he won't put his name on it. And none of the guys will act in it. They won't be in a fag play. I want to tell them I'm a fag, break some of this up, but I don't want to lose my job." Max's name isn't really Max, and he doesn't really work in New Haven, CT. I don't want him to lose his job either.

A confession. I didn't write JULIE JOHNSON because I'm gay. Perhaps the play is partly a response to my own Mormon background, a religion and culture of breathtaking beauty and warmth. Most Mormons live simply, full of love for God, for their families, and for their fellow human beings. Their faith is astounding. Every moment of their lives is about God. Every breath they take is for His Church.

Which makes it difficult for Mormons who are pro-choice, or want to pray to God the Mother, or have any opinion which is not authorized by the Church Authorities, or are gay, because all of this is apostasy. In 1979, Sonia Johnson was excommunicated for calling herself the president of Mormons for the Equal Rights Amendment. This year several women and men were excommunicated for reasons such as attending a pro-choice rally, publishing articles about unofficial Mormon history, and publicly admonishing Church Officials to "choose love not power." All of the people excommunicated are devout believers. Losing their Church is worse than if their arms and legs had been torn off.

At a writers' conference recently, I met a BYU professor, a Mormon woman who was in danger of losing her job and getting excommunicated because she wanted to pray to God the Mother. She trembled as she spoke. She blinked often and hard. Others who heard her story wondered why she didn't just stop being a Mormon. They didn't understand. Like the game of tug of war we played when I was a kid, this woman was being pulled like crazy from opposite directions. She couldn't stop being a Mormon any more than she could turn herself into a tree.

Last week I got a brochure in the mail advertising the services of a Mormon psychologist. Therapy by a Mormon for Mormons. Also, groups for adults who were sexually abused as children. Wow, I thought. I remember when Mormons didn't believe in psychologists. I turned the brochure over. Also, he offered group and individual counseling to reorient people to heterosexuality.

Can a person give up being gay to stay Mormon? Can a person give up being Mormon to be gay?

I didn't write JULIE JOHNSON because I'm gay. I wrote it because I needed to write about someone who isn't living truthfully, who begins to live truthfully, and how wonderful and terrible that is. Terrible because sometimes change means giving up one's whole world, everything one holds dear. But wonderful too because living authentically, is, well, wonderful.

—*Wendy Hammond*

CHARACTERS

Julie Johnson – 33, Hoboken accent

Lisa Johnson – 13, Hoboken accent

Frankie Johnson – 14, Hoboken accent

Claire, 33 – Hoboken accent

Mr. Miranda – older than Julie

SET:

Expressionist. Parts of rooms, as if a spotlight suddenly illuminated
one tiny piece of life.

– A middle-class living room.
– A teacher's desk.
– A screen on which slides are projected.
– A park bench.

TIME:

The Present

PLACE:

Hoboken, New Jersey, 4th and Monroe

Julie Johnson

ACT ONE

SCENE 1

Music – longing, yearning. Lights up low on a Hoboken living room.
Julie (33) is crouched between a chair and the couch. She clutches a pink piece of paper. She is crying.
Lights fade.
Lights up. Julie is still crouched on the floor, still crying, still clutching the paper. Lisa (13) and Frank (14) stand at the open front door. They hold school books.

FRANK: Mom?
> (*She doesn't answer.*)
> Mom, are you hurt?
> (*She doesn't answer.*)
> Why doesn't she answer?

LISA: I don't know.

FRANK: Look.

LISA: What?

FRANK: She's got something in her hands.

LISA: What is it?

FRANK: Beats me.

LISA: What's that in your hands, Mom?
> (*Julie doesn't answer.*)

FRANK: Maybe it says something. Maybe that's why she's crying.
> (*A beat.*)
> Maybe you should go see what it is.

LISA: You do it. You're the oldest.

FRANK: I think the youngest should do it.

LISA: No!

FRANK: Geez.
> (*Very tentatively Frank crouches down by Julie, but when he*

attempts to take the pink paper out of her hand she pulls away.)
Shit.

LISA: Mom, you need some Kleenex.

> *(Gets a box off a shelf.)*

FRANK: Mom? Did something bad happen?

LISA: I'm getting you some Kleenex.

FRANK: What happened, Mom?

LISA: Here we go. A whole box.

> *(Sets the box in front of Julie.)*

FRANK: Tell us what happened, OK? OK?

> *(They wait. Julie doesn't respond.)*

LISA: She's not taking the Kleenex.

> *(A beat.)*
>
> Why isn't she taking a Kleenex?
>
> *(A beat.)*
>
> Mom, your nose is dripping all over your shirt. You gotta take a Kleenex!
>
> *(Music. Lights fade.*
>
> *Lights up. Julie is still crouched on the floor, still crying, still clutching the paper. There are now several crumpled Kleenex on the floor around her. Claire kneels some distance away. Frank and Lisa stand behind Claire. Frank clutches a glass of water.*
>
> *Claire is a big woman Julie's age. She wears a lot of makeup, tight clothes and tall, sprayed hair.)*

CLAIRE: Julie?

LISA: She won't talk. I told you.

CLAIRE: I'm just trying it. Hey Jule, it's me.

LISA: She not gonna talk!

CLAIRE: I just wanna try it.

LISA: But WE tried it for like half an hour!

CLAIRE: Then I wanna try it again! Julie, Lisa came over. She says there's something wrong with you. What's wrong with you, Julie? . . . Honey? . . .

LISA: I told you.

CLAIRE: Is it Rick? Did ya have a fight with Rick?

LISA: Didn't I tell you?

CLAIRE: Are ya hurt?

LISA: She doesn't talk!

CLAIRE: Lisa?

LISA: What?

CLAIRE: I think you gotta go to your room, OK? I think you gotta leave us alone for a minute, OK? . . . OK?!

LISA: OK. Frankie, come on.

(*Reluctantly, Frank hands Claire the glass of water and follows Lisa off.*)

CLAIRE: So, Jule. How's things?

(*Julie doesn't respond.*)

Not so good, huh?

(*Julie doesn't respond.*)

Can ya hear me, Julie?

(*Julie doesn't respond.*)

If you can hear me, do something, OK? Wiggle your toes, something, 'cause I at least gotta know if you can hear me.

(*Slowly, Julie nods.*)

Does that mean you can hear me?

(*Julie nods.*)

Great! We're getting somewhere! We got communication! OK. Are ya hurt, Julie?

(*Julie shakes her head no.*)

Didja fall or something?

(*Julie shakes her head no.*)

Are ya sick?

(*Julie shakes her head no.*)

Watcha got in your hands?

(*Julie doesn't answer.*)

Is that the problem? What you got in your hands?

(*Julie doesn't answer.*)

Come on, Julie. We were on a roll.

JULIE: (*Barely audible*) I . . .

CLAIRE: What's this! She talks! The woman is speaking!

JULIE: (*Softly.*) I don't wanna . . .

CLAIRE: What? You don't wanna what?

JULIE: I don't wanna be stupid no more.

(*A beat.*)

CLAIRE: Julie. Like I think you should know. You're not stupid.

JULIE: Yeah I am.

CLAIRE: You're raising two kids, Julie. You can't be that stupid.

JULIE: Yeah ya can.

CLAIRE: Hm. Let's get ya up on the couch. It'll be easier to talk on the couch.

JULIE: I wanna stay here.

CLAIRE: OK. OK. Fine with me.

(*She sits in the chair next to Julie.*)

This is fine, talking like this. I like it fine. So why do ya think you're stupid?

JULIE: Because.

CLAIRE: What?

JULIE: A lotta things.

CLAIRE: Like what?

JULIE: Like . . . A lotta things.

CLAIRE: Tell me.

JULIE: A lotta things, OK? I mean . . . Like you just gotta take my word for it. I'm stupid, OK? I think I wanna . . . get up now. Will ya . . . help me up?

CLAIRE: (*Helping her.*) Sure. Lean on me. That's it.

JULIE: My legs are asleep.

CLAIRE: There we go.

(*Julie is on the couch now.*)

You want some water? Frankie got you a glass of water.

(*Claire hands her a glass of water. Julie downs half of it hungrily.*)

I'm gonna fix your face, OK Jule? You got makeup all over.

(*Using Kleenex dipped in water, Claire gently washes Julie's face clean.*)

This is definitely better. We are definitely getting somewhere.

(*Claire pats Julie's face dry with a dry Kleenex.*)

Hey, How 'bout we go see a movie tonight. Just you and me. Get ya outa the house for awhile. Give ya perspective. Maybe all ya need is a little perspective. Hellbound Two is playing at the Hoboken Cinema.

(*Julie shakes her head no.*)

Then come over later and we'll watch The Simpsons together.

(*Julie shakes her head no.*)

Come on, Jule. I mean I could use the company. I mean maybe my day's been pretty fucked up too.

JULIE: I . . .

CLAIRE: What?

JULIE: I got . . . something to tell . . . you about.

CLAIRE: OK. What?

JULIE: I hope you don't . . . think it's . . . weird.

CLAIRE: What?

    (*Julie unfolds the pink paper in her hands and hands it to Claire.*)
    What's this?

JULIE: Something I sent for.

CLAIRE: (*Reading it.*) Adult education. Hoboken High. Classes in
    English, aerobics –

JULIE: That one. The one I underlined.

CLAIRE: Introduction to computers?

JULIE: You wanna go?

CLAIRE: To THIS?

JULIE: Yeah.

CLAIRE: COMPUTER class?

JULIE: You don't even need . . . a high school diploma . . . I called up
    . . . the teacher. He said you don't even need . . . a high school
    diploma.

CLAIRE: Julie. I mean didn't you get the lowest grades of the whole
    tenth grade? I mean like school was never your thing, you know?

JULIE: This isn't . . . LIKE school. It's . . . COMPUTERS. How do you
    think . . . that rocket ship . . . Magellen . . . how do you think it
    got to Mars? And cartoons? People draw them on . . . computers
    and it's the . . . COMPUTER that makes them move.

CLAIRE: Julie. Like where did you learn that stuff?

JULIE: I been watching . . . TV . . . all day sometimes . . . Channel . . .
    13 . . . nature programs . . . beginning physics . . .

CLAIRE: Jesus.

JULIE: I been reading . . .

    (*Gets up and reaches under the couch*)
    magazines too.

    (*She pulls a stack of magazines from under the couch and plops it
    down on the coffee table.*)

CLAIRE: Christ.

JULIE: *Omni. Discovery.* You know. Science ones.

    (*She pulls another stack of magazines from under the couch.*)
    Every time I go to the . . . grocery store I buy one . . . or two . . .
    sometimes three.

    (*She pulls another stack from under the couch.*)

CLAIRE: Jesus Christ!

JULIE: I try to figure out what the . . . articles are saying. I really . . . TRY.

CLAIRE: I mean how long have you been buying these magazines?

JULIE: Couple a . . . years. Maybe . . . more.

CLAIRE: And ya never told me?

JULIE: I was . . . scared you'd think it was . . . weird.

CLAIRE: Well it is weird.

JULIE: See?

CLAIRE: I mean really weird.

JULIE: See?

CLAIRE: But still you shoulda told me. I mean Jesus Christ!

JULIE: Yeah.

CLAIRE: I mean I see you every fucking day of my life. I mean Jesus fucking Christ!

JULIE: Yeah.

CLAIRE: Like I'm afraid to ask what ELSE have you been hiding?!

(Julie pulls another stack of magazines from under the couch and plops it on the coffee table. She then goes to a cabinet and opens it. The cabinet is full of magazines. She goes into a closet and pulls out three orange crates of magazines.)

CLAIRE: More – science ones?

JULIE: Yeah.

CLAIRE: Jesus Christ.

JULIE: (*Nods.*) I try to . . . understand all kinds . . . of things but . . . well . . . But maybe if I had a teacher to . . . explain it to me.

CLAIRE: I feel I don't know you no more. My own best friend I haven't really known.

JULIE: I shoulda . . . told you.

CLAIRE: Yeah you shoulda. I mean Jesus Christ!

JULIE: Yeah.

(Silence. They regard the magazines.)

If . . . ya don't like it ya don't have to go . . . back.

CLAIRE: Where?

JULIE: The . . . class. You could even leave before the . . . end . . . if you don't like it.

CLAIRE: You really want me to do this?

JULIE: I really . . . want you to. Really. I mean really . . . REALLY.

CLAIRE: Jesus. I mean it's weird but . . . So when does it start?

JULIE: Monday 5 o'clock.

CLAIRE: So I'll come over Monday and we'll walk together.

JULIE: No, ah. I mean . . .

CLAIRE: What?

JULIE: Well. I didn't mean I was going. I mean . . . I'm not going.

CLAIRE: Then why'd you want me to?

JULIE: I thought you'd be . . . interested.

CLAIRE: And you're not?

JULIE: I can't, OK? I mean I don't know why I wanna do it so bad but I can't so what's the use even thinking about it.

CLAIRE: Oh, I get it.

JULIE: Yeah.

CLAIRE: I mean am I right? Do I get this?

JULIE: You . . . get it.

CLAIRE: But you know I don't like it. I mean I know you know I don't like it. Like you're not even gonna try with him?

JULIE: 'Course I'm gonna try.

CLAIRE: 'Cause sometimes you don't.

JULIE: I'm gonna try!

CLAIRE: 'Cause sometimes you don't even try.

JULIE: I'm gonna . . . *try* with him! OK? I'm gonna try harder than I ever tried . . . ANYthing before! OK?! OK?!!

CLAIRE: (*Her eye catches something out the window.*) Shit. He's home.

JULIE: Oh!

> (*Julie jumps to the front door and chain locks it. Then they both shove the magazines under the couch and back into the closet as fast as they can.*
>
> *The front door starts to open and gets stopped by the chain.*)

RICK'S VOICE: (*From off.*) Julie? What the fuck!

> (*The women are still flying around putting away magazines.*)

JULIE: (*Calling.*) Just a . . . minute!

> (*The door jangles against the chain.*)

RICK'S VOICE: (*From off.*) Julie? What the FUCK!

JULIE: Just a minute!

> (*At last the women are finished.*)

CLAIRE: (*Mouthing.*) I'm goin' out the back.

> (*Julie nods. Claire heads for the kitchen, then turns back to Julie.*)
> You're really gonna try?

JULIE: I'm not just gonna . . . try. OK? I'm gonna . . . DO it. OK?

> (*Claire gives a thumbs up sign then exits out through the kitchen.*

We hear the back door open and shut. Rick bangs furiously on the front door.)

RICK'S VOICE: (*From off.*) What the fuck, Julie? What the FUCK!

(Julie holds onto her pink flyer. She walks slowly to the front door and reaches up to the chain. BLACKOUT.)

SCENE 2

Spot up on Mr. Miranda who sits on top of his desk. He holds onto a slide projector control mechanism.

MR. MIRANDA: Once upon a time, when computers were young and huge as dinosaurs,

(He presses the slide projector control button. ON A SCREEN appears a cartoon line drawing of a computer that looks kind of like a dinosaur.)

there lived a man named Lorenz.

(ON THE SCREEN, a cartoon line drawing of a scientist.)

He was a scientist, a meteorologist at MIT, and he believed that computers were going to make the weather PREDICTABLE.

(ON THE SCREEN, the graphic for the Channel 4 five-day weather forecast.)

Not like those five day stab in the dark forecasts on the six o'clock news that say it's going to be sunny and warm tomorrow

(ON THE SCREEN, a snowstorm.)

and then there's a snowstorm. Lorenz meant really predictable. You, in the back row. Far right corner.

CLAIRE: (*From off.*) Me?

MR. MIRANDA: Your name, please?

CLAIRE: (*From off.*) Claire.

MR. MIRANDA: We're about to have a break, Claire. I hope you consider staying awake until then.

CLAIRE: I was listening. I was just resting my eyes.

MR. MIRANDA: Good.

(ON THE SCREEN, a cartoon line drawing of a weather machine.)

So Lorenz built a weather machine – a glassed in environment with a barometer that went up and down and winds that changed from north to south – and he hooked it up to a computer.

(*ON THE SCREEN, the weather machine hooked up to a computer.*)

But what he learned from his weather machine was this. Weather will never be predictable. It is chaotic. Tiny things change everything. A small tap on the glass of Lorenz's weather machine could – but not always – affect the air pressure just enough to affect the barometer just enough to change the direction of the wind which would bring in a storm.

(*ON THE SCREEN, rain.*)

In other words, if you go outside tonight and blow

(*Mr. Miranda blows.*)

there is a tiny, infinitesimal possibility that you could create

(*ON THE SCREEN, a tornado.*)

a tornado

(*ON THE SCREEN, the roof off a house.*)

that could tear your roof off and your life would be altered forever. Next time you go outside, blow

(*ON THE SCREEN, Mr. Miranda blowing.*)

and think about tiny things that change everything.

(*BLACKOUT.*)

SCENE 3

Lights up on a ball. Julie and Claire enter. Claire takes out a cigarette.

JULIE: So? Did you like it?
CLAIRE: I liked it.
JULIE: I loved it.
CLAIRE: Mr. Miranda's great.
JULIE: The history of the computer.
CLAIRE: The ones and zeros.
JULIE: Nobody else got the ones and zeros.
CLAIRE: Come on. You got it.
JULIE: Like . . . a half hour after you.
CLAIRE: But that Lorie – whatever. You got that Lorie whatever.
JULIE: Lorenz attractor?
CLAIRE: Nobody else got that even a little.

JULIE: It was . . . beautiful, you know? Red, purple, green.

CLAIRE: (*Lights her cigarette.*) Let's get outa here.

JULIE: I'm . . . gonna stay . . . a minute.

CLAIRE: Don't you gotta get home?

JULIE: I wanna . . . say something . . . to Mr. Miranda when he comes out.

CLAIRE: What?

JULIE: Ah . . . something.

> (*Claire shrugs. Julie takes a cigarette from Claire's pack and lights it.*)
>
> Don't tell . . . Mike about . . . the class, OK?

CLAIRE: I already told him.

JULIE: Then tell him not to . . . tell Rick!

CLAIRE: I thought you told Rick. I thought Rick said yes!

> (*Julie shakes her head no.*)
>
> You came anyway?
>
> (*Julie nods.*)
>
> At what point did he give you that bruise?

JULIE: What bruise?

CLAIRE: The one with an inch of makeup on top.

JULIE: Just . . . make sure you tell Mike not to tell Rick . . . as soon as you get home.

CLAIRE: Mike's not gonna be home when I get home.

JULIE: AGAIN?

> (*Claire nods yes.*)
>
> Claire!

CLAIRE: (*Takes out her makeup.*) Maybe we're just going through a rough period, you know? Every couple goes through rough periods.

JULIE: Yeah.

CLAIRE: (*Puts on more lipstick.*) Except that ours started the day we were married and has gotten worse ever since.

JULIE: (*Laughing.*) Claire!

CLAIRE: Maybe it's better Mike's never home nomore. I mean what did he do when he was home? Watch TV? Lie on the couch like a beached whale? He laughs at something and his big stomach starts jiggling so bad I think I'm in an earthquake.

JULIE: Rick watches TV a lot too.

CLAIRE: But does he eat pink popcorn? Remember how Mike used to eat those big huge bags of pink candy popcorn?

JULIE: But Rick drinks . . . whiskey . . . like a bottle every . . . other night.

CLAIRE: But Mike SNORES in front of the tube.

JULIE: Rick clicks . . . his teeth. Clicking teeth is worse.

CLAIRE: Not the way Mike snores. It sounds like a train is coming, his mouth wide open, little bits of pink popcorn flying out.

JULIE: Rick has dandruff.

CLAIRE: Mike gets pimples on his ass.

JULIE: Rick forgets to brush his teeth.

CLAIRE: Mike smells like a locker room.

JULIE: Rick smells good. He wears Brut.

CLAIRE: I like Brut.

JULIE: But he yells a lot.

CLAIRE: Mike doesn't talk.

JULIE: He doesn't like me doing nothing.

CLAIRE: Marry me are the only two words I ever remember him saying.

JULIE: Can I do this? No. Can I do that? No.

CLAIRE: He didn't even say I do. He just grunted.

(*Mr. Miranda enters.*)

MR. MIRANDA: Hello, Claire.

JULIE: (*Bursting.*) Mr. Miranda, your class . . . I mean, like, I *loved* it.

CLAIRE: This is Julie. We're friends.

JULIE: Like I never loved *nothin'* like I love your class.

MR. MIRANDA: Thank you, Julie. Thank you very much.

(*He tries to exit but Julie is in the way, gawking at him. He gives a nervous laugh. She then realizes what she's doing, gives a nervous laugh and gets out of the way. She watches him go, dreamy-eyed.*)

CLAIRE: THAT's the something you wanted to say?

JULIE: (*Still looking after him.*) Claire? Would you ever leave him?

CLAIRE: Mr. Miranda? Never.

JULIE: Would you ever leave Mike?

CLAIRE: I don't know . . . You know I exaggerate about Mike. It's the way I express humor.

JULIE: Yeah.

CLAIRE: I mean I wanna have kids. Mike and me, we're gonna have kids when things are better between us . . . Would you ever leave Rick?

JULIE: Are you kidding? I mean . . . you gotta be kidding!

(*BLACKOUT.*)

SCENE 4

Music – disjointed, violent. Music cuts off abruptly as lights snap on the living room. Julie is heaving Rick's things out the window. The kids are hysterical. Rick is outside screaming up to the window.

RICK: (*From outside.*) YOU GOTTA LESSON TO LEARN, JULIE! YOU GOT A MAJOR LESSON TO LEARN! I'M GONNA TEACH YOU A LESSON, BABY! I'M GONNA TEACH YOU A MAJOR FUCKING LESSON!

LISA: (*Trying to stop Julie.*) STOP IT! STOP DOING THAT! STOP DOING THAT! YOU'RE CRAZY! YOU'RE FUCKING OUTA YOUR MIND! YOU'RE A LUNATIC! STOP IT! STOP DOING THAT! YOU'RE A FUCKING LUNATIC! I GOT A FUCKING LUNATIC FOR A MOTHER!

FRANK: (*To Lisa.*) LEAVE HER ALONE! IT'S BETTER THIS WAY! LEAVE HER ALONE! IT'S BETTER THIS WAY! SHUT UP! SHUT UP!
(*Suddenly all shouting stops. Frank and Lisa watch out the window as Rick drives off.*)

LISA: I can't believe you did that. I can't believe you did that!
(*Lisa runs off in tears.*)

FRANK: It's better this way, right Mom?
(*Julie doesn't know what to answer. Frank's lip starts to quiver and he runs off too. Julie looks around the living room. Furniture has been turned over. A glass whiskey bottle lies in pieces on the floor. Julie rights the chair and lamp. She goes off to the kitchen and returns with a broom. Suddenly the front door opens. Julie shudders deeply.*)

CLAIRE: Just me.

JULIE: Oh.
(*Julie goes to the front door, puts on the chain lock, then goes back to sweeping. Claire watches, baffled.*)

CLAIRE: I heard something. The whole neighborhood heard shouting.

JULIE: Yeah.

CLAIRE: There's stuff piled under your window.

JULIE: Yeah.

CLAIRE: You OK?

JULIE: Yeah.

CLAIRE: The kids OK?

JULIE: Yeah.

(*Claire watches Julie a moment.*)

CLAIRE: It's just, you don't seem like, you know, *yourself.*

JULIE: I'm myself.

(*Clothes start flying in from off. Julie doesn't seem to notice.*)

CLAIRE: Why are these clothes flying in?

(*Julie keeps sweeping. Claire picks up a piece of clothing and sees it's an Ice T sweatshirt.*)

Lisa.

(*Calling off.*)

What are you doing, Lisa?

LISA: (*From off.*) What does it look like!

CLAIRE: (*Calling.*) It looks like your clothes flying into the living room. Why are your clothes flying into the living room?

(*A suitcase flies in. Lisa runs on after and starts stuffing clothes into the suitcase. Frank follows Lisa on.*)

JULIE: Lisa?

LISA: I'm gonna go live with Daddy.

JULIE: You . . . *can't.*

LISA: I CAN.

JULIE: You don't know where . . . he went.

LISA: I'll find him.

JULIE: How?

LISA: I'll find him! I wanna live with Daddy!

CLAIRE: Hold it! Hold everything! Let me see if I can figure this out. Daddy doesn't live here no more?

LISA: She kicked him out! She threw all his stuff out the window! Even his boxer shorts!

CLAIRE: Julie?

JULIE: He was . . . hitting on me and hitting on me –

LISA: He didn't *wanna* be hitting on you! You told him about the class!

CLAIRE: You told him about the class?

LISA: He didn't *wanna* be hitting on her!

JULIE: I . . . SNAPPED. I don't know . . . why. I just . . . SNAPPED.

LISA: It's your own fault he was hitting on you!

JULIE: And then I told him . . . what I'm gonna do . . . I told him . . .

how I had been talking to . . . Mr. Miranda after . . . the class . . . and how Mr. Miranda says I could go to another class that will teach me . . . how to pass the G.E.D. which is the same thing . . . as getting a high school diploma . . . and then I could apply to Jersey City State College as a computer science major. And I been . . . thinking about this and . . . thinking about it and now I wanna do it so bad I think my . . . heart's gonna push right outa my . . . chest.

LISA: Then Dad called her a crazy woman. Then she kicked him outa the house!

JULIE: So that's what I'm gonna do. I'm gonna get a high school diploma. And then I'm gonna go to college. I'm gonna be a computer scientist.

(*Julie looks up. Claire is glaring at her.*)

JULIE: Stop . . . looking at me.

(*Claire glares.*)

Stop looking at me!

CLAIRE: Julie. I mean, like you got two kids.

JULIE: Rick will pay for stuff. He's still . . . responsible.

CLAIRE: But what if he doesn't?

JULIE: He . . . has to.

CLAIRE: But what if he doesn't.

JULIE: I'll go to court. You're supposed to go to court.

FRANK: My friend Alicia's Mom's been going to court for three years. Her Dad hasn't paid nothin'.

JULIE: We're not gonna starve, OK? I'll get a job, OK?

CLAIRE: What kind of a job?

JULIE: Something, OK?

CLAIRE: What can you do?

FRANK: You don't know how to do nothing, Mom.

JULIE: Then I'll learn something. We're not . . . gonna starve. I can . . . learn things.

(*Goes to a drawer.*)

In the meantime we can pay for food . . . outa the checking account.

(*Takes out the checkbook, opens it.*)

Lisa?

LISA: (*Bristling.*) What.

JULIE: (*Hands her the checkbook.*) How much money is in here?

LISA: (*Looking.*) You gotta balance it first.

JULIE: You know . . . how to do that?

LISA: 'Course.

JULIE: Teach me.

LISA: *What?*

JULIE: You . . . heard me.

LISA: You don't know how to balance a checkbook?

JULIE: Claire doesn't neither.

(*Lisa looks at Claire who shrugs.*)

LISA: God, you're retarded. You're both retarded! They taught us how in the sixth grade!

JULIE: (*Pleading.*) I don't want . . . none . . . of your mouth, OK? I want you . . . to teach me . . . how to balance this.

LISA: I can't teach you. You're too retarded. Only retarded people don't know how to balance a checkbook!

JULIE: Lisa.

LISA: Only retarded people have two children and no job and no way to get a job and then kick their husbands outa the house! I mean why did you kick Daddy outa the house?! I want him back! I want him back!

(*Lisa runs off to her room.*)

JULIE: Lisa! . . . Lisa come back here!

CLAIRE: Let her be, OK?

JULIE: I can't . . . let her be!

CLAIRE: Let her be.

JULIE: She's gotta . . . BALANCE this! We gotta . . . know how much money we got!

FRANK: Mom?

JULIE: What!

FRANK: I know how to balance a checkbook.

JULIE: Thank God . . . Frankie.

CLAIRE: Thank God!

FRANK: (*Taking the checkbook.*) They taught us how in the fifth grade. It's really easy.

JULIE: Thank . . . God!

FRANK: (*Showing her.*) You add up all these numbers, here, then subtract 'em from here.

CLAIRE: That's it?

FRANK: Yeah.

JULIE: It's really . . . easy.

FRANK: Yeah.

CLAIRE: Thank God.

JULIE: I mean . . . Thank God!

CLAIRE: (*Pointing to the numbers.*) I'll do these ones. You do those.
  (*They get to work. After a moment.*)

FRANK: Mom?

JULIE: Yeah?

FRANK: How are you gonna get a job? Like, you don't know how to
  do nothing!
  (*Julie looks up at Frank. Claire looks at Julie. Lights fade.*)

SCENE 5

*Music – longing, yearning. Lights up low. Julie is sitting. In front of
her is a stack of newspaper clippings and the phone. Julie stares at
the phone. Music plays. Julie keeps staring. After a long time Julie
picks up the phone. Lights fade up full. Music fades out.*

JULIE: (*Trembling.*) Yes. Hello. Ah –
  (*Slams down the phone.*)
  I gotta do it. I gotta. I GOTTA.
  (*She picks up the phone and dials. Into the phone – *)
  The ad . . . in the paper . . . for a cleaning lady. I never done that
  before, but . . . I mean I'm not so bad at dusting. I get all the
  lamps and . . . picture frames . . . but you'll have to be . . .
  patient with my oven cleaning . . . I mean it's not like I won't
  TRY –
  (*They've hung up on her. She jiggles the phone.*)
  Hello? Hello?
  (*She slams the phone down.*)
  Damn.
  (*She reads from another clipping and dials the phone.*)
  Hello? You need . . . a cleaning lady. I'm a cleaning lady. I'm
  very good . . . Julie. Julie – ah. Ah. Julie – ah. What's my last
  name? I mean I know I know . . . my last name. I mean you gotta
  know your own . . . last –
  (*They've hung up on her.*)

Hello?

(*She slams the phone down.*)

Damn damn damn! Johnson. Julie Johnson.

(*Frank bursts through the front door with several pieces of paper.*)

FRANK: Mom! I stood by the path train! Rush hour! All those yuppies rushing off the train. I yelled "Need a cleaning lady! Who needs a cleaning lady!" Five of 'em gave me their numbers! Five yuppies in 40 minutes! You better call 'em right now.

(*Hands her the papers.*)

You call while I make dinner. Peanut butter sandwiches?

JULIE: Spaghetti.

FRANK: We had that last night.

JULIE: (*Reluctantly.*) Peanut butter sandwiches.

FRANK: Cool!

(*Starts off, turns back.*)

Oh Mom. I gotta have those basketball shoes for the practice tomorrow.

JULIE: We'll go shopping at lunch.

FRANK: Cool!

(*He runs off.*)

JULIE: Damn damn damn damn damn damn!

(*She goes to the phone, dials.*)

Mike? Is Claire there? . . . I'm sorry I keep calling but I gotta find her! . . . OK . . . Thanks. Bye.

(*She hangs up as Lisa bursts through the front door.*)

LISA: (*Excited.*) You got 'em, Mom? You got jobs?

JULIE: I'm working on it.

LISA: You said you'd get jobs today!

JULIE: I'm working on it.

LISA: You said by the time I got home you'd have your schedule full of cleaning jobs. You said we'd have money in a couple of days!

JULIE: I'll have jobs by tomorrow, OK? Next week at the latest.

LISA: But what about my science fair project. How can I do my science fair project if I can't buy an ant farm?

(*Julie goes to the shelf, picks up a large jar full of dirt and plunks it down in front of Lisa.*)

JULIE: I found millions of ants in the park.

LISA: Oh Mom.

JULIE: What?

LISA: When you buy a real ant farm it's thin so you can see the ants better and it doesn't look so retarded.

JULIE: We gotta make do, Lisa.

LISA: OK, but it really looks retarded.

JULIE: We gotta make do!

LISA: OK! So now all we gotta buy is some poster board and colored markers.

JULIE: Poster board and colored markers?

LISA: For the charts and stuff.

JULIE: Charts? Why do ya need charts?

LISA: You gotta have charts, Mom. You gotta give people information. You can't just have this retarded jar sitting on a table and call it a science fair project.

JULIE: OK, you'll have . . . charts.

LISA: But how are ya gonna pay for 'em. You don't got any jobs. You don't got any money.

JULIE: I'll get the money.

LISA: How?

JULIE: None of your business!

LISA: You think money grows on trees? Money does not grow on trees. You got to work for money. You gotta earn it.

JULIE: I know you gotta earn it! Why are . . . you telling me this?

LISA: Because you're not acting like you know it. You were supposed to spend the day getting cleaning jobs. I get home and what do I find? You don't even have one job! I bet you studied ALL DAY for your stupid classes! How are you gonna support the family and buy me charts if you study ALL DAY FOR YOUR STUPID CLASSES!?

JULIE: (*Shaking.*) You . . . go to your room. You go there and . . . stay there til you can talk . . . respectful to me.

LISA: Respectfully.

JULIE: What?

LISA: Talk respectfully. It's an adverb.

JULIE: You go to your room til you can treat me with respect!

LISA: OK. OK. (*She saunters off.*)

JULIE: (*Watches Lisa go, then by herself.*) Damn damn damn damn damn damn damn DAMN!
(*Goes to the phone, dials.*)
Is Claire back yet? . . .

(*Losing it.*)

I know I keep calling. I gotta find her!...Just tell her to call Julie as soon as possible. I mean the second she opens the door. I mean don't let her take off her coat or nothing, don't let her put down her purse, don't let her –

(*Mike hangs up on her.*)

Damn! Damnit!

(*She throws the phone on the floor and then gives it a good kick.*)

Damnit to hell!

(*She holds her toe and hops around.*)

FRANK: (*Comes in with a tray of food.*) Dinner's ready! String beans and peanut butter sandwiches! Dinner! I put sugar in the powdered milk!

LISA: (*Entering.*) Not peanut butter again!

FRANK: I like peanut butter.

LISA: On Wonder Bread? I mean besides tasting retarded it's got all the nutrition of sawdust. And this stuff the government calls peanut butter!

JULIE: Lisa.

LISA: I bet there isn't one peanut in the whole gallon jar. I bet there isn't a shell.

JULIE: It's food, Lisa.

LISA: No it isn't. The government issues this stuff as a plot to stunt poor children's brains so when they grow up they don't mind doing jobs for minimum wage.

JULIE: Just . . . eat it, OK?

LISA: I'm not gonna be part of no government plot. I'm not gonna get my brain stunted. Besides, I wanna lose more weight.

JULIE: You lost weight?

LISA: Two pounds. All my friends are so jealous.

JULIE: You're gonna . . . gain it back.

LISA: I don't wanna gain it back.

JULIE: Eat your food, Lisa.

LISA: Make me.

JULIE: I'm . . . telling you, eat your food!

LISA: You can't make me. Only Dad can make me.

JULIE: He's not here!

LISA: Then find him!

JULIE: I can't . . . find him!

LISA: Call the police station! Call Monroe Boys Social Club!

JULIE: I call the station ALL DAY LONG! I call Monroe Boys Social Club ALL NIGHT! They all say he hasn't been around even though I KNOW he's been around so I'm beginning to think . . . we're not ever gonna hear . . . from him again which leaves me as the only person you got left who's gonna pay . . . the bills and make up the rules and take care of you and put food on the table even if you think that food is stunting your brain, EVEN IF YOU THINK IT'S RETARDED!

(*She is weeping.*)

So you gotta do what I say, OK? Like when I say eat something, YOU GOTTA EAT IT!

LISA: OK. Geez.

(*The front door opens but is stopped by the chain. Everyone stares at it for a moment.*)

CLAIRE: (*Through the door.*) Julie?

JULIE: (*Opening the door.*) Claire. You're here. I'm . . . so glad you're . . . here. I'm so glad . . .

CLAIRE: Julie. I left. I mean if you can kick Rick out I can leave. So I left. This morning. You inspired me and I left.

JULIE: You left your home?

CLAIRE: Yeah. I left.

JULIE: Where are you gonna go?

CLAIRE: Well that's just it. I've been sitting in the Hoboken Cinema all day trying to figure it out. I saw "When Harry Met Sally" four times. I decided first of all, since all my other friends are married I should stay with you. And second, I would not recommend seeing "When Harry Met Sally" when you're leaving your husband.

JULIE: You're staying with me?

CLAIRE: If it's alright with you. I brought some things over just in case you said yes.

(*Claire opens the front door wide and pulls in four suitcases and a trunk.*)

I got a lotta weird looks when I was dragging this into the movie theatre.

JULIE: Do you got money?

CLAIRE: A little. Yeah.

JULIE: Good 'cause we gotta buy charts and basketball shoes first thing in the morning.

CLAIRE: You gonna let me stay?

JULIE: 'Course. Of course! Of course!

(*Julie opens her arms. Claire runs to her. They embrace. BLACKOUT.*)

SCENE 6

Music. Lights up. Streetlight comes through the window. It is night. Claire is sleeping on the couch which is made up now like a bed. Julie, wearing a nightgown, comes in from the bedroom. She is clutching a book. She looks at Claire, sees she's asleep, then goes and sits by the window. She opens her book and reads by the streetlight. Claire sits up – she wasn't asleep after all. She looks at Julie.

CLAIRE: You're not sleepin'.

JULIE: (*Jumping.*) You're not neither.

(*Corrects herself.*)

Either.

CLAIRE: So? Go to sleep.

JULIE: I'll sleep after I take . . . the G.E.D. . . . tomorrow. Maybe I should study some more. I gotta learn more . . . English by tomorrow or I'm gonna . . . flunk that part.

(*She turns on the light.*)

CLAIRE: Give it here.

JULIE: (*Hands her the book.*) Thanks.

[*Note: In the Hoboken accent, ask is pronounced "ax".*]

CLAIRE: (*Reading.*) "The woman axed me how to get to the store."

JULIE: Subject, woman. Verb, axed.

(*Imitating her teacher.*)

"Not axed, Julie! Axed is what you do to a tree. ASSSSSked, Julie. ASSSSSSSSSSSSSSked." I hate . . . Mr. Walberg. Why can't Mr. Miranda be teaching that . . . class?! Mr. Walberg shouldn't . . . be allowed to teach nothing – I mean ANYthing!

CLAIRE: If ya pass the G.E.D. you won't ever have to see him again.

JULIE: If I pass the G.E.D. I'm gonna go back to his class one more . . .

time. In front of . . . everybody I'm gonna say "You know, Mr. Walberg? I think . . . you're an ASSSSSSSSSSSSSSSSSSS."

CLAIRE: (*Looking at the book.*) You know, Jule? You know this, you know? Like you've gone over this book a hundred thousand times. What else is there to know?

JULIE: Yeah.

CLAIRE: So why don't ya go back to bed.

(*She turns off the light.*)

You're not gonna pass the test if you fall asleep in the middle.

JULIE: I know.

CLAIRE: So? Go back to bed.

JULIE: I don't . . . wanna. But don't let me stop you.

CLAIRE: I don't wanna neither.

JULIE: You want me to make you some hot chocolate?

CLAIRE: No. You want me to make you some?

JULIE: No.

(*Silence. They sit in the dark.*)

What if I fail it, Claire? They don't let you take it more'n three times.

CLAIRE: What if you pass, you know? You gotta think positive.

JULIE: Yeah.

(*Silence.*)

Sometimes . . . I get these . . . thoughts. I can't . . . get 'em outa my head.

CLAIRE: About Rick?

JULIE: No . . . About . . .

CLAIRE: What?

(*Julie doesn't answer for a moment. She looks at Claire.*)

JULIE: (*Suddenly.*) Isn't Mr. Miranda . . . funny? That joke about the decimal points?

CLAIRE: I didn't get it.

JULIE: I got it. It was really funny!

(*She looks at Claire.*)

You thinking about Mike?

CLAIRE: Yeah.

(*Pause.*)

My friends don't call no more. Not since I left.

JULIE: You always had . . . so many friends. I never knew . . . How could a person have . . . so many friends?

CLAIRE: (*Laughs.*) Mike was blue!

JULIE: When?

CLAIRE: Career day! The plumber booth and then the policeman's booth and it had all this blue crepe paper hanging off.

JULIE: In Junior High?

CLAIRE: And Mike with his blue uniform inside this blue crepe paper thing, even his face looked blue! I was 14. I was Frankie's age.

JULIE: Rick was blue too . . . the first time I saw him . . . That coffee shop? Rick was talking . . . about how he was a policeman . . . so he could make the world safe.

CLAIRE: And Mike just listened. He looked – BEAUtiful. Listening like that. Like a statue inna park.

(*Silence.*)

What happened? I don't know what happened.

JULIE: I dont neither.

(*Pause.*)

Claire? Can I . . . ?

CLAIRE: What?

JULIE: Well. It's stupid.

CLAIRE: No. What?

JULIE: Could I . . . sit next to you? Like on the couch?

CLAIRE: Sure.

(*She sits next to Claire.*)

JULIE: Feels good, sitting next to someone.

CLAIRE: Yeah. It feels good.

JULIE: Could I . . . maybe . . .

CLAIRE: What?

JULIE: Sit closer?

CLAIRE: OK.

(*Julie sits so close to Claire their arms are touching.*)

JULIE: I like . . . this.

CLAIRE: Yeah.

(*Music. LIGHTS FADE OUT.*)

SCENE 7

Lights up on Mr. Miranda doing desk work. Julie is there, books in her arms.

MR. MIRANDA: You took it?

JULIE: I took it.

MR. MIRANDA: You passed it?

JULIE: I think I passed it.

MR. MIRANDA: You think.

JULIE: The English.

MR. MIRANDA: That English.

JULIE: I'll . . . find out tonight.

MR. MIRANDA: You'll call me?

JULIE: Yeah.

MR. MIRANDA: (*Shows her.*) Crossed fingers.

JULIE: Thanks.

(*Mr. Miranda takes a book from his desk and hands it to Julie.*)

MR. MIRANDA: Study it.

JULIE: Why?

MR. MIRANDA: For the test.

JULIE: I just . . . took the test. Maybe I passed the test.

MR. MIRANDA: A different test. The S.A.T.

JULIE: S.A.T.?

MR. MIRANDA: To get into Stevens. You'll need a very high score.

JULIE: The science college? You think I could get in there?

MR. MIRANDA: There's a program. They'll pay me to tutor you. You'll need a lot of tutoring.

JULIE: I could really get into Stevens?

MR. MIRANDA: You'll need a lot of studying. Here.

(*Hands her another book.*)

There's more.

(*He begins pulling books and papers out of his desk.*)

JULIE: (*Overcome.*) Wow. I mean . . . Like . . . You know? . . . I mean . . . You're the best . . . you know . . . teacher . . . I could ever . . . I mean . . . WOW.

(*His head disappears behind the desk as he reaches way back into a bottom drawer. Occasionally his hand comes up and places another book or paper on the growing pile.*)

JULIE: Ah. Mr. Miranda?

MR. MIRANDA: Hm?

JULIE: I mean . . . like I was hoping maybe . . .

MR. MIRANDA: Yeah?

JULIE: I mean could you . . . well . . .

MR. MIRANDA: What?

JULIE: It's just . . . I mean . . .

MR. MIRANDA: Tell me.

JULIE: I don't know . . .

MR. MIRANDA: WHAT?

JULIE: See there's this person . . . like who makes me . . . I mean everything seems . . . I mean when I'm near this person . . . I mean like there's . . . you know when you . . . like I feel like . . . it makes me . . . like . . . my chest . . . I mean my heart is . . . I mean inside . . . way inside me . . . deep inside . . . I'm not explaining this very well. It's like singing, this person, like midnight mass on Christmas Eve when the church is full 'a candles I mean I think I'm in love with this person but there's reasons why I should put it outa my mind but I can't. I mean put it outa my mind. I should but I can't. I don't know what to do.

(*Mr. Miranda has now come out from behind the desk.*)

MR. MIRANDA: Julie.

JULIE: Yeah?

MR. MIRANDA: I think I know who this person is.

JULIE: (*Brightening.*) Yeah?

MR. MIRANDA: This person likes you very much, Julie. And is attracted to you. Finds you very very attractive.

JULIE: (*Ecstatic.*) Really?

MR. MIRANDA: And has actually, often, thought of you in the same way, but to confess, as a confession, I once had romance with, an affair, I guess, I guess you'd have to call it an affair, with a student, an adult student like yourself and I hurt this student badly and my wife, well, she cried, well, she still isn't over it and I'm not either, I still ask myself every morning when there's shaving cream all over most of my face which makes my eyes stand out very clearly in the mirror, I ask my eyes clearly standing out from the shaving cream every morning how I could have done such a thing to my wife.

JULIE: Mr. Miranda?

MR. MIRANDA: Students and teachers just shouldn't fall in love with each other. Well it happens. It does happen. But it's not really the teacher a student falls in love with. She's actually falling in love with the subject matter. And sometimes a teacher seems bigger than life – But when I'm not teaching I'm just a normal boring person. Take my word for it. When I'm at home not teaching I'm really very boring. I even bore myself.

JULIE: (*Cracking a smile.*) Like you think . . . like . . . I'm in love with YOU?

MR. MIRANDA: Ah. You're not?

JULIE: (*Cracking up.*) I'm sorry. I'm really sorry. I'm really, really –
(*She can't continue she's laughing so hard.*)

MR. MIRANDA: (*Humiliated.*) It's been known to happen. It's not unheard of.

JULIE: (*Through her laughter.*) I'm sorry, Mr. Miranda. I mean . . . you have to admit it's . . . FUNNY!

MR. MIRANDA: I'm sure it is.
(*Slowly Julie is able to squash her laughter.*)

JULIE: (*Very softly.*) It's Claire. I'm in love with Claire.

MR. MIRANDA: Oh.

JULIE: Yeah.

MR. MIRANDA: Mm.

JULIE: You're . . .

MR. MIRANDA: What?

JULIE: Disgusted.

MR. MIRANDA: No. Oh no.

JULIE: But it's . . .

MR. MIRANDA: What?

JULIE: Perverted.

MR. MIRANDA: You think?

JULIE: The Bible says it's . . .

MR. MIRANDA: The Bible never contradicts itself?

JULIE: Everybody says it's . . .

MR. MIRANDA: I don't.

JULIE: No?

MR. MIRANDA: Not at all.

JULIE: Why not?

MR. MIRANDA: Well. I've had many students . . .

JULIE: Yeah?

MR. MIRANDA: Yes. Many. Over the years. I don't know why they come to me. Maybe there's no one else to go to.

JULIE: Many?

MR. MIRANDA: Yes.

JULIE: What do you tell them?

MR. MIRANDA: Nothing useful, I'm sure. Some people – it's the way they are.

JULIE: This girl . . . Charlene . . . in high school . . . her hair was a crew cut almost. The other kids . . . spray painted . . . "dyke" . . . on her locker. They put things . . . on her lunch tray . . . you know . . . dirty . . . things.

MR. MIRANDA: It's hard what you're talking about. A hard life.

JULIE: They said it was . . . Charlene's fault they were . . . treating her that way. They'd stop . . . treating her that way when she . . . stopped bein' a pervert. Once, in gym, a girl punched her . . . The girl said Charlene was lookin' at her queer. Charlene's lip was . . . bleedin' and everyone . . . was laughin' at her. Even Claire was . . . laughin'.

MR. MIRANDA: Were you?

JULIE: Yeah.

(*A beat.*)

Was it wrong . . . me laughin' at her? Or should I be laughin' at myself . . . now?

(*Mr. Miranda looks at her a moment, then picks up his briefcase as if to leave.*)

MR. MIRANDA: When you're finished in here, just shut the door. It locks by itself.

JULIE: Where you going?

MR. MIRANDA: Julie. I think you've got to . . . well . . . figure this out.

(*Music. LIGHTS FADE.*)

SCENE 8

Music. Lights up on the living room. Frank is playing Nintendo on the TV set. Claire enters and begins setting up a card table with table cloth and candles. She is still wearing her waitress uniform.

CLAIRE: (*As she works.*) Coke?

FRANK: No.

CLAIRE: It's cherry.

FRANK: No.

CLAIRE: Peanut butter cookies? I brought some home from the diner.

FRANK: I'm not thirsty, OK?! I'm not hungry!

CLAIRE: You're mad.

FRANK: No.

CLAIRE: I thought you wanted to stay over at Jose's. I thought staying over at Jose's was your favorite thing in the world.

FRANK: It's not.

CLAIRE: I thought it was.

FRANK: I mean why do I have to go?! Why does Lisa have to go?! If Mom needs a night off why the fuck don't you go?!

CLAIRE: Watch your mouth.

FRANK: Why the fucking shit hell don't you go?!

CLAIRE: Because we gotta celebrate her passing the test.

FRANK: You don't know she passed the test.

CLAIRE: I know.

FRANK: Then Lisa and me should be celebrating with her! Who the fucking shit hell gave you the right to celebrate with her!

CLAIRE: Next time I hear that language coming out of your mouth you're going to your room!

FRANK: You use language.

CLAIRE: Not anymore. Your Mama made a rule.

FRANK: When Mom's here I'll do what she says but I won't fucking do what you fucking say! I mean who the fuck are you?! Who the fucking shit hell Jesus shit fucking hell are you?!

LISA: (*Bursting in.*) Claire! Claire! You wanna see my boyfriend? He gave me his picture at lunch! He said he always wants a piece a him with me so he gave me his picture at lunch!
(*Shows Claire the picture.*)
Isn't he cute? He's really cute. Chuck. His name is Chuck.

CLAIRE: What happened to Hector?

LISA: Hector's so dumb.

CLAIRE: Yesterday Hector was smart. Yesterday you wanted to live with Hector so you could pick up some of his smartness.

LISA: He's dumb. He was talking to Suzy Molnari the whole Math class, making goo goo eyes. Who needs him, you know? I don't need him. I gonna go get packed.
(*She starts to run off, then stops.*)
I'm glad Mom's taking a night off from us kids. She needs a night off from us kids. She's been working very hard. I've been very worried about her.

(*She starts to run off.*)

You've been working hard, too. I've been worried about you, too.

(*She runs off.*)

CLAIRE: Frankie, what if tomorrow night I get lost and you can celebrate with your mother.

(*Julie enters with school books.*)

JULIE: (*Entering.*) Hiya Frankie.

(*She tries to kiss Frankie but he yanks his head away and stomps off.*)

Frankie?

(*She sees the table and candles.*)

What's this?

CLAIRE: I don't know.

JULIE: I thought we were gonna . . . go have a Blimpie.

CLAIRE: You don't like it?

JULIE: Yeah I like it. It's . . . beautiful.

CLAIRE: Yeah.

JULIE: BEAUTIFUL.

CLAIRE: I wanted it to be beautiful.

JULIE: Well it is. BEAUTIFUL.

CLAIRE: Good. 'Cause I wanted it to be.

JULIE: Well it is.

CLAIRE: Good.

JULIE: Yeah.

CLAIRE: 'Cause I wanted to celebrate, you know? We got a lot to celebrate.

JULIE: I don't know yet if I passed the test.

CLAIRE: We got more'n that to celebrate. I mean, I got something to tell you.

JULIE: Yeah?

CLAIRE: Yeah.

JULIE: Well. Then maybe . . . I got something to tell you too.

CLAIRE: Yeah?

JULIE: Yeah.

CLAIRE: You go first.

JULIE: No. You.

CLAIRE: I couldn't. You go.

JULIE: I couldn't . . . neither.

CLAIRE: Maybe we better have some wine first.

JULIE: Yeah. Let's have . . . some wine first.

(*The phone rings.*)

CLAIRE: Oh, you think that's . . . ?

JULIE: I don't know.

(*Julie answers it.*)

Hello? . . . Yeah? . . . Yeah? . . . Yeah . . .

(*Hangs up.*)

CLAIRE: Well?

JULIE: Mr. Walberg.

CLAIRE: You didn't pass.

JULIE: No.

CLAIRE: I'm sorry.

JULIE: I did . . .

CLAIRE: You can always try again.

JULIE: No, I . . . passed.

CLAIRE: You passed?

JULIE: I passed!

CLAIRE: You passed! You passed!

JULIE: I passed! I passed! I passed!

CLAIRE: I can't believe it. I can't fucking believe it! I'm sorry about my language but I am living with a goddamn high school graduate! I am so fucking proud I'm gonna burst right outa this goddamn fucking uniform.

(*Lisa enters with a large bag.*)

LISA: I'm ready.

CLAIRE: Your Mama passed!

LISA: You always thought you were so stupid, Mom, but I always knew you were smart. Frankie! Frankie! (*He comes in without a bag.*) Mom passed! She passed!

FRANKIE: Yeah?

LISA: Aren't you taking nothing?

FRANK: It's only one night.

LISA: (*Shrugs.*) Bye Mom. Bye Claire. Get drunk. Get rowdy. Mom, you could use a little rowdiness, you know?

(*She kisses them and leaves. Frank follows.*)

JULIE: Don't I get a kiss, Frankie?

FRANK: No.

LISA: Frankie . . .

(*He's gone. Julie and Claire are very nervous with each other.*)

JULIE: What's with Frankie?

CLAIRE: I don't know.

JULIE: Maybe we better do something.

CLAIRE: What?

JULIE: I don't know. We'll figure something out.

CLAIRE: We'll figure something out. You want some wine?

JULIE: Yeah.

CLAIRE: Here.

> (*Hands her a glass. Takes a cigarette and offers her one.*)

JULIE: I quit.

CLAIRE: What?!

JULIE: Today. I decided. I wanna be . . . the best I can . . . be. In EVERYthing.

CLAIRE: Is this the big news?

JULIE: Something else.

CLAIRE: Well.

> (*Puts the cigarette pack down.*)
>
> Congratulations.

JULIE: Thanks.

> (*They drink.*)
>
> So . . .

CLAIRE: What?

JULIE: You gonna tell me?

CLAIRE: I don't know.

JULIE: You don't know?

CLAIRE: I mean how are you gonna reACT.

JULIE: Well. Try me.

CLAIRE: Why don't you tell me?

JULIE: Because. How are YOU gonna react?

CLAIRE: I got an idea. Why don't you give me one of your footrubs. My feet are killing me.

JULIE: Sure. Sure.

> (*They sit on the couch. Julie rubs Claire's feet.*)

CLAIRE: Thanks Jule. There. That's it. Yeah. It was wild in there today. "Miss? Miss? Ma'am? Miss? Miss?" One lady had me running back and forth so many times I almost shoved her jello up her nose. That's good. Oh.

JULIE: So maybe we both have the same thing . . . to tell.

CLAIRE: I don't think so, Jule. I mean, I wouldn't think so.

JULIE: There's always a chance.

CLAIRE: Well, maybe there's a chance.

JULIE: I'm hopin' on that chance.

CLAIRE: But I don't see how you could guess what I'm gonna say. I mean no way could you guess it.

JULIE: But still, there's a . . . chance.

CLAIRE: Maybe, but like, no way.

JULIE: So here goes. So. I mean. Like I don't miss Rick nomore . . . I mean like, I been thinking about . . . someone . . . else.

CLAIRE: Yeah? Who?

JULIE: Like all the time. Like every second.

CLAIRE: Who?

JULIE: You.

(A beat. Then Claire jumps off the couch.)

CLAIRE: What is this? I mean what is going on here?

JULIE: Claire —

CLAIRE: You're rubbing my feet 'cause you got something else on your mind?

JULIE: Forget it, OK? Let's just forget I said that.

CLAIRE: Has this been going on the whole time I been living here? You been having dirty nasty thoughts about me the whole time?

JULIE: No, OK? Can we just forget what I said?

CLAIRE: No we can't just forget what you said! I thought you were my friend!

JULIE: I AM your —

CLAIRE: I thought you liked me for me!

JULIE: I do just like you for you!

CLAIRE: OK. OK. Wait. I gotta get outa here. There is no need to DISCUSS this even. I'm going to bed. In Lisa's room. And I'm putting the dresser against the door. And first thing in the morning I'll start looking for a place of my own. I mean I can't BELIEVE this! I really can't BELIEVE it! We were having such a good time together!

(She exits.)

JULIE: *(Calling.)* Claire . . . Don't move out, OK? . . . Claire? . . . Claire!

(No answer. Julie throws herself onto the couch.)

Damn damn damn damn damn damn DAMN. DAMN IT!

(After a moment Julie gets up, blows out the candles and

dismantles the table. But the leg of the table won't go down. Julie struggles with it, then finally bursts into tears. Claire comes back in.)
Claire.
(Claire sits on the couch.)
Don't move . . . out, OK?
(Claire doesn't answer.)
I DO like . . . you for you. I mean that's the whole . . . point. I mean I like . . . you so much I think I'm in . . . love with you.
(Claire doesn't say anything.)
But don't move out because I'm not . . . gonna say no more about it. I mean we're both gonna forget the . . . whole thing. It's gone. Never happened.

CLAIRE: Can I tell you what I was gonna tell you?

JULIE: Sure.

CLAIRE: I was gonna tell you that I figured something out. I figured out I don't wanna work at Malibu Diner no more. I wanna go to Mr. Walberg's class and pass the G.E.D. And then I wanna become a police officer. I mean if Mike and Rick can do it so can I. They let women in now. I never pictured myself doing something like that but watchin' you's inspired me. Does this bother you?

JULIE: Why would it bother me?

CLAIRE: 'Cause Rick's a police officer. I thought it might bother you, me becoming one.

JULIE: It doesn't bother me.

CLAIRE: You ever been with . . . a woman . . . that way? The way you were talking?

JULIE: No.

CLAIRE: You ever . . . thought about it?

JULIE: Not til . . . these last months . . .

CLAIRE: I thought about it.

JULIE: Yeah?

CLAIRE: Since high school. On and off. Since Jr. High. On and off. I thought about you.

JULIE: Why didn't . . . you tell me?

CLAIRE: Because it's not normal, these thoughts. They gotta be put out of your head. Our heads.

JULIE: You really think so?

CLAIRE: Don't you?
(Music. LIGHTS FADE OUT.)

END OF ACT ONE.

ACT TWO

SCENE 9

Music. Lights up on Julie on a park bench. Sounds of a busy park. Julie pats her mittened hands together for warmth. It is winter dusk.

Someone off front catches Julie's eye. She smiles and waves. The person moves on. Julie checks her watch.

CLAIRE: (*From off.*) Julie?

JULIE: Claire!

(Claire runs on. Julie jumps up and almost leaps on Claire but stops herself. Awkwardly, Claire sits on one side of the bench, Julie on the other. They speak without looking at each other.)

CLAIRE: Sorry I'm late.

JULIE: That's OK.

CLAIRE: Work was crazy!

JULIE: It's OK.

CLAIRE: Three tables of kids. They wouldn't leave.

JULIE: It's OK.

CLAIRE: There's Susan.

(*She waves.*)

Fred.

(*She waves again.*) What is this?! Grand fucking Central?!

JULIE: People are walking their dogs.

CLAIRE: Can't a person have some privacy?

JULIE: It's after work. People walk their dogs.

CLAIRE: Fucking Newport Mall! I want a cigarette! Fuck! 'Scuse my language.

JULIE: You gonna have one?

CLAIRE: No I'm not gonna have one. Yolanda.

(*She waves.*)

JULIE: I . . .

CLAIRE: What?

JULIE: Thought about you.

CLAIRE: Yeah?

JULIE: All day. Every minute.

CLAIRE: Every minute?

JULIE: Every second.

CLAIRE: Come on.

JULIE: While I was wiping crumbs off Mrs. Leyners table. I thought about you.

CLAIRE: Geez. – I want a cigarette! Fuck!

JULIE: But you're not gonna have one.

CLAIRE: I told you last night. I wanna improve myself.

JULIE: Yeah?

CLAIRE: Like you're doin'. Julie?

JULIE: What?

CLAIRE: I guess I.

JULIE: What?

CLAIRE: Thought about you too.

JULIE: Yeah?

CLAIRE: While I was serving Brenden his eggs.

JULIE: Yeah?

CLAIRE: And. While I was scooping the cole slaw.

JULIE: `I wanna . . . hold your hand.

CLAIRE: No

JULIE: I know.

CLAIRE: It's a park.

JULIE: I know.

CLAIRE: It's fuckin' Macy's! Fuck! I'm not smokin' a cigarette! I don't wanna taste like no ashtray!

JULIE: You didn't taste like an ashtray . . . last night.

CLAIRE: I tasted like an ashtray.

JULIE: No, like . . . Sprite. Without the bubbles.

CLAIRE: Like an ashtray.

JULIE: Diet Sprite maybe . . . with a little . . . charcoal thrown in.

CLAIRE: See?

JULIE: I *loved* . . . the way you tasted.

CLAIRE: Yeah?

JULIE: I *loved* it.

CLAIRE: I wanna . . . hold your hand.

JULIE: It's a park.

CLAIRE: I know.

JULIE: If we were home.

CLAIRE: But the kids.

JULIE: The kids.

CLAIRE: We can't do nothin' with the kids there. Not even when they're sleepin'.

JULIE: We could be quiet!

CLAIRE: Right.

JULIE: We gotta send 'em out.

CLAIRE: Every night?

JULIE: Not every night.

CLAIRE: Once a week at the most.

JULIE: We can't even talk . . . you know . . . romantic. Not when they're there. Not even in another room.

CLAIRE: They'll feel something. They'll pick something up.

JULIE: They wouldn't understand.

CLAIRE: They couldn't understand.

> (*Pause.*)

JULIE: When the kids are grown.

CLAIRE: Whenever we want.

JULIE: All the time.

CLAIRE: That's a long way away, when the kids are grown.

JULIE: Yeah.

> (*Silence.*)
>
> I got you . . .

CLAIRE: What?

JULIE: I don't know. A present.

CLAIRE: What for?

JULIE: I don't know.

> (*Julie hands Claire a small box.*)
>
> I didn't wrap it 'cause . . .

CLAIRE: (*Opens the box.*) You can't afford this.

JULIE: They let you pay the phone bill late . . . if you call first . . . and tell 'em.

CLAIRE: Julie. It's beautiful.

JULIE: Garnet. Put it on.

CLAIRE: Not here. OK?

JULIE: Yeah.

CLAIRE: I got you something too.

> (*Claire takes a large brown bag out of her large purse and hands it to Julie.*)

JULIE: Wow!

CLAIRE: I didn't wrap it neither.

JULIE: (*Looks inside.*) I mean . . . Wow! A notebook!

   (*She pulls out a brightly colored notebook.*)

CLAIRE: Your old one was falling apart.

JULIE: I mean like . . . Wow!

   (*They look at each other.*)

   I wanna . . .

CLAIRE: Me too.

   (*Silence. They look at the people all around them in the park.*)

JULIE: I'm . . .

CLAIRE: What?

JULIE: Thinking about it.

CLAIRE: Here?!

JULIE: Nobody can stop us from thinking.

CLAIRE: What if someone sees?

JULIE: I'm not DOing nothing.

   (*Corrects herself.*)

   Anything. Last night . . .

CLAIRE: We were a mess last night.

JULIE: (*Smiles.*) At first.

CLAIRE: (*Laughs.*) A fuckin' disaster!

JULIE: But later. When I touched your face?

CLAIRE: Yeah. Yeah.

JULIE: I touch your face now.

CLAIRE: Julie!

JULIE: In my mind. I'm touching your face. Can you feel it?

CLAIRE: What if someone hears!

JULIE: They won't. They're walking their dogs. They're swinging their kids. They won't.

CLAIRE: I want a cigarette!

JULIE: Don't think. I'm touching your face. Can you feel it?

CLAIRE: Yes.

JULIE: I'm kissing your face. Can you feel it?

CLAIRE: Yes.

JULIE: I'm touching your hair.

CLAIRE: I'm touching your mouth.

JULIE: I'm kissing your mouth.

CLAIRE: Yes.

JULIE: Your lips.

CLAIRE: Yes.

JULIE: I'm touching your neck. I'm kissing your neck.

CLAIRE: I'm touching your shoulders, your arms.

JULIE: Your breasts. Soft.

CLAIRE: You're soft.

JULIE: All over.

CLAIRE: Your thighs.

JULIE: I touch you all over. I kiss you.

CLAIRE: I kiss you too.

JULIE: My lips on your skin. My tongue.

CLAIRE: I feel it.

JULIE: You smell good. Like Diet Sprite. No, like rain.

CLAIRE: There?

JULIE: Salty. Salty rain.

CLAIRE: Soft.

JULIE: My lips, my tongue.

CLAIRE: I can feel it.

JULIE: You're . . .

CLAIRE: I can feel it.

JULIE: Soft.

CLAIRE: I can feel it.

JULIE: Wet.

CLAIRE: I can feel it.

JULIE: Wet.

> (*They look at each other a long moment, then turn away.*)
> Claire?

CLAIRE: Yeah?

JULIE: You make me . . . You feel so . . . Like inside . . . and all over
. . . like going up so high on a swing the chains jerk coming
down . . . I mean . . . I never knew there could be so much
FEELING.

CLAIRE: Like I been all my life in one of them nun's hair shirts? And
last night you took it off.

JULIE: Like . . . I love you.

CLAIRE: Shit.

JULIE: What?

CLAIRE: Sally.

> (*Waves.*)
> I haven't seen Sally, I don't know, since before I left Mike.

(*Calling.*)

Hiya. How're ya doin'?

(*To Julie.*)

I used to see Sally all the time. Me and Mike, we used to see Sally and George all the time. Shit.

JULIE: What?

CLAIRE: The way she's looking at us.

JULIE: What way?

CLAIRE: She sees something.

JULIE: What's there to see?

CLAIRE: She sees! She can tell!

JULIE: We're not . . . even touching!

CLAIRE: She's not stupid. She can tell!

JULIE: There's nothing to tell!

CLAIRE: It's written all over us!

JULIE: Claire. We didn't do nothing!

CLAIRE: Right.

JULIE: Claire?

CLAIRE: Don't get near me! She's looking!

JULIE: I'm not . . . near you! She's not looking!

CLAIRE: She's looking.

JULIE: She's walking away!

CLAIRE: She's looking! I can feel it!

JULIE: Claire?

CLAIRE: I can feel it!

(*BLACKOUT.*)

SCENE 10

In black, a cigarette is lit. Spot up slowly on Mr. Miranda leaning back against his desk watching the smoke rise from the cigarette.

MR. MIRANDA: See how the smoke rises smoothly off the end of the cigarette? Until here.

(*He points.*)

Where it becomes wild and turbulent. Like a river that flows smoothly down a hill but then suddenly turns into rapids.

(*ON THE SCREEN, a picture of river rapids.*)

The trouble with turbulence is that physicists have never been able to figure it out. Like weather, there are no rules that make it predictable. Its motion never repeats. It is chaotic. Our friend Lorenz –

(*ON THE SCREEN, the cartoon line drawing of a scientist.*)

reduced the turbulence of boiling water –

(*ON THE SCREEN, boiling water.*)

into three ridiculously simple variables, and made a graph which followed these variables over time.

(*ON THE SCREEN, a multicolored Lorenz attractor. [Butterfly attractor.] It is simply beautiful.*)

This is a picture of chaos. But as you can see, it doesn't look chaotic at all. Or rather, the look of chaos has patterns to it.

(*Music. LIGHTS FADE.*)

SCENE 11

Lights up on the living room. Claire, in a robe, her hair all done, is putting on makeup. Lisa hovers over her, watching.

CLAIRE: (*After a moment.*) Do ya have to stand so close?

LISA. I wanna watch.

(*Claire goes back to work.*)

CLAIRE: I can feel your breath on my face!

LISA: I wanna learn this.

(*Claire goes back to work.*)

CLAIRE: Don't you got no girlfriends can teach you?

(*Julie bursts into the front door with books, two rolls of paper and a bag of groceries.*)

JULIE: (*Beside herself.*) Claire! Lisa! You gotta see this! You gotta see this!!

CLAIRE: Here she goes.

(*Julie unrolls a sheet of paper.*)

JULIE: A computer made this!

(*ON THE SCREEN, we see the Butterfly Attractor.*)

LISA: (*Wrinkles her nose.*) What is it?

JULIE: A strange attractor.

LISA: A *what?*

JULIE: Mr. Miranda was teaching me this. Simplified, this is a series of numbers that never repeats.

CLAIRE: I don't see any numbers.

JULIE: It's a graph of the numbers.

LISA: And it turns into a butterfly?

JULIE: Yeah! And look at this!

> (*She unrolls another sheet of paper.*
> *ON THE SCREEN, we see a leaf drawing done by a computer.*)

LISA: Is this the same thing? Numbers that never repeat?

JULIE: But different numbers.

LISA: And it turns into a LEAF?

JULIE: Yeah!

LISA: Is that what a real leaf is?! Numbers that never repeat?!

JULIE: I think it is!

LISA: Maybe that's what the whole universe is! Numbers that never repeat!!

JULIE: I think it could be!

LISA: I mean this is the freshest thing I've ever seen! I mean this is RAW!

JULIE: Raw?

LISA: I wanna go show Joe. Can I show these to Joe?

CLAIRE: Joe?

LISA: (*Rolling up the papers.*) My new boyfriend. He's gonna flip over these!

CLAIRE: What happened to Chuck?

LISA: Chuck is an asshole.

JULIE: Watch your mouth.

LISA: What else can ya call it? He tells me to meet him in the Park yesterday and then he never shows up. What an asshole!

JULIE: Lisa.

LISA: What.

JULIE: (*With authority.*) Watch your mouth.

LISA: (*Submits.*) Yes Mom.

> (*Holds up the paper rolls.*)
> I mean these are totally tight!
> (*She runs out and slams the door behind her. Julie looks at Claire all dolled up.*)

JULIE: What's this?

CLAIRE: Like it?

JULIE: You're . . . *beautiful.*

CLAIRE: I think you could use some lipstick too. Whaddya think?

JULIE: Frankie home?

CLAIRE: Out 'til six.

JULIE: (*As she chain locks the door.*) Yeah. I could use some . . .
lipstick.

*(Claire kisses Julie. When they part Julie's got Claire's lipstick all
over her mouth. Julie looks in the mirror.)*

I think you missed a part. (*Points.*) There.

(*Claire kisses her.*)

There.

(*Claire kisses her again.*)

CLAIRE: I think I need some back. There.

(*They kiss.*)

There.

JULIE: There.

CLAIRE: There.

*(Back and forth they kiss each other until lipstick is all over both
their faces and they're laughing so hard they can't move. Then –)*

The groceries.

JULIE: Leave 'em

CLAIRE: They'll spoil.

JULIE: So?

CLAIRE: Julie, come on.

JULIE: (*Realizes.*) The ice cream.

(*She picks up a grocery bag.*)

Wanna help?

CLAIRE: No I gotta finish.

(*She creams off the lipstick all over her face.*)

JULIE: What's the rush?

CLAIRE: I gotta be there in 20 minutes.

JULIE: Where?

CLAIRE: Sally's.

JULIE: Oh.

(*Julie takes the grocery bag out to the kitchen, then comes right
back out.*)

We were gonna study tonight. You're not gonna study?

CLAIRE: I'm goin' to Sally's. She's having the gang over.

JULIE: You said you were gonna study.

CLAIRE: I changed my mind, OK? Sally called and finally she invited me and I haven't been invited nowhere for months and months so I changed my mind about studying.

JULIE: You *gotta* study!

CLAIRE: Not tonight I don't.

JULIE: You're not gonna pass your G.E.D. test!

CLAIRE: The test isn't for two and a half weeks.

JULIE: Still. You got a lot to learn!

CLAIRE: I'm goin' to Sally's. You got me, Jule? I'm gonna go be with my friends.

(*Claire yanks panty hose out of a drawer and starts putting them on.*)

JULIE: You bored of me?

CLAIRE: No.

JULIE: You are. You're bored of me.

CLAIRE: I'm not bored of you.

JULIE: Then why aren't you staying home with me?

CLAIRE: 'Cause I'm sick of staying home!

JULIE: See?

CLAIRE: Normal people don't stay home every single night of the year. Normal people go out sometimes and party with FRIENDS!

JULIE: Well we're not normal.

CLAIRE: I don't know about you, Julie, but I AM *NORMAL!*

JULIE: What does that mean?!

CLAIRE: I want some FUN! THAT's what it means! *NORMAL FUN!* I mean one more night listening to you talk on and on about FRACTALS FRACTALS and semi-CONDUCTORS and I'm gonna go outa my MIND!

JULIE: Claire?

CLAIRE: I'm sorry.

JULIE: I'm *trying* . . . to *improve* myself.

CLAIRE: I MISS MY FRIENDS, Julie. All my LIFE, since KINDERGARTEN til I moved in here with YOU, these people were my FRIENDS!

JULIE: And what . . . are you gonna talk about with *your FRIENDS!* The same subjects you . . . discuss with ME? Who's having an affair with who? Hairstyles?! Maybe I go outa my mind with YOU sometimes! Maybe I think sometimes . . . you sound STUPID!

(*Claire throws two books — bang bang.*)

I didn't mean that. Claire? I didn't mean that!

CLAIRE: Julie. You are not ABOVE people! You can learn all kinds a fancy words, you can sit in the laundry spouting x's and the y's and the z's and shit but people are rolling their eyes at you, Julie. I seen 'em. It makes me wanna crawl under the folding table!
(*Julie turns and goes off.*)
What are you doing? I'm talking to you! Julie, I'm talking to you!
(*Julie comes back on with a dress. She starts undressing.*)
What are you doing?!

JULIE: You wanna be with your friends? We're gonna be with your friends.

CLAIRE: You can't go.

JULIE: Why not?

CLAIRE: You weren't invited.

JULIE: I'll go as your date.

CLAIRE: Julie.

JULIE: Your roommate.

CLAIRE: I can't believe this!

JULIE: You wanna go? I'll go with you.

CLAIRE: I don't want them seeing us.

JULIE: They won't see nothing.
(*Corrects herself.*)
Anything.

CLAIRE: They'll see, Julie.

JULIE: They'll see your roommate. I'll act like your roommate.

CLAIRE: They'll figure it out.

JULIE: I'm not gonna touch you or nothing. ANYthing. I'll keep my hands off you.

CLAIRE: The way you look at me, Julie.

JULIE: I won't even look at you!

CLAIRE: Julie, they'll feel it! They'll know!

JULIE: How're they gonna know?

CLAIRE: Julie!

JULIE: If I'm not touching you or looking at you, how're they gonna know?!

CLAIRE: They'll know! I know they'll know!

JULIE: OK?! OK?! So what if they know! It's who we are, Claire!

CLAIRE: It's not who I am to THEM!

JULIE: I LOVE you, Claire! I'm proud of you!

CLAIRE: You're scarin' me, Julie. You're talkin' like maybe you're gonna tell somebody.

JULIE: I wish we COULD tell somebody. EVERYBODY. I wanna tell EVERYBODY!

CLAIRE: But you're not gonna tell NOBODY. You hear me? 'Cause if you do I'm not gonna have not even ONE friend left. Sally, Fred, Susan, Jim, Yolanda – not even ONE of 'em! I know you KNOW that. You know I know you KNOW that!

JULIE: Claire. Look. Wouldja sit down? I want you . . . to sit down.

CLAIRE: I gotta go.

JULIE: You can go! But I gotta . . . say something first. And you're not gonna like it . . . in the beginning. But if you can keep your temper from blowin' then later, when I got the whole thing explained I think maybe you're gonna like it, I think maybe you're gonna like it a lot. So sit . . . down. Please? Wouldja . . . sit down?

(*A beat. Then Claire sits.*)

Thank you. Thank you. So here it is. I've been thinking and thinking about this. We get new friends.

CLAIRE: *What?*

JULIE: You gotta hear me out! Mr. Miranda says there's a lotta people like us and we could make friends with them.

CLAIRE: You told Mr. Miranda?

JULIE: You gotta keep your temper from blowin'!

(*With all her might, Claire contains herself.*)

So we make new friends, New York City kinda friends. And next year, knock on wood, I'll be goin' to college, Stevens maybe. And you could be goin' to college too. Jersey City State. Or wherever you want. See? I made this chart.

(*She takes a giant paper roll from under the couch.*)

Like you always say how you'd make a good lawyer, and I think it's true, you got great arguing skills, so I got to thinking, would that be possible? Is it possible us goin' to college together? Just let me show you.

(*She gets down on her hands and knees and spreads out a giant chart on the floor.*)

See, you go to classes three nights a week, study the other two nights and on Saturday. Then weekend nights and all day Sunday we both spend with the kids. You can see how I divided up the chores. Lisa and Frank will have to do some of the chores.

(*Claire grabs her purse.*)

Then over here I listed the cost of both our colleges and how we're gonna pay for it. Here's information about Stevens where I wanna go. The cost of tuition and grant and loan possibilities. And here's information for you about NYU and Columbia. I asked Mr. Miranda. They got real good pre-law programs.

(*Claire takes a cigarette pack out of her purse. Julie doesn't see her.*)

I put our living expenses and tuition expenses in this column. Then against that, I listed our incomes and available grants and loans. It's tight. I admit it's tight. But it's poss –

(*Claire lights a cigarette. Julie hears it, looks up.*)

Claire?

(*Claire takes a deep drag.*)

But you quit, Claire.

(*Claire blows a smoke ring.*

The door opens and gets caught by the chain. Furious banging.)

FRANK: (*From off.*) Open the fuckin' DOOR!

(*Julie opens the door. Frankie charges into the living room.*)

JULIE: Frankie?

FRANK: Fuck you fuck you fuck you FUCK YOU!

(*Frankie runs off to his room knocking over a lamp on his way. Lisa bursts into the room.*)

LISA: Mom? Something's wrong with Frankie. He was lightin' trash on fire in the park. I gotta go see what's wrong with Frankie.

(*She runs off to his room.*)

JULIE: What's with . . . ?

CLAIRE: I don't . . .

JULIE: He was fine this . . .

CLAIRE: This morning there wasn't nothin' . . .

JULIE: What could . . . ?

CLAIRE: I don't know.

(*Frankie enters with his backpack. Lisa follows.*)

FRANK: Kevin Smith says I'm living with perverts.

LISA: Kevin Smith is an asshole!

JULIE: Lisa!

LISA: OK, idiot!

JULIE: (*To Frankie.*) We're not perverts!

FRANK: He saw you two holding hands down by the docks.

CLAIRE: We weren't holdin' hands!

LISA: He's an IDIOT! STUPID IDIOT!

FRANK: Is he right? Are you dykes?

CLAIRE: 'Course not, Frankie.

JULIE: 'Course not.

FRANK: I think he's right. I think you are dykes.

CLAIRE: We're not no dykes!

FRANK: I'm gonna go live with Dad.

JULIE: Frankie! No!

FRANK: You said I could choose who to live with! I'm gonna go live
with Dad!

(*He runs out the front door.*)

JULIE: (*Chasing him out the door.*) Frankie! FRANKIE! (*From off.*)
FRANK – IE!

LISA: Kevin Smith is the stupidest idiot I ever knew in my LIFE!

(*Lisa runs off to her room in tears. Furiously, Claire throws on the
rest of her clothes, stomps into her heels and lights another
cigarette. Julie re-enters out of breath.*)

JULIE: Claire. Like . . . Mr. Miranda says smokin's like . . . putting
carcinogens right into your lung tissue!

(*Claire throws on her coat and crosses to the door.*)

You're goin'?

CLAIRE: No one's ever gonna call me that again, Julie.

JULIE: What?

CLAIRE: I'm not no DYKE!

JULIE: No! We're not . . .

CLAIRE: No one's ever gonna call me dyke again!

(*Claire slams the door behind her. Dazed, Julie goes to the window
and watches her walk away. Lisa enters.*)

LISA: Mommy?

JULIE: Yeah?

LISA: Is it true?

JULIE: What?

LISA: You and Claire?

JULIE: We love each other. That's true.

LISA: What way?

(*A beat.*)

JULIE: Lovers.

LISA: (*Her face crumpling.*) Shit.

JULIE: I shouldn'a told you?

LISA: No. You shoulda.

JULIE: You want a hug?

LISA: No. I wanna sit.

(*Lisa sits on the couch.*)

JULIE: You wanna?

LISA: I just wanna sit.

(*Lisa cries. Julie watches her. Music up. Lights fade out.*)

SCENE 12

Music – longing, yearning. Lights up low on the living room. Night. Streetlights through the window. Julie stands watching out the window.

JULIE: (*Seeing him out the window.*) Frankie? Frankie!

(*She runs to the front door and opens it wide.*)

Frankie!

(*He comes in. He is sullen, not looking at Julie.*)

FRANK: Dad was havin' a woman over. He said I couldn't stay with him when he was havin' a woman over.

JULIE: I'm glad, Frankie. I mean . . . I'm glad you're back.

(*Frankie moves off toward his room.*)

You got a game tomorrow?

(*Frankie shrugs.*)

Can I watch? I haven't watched you for awhile.

(*Frankie doesn't answer.*)

Then maybe we'll go to the Castle Rock Coffee Shop and I'll buy you one of those things you like, that Pineapple Cherry Chocolate Supreme thing, and we'll talk. I think maybe we got a lot to talk about.

(*He thinks.*)

FRANK: Yeah.

(*He goes off.*)

JULIE: (*Calling after him.*) Thanks Frankie.

(*Julie goes back to the window. She watches a moment, then goes to the door and opens it. After a moment, Claire enters.*)

Have fun?

CLAIRE: Yeah. I'm tired. 'Night.

(She takes out sheets from her drawer and tosses them onto the couch. Julie sits in the chair.)

I said I'm tired.

JULIE: I know.

(Claire starts to unfold the sheets, but then stops. She sits on the couch and puts her head in her hands.)

It's not gonna work, is it?

CLAIRE: What?

JULIE: Us.

(Claire doesn't answer for a long time.)

CLAIRE: It's just. Julie, you're goin'. Zoom. You're flying out somewhere. The ozone maybe. I don't know and I don't know if I wanna know. I think I just wanna stay back here on the earth and wave to you every once in awhile.

JULIE: I wanna . . . I gotta MAKE something outa myself. Don't you wanna make something outa yourself?

CLAIRE: No, you know? Like. I already am something.

(Pause.)

Mike was at the party.

JULIE: Claire, you didn't –

CLAIRE: We had a conversation.

JULIE: You're not gonna –

CLAIRE: We're gonna have some more conversations.

JULIE: You're not thinking of . . . You couldn't . . . Claire, when you and me, when we're alone. It was never like that with Mike.

CLAIRE: None of your business, OK?! What I think, what I feel, what I'm gonna do with my future, ALL of it, it's none of your goddamned BUSINESS!

JULIE: OK! It's none of my business!

(Julie gets up to leave.)

CLAIRE: Julie? Would you . . . ?

JULIE: What?

CLAIRE: Sit next to me.

JULIE: 'Course. Of course!

(She sits next to Claire on the couch.)

You want me to sit closer?

CLAIRE: No.

(Silence.)

Julie?

JULIE: Yeah.

CLAIRE: Maybe there's a lotta stuff wrong with my life.

JULIE: Yeah!

CLAIRE: But it's mine, you know?

(*Silence. They sit.*)

JULIE: I'm always gonna love you, Claire. I never loved nobody like the way I love you.

(*Music. Lights fade out.*)

SCENE 13

Lights up on Mr. Miranda at his desk, searching through an algebra book. Julie enters.

JULIE: Mr. Miranda?

MR. MIRANDA: Hi Julie. I'm just about ready for you.

JULIE: You know those gay dances you told me about? For gay women?

MR. MIRANDA: Yeah?

JULIE: How wouldja like to go with me to one?

MR. MIRANDA: Well.

JULIE: Then after that we could go to the Liberty Science Museum. I've never done anything like that before.

MR. MIRANDA: Could my wife come with us? She's been pretty touchy since I . . . well . . . that affair.

JULIE: You just better hope she doesn't pick someone up.

MR. MIRANDA: I'll take my chances.

JULIE: Good. So let's work.

MR. MIRANDA: OK. Today we're going to do some factoring. Start off by reading –

(*Her face stops him.*)

What's wrong? Something's wrong.

JULIE: Would you . . . ?

MR. MIRANDA: What?

JULIE: Have you ever hugged a student? Not like an affair type hug. Like a comfort . . . hug.

MR. MIRANDA: Well. I don't think so.

JULIE: Oh.

MR. MIRANDA: There's always the first time.

> (*He opens his arms. They hug awkwardly at first. Then Julie weeps.*)

JULIE: She's gone, Mr. Miranda. She went back to her husband.

MR. MIRANDA: Yeah.

> (*He holds her for a long time. Finally Julie breaks it off.*)

JULIE: I wanna get to work.

MR. MIRANDA: You don't want to talk about it?

JULIE: I'd rather work.

> (*She sits.*)
>
> Mr. Miranda?

MR. MIRANDA: What?

JULIE: I'm gonna be the best computer scientist in Hoboken, right? Maybe in all of New Jersey.

MR. MIRANDA: (*Smiles.*) Tell you what. No algebra today. I was going through some old disks and I found a program I'd like you to try. It'll help you with geometry. You got your S.A.T.'s in a month and you need to do more geometry.

> (*He opens his desk drawer, pulls out a disk and sticks it in the computer. ON THE SCREEN appears the night sky full of stars.*)
>
> Here's the instructions.
>
> (*He hands Julie a small manual. Julie sits in front of the computer.*)
>
> The bright star just right off center? You see it?

JULIE: Yeah.

MR. MIRANDA: I want you to figure out how many light years it is from the earth.

JULIE: Sure.

> (*Mr. Miranda goes back to sorting papers. Julie looks at the instruction manual and taps on the computer. ON THE SCREEN, lines appear marking a right triangle between the star and two points on earth. Music up. ON THE SCREEN, the distance of two sides of the triangle is noted. Lights fade out on Mr. Miranda and Julie. The stars stay bright.*)

END.

Betty the Yeti

by Jon Klein

For Steitzer.

BETTY THE YETI was directed by Jeff Steitzer with the following cast (in order of appearance) :

CLARE KUTZ	Adale O'Brien
IKO	Mary Lee
TERRA SAWYER	Mia Dillon
TREY HUGGER	V. Craig Heidenreich
RUSS T. SAWYER	Stephen Yoakam
THE CREATURE	Caroline Swift

Scenic Designer	Paul Owen
Costume Designer	Laura Patterson
Lighting Designer	Kenneth Posner
Sound Designer	Casey L. Warren
Props Master	Ron Riall
Stage Manager	Carey Upton
Assistant Stage Manager	Michele Kay
Dramaturg	Michael Bigelow Dixon
Casting	Laura Richen Casting

BETTY THE YETI was commissioned by A Contemporary Theatre, in association with The Seattle Arts Commission, directed by Jeff Steitzer with the following cast (in order of appearance) :

CLARE KUTZ .... Dee Maaske
IKO .... Kristine Goto
TERRA SAWYER .... Sarah Brooke
TREY HUGGER .... Jeff Cummings
RUSS T. SAWYER .... Wesley Rice
THE CREATURE .... Amy Perry

Scenic Designer .... Bill Forrester
Costume Designer .... Carolyn Keim
Lighting Designer .... M. L. Geiger
Sound Designer .... Steven M. Klein
Stage Manager .... Jeffrey K. Hanson
Dramaturg .... Steven E. Alter

JON KLEIN is a native of Kentucky now living in Seattle, and is the author of thirteen produced plays. His most frequently produced work is T BONE N WEASEL, which premiered at the ATL Humana Festival in 1987, and has since received over fifty productions nationwide. Winner of an HBO Playwrights USA Award, T BONE N WEASEL was also adapted by the author for the TNT film version, starring Gregory Hines and Christopher Lloyd.

Other plays include an adaptation of Stendhal's novel THE RED AND THE BLACK, FOUR OUR FATHERS, SOUTHERN CROSS, PEORIA, LIFE CLASS (THE FINAL LESSON OF THOMAS EAKINS), THE EINSTEIN PROJECT (co-author) and LOSING IT (winner of an FDG/CBS New Play Award). These plays have been produced Off-Broadway and at such prominent regional theatres as Center Stage in Baltimore, Alley Theatre in Houston, and the Alliance Theatre in Atlanta.

He is also the author of a children's play, THE HARDY BOYS IN THE MYSTERY OF THE HAUNTED HOUSE, which recently premiered at Seattle Childrens' Theatre and is scheduled for production at the Emmy Gifford Childrens' Theatre in Omaha.

He has received fellowships from the National Endowment for the Arts, and the Bush, McKnight and Jerome Foundations. Four of his plays have been developed at Midwest PlayLabs, and one at Robert Redford's Sundance Institute in Utah.

Klein is an alumnus of the Playwrights' Center in Minneapolis, and was a Playwright-In-Residence at the Alliance Theatre in Atlanta. He has also taught playwriting at the University of Washington and the Cornish School of the Arts, both in Seattle.

Production History

BETTY THE YETI was first commissioned by A Contemporary Theatre in Seattle. It received its world premiere in the Humana Festival of New Plays at Actors Theatre of Louisville in March, 1994. The Seattle production opened one month later at A Contemporary Theatre. Both productions were directed by Jeff Steitzer. At the time of publication, BETTY THE YETI is scheduled for production at Stamford Theatre Works in Stamford, Connecticut.

Author's Note

Satire in the 90's is a risky business. It's a dangerous time to risk offending people, because—well, somebody might just object. And we certainly don't want that. Do we?

As in my play T BONE AND WEASEL, I employ satiric humor because I believe it illuminates social issues in a truthful and effective way. BETTY THE YETI reveals all sides of the Environmental Crisis to be equally valid—and equally absurd.

It would be dishonest for me to suggest that there are solutions that would satisfy all parties, and downright stupid to promote one viewpoint over all the others. The U.S. Government has been trying to come up with a timber compromise for two years now—without success. If there ever was a subject appropriate for satire, this is it.

So I chose to create this "Eco-Fable." With a creature that represents all the mystery and beauty of the ancient forests—and the same threat of extinction. It's a fairytale for adults.

One final comment. I don't believe theatre audiences turn their brains off when they're laughing (though some critics disagree). My hope is that the themes of this play continue to linger, long after the laughter subsides. About our own responsiblity to the natural world...and second chances.

Special thanks to William Dietrich, author of *The Final Forest*, for his support and inspiration.

—Jon Klein

FOR CAUTION NOTICE SEE PAGE OPPOSITE TABLE OF CONTENTS.

BETTY THE YETI by Jon Klein. ©1994 by Jon Klein. Reprinted by permission of the author. All inquiries should be addressed to Lois Berman and Judy Boals, Writers' Representatives, 21 W. 26th St., New York, NY 10010.

CHARACTERS

Iko – a forest ranger. Early twenties. Japanese-American woman. Wears uniform of the National Forest Service.

Clare Kutz – a logging contractor. Mid-fifties. A hearty, robust woman. Wears jean jacket, flannel shirts, jeans, work boots.

Trey Hugger – Founder of "Timber Watch," a watchdog organization. About thirty. Long hair, quite handsome, has short ponytail. Wears fashionable, expensive Northwest "outfitter" clothes.

Terra Sawyer – an environmental activist, and Clare's daughter. Mid-thirties. Wears sweatshirts, tight jeans, hiking boots.

Russ T. Sawyer – an unemployed logger, and Terra's husband (separated). Early forties. Short, unkempt hair and a week's worth of beard growth. Wears logger's work clothes: short pants, high work boots, suspenders over two layers of shirts.

The Creature – a yeti. Between five and six feet tall, slightly stooped. Though not quite human, a female form is slightly apparent under a layer of reddish-yellow fur and somewhat simian face.

PLACE:

A grove of old-growth in the Willamette National Forest, not far from the Santiam River.

A thick canopy of mossy trees that keeps daylight out and moisture in. The undergrowth is thick with ferns, flowering plants and downed trees. There is an enormous Douglas Fir, centuries old, that dominates the scene.

In a clearing, a small tent has been erected. A small amount of camping equipment and fishing gear sits outside the open tent, including an oil lantern. A fire ring has been built from stones, and the charred remains of a fire are evident.

A dark, mysterious, and beautiful place.

TIME:

Maybe never. Maybe tomorrow.

PRODUCTION ELEMENTS:

Since this play is a "fable," the production elements can and should emphasize a movement away from what is "real." Any attempt to construct a Natural History Museum panorama of the ancient forest is probably ill-advised. Designers should be encouraged to explore ways to suggest this atmosphere, rather than recreate it.

BETTY:

Remember, Betty is a mythical creature. Whatever costume is devised needs to allow flexibility, comfort and ease of movement. She's not quite human, and not quite an animal – and yet there are times she must seem to be very much like one or the other. It's important to emphasize that she has many animal modes – not always that of an ape. Though Betty has little "dialogue," the performer who plays her needs to be able to express thought and emotion in other ways. Her "character" needs to be as fully developed and considered as anyone else in the play – this is *not* just an actor in a monkey suit. Training in mime, movement and voices should be desirable qualities in casting the role.

The mythic Pacific Northwest is dead. Relics of it, human and otherwise, are scattered about the landscape, but it is unmistakably gone. In its place is a different country filled with factory outlets, Thai restaurants and tree farms; car dealerships, software designers and airplane factories; opera companies, beds and breakfasts.

This isn't of itself good or bad. It just is.

—Terry McDermott and Sylvia Nogaki
Seattle Times reporters

Betty the Yeti

ACT ONE

SCENE 1

A late March afternoon. A few thin shafts of sunlight manage to slice their way through the dense canopy of the ancient forest. Clare is situated some distance from the Douglas Fir, peering up into its tallest branches with binoculars. Iko is seated on a log speaking insistently into a portable communication device.

CLARE: Can't find him.

IKO: (*Into phone.*) Well, what did they expect?

CLARE: What's he look like again?

IKO: (*To Clare.*) Hold on a minute. (*Back to phone.*) Look, they don't have a backcountry permit, they take their chances . . . Let me guess, they couldn't find any pencils at the trailhead. If I've heard it once, I've heard it a hundred . . . No, it's okay, go ahead and fill one out for them. Which way are they heading? . . . No good. That site's overflowing already. Do they know how cold it gets up there? Did they bring an oil stove? . . . I knew it. Where are they from? Portland? . . . Seattle. Even worse. They'll build a fire in the alpine just to cook their turkey wieners. Send them back down to the Santiam for the night. Anything else? . . . I don't know. I'm still monitoring the situation here. . . . Not yet. I'll let you know when it happens.

(*She puts down the communicator and stands.*)

Honestly, some people walk into a National Forest and act like they *own* the place.

CLARE: Don't see him. Must have hopped away.

IKO: You would have seen any movement. He knows we're down here, so he's just trying to blend in. Look for the coloring.

CLARE: Tell me again.

IKO: Sort of a mottled grey . . .

CLARE: "Mottled?"

IKO: You know, spots.

(*Clare lowers the binoculars to take a look at Iko.*)

Um . . . spotty.

CLARE: Field biologist, right?

IKO: Well, graduate studies . . .

CLARE: Don't sell yourself short, hon. Anyone who can use the word "mottled" is at the advanced level.

(*She raises the binoculars.*)

Now help me find this creature.

IKO: Where are you at?

CLARE: Pretty high. I think lightning hit the trunk.

IKO: And up above, three branches shooting out on the same side?

CLARE: Right.

IKO: And a big squirrel's nest?

CLARE: Yeah! I've got it!

IKO: Wrong tree.

(*Clare glances at Iko in annoyance.*)

Now move to the left, and you'll see the top of a young hemlock. Keep going left, and the very next tree is the Douglas Fir.

CLARE: All right.

IKO: Now up about three branches.

CLARE: Well I'll be damned.

IKO: Find him?

CLARE: Looks asleep.

IKO: Not injured?

CLARE: Don't think so. How'd you identify him?

IKO: He dropped his wallet.

(*She produces a wallet from an inside pocket and shows it to Clare.*)

CLARE: Yep, that's Russ all right.

IKO: (*Pointing.*) An employee ID for Kutz Contractors. The only phone number I found.

CLARE: Ain't had work for him in months. I suspect that's part of the reason he's up there.

IKO: Oh no. Not an unemployed logger?

CLARE: That ain't all. His wife left him.

IKO: Oh God.

CLARE: Not the kind to kill himself, though. Not Russ.

IKO: You're sure about that?

CLARE: Nah. More likely to don a flak jacket and an AK-47 and take out a fast-food outlet.

IKO: Oh God, oh God.

CLARE: Never worked for the post office, though. So he's got that goin' for him.

(*She calls up to the top of the tree.*)

You stay awake up there, Russ! She'll be here soon!

IKO: Who'll be here?

CLARE: His wife, Terra. Called her right after I heard from you. Course she's gotta find a car, and it's a long drive . . .

IKO: Is that a good idea? To bring her here?

CLARE: Believe me, hon. If anybody knows how to bring him down, it's her.

IKO: How well do you know her?

CLARE: Not well.

IKO: Oh.

CLARE: She's my daughter. But we don't talk much anymore. Accused me of participating in – what did she call it? – the "last great buffalo hunt." Left her husband – one of the best cutters around, mind you . . . walked out on the family business – which she would have inherited . . . and moved to Portland. Works for one of those preservationist groups. You know the kind I mean, don't you? Beauty, Bambi and backpacking.

IKO: You cut mostly Old Growth, don't you?

CLARE: It's a living, hon. Used to be a good one, too. Just ask your employer – the Forest Service. These reserves were the best tree farms in the country till twenty years ago, when they started putting up barbecue grills and campgrounds.

IKO: You know, this is probably not the right time to discuss forest management. Not while we've got an emotionally disturbed man in a treetop.

CLARE: Seems like a good time to me. I was just thinkin' how nice it would be for the Department of Agriculture to be in on this. Think we should give 'em a call?

IKO: Please –

CLARE: All right, hon. Where'd you find the wallet?

IKO: I saw it fall. Heard it dropping through the branches.

CLARE: Must have taken him by surprise.

IKO: Well, I came up the trail and noticed this unauthorized campsite –

CLARE: Not the kind of man to bother with permits.

IKO: And I was afraid it might be another yew thief –

CLARE: A what?

IKO: Someone stripping bark off the Pacific Yew trees.

CLARE: There's money in that?

IKO: Quite a bit. It's a key ingredient in taxol – a remedy for cancer.

CLARE: Poaching tree bark. Thought I'd heard everything . . .

IKO: We do some hiring at yew season. Might even mean some work for your loggers.

CLARE: I'll keep that in mind, hon.

IKO: My name is Iko.

CLARE: Tell the boys at the Forest Service to give me a call. What they won't let me cut, I'll be happy to strip. I just can't stand the idea of all these trees just . . . standing here.

IKO: Providing oxygen and scenery –

CLARE: Right. What a waste of timber.

(*Terra enters, followed shortly by Trey. Terra is angry and breathless, while Trey is controlled and somewhat condescending, given the situation.*)

TERRA: Where is he?

(*Iko and Clare point to the top of the tree. She yells in that direction.*)

All right, Russ, you've had your fun. Now come down here!

IKO: Maybe a gentler approach –

TREY: Oh, I think when it comes to handling Mr. Sawyer, Terra is the acknowledged authority. May I?

(*He takes the binoculars from Clare and peers skyward.*)

CLARE: Did you have to bring him along?

TERRA: Hello, Mother.

TREY: I have a rule about other people driving my Range Rover.

CLARE: Shoulda guessed.

TERRA: Why is it that the only time I ever hear from you is when Russ has some sort of emotional crisis?

CLARE: You gotta admit, he's doin' his best to keep the family together.

TERRA: I can think of other ways.

(*She yells above again.*)

You hear me, Russ? This is the last time!

TREY: Remarkable agility for a man his age. How does he do it?

(*He hands the binoculars back to Clare.*)

CLARE: Experience, boy. You're lookin' at the best spar-climber in Willamette County. To this day I'd put my money on him over any young highballer in a grippin' contest.

TREY: Sounds like a perfect candidate for the demonstration job at the Museum of Science and Industry.

TERRA: Don't start, Trey.

TREY: Why not? I think a museum would be the perfect spot for the old boy. Along with the other relics of civilization. Whaling techniques on Tuesday, the Pony Express on Wednesday, Russ and his chain saw on Thursday . . .

CLARE: No call to be cruel, boy.

TREY: Cruel?

TERRA: Yes, Trey, you could give us a little help here.

TREY: Hey, I'm totally sympathetic.

(*He moves directly under the tree, next to the trunk. He calls up.*)

You hear me, Russ? I care about you too, you poor miserable unwanted bastard! You're not just one more casualty of federal mismanagement and industrial decline! Well, okay, so you are. Tell you what – when you come down I'll interview you for "Timber Watch!"

(*He turns to Iko.*)

That's my newsletter. Circulation increased by three thousand this year alone.

CLARE: I wouldn't stand so close, boy.

TREY: Close to what?

CLARE: To the tree. See, he's been up there for several hours, and I assume he took a full canteen . . .

TREY: What are you talking about?

(*A small amount of yellow liquid falls in a narrow stream from above onto Trey's head.*)

CLARE: Never mind.

TERRA: Ewww.

TREY: That son of a bitch . . .

CLARE: Still got the aim of an eagle.

TREY: Of all the sick –

IKO: You better wash out that jacket before the insects get you.

TERRA: Please do.

IKO: The river's down trail about a quarter mile.

TREY: Of all of the disgusting, juvenile –
TERRA: Go ahead, Trey. We'll be here a while.
    (*Trey begins to move off.*)
CLARE: Hey Trey.
    (*Trey stops and turns.*)
TREY: What now?
CLARE: What's the difference between a truckload of spotted owls and
    a truck full of bowling balls?
TREY: (*Resigned.*) What.
CLARE: You can't unload the bowling balls with a pitchfork.
TREY: Is that what passes for humor in the logging towns?
CLARE: Not much else to laugh about.
    (*Trey leaves furiously, taking off his jacket.*)
IKO: I guess he's got no intention of coming down.
CLARE: You know what it takes, don't you, Terra?
TERRA: Let's see what he brought along.
    (*Terra goes into the tent and pulls out a large backpack, which she
    begins to search through.
    Iko takes the binoculars from Clare and peers upward.*)
CLARE: Can't say that boy helped any.
TERRA: It's become a personal issue with him.
CLARE: Personal?
    (*Terra looks up from her search at her mother. A pause as she
    considers her answer.*)
TERRA: He's asked me to live with him.
CLARE: Oh, Lord, Terra.
TERRA: Just until the divorce is final.
CLARE: Then what? Another wedding?
TERRA: That's the general idea. According to Trey, anyway.
CLARE: My own daughter. And a green freak. Your father would turn
    over in his grave. If he hadn't been cremated.
TERRA: I haven't said yes, Mother. So there's no need to mention it to
    Russ. He gets easily upset.
IKO: (*Looking through binoculars.*) I've noticed.
TERRA: Don't worry, I'll get him out of your precious fiber farm in time
    for market.
IKO: Is it my imagination, or do people dislike federal employees?
CLARE: I take it you're not from around here.
IKO: No. Japan.

(*Pause.*)

CLARE: Yep. You're gonna have some trouble making friends.

(*Terra pulls a hand ax out of the pack and stands up.*)

TERRA: Here's what I'm looking for.

CLARE: Ain't met a cutter yet who won't respond to that.

(*Terra approaches the tree and yells skyward.*)

TERRA: TIMBER!

(*She gives the tree one good whack with the ax. Then she walks back to the pack, lays down the ax and sits on a log.*

Long pause. Iko looks up in disbelief.)

IKO: You gotta be kidding.

CLARE: Wait and see.

TERRA: It has a kind of subconscious effect.

(*Iko heads for her communicator.*)

IKO: This is ridiculous. I'm calling the state patrol. (*She picks up the phone.*) Come in, Shawn. Come in . . . The situation here is unchanged. Can you reach the Santiam station and tell them I need –

(*She stops at the sudden appearance of Russ, who has walked into the area from behind the tree. He is in full climbing gear. Russ surveys the three women, then looks at the ax.*)

RUSS: Who did that?

(*Pause.*)

IKO: Forget it, Shawn.

(*She puts down the communicator, stunned.*)

RUSS: Come on, now. Who was it?

IKO: How did you –

(*Terra confronts Russ.*)

TERRA: Who do you think.

RUSS: Haven't I told you . . . the *worst* thing to do to a logger –

TERRA: So when's your next stunt scheduled?

IKO: But how did –

RUSS: Don't change the subject.

IKO: But just how . . . where did . . . how did you . . .

(*Russ turns to Iko in agitation.*)

RUSS: What is your *problem*?

(*Terra turns to Iko and Clare.*)

CLARE: (*To Iko.*) What'd I tell you? Best climber in the county.

TERRA: Would you mind giving us a minute alone?

(*Clare and Iko begin to move off.*)

IKO: Sure. I need to check something over the ridge.

CLARE: And I'll head down to the river to look for old Yellow Jacket. (*To Iko.*) Say, any salmon left in the Santiam?

IKO: They're endangered.

CLARE: Who isn't?

(*Iko and Clare exit in opposite directions.*)

RUSS: He's at the river? Did I get him?

TERRA: Bull's eye.

RUSS: At least the day isn't a total loss.

TERRA: Oh, Russ. Why do the two of you bring out the worst in each other?

RUSS: Can't speak for Golden Boy. But as for me – gosh, why don't I like that guy? After all, he *is* a friend of yours. Assuming "friend" is still the appropriate word . . .

TERRA: Russ –

RUSS: Now let's see – could it be his flatlander attitude, or his perfectly groomed appearance, or his ever so trendy Northwest apparel, or his logger-hating magazine, or his new four-wheel drive with the cellular phone . . . or could it possibly just be that damn ponytail? Nope, I got it. It's his teeth. They look like the originals. Which means he never got hit by a runaway choker, or knocked down by a slipped cable. Hell, you can't even get near a tree with a sawblade without getting hurt somehow. I've seen them explode, you know that?

TERRA: I know –

RUSS: It's true. Trees can explode. Blow up right in your face before you even finish the diagonal cut. Took out Chuck Hodge's eye.

TERRA: I remember –

RUSS: Won't find a man in this county ain't been hurt somehow. Insurance companies won't even return our calls. Say the only job more dangerous is professional football. Course those guys get paid a little better.

TERRA: Calm down, Russ. You're gonna have a rigging fit.

RUSS: My own father, God rest his soul, lived to the ripe old age of forty-nine until a rotted-out cedar came down on his back. Ten years of white finger never kept him from a day's work.

TERRA: I was talking about you and Trey –

RUSS: And so am I. If he had just one little scar on his face, just one finger missing, hell, I'd settle for a slight limp! – I'd have some respect for that pissant tree lover. I'd even give him permission to talk about shutting down a way of life for which my father contributed his last breath. But no – he's just too damn pretty.

TERRA: So that's what it comes down to. Jealousy.

RUSS: You don't think he's pretty?

TERRA: We're not talking about me.

RUSS: We are now. Why *do* you hang around with him?

TERRA: We have common interests.

RUSS: Really? What position?

TERRA: You're impossible. The divorce isn't even final and you're already worrying about other men –

RUSS: You tryin' to tell me he's never laid a hand on you? Never even tried?

(*Pause.*)

Funny how quiet the forest can get.

TERRA: You know, you'll find this hard to believe, but sometimes late at night, I can manage to remember a few good times. Sometimes I even miss you.

RUSS: So what keeps you from comin' home?

TERRA: You know what keeps me. I can't reconcile my beliefs –

RUSS: Here we go. Politics.

TERRA: Use whatever word you want, it's still the most important thing in my life, to try and preserve this planet. Not so much for myself as for the children.

RUSS: Meaning, I suppose, the children we never had.

TERRA: Oh God, Russ, just listen to yourself. Not everything in the world has to do with you and me. There are more important things happening out there.

RUSS: More important than us.

(*Pause.*)

TERRA: At the moment. Yes.

(*Pause.*)

RUSS: Another exploding tree.

TERRA: Why do you make me say these things?

RUSS: You're right. I should know better.

TERRA: It's not like you don't have a choice, Russ. Anything's better than sitting around feeling sorry for yourself.

RUSS: So what do you suggest?

TERRA: Eco-tourism.

RUSS: Aw jeez, not this again.

TERRA: It's a growing field.

RUSS: Come on, Terra. Do you see me renting mountain bikes? Handing out soft yogurt to people from Long Island?

TERRA: You know the backcountry better than anyone around.

RUSS: A trail guide. Ah, there's the life. "Just look at them big trees, folks. Bet you ain't ever seen the likes of those back in Ohio. And don't forget, we forced hundreds of local folks out of their jobs just so you can run your videocams and tell the neighbors back home how you spent your vacation 'roughing it.' "

TERRA: That's hardly fair –

RUSS: "And while you're at it, just help yourself to all the fish and game. After all, you don't mind taking our lumber to build your hot tubs and wipe your asses, so why not finish the job and take *all* of our natural resources. But be sure to tell the folks back home in Saginaw how we're raping the environment. Okay, group photo!"

TERRA: Why do you have such a closed mind? I don't think it would be such a bad life, maybe running a little bed and breakfast on the edge of the forest. I wouldn't have to worry about you being killed or injured every hour of the day.

RUSS: Oh, stop it, Terra. That's not why you left and you know it. You were ashamed of me.

TERRA: Well, I don't think displacing wildlife and butchering the landscape is anything to be proud of.

(*Russ stands up, stung. Iko enters the area, cautiously.*)

RUSS: You know, there was a time you didn't even care about the forest.

TERRA: I didn't have to care. Not until Mom started sending crews into the Old Growth.

RUSS: And I became a butcher.

(*Terra notices Iko's presence and changes her tone.*)

TERRA: I didn't mean that.

RUSS: Then why did you say it?

TERRA: Bad choice of words –

RUSS: Sure, whatever.

IKO: Should I . . . is this . . .

RUSS: It's all right, lady. At the end of a long, hard day of slaughter and destruction, this little Hitler gets tired. So if you two will excuse me –

(*He heads for the tent. Iko approaches him.*)

IKO: Mr. Sawyer. I'm afraid you've camped on an unauthorized site. No offense.

(*Russ stops and gives her a hard look.*)

RUSS: And I'm afraid the most likely person to encounter serious injury at this particular moment is some . . . pellet counter, telling me where I can or cannot take a nap. No offense.

TERRA: She's just doing her job, Russ.

RUSS: At least she's got one.

(*Russ goes in the tent and zips it shut, not acknowledging either of the women further.*)

TERRA: Sorry.

IKO: What's he so sensitive about?

TERRA: Russ is a vet. Words like "butcher" have a different resonance for him.

IKO: Vietnam?

TERRA: That's why he became a cutter – not for the scenery, not for the fresh air, not even for the money. It was the solitude. Now all of a sudden he's the killer of spotted owls and ancient forests. It's like he just stepped off the plane in his uniform, facing the protesters.

(*Iko looks toward the tent.*)

IKO: What do you want me to do?

TERRA: You can cut him a break. If he wants to spend some time alone in the woods, who's he gonna hurt? And who's gonna hurt him?

IKO: There are designated sites –

TERRA: All swarming with people who can't spend more than one night away from their hot showers and blow dryers. You know what they're like.

IKO: But the rules –

TERRA: Rules are meant to be changed. This is America, know what I mean? Don't be so . . .

IKO: Japanese?

TERRA: Sorry. It's just that . . . well, maybe I should just come right out and ask you.

IKO: Please do.

TERRA: Life in Japan . . . for a woman, I mean . . . isn't it a little like
. . . slavery?

IKO: It's a cultural thing.

TERRA: Right.

IKO: A really *male* culture.

TERRA: I hear you.

(*Pause. The wind blows through the trees.*)

IKO: I wonder. Why do unhappy people like to go to the woods? Why
not a bar?

TERRA: You know the saying. If a tree falls in the forest . . .

(*Trey enters with Clare. He carries his wet jacket.*)

TREY: If a tree falls in the forest, and no one is there to hear it – you
can still get an injunction in federal court. Has the noble warrior
returned?

TERRA: He's resting. So leave him alone, Trey.

TREY: I kind of liked the tree-sitting bit. Reminded me of the early
days of the movement.

CLARE: Hardly the same.

TREY: Oh, I don't know. Earth First used to do things like that.

CLARE: Along with spiking trees. And putting sugar in the gas tanks of
bulldozers.

TREY: Renegades. No one ever approved of tactics that could cause
injury.

CLARE: Officially, anyway.

TREY: Besides, now we know that sitting in a courtroom is more
productive than sitting in a tree.

CLARE: Really? I just thought your generation was scared of heights.

TREY: I'm beginning to see where sympathies lie around here. Not
with the pissee, but with the pisser.

TERRA: He *has* been through a lot, Trey.

TREY: This is truly amazing. Here's a guy who sends four people
running all over the state just to come and hold his hand. Yet *I'm*
the one that's out of line. Would it be too sullen of me to suggest
that what he really needs is a good therapist?

TERRA: Yes it would.

IKO: You know, Mister, I hope you care more about trees than you do
for people.

CLARE: Good one, hon.

TREY: You know, I've been wondering about something. What in the world is a Japanese girl doing in a U.S. National Forest? Shopping?

TERRA: Stop it, Trey.

(*Trey looks around at the trees, making his selections.*)

TREY: Let's see, there's a red cedar, what a lovely deck for your Dad's ranch house. And over there's a young redwood! How perfect for that dining room table Mom's been searching for. And what about this Douglas Fir? I know – a teahouse!

IKO: Is this the only common ground you people can manage to find? Japan-bashing?

CLARE: The great American pastime, hon. It makes us feel all warm inside.

TERRA: Lay off, Trey. It's not like her own family is responsible for the trade wars.

TREY: How do you know? Did she give you her background?

TERRA: Go ahead and ask her.

(*Iko looks at Terra wide-eyed.*)

I know, it's none of his business. But trust me, it will just put an end to the argument.

TREY: Okay. What's your father do?

IKO: Do?

TREY: You know. For a living.

IKO: Well, he has his own business.

TREY: Which is?

(*Pause.*)

IKO: Imports.

CLARE: Uh oh.

TERRA: It's okay, Iko. It's not like he buys raw logs or anything.

(*Iko freezes up. Pause.*)

Right?

IKO: Umm . . .

TERRA: Oh no.

TREY: I knew it.

(*He turns back to Iko.*)

Four billion board feet of untouched lumber in Japan, but do they dare cut any of their own precious forests? No, it's easier to just wage economic war.

CLARE: Don't you listen to him, hon. You people are the only ones keepin' our heads above water.

TERRA: I've pointed this out to you many times, Mother. Every raw log sent overseas equals four lost jobs in the States. So whose heads are you talking about?

CLARE: Oh, hell, Terra. Name one job that don't hurt the environment or exploit its workers . . .

TERRA: There are hundreds of –

CLARE: . . . and where you can make a living wage.

TERRA: Well, now you're just being unreasonable.

(*Russ' voice comes from inside the tent.*)

RUSS: (*Shouting.*) Will you all shut the fuck up?

(*Pause. Everyone considers this for a minute.*)

TREY: You know, I used to have trouble understanding Russ.

TERRA: He's right. We should go.

TREY: No, I want him to hear this. And all of you too. Just to show I'm not completely insensitive. (*To Iko.*) Trees more than people, isn't that what you said?

IKO: Maybe I shouldn't have –

TREY: No, no, you were right. And you helped me gain some terrific insight into Sawyer's predicament. After all, isn't he a lot like the very trees that he cuts down? Trees that serve their purpose well for half a century or so, but then – (*Gesturing to Clare.*) according to the industry, at least – trees that outlive their usefulness.

TERRA: Don't do this, Trey.

(*Trey walks over to the Douglas Fir, raising his voice to make sure Russ can hear every word.*)

TREY: He must feel a lot like this big old Douglas here. Needles thinning out on top. Bulging out in the middle with fatty tumors. Infected with all the rot and disease that naturally come with age. A home for various parasites and microbes. Losing its ability to keep its appendages . . . erect. Maybe he's right. Maybe it's better to just – cut it down.

(*The tent flap zips open, as Russ comes out with a large hunting knife.*)

RUSS: You're gonna see some cutting now, you self-righteous little prick.

TERRA: I knew this would happen.

(*Russ and Trey face off.*)

IKO: Not on federal property!

TREY: Come on, Pops. I'm ready for you.

TERRA: Put it down, Russ.

RUSS: Oh, I know where to put it.

IKO: Please. Stop it!

TREY: "Pardon me, thou bleeding piece of earth, that I am meek and gentle with these butchers." Shakespeare.

RUSS: "Kiss your ass goodbye, college boy." Russ Sawyer.

IKO: I mean it! You'll scare away the owl!

(*Everyone stops and turns to Iko. Russ and Trey immediately forget about the fight, and Russ unconsciously lowers the knife. Long pause.*)

Oh shit.

TERRA: Owl?

CLARE: There's an owl around here?

TREY: A *spotted* owl?

IKO: I didn't say owl.

RUSS: Oh yes you did.

IKO: I said "bowel."

TERRA: "You'll scare away the 'bowel'?"

IKO: It's an old Japanese saying. It means . . . "do not agitate my upset stomach."

CLARE: No, I heard you too.

TERRA: You distinctly said "owl."

TREY: All right, come clean. Where's the nest?

IKO: I don't know.

TERRA: Then where'd you see it last?

IKO: (*Pointing.*) Well, I was up on that ridge yesterday –

TERRA: The ridge!

CLARE: Damn it.

(*Clare sits on a log despondently.*)

TERRA: Come on. Let's take a look.

(*Trey approaches Clare, gloating.*)

TREY: You know what that means, don't you, Clare?

CLARE: I know what it means.

IKO: All right. I'll show you where I saw it if you promise to approach quietly.

TREY: Believe me, miss. When it comes to spotted owls I can be as quiet as the mice they consume. Lead the way.

(*Iko reluctantly guides the excited Terra and Trey off.*)

CLARE: Another three thousand acres that I can't touch. That's what it means. And the sale on this timber is slated for next year. If she ever finds that nest . . .

RUSS: She won't find the nest. Not up on the ridge.

CLARE: How do you know?

RUSS: Because . . . I know where the nest is.

(*Pause. Clare looks at him with intensity.*)

CLARE: Keep your voice low.

(*She stands up and slowly moves toward him, looking off in the others' direction, to make sure they're still alone.*)

Where?

(*Russ points to the top of the Douglas Fir.*)

You saw it up there?

RUSS: I was sitting next to it.

CLARE: Was there a pair?

RUSS: Just one. And you know the strangest thing about it?

CLARE: What?

RUSS: You promise not to tell anybody –

CLARE: Yes, yes, what is it?

(*Pause. Russ walks away from her, embarrassed.*)

RUSS: I kind of . . . *liked* it.

(*Pause.*)

CLARE: I'm not quite following you, son.

RUSS: I . . . liked the owl. I thought it was . . . cute.

(*Pause.*)

CLARE: Let me see if I understand this. You mean to tell me you were close enough to stare right into the eyes of the very creature that . . . that represents the end of a century of tradition and prosperity – and you thought it was *cute?*

RUSS: I'm so embarrassed.

CLARE: You're a disgrace to the state of Oregon.

RUSS: I know, I know. But it had these big brown eyes, like a sweet little spotted pussycat or something, and it wasn't afraid at all. I mean, I could have leaned over, put my hands around its little grey neck, and slowly squeezed the breath out of the poor little thing – and *it would have let me.* That's how trusting it was, how sure that I meant it no harm.

CLARE: Good Lord, Russ . . .

RUSS: I know, I know, I feel like I've lost my manhood.

CLARE: At the very least.

(*Russ looks skyward.*)

RUSS: Oh, God. Why did it have to be an *owl?* Why couldn't you have made it some kind of endangered forest *rat,* or some kind of disgusting beetle that lives on its own dung? The public relations would never have worked: "Save the Pacific Dung Beetle – It Gives a Shit. Won't You?" But no, you had to make it an owl. The wise old owl. The protector of the forest. The master hunter. Hell, even Merlin had an owl.

CLARE: Who, Merlin Crabbe? Down at the sawmill?

RUSS: No, no. King Arthur's Merlin. Remember the Disney cartoon?

CLARE: Oh, right. Well, look, boy, don't punish yourself. It's not just owls anymore. Now they've added salmon to the list, and that weird fuzzy seabird . . .

RUSS: The marbled murrelet.

CLARE: That's it. Hell, Terra goes even further than that, says everybody has to start looking at the big picture. According to her it all connects somehow – trees, animals, even plants –

RUSS: The ecosystem.

CLARE: That's the word.

RUSS: She uses it a lot.

CLARE: Look. Let's just keep this owl nest our little secret. I'll figure out something. In the meantime I'll drop a few names from the Forest Service and talk that gal into letting you keep your tent here.

RUSS: Thanks.

CLARE: Don't mention it.

(*She starts off after the others. Russ looks up into the tree.*)

RUSS: That's the life.

(*Clare stops and turns.*)

CLARE: What?

RUSS: Three thousand acres. Per pair. Did you know they mate for life?

CLARE: Listen up, boy. I like animals as much as the next person. But you gotta know where to draw the line.

(*Clare turns and exits.*

Russ reflects for a moment, then goes into his tent.

A beat.

At the far upstage corner, The Creature appears. It enters slowly, then remains still, watching the tent. Lights out, fast.)

SCENE 2

A few days later. Evening. The lantern is lit.
Iko is in the area, hooting in imitation of the spotted owl. She looks
up in the trees, waiting for a response.
She hoots again, then waits.
Russ enters from the direction of the river, carrying fishing gear
and two mid-sized salmon.
Iko doesn't see him, and hoots again.

RUSS: So this is our tax dollars at work.
  (*She turns, slightly startled.*)
IKO: Oh, it's you. Did you see the owl down there?
RUSS: Nothing but a couple of flatlanders.
IKO: That reminds me. I'm getting some reports that you're warning
  hikers away from the Santiam. With stories of cottonmouths.
RUSS: So what?
IKO: They're not indigenous and you know it.
RUSS: Anyone who doesn't know which snakes to watch for has no
  business hiking here anyway.
  (*He lays out the salmon on a cloth.*)
  Besides, I didn't want anybody spooking my supper.
  (*She approaches the fish and examines them.*)
IKO: Those are coho salmon! You're not allowed to catch those!
RUSS: Damn. And here I thought they were cutthroat trout.
IKO: You know very well what they are – a threatened species.
RUSS: Wouldn't it be nice if loggers got the same protection as owls
  and fish?
IKO: Do you know how many times I've heard that question?
RUSS: Obviously not enough to come up with a good answer.
  (*He looks up and sees her look of disapproval.*)
  Look, it's a little late for throwing them back. What do you want
  me to do?
IKO: I want you to start respecting my authority. I'm already breaking
  enough rules just letting you stay.
RUSS: All right, I appreciate it. Okay?
IKO: How long do you plan on camping here?
RUSS: I don't plan to plan any plans.

IKO: What?

RUSS: I'll let you know.

IKO: No more salmon. And no more scaring off hikers with fake snakes.

RUSS: Yes, Mom. Join me for supper?

IKO: They do look good.

RUSS: Wait till you see how I prepare them. A little garlic, a little white wine – one taste and you'll think you're back in Yokohama.

IKO: I've never been to Yokohama.

RUSS: All right then. Portland.

(He starts pulling out ingredients and cookware from his backpack.

Iko turns and takes her position, then hoots. She looks and listens for a response from the trees. She hoots again.

A beat.

A loud, nearby hoot of forceful proportions comes from nearby – at ground level.

Russ stops what he's doing as Iko freezes.)

That sounds like one big owl.

IKO: Where'd it come from?

RUSS: Try it again.

(Russ slowly stands, looking around. Iko nervously hoots again. The Creature slowly comes into view. It hoots, rather ferociously. Pause.)

(Softly.) We're both going to die.

IKO: Be very still.

RUSS: What the hell *is* it?

IKO: I don't know.

RUSS: That smell –

IKO: I know.

RUSS: It's a bear, right? What else could be that size . . . except some kind of weird albino bear.

(The Creature throws back its head and gives a high-pitched shriek.

Pause.)

Or there may be other choices.

IKO: That was an eagle cry.

RUSS: I think we need an Audubon Guide.

IKO: It has some sort of mimetic ability. Fascinating.

RUSS: Those things on its . . . chest.

IKO: Yes, I think so too. A female.

RUSS: Hey, are we positive this thing is by itself?

IKO: I think it's alone.

RUSS: For all we know, this could be the runt of the litter.

IKO: Whatever it is, animals don't approach campsites unless they're hungry.

RUSS: That's reassuring.

IKO: Just don't run. That's the worst thing you can do.

RUSS: I hate it when people say that.

IKO: Do you have any food on you?

RUSS: Some beef jerky.

IKO: What kind?

RUSS: I don't know. Why? You think this thing is brand-conscious?

IKO: I want to make exact notes on what food she eats and rejects.

(*Russ slowly pulls the plastic bag out of his jacket pocket. The Creature snorts and cocks its head.*)

Don't startle it.

RUSS: Oh, there's good advice.

IKO: Give her some.

RUSS: All right. Don't rush me.

(*He lays a strip of jerky down on the ground and slowly backs away.*)

There.

(*The Creature looks at the jerky, looks at him, looks back at the food.*)

IKO: It's not working. You have to establish permission, form a bond with the animal.

RUSS: Well what do you expect me to do, feed it by hand?

(*Iko doesn't reply, but just looks at him. He responds to her look.*)

No. No way. Forget it.

IKO: Take a bite of it first to show that it's food. With that stuff it's hard to tell.

RUSS: You do it.

IKO: I don't eat meat.

(*Russ pulls out another strip of jerky and takes a bite of it, focusing on The Creature.*)

RUSS: Yum. Tasty. Much better than human flesh.

IKO: Now hold it out.

(*The Creature cocks its head, takes one step toward Russ and stops.*)

So far so good.

RUSS: As long as it doesn't do anything unpredictable, like –

(*The Creature saunters over to Russ without hesitation, smells the meat and takes the strip of jerky by its mouth.*)

Oh please God not the fingers not the fingers not the fingers –

IKO: Shhh. See what it does.

(*The Creature starts to chew on the end of the strip, then stops abruptly. Its expression suddenly changes to one of displeasure. It starts growling, and shaking its head back and forth like a dog with a rope.*)

RUSS: Give it a chance. It's an acquired taste.

(*Finally The Creature lets loose of the jerky, flinging it across the area into oblivion. It eyes Russ suspiciously, still growling. Pause.*)

Oh Christ. You know that rule about not running?

IKO: Yes.

RUSS: I say fuck it.

IKO: Not a good idea. We become instant prey.

RUSS: What are we now?

IKO: She's not sure. Better to keep her guessing.

(*The Creature begins to sniff and look around the campsite. It moves over to the salmon, laid out on the ground.*)

She wants the salmon.

RUSS: But that's our dinner.

(*Russ moves cautiously toward the salmon. The Creature begins to growl again, eyeing Russ. Russ backs away.*)

Feel free. As much as you want.

(*The Creature stops growling, takes the fish and quickly moves off, crashing through the brush.*)

IKO: I'm gonna follow it.

(*Iko sprints off.*

Russ' legs finally give out, and he sits down hard on the ground. He starts to hyperventilate, and puts his head between his knees. Finally, as he catches his breath, an idea occurs to him.)

RUSS: Oh my God. It's from Hanford.

(*He stands up, looking around uncertainly.*)

They said there were leaks. Some . . . raccoon, or maybe a big marmot . . . wandered onto the reservation, and turned into this

. . . atomic mutant.

(*He surveys the tent.*)

Definitely time to pack.

(*He goes to the tent and squats, wrapping up the fish and restoring items to his backpack.*)

Yep. A soft couch, a six-pack, a pizza, and a long night of watching Ronco products. That's what I want.

(*The Creature has reappeared, coming up behind him. It approaches Russ without fear. Russ doesn't notice.*)

No owls, no hikers, no rangers, and best of all, no –

(*He senses a presence behind him.*)

. . . chance of surviving.

(*Russ turns his head and noticing how close The Creature is to him, steps backwards and loses his balance. He sits down hard on the ground, and tries to protect himself with his pack.*

The Creature takes the pack from him, searching inside of it. Then she goes to the tent and marks her territory.

It goes inside, taking the pack with her. Russ doesn't dare move, allowing The Creature to settle itself.

A beat.

Russ slowly approaches the tent and looks inside.

Iko enters the area, in agitation.)

IKO: I lost it. Now no one will ever believe –

RUSS: (*Softly.*) Shh.

(*Iko stops in her tracks.*)

She's sleeping.

(*Lights out.*)

SCENE 3

Three days later.

The area is now littered with bags – duffel bags, backpacks, etc. Some are plastic, some are nylon, some seem new, some quite old. All seem to contain at least some items.

Terra and Trey are there, Terra scanning the area, Trey sticking his head in the tent.

TERRA: Any sign of him?

(*Trey pulls his head out, grimacing.*)

TREY: Only the smell. Man, that is intense.

TERRA: Russ never washed much during camping trips.

TREY: That must have been fun.

TERRA: It can be. I wonder what all these bags are doing here.

TREY: It proves he's not lonely. Maybe some of his logging buddies –

TERRA: Don't think so. Loggers don't hang with other loggers. Not during a layoff. And Russ isn't exactly renowned for his social skills.

TREY: Well, I didn't drive an hour and hike three miles for nothing. We'll just wait till he gets back.

TERRA: This isn't necessary, Trey. I can always mail him the divorce petition.

TREY: Are you kidding? He moved up here to *escape* mail delivery. I know how his mind works. This way I'll see you put those papers right into his grubby little fingers.

TERRA: He won't even bother to read them.

TREY: That's alright. At least he'll know you mean business.

TERRA: You know, I *am* capable of handling this myself. I don't need your help.

TREY: Well, can you blame me? You won't take my offer seriously until the marriage is dissolved.

TERRA: That's true.

TREY: And you refuse to move in with me. You'd rather stay in that lousy basement apartment.

TERRA: I like having my own space.

TREY: You don't even have any windows, Terra.

TERRA: I have my posters. Of the ancient forest.

TREY: Great. You know how many trees were cut to make those?

(*Terra holds her hands to her head and groans furiously.*)

TERRA: Aaarrrgghhh . . .

TREY: I know. It gets complicated.

TERRA: You never let loose, do you?

TREY: Not when it comes to the issues. Do you know how many environmentalists have already lost their credibility? Half of them are working as consultants for the timber industry.

TERRA: I'm not talking about the movement, Trey.

TREY: You're not?

TERRA: It's just that you're so . . . hard on everybody. Especially Russ . . .

TREY: Sawyer again. It always comes back to Sawyer.

TERRA: I was married to him, you know. For ten years.

TREY: You're too sentimental about these things. So he's stuck in the middle of a national crisis. That doesn't mean he can't find something else to do. And make himself more useful.

TERRA: Useful. Right.

TREY: What's the matter? Did I say something wrong?

TERRA: Of course not, Trey. You say everything right. It's impossible to try and argue with you.

TREY: Why would you want to?

TERRA: I don't know. You're the best activist I've ever met . . . I have the greatest admiration for what you do . . .

TREY: But?

TERRA: But what do you feel?

TREY: Feel? About what?

TERRA: About the trees? Or the wildlife? Look around and above you at this ancient forest . . .

TREY: It's very nice.

TERRA: Nice? It's awe-inspiring. It's stunning. Words can't do it justice . . .

TREY: Then what do you want me to say?

TERRA: I don't know. Something . . .

TREY: Look, why do you think I'm protecting the spotted owl? Not because I think it's a spectacular animal. If you ask me, it's not very bright, doesn't fly very well and is far too tame for its own good. But it *is* an excellent indicator for the environment.

TERRA: But look around. Doesn't this make you feel more . . . alive? Don't you wanna just rip your clothes off and make love in the dirt? Or are you afraid of bugs?

TREY: Of course not. I don't care about bugs.

TERRA: Good.

TREY: It's erosion. We'd just be adding to the problem.

TERRA: Oh, Trey . . .

TREY: And these ferns look pretty delicate . . .

TERRA: Never mind.

TREY: Oh, I get it. You wish I were more like Sawyer.

TERRA: God no. He'd make love in the forest, then clear cut it the next day.

TREY: I suppose I could be a little . . . looser.

TERRA: It's all right, Trey.

TREY: No, I should learn how to do this. Just let me find an appropriate spot . . .

(*Trey walks around the area, checking the layout, uncomfortably removing his jacket and laying it neatly over a log. Terra is amused. She approaches him, puts her arm around him, and kisses him affectionately.*)

TERRA: Let's go back to your place. We'll be more comfortable.

TREY: Tell you what. I'll let you drive the Range Rover.

TERRA: This is a big step, Trey. I'm proud of you.

(*Iko enters, and looks around for signs of Russ and The Creature, confused by the bags.*)

IKO: Where's Russ?

TERRA: We haven't seen him. Maybe the river?

IKO: It's possible.

TREY: With a little luck, something dragged him away and ate him for supper.

IKO: Even more possible.

TERRA: Tell him . . . no, forget it. Don't mention you saw us.

IKO: Whatever.

(*Terra and Trey exit. Russ and The Creature enter from the opposite side, carrying three or four more bags to add to the collection.*)

RUSS: Thought they'd never leave.

IKO: What's all this?

RUSS: She's been keeping them stashed somewhere. Now she wants to show them to us.

IKO: The instincts of a packrat, or a ground squirrel. I'm not sure this animal has any idea what she is.

RUSS: Do you?

IKO: Well, I called the Society of Cryptozoology . . .

RUSS: The what?

IKO: The scientific study of hidden animals.

RUSS: There's a club for everything, isn't there?

(*She pulls out a small notebook and consults her notes.*)

IKO: They keep records of any mysterious animal sightings, such as the Loch Ness Monster, or Ogopogo in British Columbia . . . or the Sasquatch.

RUSS: Is that what she is?

IKO: I don't think so.

(*The Creature suddenly dumps the contents of a bag onto the ground, picking up camping and personal items, examining them.*)

This animal is much too small. Her arms don't drag on the ground, and look at her paws. Hardly a "Bigfoot."

RUSS: Then what is she?

IKO: I think what we have here is an American version of the Tibetan yeti.

RUSS: A yeti?

THE CREATURE: Ett . . . tee?

IKO: My God. She's starting to emulate human language.

RUSS: Wait a minute. Are you talking about the Abominable Snowman?

IKO: Sort of. Her size and coloring matches descriptions of creatures seen in the low Himalayan forests. Which have similarities to the Old Growth forests of the Pacific Northwest.

RUSS: A yeti.

THE CREATURE: Ett . . . tee.

IKO: No, no. Yeh. Yeh-tee.

THE CREATURE: Yett . . . tee.

RUSS: Better.

THE CREATURE: Bet . . . tee.

IKO: Yeh . . . tee.

THE CREATURE: Bet . . . tee.

RUSS: Hold on. If that's what she wants to call herself, why not? Betty.

THE CREATURE: Bet-tee.

RUSS: It's a good name.

(*The Creature is overjoyed, hopping around the campsite.*)

THE CREATURE: Bet-tee. Bet-tee. Bet-tee. Bet-tee. Bet-tee. Bet-tee. Bet-tee. Bet-tee.

RUSS: Hey!

(*The Creature stops and looks at Russ, slightly cowed.*)

It's not *that* good.

IKO: You two seem to have developed quite a rapport.

RUSS: Oh, I've gotten way beyond yes and no. Watch this. Betty.

(*The Creature becomes alert, watching Russ carefully.*)

Game?

(*The Creature gets excited, throwing her arms over her head and*

snorting.)
Listen. Listen.
(*The Creature stops and watches Russ attentively.*)
Owl.
(*The Creature widens her eyes and swivels her head, keeping her body perfectly still.*)

IKO: Unbelievable.

RUSS: Hold on. (*To The Creature.*) Bobcat.
(*The Creature arches her back and growls low.*)

IKO: Like the animal version of a street mime.

RUSS: Fish.
(*The Creature swims against an unseen current, puffing her cheeks.*)
Now get a load of this. Abstract concepts.

IKO: What do you mean?

RUSS: Just watch. Pain.
(*The Creature licks her paw.*)
Happy.
(*The Creature rubs her crotch on a log.*)

IKO: I wish *I* could be that happy.

RUSS: Let's try something really complex.

IKO: Like what?

RUSS: I don't know . . . how about combining the concepts?
(*To The Creature.*)
Happy Pain Fish.
(*Pause. The Creature stares at Russ, then picks up a scoop of loose dirt and throws it at him.*)

IKO: Happy Pain Fish?

RUSS: Too advanced, huh?

IKO: Too stupid.

RUSS: All right, all right. Cold.
(*The Creature curls up on the ground and begins to sleep.*)
What's that supposed to be?

IKO: I think she's showing us hibernation. She must have a winter shelter.

RUSS: I've been following her back and forth. To what I think must be her home.

IKO: Where is it?

RUSS: The lava flow. But I lost her among the boulders.

Iko: So that's where she's been keeping these bags. Hidden in some lava tube.

Russ: Couldn't keep up with her. She sprang from rock to rock like a goat.

(*The Creature stands up and hops with agility.*)

Yeah, right. Goat. Enough.

(*The Creature settles down again.*)

I just kept falling down and cutting my legs.

Iko: That's the obsidian flow – black glass. And it explains why she's been protected all this time from hunters and predators. They can't walk on it any better than you. Even the original surveyors never returned.

Russ: You mean these guys?

(*Russ goes to an old duffel bag and pulls out a couple of surveying tools from the late 19th century.*

Iko looks it over and reads an inscription.)

Iko: "James J. Hill, proprietor. 1886." Whoever owned this equipment was surveying for the Northern Pacific Railroad.

Russ: Railroad? There's no railroad around here.

Iko: That's right. In 1900 Hill suddenly sold all the timberland to Frederick Weyerhauser. For six cents an acre.

Russ: But he never cut these trees.

Iko: Something kept dissuading them. I wonder what.

Russ: I think I have an idea.

(*Russ reaches into the bag and pulls out a human skull.*

Pause. They both slowly turn and stare at The Creature.

The Creature belches.)

Iko: I should report this.

Russ: Now hold on. Let's think this through.

(*He puts the items back in the bag and closes the bag, reflecting.*)

Look. There's no proof it was her that . . . discouraged . . . these land developers.

Iko: Probably her ancestors. It was over a hundred years ago.

Russ: So why make her pay for what they did? What do you think would happen if we reported her to the authorities?

Iko: These woods would swarm with biologists and wildlife agents. Armed with tranquilizer darts.

Russ: And what if Betty isn't too keen on the idea of being captured alive? What if she uses those claws to do a little damage in the process?

IKO: They'd destroy her.

RUSS: On the spot.

IKO: So what do you suggest?

RUSS: I suggest we keep her our own little secret. In the meantime, you can do your own private observations on her. Studying her habits in the wild.

IKO: Ideal conditions, that's true.

RUSS: Without a hundred scientists watching her every move and telling you to stand out of the way.

IKO: So what's your angle?

RUSS: No angle. I just want to help.

IKO: Why?

(*Pause.*)

RUSS: I don't have much to keep me going right now, you know? This would give me . . . I don't know, a goal . . . something I can do.

(*Pause.*)

What do you say?

(*Iko holds out her hand. Russ shakes it with pleasure.*)

IKO: First thing. We have to protect her sanctity.

RUSS: How?

IKO: Oh, we can start with a little trail maintenance. You know that log bridge over the Santiam?

RUSS: Yeah.

IKO: It just washed out.

RUSS: I love it! What else?

IKO: A few variations on your snake tales. Only this time let's use animals that actually live in the forest. Maybe a bear chasing hikers . . .

RUSS: Or a rabid bobcat . . .

(*Betty begins to respond to the word, but is immediately silenced by a gesture from Russ.*)

IKO: Now you're talking. But the worst problem is Betty herself.

RUSS: You mean she's too friendly.

IKO: Too conspicuous. There's an old saying in Japan. "Deru kugi wa utareru."

RUSS: What's it mean?

IKO: "The protruding nail gets hammered down."

(*The Creature perks up, listening carefully. Suddenly, she springs to her feet and runs off.)*

RUSS: Someone's coming.

IKO: Still afraid of strangers. That's good.

(*Clare comes into the clearing. She looks around at the collection of bags.*)

CLARE: What the hell is this?

RUSS: This?

CLARE: All these bags.

IKO: New forest service policy.

CLARE: Which is —

IKO: Confiscation. Anyone caught on federal land without a permit, gets his property seized by the Government.

CLARE: What?

IKO: Gentle persuasion doesn't work.

CLARE: This is a National Forest. Not the Mexican border.

RUSS: What are you doing here, Clare?

CLARE: Your landlord called me. Rent's overdue.

RUSS: What'd you tell him?

CLARE: Told him you don't work for me anymore. (*To Iko.*) Oh, guess what I saw on the way up here. A rare and mystical creature.

(*Russ and Iko respond simultaneously, with great nervousness.*)

IKO: What?

RUSS: What are you talking about?

CLARE: The spotted owl.

IKO: (*Relieved.*) Oh, that.

CLARE: Excuse me. I thought it was in your job description to get excited about endangered species.

IKO: All right, all right. Where'd you see it?

CLARE: In a silver fir about five minutes down the trail.

IKO: I guess I'll take a look. (*To Russ.*) You should tell her about the bear sightings. (*Iko unenthusiastically exits.*)

CLARE: That girl's losing her drive.

RUSS: You shouldn't be here, Clare. There's been some reports of bear maulings —

CLARE: No bear ever kept me from a day's work. And work is why I'm here.

RUSS: What do you mean?

CLARE: I mean I made up that story about the owl to get rid of her. I got a business proposition for you. Feel like makin' a little money? How's five thousand sound?

RUSS: (*Interested.*) Sounds pleasant. Real pleasant. You're talking about a new cut, aren't you?

CLARE: You'd supervise the entire operation.

(*She produces a small flask, which she hands to Russ with congratulations. Russ hoots and takes a sip.*)

Wouldn't even have to pick up a saw. But I need it done fast.

RUSS: How's the territory?

CLARE: You tell me. You've been living in it all week.

(*Pause.*)

RUSS: Here? You're going to cut here?

CLARE: Clear down the slope to the river road. That boy Trey filed a petition in federal court against any cutting in this area. Well, that don't make the Forest Service none too happy, especially since the injunction would be based on mere *speculation* of an owl. So we decided to work out a deal for a quick timber sale. They get the cash and I get the trees. By the time the court makes a decision it will all be too late. Hell, even if they slap me with a fine I'll come out way ahead.

RUSS: You're going to cut these trees?

CLARE: That's what I've been saying, son. Before somebody else finds that owl. And I expect you to keep quiet about your treetop encounter.

RUSS: If it were anywhere else –

CLARE: What are you worried about? That damn owl? Tell you what, we'll make it a Franklin cut, leave a few trees behind for wildlife. You can even keep this Douglas Fir for your owl. Now that's one expensive nest, sitting in some prime timber, but I'm willing to make the sacrifice for my son-in-law.

RUSS: It's not the owl.

CLARE: Then what is it? Is there something else you need to tell me about?

(*Pause.*)

RUSS: No.

CLARE: Then why not put a little cash back in your pocket? Pay your landlord. And come back to the productive world of gainful employment. Slightly illegal, I'll grant you, but still gainful.

RUSS: Can I think about it?

CLARE: Time is not an option here, son. Let me put it to you this way.

Either I hear the word "yes" in the next couple of seconds, or I'm gonna go find someone else. Either way these trees will be gone within two months. With you or without you. Now what's it gonna be?

(*Pause. Russ turns away from her.*)

RUSS: (*Resigned.*) Who's the siderod?

CLARE: Your pick.

RUSS: Willy.

CLARE: Consider it done.

(*Russ continues to sip from the flask without much pleasure.*)

Cheer up, boy. I've got some shake rats and hook tenders been out of work longer than you. They can't wait to hear the sound of chain saws again. Now they'll get the chance.

(*Iko enters.*)

IKO: I didn't find it.

CLARE: Must have heard you coming. Well, no rest for the wicked. Time to get back.

IKO: I wouldn't advise coming back for a while. At least, not until this bear problem is resolved.

(*Clare has recognized one of the backpacks.*)

CLARE: Where'd you find that?

IKO: Like I said, one of the hikers –

CLARE: That's not a hiker's bag. That's a cutter's satchel.

(*She picks it up and opens it.*)

Spurs and hickorys. My husband issued this gear thirty years ago. The satchel too.

IKO: Someone must have found it.

CLARE: Not even rusted.

(*She notices some of The Creature's paw prints in the ground.*)

What kind of print is this? Can't make it out.

IKO: Must be the bear.

CLARE: Ain't no bear. Look at it, it's almost human.

RUSS: That's you isn't it, Iko?

IKO: It is?

RUSS: Remember going barefoot for a while this morning?

IKO: Right, right.

CLARE: Time to cut your toenails.

IKO: I'll head down with you. That bridge isn't too stable over the Santiam.

CLARE: Seemed strong to me.

IKO: That could change.

(Iko and Clare exit, both giving clandestine signals to Russ as they go.

Pause.

Russ sits on a log and takes a long, hard swig. He clears his throat harshly.

The Creature is heard, imitating Russ' vocalization.)

RUSS: Hi, Betty.

(The Creature comes into view, curious about Russ' drinking.)

You gotta stop coming around here now. Go back to your lava tube before the crews come in.

(He drinks again.)

As for me, the destroyer of worlds, I'm gonna get stinking drunk until I pass out on the ground. With a little luck maybe there really is a bear around here. Put me out of my misery.

(He drinks again, then coughs hard, spitting up a little of the liquor.)

Oh, Terra. If you could only see me now, you'd fall in love with me all over again.

(He laughs without humor.

The Creature approaches Russ, curious about his mood. She examines the bottle.)

No, none for you. Liquor's reserved for the politically incorrect.

(He drinks again.)

Listen to me, Betty. Go back home to the lava field. It's not safe here.

(The Creature strokes and kneads his shirt, under his open jacket.)

That's flannel, not fur. Keeps you warm. Don't it . . .

(The Creature nuzzles his chest.)

. . . feel good?

(He gently tries to push her away.)

I mean it, Betty. You better get out of here before –

(The Creature looks up into his face.)

Your eyes. They're . . . beautiful.

(The Creature slowly brings her face to his. Russ is uncertain but too amazed to pull away. She purses her lips in imitation of a kiss, but at the last second, licks his face all over. Russ sputters and stands up.)

Look, you're an attractive . . . creature. But there are certain things a guy just can't do, no matter how long it's been, or . . .

(*The Creature gets down on all fours and exposes her haunches to Russ. She starts to purr.*)

I can't. It's perverse. It's unnatural. It's unethical. It's immoral. It's . . . strangely tempting.

(*Russ takes a very long swig from the bottle, mesmerized.*)

Why should I give a damn about what society says. Society never gave me anything I could use . . .

(*The Creature howls softly and plaintively.*

One last swig, then he slowly puts the bottle down, then stands back up.)

I just hope to hell nobody tells Greenpeace.

(*He begins to unbuckle his belt as lights quickly fade out.*)

END OF ACT ONE

ACT TWO

Transition –
The sounds of heavy machinery and chain saws are heard during
the intermission. The sound suddenly stops as lights come up.

SCENE 1

Four months later. A hot day in July.
The view has changed greatly. The first thing one notices is the
light – bright, almost oppressive sunlight spills freely over the entire
area. And although there is a certain amount of debris on the
ground, the trees have been cut to stumps. The lone visible
exception to the harvesting is the Douglas Fir, which remains
standing with a wooden or metal plaque crudely constructed and
nailed into the bark. The sign has a large blue "W" with the
smaller word "WILDLIFE" underneath.
The tent is still there, but with the addition of a lot of camping
accessories and luxury items: a barbecue grill; a picnic table
containing various used plastic dishes and glasses; a boom box
and magazines; a small stack of wood for the fire; an umbrella
over the table; a lawn chair; a cooler – and a brightly colored
wind sock at the front of the tent. But there is no wind.
As lights come up, The Creature is lying in the lawn chair,
wearing sunglasses and sipping on a tall drink with a straw. She is
looking at a coffee-table book on the National Park System. Russ
watches Terra, who is sitting on a log, doubled over in apparent
distress. A long beat before she speaks.

TERRA: Okay. I'm trying to stay calm.
RUSS: I know, it's a little weird –
TERRA: That's how you describe it?
RUSS: I didn't think you'd get so upset.
TERRA: First I come out here to find you sitting in a treetop. Next thing
    I know there's an illegal harvest in this very same area –
RUSS: Legal, mostly legal –
TERRA: – with you in charge. Then you tell me about you and this . . .

thing . . .

RUSS: She's a yeti.

TERRA: I think I'm going to be sick.

RUSS: Maybe I shouldn't have told you.

TERRA: Is this your solution to a mid-life crisis: Sex with animals?

RUSS: (*Bitterly.*) Oh, like there's a *better* way . . .

TERRA: Trey was right. You're in need of professional help.

RUSS: Look, it just happened once . . . or twice. And that was months ago.

TERRA: I don't think frequency is the issue here, Russ. I'm talking about mental deterioration.

RUSS: Jeez. Sorry I mentioned it.

TERRA: They could put you away for this. I mean, this is Oregon. Having sex with other *people* is considered subversive, much less the animal kingdom.

RUSS: I thought you might understand.

TERRA: You're gonna have trouble finding anyone in the *solar system* who would understand this.

(*The Creature has reached the bottom of her drink, and makes a loud sucking sound with her straw.*)

Mother once told me that men need a little strange now and then. I had no idea *how* strange.

RUSS: You've made your point.

TERRA: I kept telling you not to screw with nature. Did that just give you *ideas?*

RUSS: Are you done?

TERRA: No. Not by a long shot. Did you ever stop to consider the health risks?

RUSS: What do you mean?

TERRA: Well, did you use anything?

(*Pause. Russ stares at her as though she's gone insane.*)

RUSS: Gee, it would have just spoiled the moment . . .

TERRA: Don't get smart. You might have just discovered a whole new strain of sexually transmitted disease. Does that make you proud?

RUSS: Would they name it after me?

TERRA: Something's happened to you, Russ.

RUSS: What are you looking for, a reasonable explanation?

TERRA: Absolutely. This just confirms my belief that men without women turn into barbarians.

RUSS: Is that so? And what does that make women without men?

TERRA: Enlightened.

RUSS: I'm just trying to be honest. Isn't that what you used to ask for? More – what was that word you used – intimacy?

TERRA: With *me*, Russ. Not woodland creatures.

(*The Creature, by now tired of the arguing, snarls at Terra and goes into the tent.*)

RUSS: You could make more of an effort with her, you know.

TERRA: With who?

RUSS: With Betty. Get to know her a little. You'd find you have a lot in common.

TERRA: Like what?

RUSS: Like . . . love of the outdoors . . .

TERRA: She doesn't have a *choice*, Russ. She's a wild animal.

RUSS: Well, if you're gonna be judgmental –

TERRA: Do you know how that makes me feel? Comparing me to that . . . thing? What's next for you? Mountain goats?

RUSS: You make it sound so . . .

TERRA: Psychotic.

RUSS: Why can't you just look at it like . . . "Beauty and the Beast"?

TERRA: What?

RUSS: You cried when you saw that movie.

TERRA: That's because I felt sorry for the *Beast*. Like that poor creature. She doesn't belong here.

RUSS: Of course not. Don't you think I know that? She took over my tent right after the harvest. I can't get near it now. Just watch.

(*Russ unzips the tent, but backs away when The Creature snarls and nips at him.*)

I'm sleeping out here now. Without any cover.

TERRA: Serves you right. For destroying the forest.

RUSS: Will you give me a break? I had no choice. You know your mother. She would have cut it with or without me. Am I right?

TERRA: I suppose.

RUSS: And I kept thinking about the cutters who like to bring rifles along, hoping to bag a deer during lunch break. I figured if I took the job myself, Iko could help me keep her out of sight while I kept the crew too busy to notice. I completed the cut in record time.

TERRA: What's all this junk? She doesn't need this stuff.

RUSS: Betty likes catalogs. She points to pictures, and I order the things she wants.

TERRA: Whatever for?

RUSS: It makes her happy.

TERRA: She wanted a wind sock?

RUSS: You'd be surprised.

(*The Creature comes out of the tent, making a grunting sound. She shows the book to Russ and points to a picture. Russ looks at the book.*)

That's a moose. I can't order a moose.

(*The Creature points and grunts.*)

No.

(*The Creature snarls and nips at him, making him jump back. She goes back into the tent.*)

TERRA: She doesn't seem to like you very much.

RUSS: She's a little testy lately. Doesn't like it when I get too close.

TERRA: At least one of you has standards. Does Iko know about you and –

RUSS: God, no. Do you think she might suspect?

TERRA: I don't think it would enter a normal person's mind, Russ.

RUSS: You gotta help us, Terra. I don't know how much longer we can keep her a secret. A few hikers have already ignored the bridge and bear warnings and spotted her up here. So far we've been trying to camouflage her as just another camper, but our luck can't hold forever.

TERRA: People accept her as a camper?

RUSS: Well, we've taught her to dress appropriately. And this accumulation of stuff actually helps with the disguise. But most people don't really want to get that close.

TERRA: I believe you.

RUSS: Will you help us protect her?

TERRA: You know, it's odd to see you so concerned about the welfare of an animal. Weren't you the one who posted recipes for owl soup all over the forest?

RUSS: I know. I don't really get it myself.

TERRA: Well, you're not off to a good start, the way you've corrupted this creature already.

(*She looks around the area with disgust.*)

How can she even stand it around here? Hundreds of years of

natural history reduced to . . . a pile of slash.

RUSS: We did leave a couple of trees standing, you know. For wildlife. (*Terra peers up into the high branches of the Douglas Fir, laughing bitterly.*)

TERRA: And what attractive specimens they are. Anything up there would turn into a target for predators within minutes. Have you ever seen anything up there? Even a squirrel?

RUSS: There used to be something. But it left.

TERRA: Of course it did, animals aren't stupid. There's no protection from anything here. Not even the sun.

RUSS: Betty likes the sun.

TERRA: Betty? Oh, there's a healthy example of adaptation in the wild. They can just build a shopping mall around her. Give her a charge card and she'll be completely assimilated. You've done wonders for her quality of life, haven't you?

RUSS: So we made a few mistakes –

TERRA: Let me ask you something. What went through your mind as you cleared this land? Anything? I'm just curious.

RUSS: To tell you the truth, I thought about . . . Betty. Whether she'd come back, or return to her lava tube forever. So when the trucks had left and the slash was piled, I set up my tent again. And I waited. She showed up the first night.

TERRA: I can't understand why. There's nothing about this place that's conducive to wildlife.

RUSS: I think it was me. She wants to be near people.

TERRA: I think you've got it wrong. She wants to *be* people. (*Iko enters, in simple civilian hiking clothes and backpack.*)

IKO: (*To Terra.*) Good, you're here. Russ wasn't sure you'd come.

TERRA: Iko? Is that you? I didn't recognize you in your civvies.

IKO: You better get used to it. I lost my job.

TERRA: Oh, no . . .

RUSS: Welcome to the club.

TERRA: How come?

IKO: Oh, several reasons. Not maintaining this trail properly, such as the mysterious vandalism at the log bridge. Discouraging hikers from entering the area. Spending too much time away from the designated campsites to do – how did they put it? – "unknown research of an entirely personal nature, apparently unrelated to the job description."

RUSS: (*To Terra.*) Betty.

IKO: I've got to know what will happen to her.

RUSS: Terra said she'd help us.

TERRA: Now hold on. There's not much I can do. Like any endangered species, you need to petition for federal protection in the courts.

RUSS: Fine. File a petition.

TERRA: Look, guys. I'm just a beginner at this. For the petition to be taken seriously, it should be filed in the name of one of the environmental rights organizations. And that means telling them about her first.

RUSS: Why?

TERRA: You can't keep Betty a secret and seek legal protection too.

RUSS: No. Forget it.

IKO: It might be the best thing now, Russ.

RUSS: I know who she's talking about. She wants to tell Trey.

TERRA: Listen. No group has been more successful in wildlife injunctions than Timber Watch. And that's entirely due to his expertise.

RUSS: And the friends he's made in high places.

TERRA: So? Friends are helpful. Don't you think Betty needs friends?

RUSS: She's got friends. Two of them.

TERRA: But look what you've done to her.

IKO: She's right, Russ.

(*She opens her backpack and takes out her journal, now almost full. She shows it to Terra.*)

Look at this journal. Four months of observations.

(*She opens it to an early page.*)

"Day Seven. Betty shows us how she catches salmon in her paws as they jump the cascades. She eats the fish whole, evidently having a stomach lining that protects against the sharp points of the bones."

(*She turns about midway.*)

"Day Forty-seven. Curious about our preference for cooked food over raw, Betty communicates to us that she would like to try her salmon baked over a fire. Russ obliges, and she is delighted with the taste of the finished product."

(*She turns toward the end.*)

"Day Eighty-seven. Betty uses mesquite chips and dill sauce to create a delicious new recipe."

(*She closes the book and turns to Russ.*)

RUSS: We meant well.

IKO: But we screwed up.

(*She turns back to Terra.*)

And now that I've lost my authority here, Betty's in more danger than ever.

RUSS: Hey, speak for yourself. I'm not going to leave her until I'm sure she has the same protection as the bald eagle.

TERRA: Or the spotted owl?

RUSS: You've just been waiting to say that, haven't you?

TERRA: There's no better feeling than ironic satisfaction.

RUSS: All right, sure. Like the owl. Whatever it takes to make it a crime to harm her.

TERRA: That takes a Federal Court, Russ. I suggest we consult with Trey.

(*Pause. Russ looks at Iko.*)

RUSS: Okay.

TERRA: Can I have the journal? Any scientific data would help convince the judge.

(*Iko hands Terra the journal.*)

IKO: Sure.

TERRA: Do you have a place to stay now?

IKO: Oh, there's always another campsite. If they give me a permit.

(*Terra removes a cellular phone from her pack and hands it to Iko.*)

TERRA: Here. We need an easier way to stay in touch.

IKO: Good idea.

(*Russ regards the phone suspiciously.*)

RUSS: Hey . . . haven't they connected those things to some kind of cancer?

TERRA: You believe everything you hear? Ronald Reagan said trees cause pollution.

IKO: Look around. He may have been on to something.

(*They grimly survey the scene. Iko exits. Betty begins to come out of the tent to follow Iko. Russ turns and scolds her.*)

RUSS: Stay, Betty.

(*Betty snarls and goes back in the tent.*)

TERRA: Still have that magic touch with the ladies, don't you?

RUSS: Will you stop it?

TERRA: Let's see, how did you resolve our little spats? Flowers? Chocolate? No, as I remember, petulant sulking usually did the trick.

RUSS: Is it even possible for you to stop it?

TERRA: I was just going to ask you the same thing.

RUSS: What's this about really? Jealousy?

TERRA: What's to be jealous of? Animals don't care about political inconsistencies. This is the perfect relationship for you. I hope you'll be very happy together. Which reminds me.
(*She produces a legal document.*)
Sign this and you're free to fuck with the fauna.
(*She hands it to Russ.*)

RUSS: So this is it.

TERRA: Too bad I didn't wait a little longer. Bestiality would have made such interesting grounds for divorce.
(*She hands the papers to Russ, who reads the papers.*)

RUSS: "Petition to the Ninth Circuit Court of Appeals – Request for Injunction to suspend BLM timber sales in Willamette National Forest . . . "

TERRA: Oops. Wrong lawsuit.
(*She grabs the document back from him.*)

RUSS: Glad to hear it. I'd hate to think all those signatures are people who want us to get divorced.

TERRA: I must have picked up the wrong papers.

RUSS: Hell, why don't I just sign that one? Either way my life is over.

TERRA: Stop it, Russ. Melodrama's not your strong suit.

RUSS: You don't even know who I am anymore.

TERRA: Don't know you? Don't you get it yet? This isn't about who you are. It's about the things you *do.*

RUSS: All right, sure, I made some mistakes. A lot of us did. But we had to survive.

TERRA: What kind of survival will it be when the whole planet looks like this?

RUSS: That's so tired, Terra. We've got enough trees to last into the next century.

TERRA: Not unless you include those industrial farm mutants. And you can't even call them real trees. More like a collection of . . . oversized safety matches.

RUSS: With lower grade lumber. So we'd be happy to keep cutting the old growth, if you prefer.

TERRA: See how you twist the things I say?

RUSS: Well, when you're not being logical –

TERRA: Don't talk to me about logic, you stubborn, narrow-minded . . . (*Realizing.*)

God, I miss this.

RUSS: We do sort of slip into automatic pilot, don't we?

TERRA: Like riding a bicycle.

RUSS: So I take it you don't get to do this with Boy Wonder?

TERRA: Trey? Oh, no. He's much too earnest. Everything's a matter of policy with him. If we disagree on something, we discuss the policies behind the decisions. Even when picking a restaurant.

RUSS: Tsk, tsk.

TERRA: Although, come to think of it . . . for some reason he always seems to get his way. How does he do that?

RUSS: Oh, hell, Terra. Just look at the guy. Everything about him spells out "I win." He's got the courts on his side, the politicians on his side, the newspapers on his side . . . and he's got you.

TERRA: Is this what you want now? To talk about Trey?

RUSS: You started it.

TERRA: All right then, try to understand this time. I need to be able to share my beliefs with someone. Not to be constantly forced to defend them. That's a refreshing change.

RUSS: Bullshit. He's got the future in his hands, and you both know it. Hell, I know it too – I'm out of date. Like the whalers and steamboat captains. From another era, isn't that what he says? He's right. What have I got left to offer you anymore: Is this . . . (*Gesturing around the area.*)

. . . any woman's idea of a home?

TERRA: Is it yours? Or are you just punishing yourself?

RUSS: Oh, this is my favorite part. Amateur psychoanalysis. See the Vietnam vet suffer from post-combat syndrome.

TERRA: Well, look around you, Russ. What does this remind you of?

(*Russ looks around, eventually realizing her point.*)

RUSS: Napalm. (*Pause.*)

TERRA: I better head back to Portland. Trey will be missing his Range Rover.

RUSS: You really think he has all the answers?

TERRA: Trey will know what to do. He'll make sure that Betty will

receive full protection under the law. No one will bother her.
(*She turns and walks off. Russ sits in the lawn chair.*
Betty comes out of the tent. She goes behind Russ and covers his
eyes with her paws. Russ removes them.)

RUSS: Not now, Betty.
(*She begins to groom his head, looking for insects in his hair.*)
It's all right, girl. Did you hear what she said? We're safe.
(*Lights down.*)

SCENE 2

Three weeks later. A cloudy day.
Trey is facing the audience, holding a cordless microphone. Iko is
back in her Forest Service uniform, cordoning off the front of the
stage with a rope. The Creature is unseen inside the tent. Terra is
placing a box of pamphlets near Trey. Russ sits glumly at the
picnic table.
Trey addresses the unseen crowd.

TREY: Welcome to Willamette National Forest – home of the North
American yeti. Obviously, the welfare and comfort of the creature
comes first. So let's all do our part to keep this area as natural
and undisturbed as possible.
(*The sound of cameras clicking and whirring.*)
Now, let me introduce the wilderness team that first brought the
creature to my attention. Iko Sumiko is a highly respected
member of the U.S. Forest Service, recently reinstated – I mean
returned – from a short sabbatical. Iko?
(*Iko waves to the crowd, smiling.*
The sound of cameras clicking and whirring.
Trey reaches into the box and pulls out a small booklet.)
Iko is also the author of the first edition of the *Yeti Field Guide*. A
Timber Watch publication, just $6.95 each.
(*He puts the pamphlet away.*)
Next, Terra Sawyer is a well-known environmental activist,
currently drafting a petition to suspend all timber sales in the
region – until studies on the habitat and range of the creature are
completed. Terra?

(*Terra waves to the crowd, smiling. The sound of cameras clicking and whirring.*)

I expect to be working very closely with her –

RUSS: Hah.

TREY: – to ensure that this animal will be declared an endangered species and will receive full protection under the law. Finally, Russ Sawyer –

(*Russ gives the crowd the finger, smiling. The sound of cameras clicking and whirring.*)

– no relation to Terra –

(*Russ makes a move for Trey but is restrained by Iko and Terra.*)

– was also part of the original discovery. His credentials . . . well, he has no credentials.

(*More holding Russ back at the picnic table.*)

But he has somehow managed to bond with the animal in a unique way.

(*Russ looks at Terra accusingly.*)

TERRA: I never said a thing.

TREY: So Mr. Sawyer has agreed to stay in order to provide companionship and security. Now, I've been handed some of your questions in advance . . .

(*He produces some index cards, and sifts through them.*)

"You're proposing to prohibit the logging of over one million acres of prime timber. For how long?" I'll give you the same answer I gave on the spotted owl – as long as it takes.

(*He reads another card.*)

"Has there been any previous evidence of the creature in this area?" I believe Iko can address this question.

(*He signals Iko to come forward, handing her the microphone.*)

IKO: Well, this area has had many sightings of ape-like creatures by hunters and loggers. But I'm most interested in some Native American legends. One in particular . . .

(*She pages through her journal, looking for an entry.*) . . .

Let's see. Here it is. From an early explorer among the Nisqually: "They wear no clothes, but the body is covered with hair like that of a dog, only not so thick . . . They are said to live in the mountains, in holes underground, and to smell bad. They come down chiefly in the fishing season, at which time the Indians are excessively afraid of them . . . Their voices are like that of an owl, and they possess the power of charming, so that those hearing them become demented or fall down in a swoon."

TERRA: That would explain a few things.

RUSS: Keep it down, will you?

TERRA: Russ has something to add about that last part.

TREY: What is it, Sawyer?

RUSS: Just that it sounds – familiar. Except Betty doesn't smell that bad.

TERRA: You *would* say that.

(*Trey takes the microphone away from Iko and consults the cards.*)

TREY: Next question. "Is it true that you have been approached as a possible candidate for the State House of Representatives?" No comment at this time. But thanks for asking.

(*The tent starts to unzip.*)

IKO: Trey –

TREY: What is it now?

IKO: She's coming out.

(*Pause. All turn to look at the tent. A paw appears through the opening.*)

TREY: Please, everyone remain still. Allow the creature to behave as it normally does in the wild.

(*The tent flap opens and The Creature sticks her head out, scanning the area. She still wears the sunglasses. Satisfied, she comes out of the tent.*

She has added a few more items of clothing, including an oversized jogging outfit, sandals and a Blazers cap.

There is a barrage of flash bulbs and camera noises. Startled, she rushes back into the tent. She quickly returns with a camera of her own, taking pictures of the crowd. She drops the camera and steps forward. She carries a supermarket tabloid with a cover picture of a monster. (Anything with the word "Bigfoot" would be ideal and not difficult to find.)

She goes over to the picnic table and turns on the boom box. An environmental tape of forest sounds is heard – the first birds, insects, wind and leaves to be heard in this act.

Then she picks up a large can of Deep Woods insect repellent and sprays the area around the lawn chair. She settles into the chair, looking at the tabloid.

She puts the tabloid on her lap and picks up a "Game Boy" on the ground next to the chair. She begins to play the miniature computer game, growling when she makes an error.

Suddenly Betty sneezes violently. She reaches to the ground for a large box of Kleenex, and manages to empty about half the container as she pulls one out. Letting them all but one fall to the ground, she daintily dabs at her nose in imitation of human ritual.

Then she eats the Kleenex.

Trey turns back to the crowd.)

TREY: Umm . . . any questions?

(Lights down.)

SCENE 3

Two weeks later.

The general area is now surrounded by chain link fence, topped by barbed wire.

Terra and Iko are at the picnic table. The tent is closed, The Creature apparently inside.

The table contains piles of magazines and correspondence, an appointment book and the cellular phone.

Iko sorts out correspondence as Terra finishes a phone conversation.

TERRA: Nope. Can't do it . . . She's booked through next week. Just take their number.

(Russ enters, carrying a grocery bag stuffed with foodstuffs.

He yells behind him as he enters.)

RUSS: Don't you people have jobs?

(He reaches the gate.)

Come on, open up.

(The gate is opened for Russ.)

How's she doing? Still recuperating?

IKO: Haven't seen her all day.

RUSS: I don't blame her, with all the commotion around here. They've even started to sell Yeti shirts at the general store. Took me forever to pick up a few supplies.

(He puts the bag on the table.)

TERRA: You still don't get it, do you, Russ? Paper *and* plastic?

RUSS: Another article.

(*He pulls out a news magazine and shows them an article.*)

TERRA: Let's see it.

IKO: I'm not crazy about this photo.

RUSS: Yeah, too bad they cropped me out of the shot.

TERRA: It is a family magazine.

IKO: I mean Betty. There's something about the way she . . . I just wish she'd seem a little more vulnerable. At least enough to warrant protection.

RUSS: I know. It would help if she'd take off the Blazers cap.

IKO: Doesn't she know we're trying to help her?

TERRA: Well, she *is* just an animal. How much can she possibly understand?

(*Pause. Iko looks at the tent.*

The cellular phone rings. Terra answers it.)

This is Terra . . . Who wants her now? . . . CNN. (*To Iko.*) Hand me that schedule.

(*She turns the page and shows it to Iko.*)

Who should I ditch? Scientific American or the National Enquirer?

IKO: (*Looking.*) It's the same reporter.

TERRA: Problem solved.

(*Into the phone.*) Two o'clock tomorrow. Right.

(*She hangs up.*)

RUSS: Only if she's feeling better. If she's not –

TERRA: Then they can interview Trey.

RUSS: Of course. Just let Mr. Media work his magic.

TERRA: At least he's never made a kindergarten class cry. By telling them the yeti eats children.

RUSS: They were feeding her gummi bears.

(*Clare approaches the gate of the fence. Russ lets her in.*)

CLARE: Let me in there. It's safer in the cage.

IKO: That's the idea.

(*Clare notices the closed tent.*)

CLARE: So where's the hairball? Not up for visitors today?

TERRA: What are you doing here, Mother?

CLARE: Wanna talk to you and Trey. Where is he?

TERRA: Conferring with the Sierra Club. Talk about what?

CLARE: This injunction you're threatenin' to slap on the Willamette. It ain't gonna wash and you know it.

TERRA: I think we'll just let the courts decide that.

CLARE: That critter ain't livin' in the old growth. What's the point of shuttin' down all the timber sales?

TERRA: An animal finds what shelter it can. You're the one who cut these trees –

CLARE: And she's doin' pretty damn well without 'em, if you ask me.

IKO: We don't know that for sure. With a little more study . . .

CLARE: Study all you want. In the meantime why don't you take a couple of spotted owls and set 'em up in a nest downtown on top of the Portland Savings and Loan? For all you know they might thrive there.

IKO: Taking an animal out of the wild –

CLARE: Might be just what they need. Maybe it's too damn hard to live in the forest.

(*Trey enters, newspaper in hand.*)

TREY: The White House responded.

TERRA: Finally!

(*They let him in the enclosure.*
Terra eagerly snatches the paper from him.)

TREY: Yeah, well don't get too excited

IKO: How come?

(*Terra skims the front page article.*)

TERRA: "Asked to comment on the yeti's status, the Department of Interior released this statement: 'Environmental policy requires an acceptable balance between the needs of the timber industry, the preservation of jobs and the concerns of wildlife advocates.' "

IKO: Sounds familiar.

TERRA: "In the meantime, the Forest Service is handling the situation to our satisfaction."

IKO: What's that supposed to mean? We haven't done anything.

TERRA: That *is* what they mean.

(*Terra lowers the paper in disgust.*)

RUSS: That's it? That's all we managed to buy with this circus?

TERRA: Hey – it's not like you had a better solution.

IKO: Where do we stand now?

(*Trey approaches the cooler.*)

TREY: We've got trouble.

TERRA: Why?

TREY: I've been talking to the other organizations . . .

(*Trey opens the lid of the cooler. The others immediately react by covering their noses and mouths.*)

Here, take a look at this.

CLARE: No thanks.

TERRA: Close the lid!

RUSS: The fish? What about them?

(*He replaces the lid.*)

TREY: She catches more than she can eat in a day. Coho salmon – completely endangered. And at the rate she pulls them out of the Santiam, she'll exceed last year's count in a matter of weeks.

RUSS: But they're just fish – they can't be more important than, than . . .

TREY: Than what? A yeti?

TERRA: What are you trying to say, Trey?

TREY: Think about it, Terra. I mean, it's a nice animal and all, but exactly what *good* is it? What significance does it have? Those salmon represent fisheries and canneries that depend on the survival of the species. What industry does a yeti support?

RUSS: Well . . . she goes through a lot of batteries.

TREY: Sorry, folks. The only thing that would completely protect her is endangered status. And you can forget about that.

IKO: Why?

TREY: Most of the environmental groups think she's . . . hurting the cause.

CLARE: Let me see if I got this straight. The loggers don't want her. The fishermen don't want her. The government doesn't want her. And the environmentalists don't want her.

TERRA: The beast without a country.

TREY: If only we could come up with something that would show her worth. If only she could contribute something to society . . .

RUSS: You're making this sound like welfare fraud. What about being one of a kind? Isn't that worth anything?

TREY: Not much.

RUSS: She has a life, equal to any other life.

TREY: Not when the balance is upset. Some species get more protection than others.

RUSS: What the hell are you saying here? She's being threatened?

TREY: You can't save every animal, Sawyer. It's not in the natural order.

RUSS: This stinks.

TREY: Now don't get bent out of shape. We can still save a few trees –

RUSS: Fuck the trees!

> (*Pause. Russ starts for Trey and the two men cause a melee as they grapple.*)

TERRA: Stop it, Russ!

CLARE: Calm down, son!

IKO: Russ, don't!

> (*Trey falls in the midst of the camp debris, as Russ stands over him.*)

TERRA: It's not his fault, Russ!

> (*Russ hears this and looks at Terra. He pulls away from the others, heading for his backpack.*)

RUSS: Everything . . . everything we touch . . .

> (*He begins to roll up his sleeping bag.*)

TERRA: Russ, what are you doing?

RUSS: Getting the hell out of here. And I'm taking Betty with me.

IKO: Where, back to the lava tube?

RUSS: Never you mind.

IKO: It's too late, Russ. They'll just follow her wherever you take her.

RUSS: We'll just see about that. Betty?

> (*He leans down to the tent entrance, speaking softly.*)

Come on, girl. Time to leave. Let's find a safer place.

> (*Concerned, he slowly unzips the tent entrance and peeks in.*)

Betty?

> (*Startled, he quickly unzips the flap the rest of the way and throws it open. The tent is empty.*)

Who was watching her? Anybody?

> (*Terra and Iko look at each other. Russ scans the area.*)

She's gone.

> (*Lights down.*)

SCENE 4

Night, two days later. There is a light shower.
The lantern on the table is lit, providing the only illumination other than the full moon.

Russ and Iko are seated under the umbrella at the table. Iko has rain gear on, and a large flashlight next to her pack on the table.

RUSS: I know, I know. Two days is enough. I would have packed out today if not for this rain.

IKO: You shouldn't wait for her, Russ. She probably just went back to the lava tube. She'll be safer there . . . the way she was before.

RUSS: You're right, it's better this way. No long, drawn out good-byes. Like "Casablanca."

IKO: Or "Call of the Wild."

RUSS: What are your plans now?

IKO: I want to find another place, completely isolated, where I can continue my research on endangered species. And where there aren't any trees.

RUSS: Maybe I'll join you.

IKO: I'm thinking about the Mojave Desert.

RUSS: Maybe I won't join you.

(Iko stands up and puts on her pack.)

IKO: You'll pack out tomorrow?

RUSS: I'll see you in the morning.

(Iko turns on her flashlight and starts to move off.)

She took a shirt.

(Iko turns back.)

IKO: What?

RUSS: One of my flannels. She took it with her. Liked the way they felt.

IKO: See? She won't forget you.

RUSS: Yeah. Goodnight.

IKO: See you tomorrow.

(Iko leaves.

Russ picks up his flashlight from the table, turns it on, and shines the beam in a circle around the campsite.)

RUSS: Betty? Here girl. Come on. Want some nice fish? Betty!

(He listens for some response, but hears none.

He heads for the tent, changes his mind, and carries the flashlight offstage for one more search before retiring for the night.)

Betty!

(A beat. The storm increases in intensity. Thunder is heard, it begins to rain harder, there is some distant lightning. The only

other light comes from the moon.

The Creature stealthily approaches the campsite, no longer wearing any of her exterior clothing. In one paw she carries something wrapped in Russ' flannel shirt.

She checks the tent and looks around the campsite.)

THE CREATURE: Rrrusss . . .

(More lightning, closer. She goes behind the Douglas Fir.

Dogs are heard howling in the distance over the storm.

Betty comes out from behind the tree, no longer carrying the bundled shirt. She approaches the sound of the dogs with curiosity. She imitates their howling as they get closer.

A shot rings out, ricocheting off the nearby picnic table.

Betty shrieks in fear and runs to the tree, pulling the "Wildlife" sign off the tree and holding it out in front of her, as if for protection.

She steps forward, holding the sign with confidence above her head.)

Bettee!

(Another shot is heard as lights quickly snap out.)

SCENE 5

The following afternoon. Terra, Iko, Trey and Clare are sitting, waiting for the return of Russ.

The "Wildlife" sign is on the ground away from the tree. It is stained with blood.

Iko looks offstage with concern.

IKO: Shouldn't one of us have gone with him?

TERRA: No. I know Russ. He wants to do this alone.

IKO: I can't understand it. Who had reason to kill her?

CLARE: Hell, who didn't?

TREY: I'm afraid that's true. She was of little use to either side of the environmental crisis. She just confused the issue.

CLARE: On the other hand, it might have just been a hunter.

TERRA: That's a comfort.

TREY: Let's face it, folks. She just wasn't a good example of an indicator species.

(*Russ enters during Trey's line, carrying a shovel. His mood is intense, focused.*

Russ drops the shovel on the ground, staring down Trey.)

TERRA: Russ . . . are you okay?

(*He doesn't acknowledge the question, and starts to dismantle the tent.*)

IKO: Did you find a nice place for her?

(*Russ nods, continuing his activity.*)

TERRA: We'll leave you alone, Russ. Call me when you're ready to . . . just call when you're ready.

TREY: Don't tell me . . . you're leaving without his signature again?

TERRA: This isn't the day, Trey.

TREY: Come on, Terra. You've been up here ten times in the last month, but either nobody has a pen, you forgot the papers, or something distracts you.

TERRA: We'll discuss this later.

(*Without further hesitation, Russ heads for Terra's pack. He searches through it for the divorce papers.*)

TREY: I don't think so. We'll discuss it now.

TERRA: Don't push this, Trey. I don't . . .

(*Terra has noticed Russ, who is in the process of signing the divorce papers on the table.*)

Russ . . . what are you doing?

(*Russ puts down the pen and looks at her.*)

RUSS: Just making room. For the superior species.

(*Russ returns to the tent and his backpack.*

Terra moves to the divorce papers, staring hard at them.

She picks them up.)

TERRA: I'm sorry, Russ.

RUSS: Yeah. I know.

TERRA: I don't feel like doing this today.

(*She tears up the papers.*)

TREY: You gotta be kidding. You expect me to keep standing around, waiting for you to make up your mind?

TERRA: No, Trey. I don't.

TREY: Oh.

(*Pause.*)

Oh.

(*Pause.*)

Well . . . this really sucks.

CLARE: Now this is more like it. You two together again. Why don't the two of you drop by next Sunday for brunch? We'll have it on the back porch, where we can watch the deer.

TERRA: Back off, Mother. I'm not making any promises.

RUSS: Me either.

TERRA: No one's asking you to.

TREY: But what about the trees?

(*Terra walks over to Trey and takes his hand.*)

TERRA: You've got them covered, Trey. I'll find something else to save. Even if it's not useful.

TREY: Like what?

TERRA: I'll let you know.

(*She kisses him, gently, and walks away.*)

TREY: It's a weird feeling.

CLARE: What's that?

TREY: Losing. I'm not used to it.

(*Clare approaches Trey and gently pats him on the back.*)

CLARE: You'll bounce back, boy. There's other endangered fish in the sea.

(*They exit together.*

Terra turns to Iko, as Russ finishes packing up.)

IKO: Guess I'll pack out myself.

TERRA: Already?

IKO: There's nothing more for me here. I need something new to study.

(*Terra picks up the "Wildlife" sign and looks up into the tree.*)

TERRA: You think life can ever return to this old tree?

RUSS: I don't know. But the least we can do . . . is give it some help.

(*He picks up the hand axe and carries it over to Terra. Taking the sign from her, he pounds it back onto the tree with the back of the axe.*

Suddenly a sound is heard. It sounds like the cry of a small animal.

Russ backs away, startled by the noise.

Iko and Terra also hear the cry, and they look around, trying to pinpoint the source.

Russ looks around the trunk, moves to the back of the tree, and finds a cavity in the trunk. He reaches inside and pulls out a

bundle, wrapped in one of his own flannel shirts.
He cautiously lays it on the picnic table. The crying increases.
He stares at the bundle. Iko and Terra are on either side of Russ,
staring at him. He looks at Iko. He looks at Terra.
Finally, all three return their focus to the crying bundle below.
Russ reaches down and begins to unwrap the cloth.
Lights out, fast.)

END.

Slavs!

Thinking About the Longstanding Problems of Virtue and Happiness

by Tony Kushner

This play is for Oskar Eustis, beloved comrade.

SLAVS! was directed by Lisa Peterson with the following cast (in order of appearance):

VASSILY VOROVILICH SMUKOV	Michael Kevin
SERGE ESMERELDOVICH UPGOBKIN	Gerald Hiken
ALEKSII ANTEDILLUVIANOVICH PRELAPSARIANOV	Ray Fry
IPPOLITE IPPOPOLITOVICH POPOLITIPOV	Fred Major
YEGOR TREMENS RODENT	Steven Culp
KATHERINA SERAFIMA GLEB	Kate Goehring
BONFILA BEZHUKHOVNA BONCH-BRUEVICH	Mary Shultz
VODYA DOMIK	Annie Laurie Adenart
MRS. SHASTLIVYI DOMIK	Barbara eda-Young

Scenic Designer	Paul Owen
Costume Designer	Esther Marquis
Lighting Designer	Mary Louise Geiger
Sound Designer	Casey L. Warren
Props Master	Mark Bissonnette
Production Stage Manager	Debra Acquavella
Assistant Stage Manager	John David Flak
Dramaturg	Michael Bigelow Dixon
Casting	Jay Binder

TONY KUSHNER'S other plays include A BRIGHT ROOM CALLED DAY, THE ILLUSION, and ANGELS IN AMERICA, Part One: MILLENNIUM APPROACHES, and Part Two: PERESTROIKA. His work has been produced at theatres around the United States, including New York Theatre Workshop, the New York Shakespeare Festival, the Mark Taper Forum, Berkeley Rep, and Hartford Stage Company; on Broadway at the Walter Kerr Theatre; at the Royal National Theatre in London; and around the world. ANGELS IN AMERICA has been awarded the 1993 Pulitzer Prize for Drama, the 1993 and 1994 Tony Awards, the 1993 and 1994 Drama Desk Awards, The 1992 Evening Standard Award, two Olivier Award nominations, the 1993 New York Drama Critics Circle Award, the 1993 Los Angeles Drama Critics Circle Award, and the 1994 LAMBDA Literary Award for Drama, among others. Mr. Kushner is the recipient of grants from New York State Council on the Arts and the National Endowment for the Arts, a 1990 Whiting Foundation Writers' Award, and an Arts Award from the American Academy of Arts and Letters, among others. THE ILLUSION is being adapted for film for Universal Studios; and ANGELS IN AMERICA for New Line/Fine Line Films. SLAVS! is currently appearing at Steppenwolf Theatre in Chicago, and will be produced next year at New York Theatre Workshop, Center Stage in Baltimore, Yale Rep, and elsewhere. Mr. Kushner was born in Manhattan and grew up in Lake Charles, Louisiana. He has a B.A. from Columbia University and an M.F.A. in directing from NYU, where he studied with Carl Weber. He lives in Manhattan.

FOR CAUTION NOTICE SEE PAGE OPPOSITE TABLE OF CONTENTS.

SLAVS! by Tony Kushner. ©1994 by Tony Kushner. Reprinted by permission of the author. All inquiries should be addressed to Joyce Ketay, The Joyce Ketay Agency, 1501 Broadway Suite 1910, New York, NY 10036.

For the information on the Soviet nuclear catastrophe which is addressed in Act Three, I am indebted primarily to a series of articles by John-Thor Dahlburg which ran in the Los Angeles Times, September 2-4, 1992; to Grigori Medvedev's *The Truth About Chernobyl;* and to Dr. Don Pizzarello of New York University Medical Center.

CHARACTERS

First Babushka – A Snow-Sweep of indeterminate age.

Second Babushka – Another Snow-Sweep of indeterminate age.

Vassily Vorovilich Smukov – A high-ranking Politburo member, a pessimistic man in his seventies.

Serge Esmereldovich Upgobkin – A high-ranking Politburo member, an optimistic man in his eighties.

Aleksii Antedilluvianovich Prelapsarianov – A Politburo Member of incalculable rank, the world's oldest living Bolshevik, considerably older than ninety.

Ippolite Ippopolitovich Popolitipov – An apparatchik of some importance, a sour man in his sixties.

Yegor Tremens Rodent – An apparatchik of less importance, attached to Popolitipov; a nervous type in his fifties.

Katherina Serafima Gleb – A security guard at the Pan-Soviet Archives For The Study of Cerebro-Cephalognomical Historico-Biological Materialism (also know as PASOVACERCEPHHIBIMAT). An inebriated young woman in her twenties.

Bonfila Bezhukhovna Bonch-Bruevich – A pediatric oncologist, a pleasant woman in her thirties.

Big Babushka – Yet another Snow-Sweep of indeterminate age, garrulous, large, with a mustache.

Mrs. Shastlivyi Domik – An unhappy angry woman in her forties.

Vodya Domik – A silent little girl, eight years old.

PLACE:

The play takes place in Moscow, March 1985, and Talmenka, Siberia, 1992.

IN PERFORMANCE: The actors should probably use very, very mild Russian accents – standard American accents, really, lightly perfumed with something Slavic. But intelligibility is paramount – so don't eliminate diphthongs or replace too many "w"s with "v"s.

ALSO IN PERFORMANCE: The First and Second Babushkas should be played by the actresses playing Dr. Bonch-Bruevich and Mrs. Domik. The Big Babushka should be played by the actor playing Smukov.

AND ANOTHER THING: Status is very important. Prelapsarianov is the highest-ranking Politboro member of the five; Upgobkin is next, then Smukov (probably a military man), then, by several degrees lower, Popolitipov, then, lowest of all, Rodent. The lesser are careful with, and polite to the greater. Popolitipov is incomparably more powerful than Katherina, who pays no attention to the fact. He is more powerful than, and also dangerous to Bonfila, who is acutely aware of it. In Act Three, Rodent is now the good-will ambassador of a democratically-elected Federal government, the problem being that Rodent has no good will, and he both bitterly resents and desperately needs his job; and, in addition to the coward he has always been, has become a closet fascist. For Bonch-Bruevich and Mrs. Domik, he is the first representative of real power they've seen, and as such is both an opportunity and a target for their great frustration, rage and grief.

I suggest a rather hieratic staging of the scenes in Act One, according to which the actors are grouped statically in arrangements that help make the argument clear, that reveal the position each represents on the political spectrum. The leaping is the kinetic that disrupts the stasis.

These are all people who speak their thoughts, rather than people who think and then speak. There is no need for pausing to arrive at an idea or an articulation—the rhetorical grandeur is second nature for them, expressive of great slavic passion. They shift moods as quickly and with as much polarity as Ralph Cramden. Politics is the air they breathe, as is love. The stakes are very high.

Slavs!

Thinking About The Longstanding Problems Of
Virtue And Happiness

PROLOGUE

"The idea of socialism, as the word itself indicates, is based on the idea and the practice of *a society*. This may seem, at first sight, to do nothing to distinguish it from other political ideas, but that is only because we haven't looked closely enough. The very idea of *a society* – that is, a definite form of human relationships in certain specific conditions at a particular moment in history – is itself comparatively modern. *Society* used to mean mainly the company of other people. The idea of *a society* was to distinguish one form of social relationships from another, and to show that these forms varied historically and could change. Thus, in thinking about the longstanding problems of virtue and happiness, people who began from the idea of a society did not immediately refer the problems to a general human nature or to inevitable conditions of existence; they looked first at the precise forms of the society in which they were living and at how these might, where necessary, be changed.

> *"Walking Backwards Into The Future"*
> – Raymond Williams

Two babushkas, dressed in knee-length cheap winter coats, their legs encased in thick white support hose, their feet shod in rubber galoshes, their heads of course wrapped in floral- or geometric-print scarves tied under the chin, are sweeping snow from the entrance steps of the Hall of the Soviets, the Kremlin, March 1985. As they sweep, the snow falls; they talk.

FIRST BABUSHKA: However reluctant one may be to grant it, history and the experience of this century presses upon us the inescapable conclusion that there is a direct continuum from Dictatorship of the Proletariat and the embrace of violence as a means of effecting change that one finds in later Marx and Engels to dictatorship plain and simple – you missed a spot – and state terror.

SECOND BABUSHKA: True enough. But Marx's defense of revolutionary violence must be set in its proper context, namely: the 19th Century evolutionary socialist error of belief in the Inevitability of Gradualism, which sought not so much to transform society into something new . . .

FIRST BABUSHKA: . . . But rather to create an "improved" version of the society one sought to change.

SECOND BABUSHKA: Exactly.

FIRST BABUSHKA: But is it not a false antinomy to predicate as the only alternative to Reformism or Gradualism a vanguard-driven . . .

(*Two Politburo members, V. V. Smukov and S. E. Upgobkin, very impressive in greatcoats and big fur hats, enter.*)

SECOND BABUSHKA: (*Seeing them.*) Shhhh! Shhhhhh!

(*The babushkas clam up tight. They sweep.*)

VASSILY VOROVILICH SMUKOV: Morning grandma.

BABUSHKAS: (*Suddenly becoming sweet, toothless old ladies, smiling, head-bobbing, forelock-tugging mumblers.*) Good morning sirs! How-de-doo! Mind the ice, don't slip!

(*Smukov and Upgobkin climb the stairs and disappear into the Hall.*)

SECOND BABUSHKA: You missed a spot.

FIRST BABUSHKA: Thanks.

So where was I?

ACT ONE

"O tell me of the Russians, Communist,
my son!
Tell me of the Russians, my honest
young man!"
"They are moving for the people, mother;
let me alone,
For I am worn out with reading and want
to lie down!"

"Communist"
– John Berryman

SCENE 1

*In an anteroom outside the Politburo Chamber in the Hall of the
Soviets in the Kremlin. March 1985. Smukov and Upgobkin, in
suits now, are talking. A samovar stands nearby, brewing tea.*

VASSILY VOROVILICH SMUKOV: People are not capable of change.
   They used to be, maybe, but not anymore. In the old days you
   could ask anything of the people and they'd do it: live without
   bread, without heat in the winter, take a torch to their own
   houses, as long as they believed they were building socialism
   there was no limit to how much they could adapt, transform.
   Moldable clay in the hands of history.
SERGE ESMERELDOVICH UPGOBKIN: And you feel it's different now?
VASSILY VOROVILICH SMUKOV: Well, you see.
   We are all grown less pliable, unsure of our footing, unsure of
   the way, brittle bones and cataracts . . .
   How are your cataracts, by the way, Serge Esmereldovich?
SERGE ESMERELDOVICH UPGOBKIN: Worse, worse.
VASSILY VOROVILICH SMUKOV: They should operate.
SERGE ESMERELDOVICH UPGOBKIN: They have.
VASSILY VOROVILICH SMUKOV: But . . . ?
SERGE ESMERELDOVICH UPGOBKIN: But I still have the cataracts.

VASSILY VOROVILICH SMUKOV: It grieves me to hear that, Serge Esmereldovich.

SERGE ESMERELDOVICH UPGOBKIN: Old eyes get tough, cloudy. This one (*Points to one eye.*) is not really an eye anymore, it's a bottle-cork, it's a walnut. This one (*Points to the other eye.*) lets in milky light. I live in a world of milk white ghosts now, luminous beings, washed clean of detail. And I hear better, Vashka: in every voice, a million voices whispering. (*Imitates whispering.*) Sssssshhhhh, shhssshhh . . .

More tea?

VASSILY VOROVILICH SMUKOV: No; I'll have to get up to pee in the middle of Aleksii's speech.

SERGE ESMERELDOVICH UPGOBKIN: Whereas I intend to drink two more cups, so the pressure on my bladder will keep me awake.

VASSILY VOROVILICH SMUKOV: At least in the bad old days you could sleep through the speeches and not worry that you'd miss a thing. Now the speeches are longer and you have to stay awake to boo. It's miserable: democracy. I am a true apostle of the old scientific creed: Geriatrical materialism. Our motto: Stagnation is our only hope. Our sacred text: silence. Not this interminable debate, blah blah blah, my side, your side – really, this is logorrhea, not revolution.

SERGE ESMERELDOVICH UPGOBKIN: Patience.

There are no shortcuts to the new era. The terrain is vast. Aeons to traverse, everything is implicated, everything encompassed, the world, the universe . . .

A harsh and unnaturally protracted winter is losing its teeth. A great pressure has built up to this, Vashka, a great public desperation. There is no choice. You'll see that people can change, and change radically. From crown to toe, every cell formed anew. We set the process in motion with our words.

VASSILY VOROVILICH SMUKOV: People, I think, would rather die than change.

SERGE ESMERELDOVICH UPGOBKIN: Do you really think so?

I believe precisely the opposite.

We would rather change than die.

We have been ordered into motion by history herself. Vashka.

When the sun comes out the sky cracks open, the silent flowers twist and sway . . .

SCENE 2

Aleksii Antedilluvianovich Prelapsarionov, the world's oldest Bolshevik, speaking in the Chamber of Deputies. He is unimaginably old and totally blind; his voice is thin and high, but he speaks with great passion:

ALEKSII ANTEDILLUVIANOVICH PRELAPSARIANOV: And *Theory? Theory?* How are we to proceed without *Theory?* Is it enough to reject the past, is it wise to move forward in this blind fashion, without the Cold Brilliant Light of Theory to guide the way? What have these reformers to offer in the way of Theory? What beautiful system of thought have they to present to the world, to the befuddling, contrary tumult of life, to this mad swirling planetary disorganization, to the Inevident Welter of fact, event, phenomenon, calamity? Do they have, as we did, a beautiful Theory, as bold, as Grand, as comprehensive a construct . . . ? You can't imagine, when we first read the Classic Texts, when in the dark vexed night of our ignorance and terror the seed-words sprouted, and shoved incomprehension aside, when the incredible bloody vegetable struggle up and through into Red Blooming gave us Praxis, True Praxis, True Theory married to Actual Life . . . You who live in this Sour Little Age cannot imagine the sheer grandeur of the prospect we gazed upon: like standing atop the highest peak in the mighty Caucasus, and viewing in one all-knowing glance the mountainous, granite order of creation. We were One with the Sidereal Pulse then, in the blood in our heads we heard the tick of the Infinite. You cannot imagine it. I weep for you.
And what have you to offer now, children of this Theory? What have you to offer in its place? Market Incentives? Watered-down Bukharinite stopgap makeshift Capitalism? NEPmen! Pygmy children of a gigantic race!
Change? Yes, we must must change, only show me the Theory, and I will be at the barricades, show me the book of the next Beautiful Theory, and I promise you these blind eyes will see again, just to read it, to devour that text. Show me the words that will reorder the world, or else keep silent.

The snake sheds its skin only when a new skin is ready; if he gives up the only membrane he has before he can replace it, naked he will be in the world, prey to the forces of chaos: without his skin he will be dismantled, lose coherence and die. Have you, my little serpents, a new skin?
Then we dare not, we cannot move ahead.

SCENE 3

Outside the Hall of Deputies again, the Kremlin. Ippolite Ippopolitovich Popolitipov and Yegor Tremens Rodent, two middle-aged deputies, are talking. Popolitipov is in a rage over the debate in the adjoining chamber. Rodent is freaked out. Rodent is Popolitipov's protege, and is profoundly deferential.

IPPOLITE IPPOPOLITOVICH POPOLITIPOV: The heart is not progressive. The heart is conservative, no matter what the mind may be. Why don't they get that? The mind may make its leaps ahead; the heart will refuse to budge, shatter at the prospect. Yearn to go back to what it loves. That's the function of the organ, that's what it's there for: to fall in love. And love is profoundly reactionary, you fall in love and that instant is fixed, love is always fixed on the past.

YEGOR TREMENS RODENT: Oh true. Oh I am all terror these days. Sleep with the light on. No idea of what: just terror. Popolitipov, look! I'm shaking!

IPPOLITE IPPOPOLITOVICH POPOLITIPOV: Now debate that, reformers! The conservative, fractable human heart!

(*Serge Esmereldovich Upgobkin enters, leading Aleksii Antedilluvianovich Prelapsarianov to a comfy chair.*)

YEGOR TREMENS RODENT: (*To Popolitipov.*) Sssshhhh.

(*Popolitipov and Rodent move a discreet distance away from the two old Bolsheviks.*)

ALEKSII ANTEDILLUVIANOVICH PRELAPSARIANOV: (*As Upgobkin helps him to his chair.*) Stop hovering, Serge Esmereldovich, you're practically buggering me!

SERGE ESMERELDOVICH UPGOBKIN: I have to stand this close, otherwise I don't see . . .

ALEKSII ANTEDILLUVIANOVICH PRELAPSARIANOV: Nothing to see! I'm fine! And your breath is terrible. Please, you give me the fidgets. It's just a vein, just a weak vein in my head.

SERGE ESMERELDOVICH UPGOBKIN: I'll get some tea for you . . . (*Looking about.*) If I can find the samovar.

YEGOR TREMENS RODENT: There, comrade Upgobkin, it's over there . . .

ALEKSII ANTEDILLUVIANOVICH PRELAPSARIANOV: *I'm* the blind one! You just have cataracts! I'm *blind!*

IPPOLITE IPPOPOLITOVICH POPOLITIPOV: Is Comrade Minister Prelapsarianov not feeling well?

ALEKSII ANTEDILLUVIANOVICH PRELAPSARIANOV: HOURS! HOURS OF TALK! What do they think they have to say! Such pretentiousness, they fart and they whinny and I HAVE AN ANEURISM! (*He has gotten overexcited.*) Oh, oh, oh . . .

SERGE ESMERELDOVICH UPGOBKIN: Some hot tea . . . (*He pours a stiff shot of vodka in from a hip flask.*)

IPPOLITE IPPOPOLITOVICH POPOLITIPOV: (*Quietly, to Rodent.*) For decades a mostly respectable torpor. Now: expect madness.

YEGOR TREMENS RODENT: (*Also quiet.*) In Omsk thousands saw a radiant orb in the sky, larger than the moon. Sea monsters were seen swimming in some Kazakhstan lake. Strange space creatures reported landed in Gorkii . . .

IPPOLITE IPPOPOLITOVICH POPOLITIPOV: With three eyes. And they marched about the square.

YEGOR TREMENS RODENT: Six eyes. Tiny tiny head, big big body, six eyes.

IPPOLITE IPPOPOLITOVICH POPOLITIPOV: I really think it was only three.

YEGOR TREMENS RODENT: Two rows of three each, which makes six.

IPPOLITE IPPOPOLITOVICH POPOLITIPOV: Aha.

SERGE ESMERELDOVICH UPGOBKIN: (*Offering the teacup to Prelapsarianov.*) Can you swallow it?

ALEKSII ANTEDILLUVIANOVICH PRELAPSARIANOV: My head, my head, inside my brain, there's an itch, a little worm . . . Sssshhhh. Sssshhhh . . . (*He cradles his head.*)

YEGOR TREMENS RODENT: The theory is that radioactivity escaped from the explosion at the plutonium plant at Mayak is calling to them, the creatures, from across space, and they come perhaps with food and magic farm equipment, or personal computers, or with death rays to kill us all, and in Novy Sibirsk, people whose grandparents were merely babies when the Tsar was killed are rumored to have used black arts to resurrect . . . Rasputin. *Rasputin.*

IPPOLITE IPPOPOLITOVICH POPOLITIPOV: This cannot be what Lenin intended.

YEGOR TREMENS RODENT: Fantasy is the spiritual genius of Slavic peoples. And icons weep blood again. As if seventy years of socialism had never happened at all.

ALEKSII ANTEDILLUVIANOVICH PRELAPSARIANOV: (*Sitting suddenly bolt upright.*) Wait. Wait. OH! OH!

SERGE ESMERELDOVICH UPGOBKIN: Aleksii? Aleksii!

YEGOR TREMENS RODENT: Is Comrade Minister alright, is . . .

(*Aleksii Antedilluvianovich stands, staring ahead, dropping the tea cup.*)

IPPOLITE IPPOPOLITOVICH POPOLITIPOV: Serge Esmereldovich, is he . . . ?

ALEKSII ANTEDILLUVIANOVICH PRELAPSARIANOV: I see it now! Now I see! For ninety years I have wondered and wondered and wondered WHY is the Good Cause always defeated by the Bad, WHY Injustice and never Justice anywhere, WHY does Evil always always triumph and Good cast down in the gutter to be shat upon, WHY THIS HORROR AND WHY THIS HEARTACHE and NOW I GET IT! Because God . . . is a Menshevik! Because God . . . is a Petty-Bourgeois! Because God is a Reactionary, and Progressive People are THE POLITICAL ENEMIES OF GOD! He HATES US! Now! Now AT LAST I SEE –

(*He collapses and dies.*)

SERGE ESMERELDOVICH UPGOBKIN: Aleksii? Aleksii!?

YEGOR TREMENS RODENT: Oh my God . . .

SERGE ESMERELDOVICH UPGOBKIN: Oh help, oh help, oh somebody, somebody, Aleksii Antedilluvianovich Prelapsarianov is dead!

SCENE 4

Smukov enters.

VASSILY VOROVILICH SMUKOV: Did I hear . . . ? Oh my. A dead body.

SERGE ESMERELDOVICH UPGOBKIN: Aleksii Antedilluvianovich Prelapsarianov is dead.

VASSILY VOROVILICH SMUKOV: Oh dear, he spoke too long. So many words, we were afraid this might happen.

IPPOLITE IPPOPOLITOVICH POPOLITIPOV: The strain on the heart.

YEGOR TREMENS RODENT: No, it was his brain. A vessel popped upstairs. His face is royal purple.

IPPOLITE IPPOPOLITOVICH POPOLITIPOV: But popped because: the grieving heart avenged itself on the forward moving mind. The heart drowned the brain in blood. So that the whole animal could rest, safe from the future, secure in the past. As I was saying, the mind may . . .

YEGOR TREMENS RODENT: Someone ought to call security, we can't leave him lying . . .

SERGE ESMERELDOVICH UPGOBKIN: His heart had little reason to murder his mind, Ippolite Ippopolitovich, Aleksii's mind was hardly moving in a forward direction.

VASSILY VOROVILICH SMUKOV: I thought in the main his arguments were sound. As I understood it . . .

IPPOLITE IPPOPOLITOVICH POPOLITIPOV: The brain inhabits the body like a virus inhabits a cell. It takes control of the nucleus and selfishly mismanages the entirety till disaster results. It does not do to think too much! You reformers, you vanguard, you taskmaster brain . . .

YEGOR TREMENS RODENT: Oh you are making too much of this, Poppy, Comrade Minister Prelapsarianov was ninety-five years old. No wonder, it was past his time.

IPPOLITE IPPOPOLITOVICH POPOLITIPOV: Illness is a metaphor, Yegor; the human body, the body politic, the human soul, the soul of the state. Dynamic and immobile all at once, lava and granite, the head and the heart. It's all tension and tearing, and which will win? An infarction (*Clutches his heart.*) or a stroke (*Clutches his head.*)?

VASSILY VOROVILICH SMUKOV: I don't know what you're talking about, Popolitipov, but one thing is clear: we should not move until we know where we're going. They should chisel that on poor Aleksii's tombstone, that was his best bit. Wait patiently till the way is clear.

SERGE ESMERELDOVICH UPGOBKIN: And imagination? That faculty? Which Angels are said to lack, but people possess? Dialectics can only lead us so far, to the edge of what is known. But after that . . . ?

We see so poorly, almost blind. We who . . .

YEGOR TREMENS RODENT: Careful, Serge Esmereldovich, if you're going to make a speech, look at what happened to poor Comrade Minister, and you're almost as old as he is . . . was.

SERGE ESMERELDOVICH UPGOBKIN: Then let me follow him into oblivion. Let me make that leap. Because you can only creep so far, and then you must leap, Rodent, you must use your own legs and your own will, or life itself will simply toss you in the air, but willing or resisting, I promise you all, you will leap! Does the heart plot to kill the mind, does it shatter that non-sprouted seed, the brain, before the New Blooms blossom? Then let the heart beware, for my brain will dream the New, I will make that leap, and let the strain be too much, let the strain explode my recalcitrant heart, let my heart burst like a bomb while my sparks leap their synapses! We must dream the New! And by Caution we never can! By Leaping!

(*Serge Esmereldovich Upgobkin begins to leap in the air, over and over, going higher and higher.*)

IPPOLITE IPPOPOLITOVICH POPOLITIPOV: Stop it, Serge Esmereldovich Upgobkin, you'll . . .

SERGE ESMERELDOVICH UPGOBKIN: (*As he leaps:*) Leap, you unregenerate Stalinist! Leap, you bursitic Brezhnevite! Leap, leap, procrustean, legless Legachevite, leap! So what if they dissolve the entire Union, so what if the Balkans are all re-Balkanized, so what if the Ukraine won't sell us their wheat, and Georgia secedes, and Germany reunites, and all our reforms go only to squelch real revolution!

VASSILY VOROVILICH SMUKOV: Oh, well, now that would really be terrible, we . . .

SERGE ESMERELDOVICH UPGOBKIN: (*Still leaping, continuing over the above:*) LEAP! HIGH! See if you can see it! The NEW! The UNIMAGINED! The THAT FOR WHICH OUR DREAMS ARE ACHING! For what is hope but desiring forwards!? (*To Rodent:*) Are you a man, or are you a mollusk? Will you never dare? Will you be dead forever?

YEGOR TREMENS RODENT: No!

SERGE ESMERELDOVICH UPGOBKIN: Then LEAP!

(*Upgobkin and Rodent leap and leap.*)

VASSILY VOROVILICH SMUKOV: Serge, Serge, please don't over-exert yourself, what has gotten into you?

SERGE ESMERELDOVICH UPGOBKIN: The NEW! The NEW! The NEW!

IPPOLITE IPPOPOLITOVICH POPOLITIPOV: (*Over the above:*) Yegor Tremens
Rodent, stop that at once!

(*Popolitipov stops Rodent, pulls him down to earth.*)

Control yourself, dammit.

VASSILY VOROVILICH SMUKOV: *Look* at him! Serge . . .

(*Upgobkin is leaping higher and higher. His face is upturned, he is
no longer with his comrades, he is beatific, he is smiling
enormously. From above there is a violently brief burst of
radiance, and the instant it falls on Upgobkin he collapses and
dies. And the light is gone.*)

YEGOR TREMENS RODENT: *Now* I am calling security. And no more
metaphors, anyone, please. Two bodies, two bodies, what a
scandal this will make.

IPPOLITE IPPOPOLITOVICH POPOLITIPOV: Was it his heart, or was it his
head?

YEGOR TREMENS RODENT: Heart.

VASSILY VOROVILICH SMUKOV: Still smiling. That smile. What on earth do
you suppose he saw?

END OF ACT ONE

ACT TWO

"That's why I loved you, for your magnificent heart!
And you do not need my forgiveness, nor I yours; it's
all the same whether you forgive or not, all my life
you will remain a wound in my soul, and I in yours
– that's how it should be."

The Brothers Karamazov
– Fyodor Dostoevsky

"And, oh, how blue the cornflowers, how black
the earth, how red the kerchief of the female
comrade!"

A History Of Soviet Organ Music
– John Ash

SCENE 1

*In the small, dank, dark, dismal room that serves as the guards'
chamber of the Pan-Soviet Archives For The Study of Cerebro-
Cephalognomical Historico-Biological Materialism (Also known as
PASOVACERCEPHHIBIMAT). The night following the afternoon of
Act One. A table for a desk, an old swivel chair missing a wheel,
and a security-system video monitor surveilling an adjoining
room in which big glass jars sit in neat rows on shelves. In the jars
float human brains. (We only see this room on the video screen.)
In the guardroom, Katherina Serafima Gleb, a young woman in
her twenties who is wearing the uniform of a security guard, is
sitting, staring into space. An old samovar, much less impressive
than the samovar in Act One, stands on the table, brewing tea.
Popolitipov, wearing a voluminous greatcoat and a big fur hat,
covered in snow, bursts in, carrying an ancient, battered guitar
case.*

IPPOLITE IPPOPOLITOVICH POPOLITIPOV: You.
KATHERINA SERAFIMA GLEB: What?
IPPOLITE IPPOPOLITOVICH POPOLITIPOV: Have replaced myself in me.

KATHERINA SERAFIMA GLEB: What?

IPPOLITE IPPOPOLITOVICH POPOLITIPOV: The soul in me that on Judgment Day looked to ascend to bright Heaven has been smitten, obliterated, replaced in me by you.

KATHERINA SERAFIMA GLEB: Too creepy.

IPPOLITE IPPOPOLITOVICH POPOLITIPOV: I am not merely yours, Katherina, I *am* you, I have *become* you.

KATHERINA SERAFIMA GLEB: I said, too creepy.

IPPOLITE IPPOPOLITOVICH POPOLITIPOV: I would like to run my tongue against the salty soft shag covering your upper lip.

KATHERINA SERAFIMA GLEB: Too personal.

IPPOLITE IPPOPOLITOVICH POPOLITIPOV: I want to fuck you.

KATHERINA SERAFIMA GLEB: Don't try anything, Poppy, I'm warning you.

IPPOLITE IPPOPOLITOVICH POPOLITIPOV: Can I sing you a song?

KATHERINA SERAFIMA GLEB: Your voice is repulsive. No. Do you have cigarettes?

IPPOLITE IPPOPOLITOVICH POPOLITIPOV: No. In me there is a yearning, and it complains to me of wanting you, it strains against my skin towards you, it is like the wet lapping of the tide, the pull of the moon on the ocean, like the rise of sap through frozen wood when winter is shattered by the brunt thrust of spring.

KATHERINA SERAFIMA GLEB: Too romantic.

IPPOLITE IPPOPOLITOVICH POPOLITIPOV: Like the hydraulic rush of the river through the dam, the whine of turbines, voltage coursing across a continent of wire.

KATHERINA SERAFIMA GLEB: Too technological.

IPPOLITE IPPOPOLITOVICH POPOLITIPOV: Like the inchoate voluptuous seething of the masses as they surge towards revolutionary consciousness.

KATHERINA SERAFIMA GLEB: (*Overlapping on "surge":*) Too political. Too corny.

IPPOLITE IPPOPOLITOVICH POPOLITIPOV: When I was a child . . .

KATHERINA SERAFIMA GLEB: Too psychological.

(*Popolitipov screams, then:*)

IPPOLITE IPPOPOLITOVICH POPOLITIPOV: Give yourself to me, I beg you, Katherina Serafima, or I will blow my brains out I will lie down in a snow bank or under a train or . . .

KATHERINA SERAFIMA GLEB: You were supposed to bring cigarettes, Poppy.

IPPOLITE IPPOPOLITOVICH POPOLITIPOV: I burn my flesh with cigarettes, dreaming of you, I scrape my knuckles along roughcast walls, look, bloody scabs, I deliberately lace my shoes too tight, and cinch my belt till my intestines squirm under pressure, in pain, I refuse myself sleep, dreaming of you, I've slept maybe six, maybe seven hours this whole month, sleep-deprived, trussed and hobbled and why? I mean, are you clever? No. Are you kind? Most certainly not. And yet there is in all your attributes considered and parts taken together a summational, additive kind of perfection: I love you.

KATHERINA SERAFIMA GLEB: You're old.

IPPOLITE IPPOPOLITOVICH POPOLITIPOV: I love you.

KATHERINA SERAFIMA GLEB: I hate you.

IPPOLITE IPPOPOLITOVICH POPOLITIPOV: (*Shouting:*) *I LOVE YOU!*

KATHERINA SERAFIMA GLEB: I'm a lesbian.

IPPOLITE IPPOPOLITOVICH POPOLITIPOV: Pervert.

KATHERINA SERAFIMA GLEB: Asshole.

IPPOLITE IPPOPOLITOVICH POPOLITIPOV: Abomination!

KATHERINA SERAFIMA GLEB: Exploiter!

IPPOLITE IPPOPOLITOVICH POPOLITIPOV: Wanton! Abuser!

KATHERINA SERAFIMA GLEB: Harasser! Torturer! *Apparatchik!*

(*He lunges for her. She dodges easily. He falls heavily. She steps on his neck.*)

I warned you.

IPPOLITE IPPOPOLITOVICH POPOLITIPOV: Get off.

KATHERINA SERAFIMA GLEB: Cigarettes.

(*He hands them to her.*)

I'm tired of this, Poppy, I'm going to find an easier way to get a decent smoke. I really am a lesbian, you know. I have a new girlfriend. I'll never have sex with you, I don't want to touch you, and frankly, Poppy, it's not fair you should make me go through this mortifying business over and over and over again, night after night after night; know what? You're a pig.

IPPOLITE IPPOPOLITOVICH POPOLITIPOV: I cannot help myself. (*He begins to remove an ancient guitar from the guitar case.*)

KATHERINA SERAFIMA GLEB: Just because you got me a soft job. A soft, *boring* job. Which I hate. This place is creepy. Know what? At night I hear them slithering.

IPPOLITE IPPOPOLITOVICH POPOLITIPOV: Who?

KATHERINA SERAFIMA GLEB: The brains. They rub their spongy rivules and volutes against the smooth glass sides of their jars. Sometimes they bubble. As if breathing.

IPPOLITE IPPOPOLITOVICH POPOLITIPOV: The brains are dead brains, Katherina.

KATHERINA SERAFIMA GLEB: Then why don't they throw them out?

IPPOLITE IPPOPOLITOVICH POPOLITIPOV: They study them. The great minds of the Party. Political minds. Scientific minds. Even an artist or two.

KATHERINA SERAFIMA GLEB: In my opinion they should throw them out. Most of the older ones are falling apart. No one could make a proper study of them. Sometimes when I get bored, I grab the jars and shake them up. The brain cells of Vyshinsky. The brain cells of Iron Feliks Dzerzhinsky. Whirl like snowflakes in a crystal snowball.

IPPOLITE IPPOPOLITOVICH POPOLITIPOV: Become my mistress or I will report you.

KATHERINA SERAFIMA GLEB: When you die, Poppy, will they put your brain in a jar?

(*Popolitipov begins to play softly, serenading her.*)

KATHERINA SERAFIMA GLEB: (*Listens to the music a beat, then:*) Some nights I pretend that I am not simply night watchman but I lead midnight tours through here for insomniac Muscovites whose anxieties or guilty consciences keep them awake. This is my speech:

(*To audience:*)

Welcome to the Pan-Soviet Archives For The Study of Cerebro-Cephalognomical Historico-Biological Materialism, also known as PASOVACERCEPHHIBIMAT. Here the Party has stored the brains of its bygone leaders, an unbroken line of brains stretching back to Red October. Beginning of course with Lenin, most people think his brain is still in his body in the crypt, but it's not, it's here, it is MASSIVE, 1,340 grams of solid brainflesh, the heaviest brain ever extracted, it's a wonder the poor man could hold his head up his brain was so grotesquely HUGE. Ranked beside it are many other famous brains, all floating in some sort of sudsy lime-green mummifying juice, all the famous Bolshevik brains except for those which got flushed in the notorious dead-brain purges of 1937. Stalin's brain is here; Brezhnev's which is dingy-yellow like an old tooth; Andropov's, and now I suppose Chernenko's brain, which hasn't been delivered yet. Maybe they couldn't find it.

Let's talk politics.

IPPOLITE IPPOPOLITOVICH POPOLITIPOV: (*Strumming.*) I don't want to talk politics with you, my Katushka, I want to pluck my guitar for you, pick pick pick I pick my heart to pieces.

KATHERINA SERAFIMA GLEB: Gorbachev will replace Chernenko.

Right?

Come on, Poppy, Tell me! Gorbachev will be our honored leader next?

His wife is a Jewess.

IPPOLITE IPPOPOLITOVICH POPOLITIPOV: (*Continuing to strum:*) No she . . .

KATHERINA SERAFIMA GLEB: That's what they say: Jewess.

(*Popolitipov continues to play under this.*)

KATHERINA SERAFIMA GLEB: I'm not an anti-semite, I have nothing to do with Jews, but that's what they say.

Tea?

(*Popolitipov nods his head "yes." Katherina goes to the samovar, lifts the lid, reaches within and withdraws an alarmingly large bottle of vodka. She takes a huge swallow, and hands it to Popolitipov, who does the same, and then starts playing again.*)

IPPOLITE IPPOPOLITOVICH POPOLITIPOV: Gorbachev isn't a Jew. Nor is Raisa Maximovna. He'll never be General Secretary. He's only fifty-four, much too young.

(*Little pause.*)

A strange lust for the sort of pleasures one associates with adolescence seems to have overtaken everyone: panic, mania, nausea, rage. The pleasures of adulthood are forsaken.

KATHERINA SERAFIMA GLEB: What are the pleasures of adulthood?

IPPOLITE IPPOPOLITOVICH POPOLITIPOV: Heartbreak. Agony deep as bone marrow. Quiet, nuanced despair.

(*A pause. He looks at her. She drinks vodka. He drinks vodka.*)

KATHERINA SERAFIMA GLEB: Gorbachev will come, trailing free market anarchy in his wake! Burger King! Denny's! The International Monetary Fund! Billions in aid will flow! Solzhenitsyn will come back from Vermont to thrash and purify us! Kentucky Fried Chicken Franchises! Toxic waste! Everything will change then because Gorbachev is crafty and sly in the manner of Jews. He'll defeat the deadbeat nomenklatura, every last one, including you, Poppy, and then there will be no more politics, we will become like Americans, I will be in a heavy metal band! There will be *surprises:* most of them unpleasant, but at least unanticipated, and the Great Grey Age of Boredom will finally lift.

(*She takes a swig of vodka, he takes a swig of vodka.*)

IPPOLITE IPPOPOLITOVICH POPOLITIPOV: To the Great Age of Boredom.

KATHERINA SERAFIMA GLEB: I am inexpressibly, immeasurably sad. Sad sad.

IPPOLITE IPPOPOLITOVICH POPOLITIPOV: Because you are a Slav. Sorrow is the spiritual genius of Slavic peoples.

KATHERINA SERAFIMA GLEB: Bullshit. I don't believe in national identities. Reactionary! I am an anarchist.

IPPOLITE IPPOPOLITOVICH POPOLITIPOV: You are a nihilist.

KATHERINA SERAFIMA GLEB: I am an internationalist. (*Swig of vodka.*) Like Trotsky! (*Swig of vodka.*) The Jew!

(*Pause. He looks at her.*)

IPPOLITE IPPOPOLITOVICH POPOLITIPOV: When I was a child, I was an ugly child, a graceless child, and did not believe I would be loved and was in fact not loved by anyone.

KATHERINA SERAFIMA GLEB: Poor Poppy. Poor Poppy the Slav.

IPPOLITE IPPOPOLITOVICH POPOLITIPOV: My mother dead in the Great Patriotic War, in the snow, German bullet through her spine, her belly, but I was already a young man by then so it can't have been then that I lost her love, but earlier, earlier, a point towards which my memories refuse to travel – I cannot blame them. My father was a bastard, the Germans got him too.

KATHERINA SERAFIMA GLEB: (*Swigging vodka.*) Poppy, the orphan.

IPPOLITE IPPOPOLITOVICH POPOLITIPOV: The Party adopted me. The Party was not Love, but Necessity; it rebuilt the ruined world. Through the Party I came to love.

KATHERINA SERAFIMA GLEB: Love.

(*Vodka. Sorrow.*)

IPPOLITE IPPOPOLITOVICH POPOLITIPOV: The Party dispenses miracles. The Party drove away the Czar, immortalized Lenin, withstood France and Britain and the United States, made Communism in one country, electrified Russia, milled steel, built railways, abolished distance, defeated Germany, suspended time, became Eternal, dispersed the body of each and every member, molecule by molecule, across an inconceivably vast starry matrix encompassing the infinite: so that, within the Party, everything is; so that everything human, even Marx – was shown as limited and the Party, Illimitable; and through the illimitable Party the human is exalted, becomes Divine, occupant of a great chiming spaciousness that is not distance but time, time which never moves nor passes, light which does not travel and yet is light: and love, pure love, even in a degraded, corrupt and loveless world, love can finally be born.

(*Little pause, more vodka.*)

Do you understand what I am saying to you, Katushka?

KATHERINA SERAFIMA GLEB: Not a word.

IPPOLITE IPPOPOLITOVICH POPOLITIPOV: (*Very tenderly:*) That night, that night, when I saw you that night, I was walking in the Arbat, you had fallen in the snow, sleeping in the gutter, dirty, drunk, rude, radiant: I was overwhelmed with lust, and then followed – love. Love. Love. Love. Love. Even in a corrupt and loveless world, love can be born.

(*Katherina leaps to her feet and screams, a long, loud, howl of joy; she rushes across the room at Dr. Bonfila Bezhukhovna Bonce-Bruevich, who is just entering the room, carrying a wrapped parcel, wearing hat and coat, covered in snow. Katherina kisses Bonfila passionately.*)

IPPOLITE IPPOPOLITOVICH POPOLITIPOV: (*Aghast!*) Good God!

BONFILA BEZHUKHOVNA BONCH-BRUEVICH: (*Seeing Popolitipov:*) Oh my God.

KATHERINA SERAFIMA GLEB: God I'm happy! Hello, Poppy!

BONFILA BEZHUKHOVNA BONCH-BRUEVICH: (*Bowing her head slightly:*) Comrade Commissar, I . . .

KATHERINA SERAFIMA GLEB: See? Lesbians! This is my girlfriend, Doctor Bonf . . .

BONFILA BEZHUKHOVNA BONCH-BRUEVICH: (*Cutting her off:*) I'm interrupting.

(*Bonfila turns to leave, Katherina grabs her arm.*)

KATHERINA SERAFIMA GLEB: No, Poppy was interrupting, Poppy is always interrupting, but now he's going. Aren't you, Poppy? (*Screaming with rage:*) GO, POPPY!!!

BONFILA BEZHUKHOVNA BONCH-BRUEVICH: (*To Katherina:*) You're drunk.

KATHERINA SERAFIMA GLEB: No I'm not.

BONFILA BEZHUKHOVNA BONCH-BRUEVICH: Yes you are!

KATHERINA SERAFIMA GLEB: You're mad at me.

(*To Popolitipov:*) See what you've done.

I need a drink.

(*To Popolitipov:*) See, my sadness is gone, I must not be a true Slav after all. I'm happy you can see her, now maybe you will know that I cannot love you: ever, ever. And she is a physician, she cures people, not an ineffectual aged paperpushing-timeserver-apparatchik-with-a-dacha like you who only bleeds the people dry.

(*Awkward pause.*)

BONFILA BEZHUKHOVNA BONCH-BRUEVICH: Did I interrupt . . .

(*Pointing to the guitar that Poppy clutches:*) Comrade Commissar was playing the . . .

IPPOLITE IPPOPOLITOVICH POPOLITIPOV: (*Putting the guitar away:*) Not anymore.

Doctor . . . ?

KATHERINA SERAFIMA GLEB: Bonch-Bruevich!

BONFILA BEZHUKHOVNA BONCH-BRUEVICH: (*Simultaneously:*) Comrade Commissar, I . . .

(*To Katherina, hearing that she has said her name:*) Shut up

I'll go.

I'll go.

Somebody should go

This is mortifying.

IPPOLITE IPPOPOLITOVICH POPOLITIPOV: Is it?

(*Pleasant:*) Things change. Some things. We are all liberals.

(*Homicidally angry, to Katherina:*) Horseleech! Viper's spawn!

(*Pleasant again:*) You are a doctor. Of . . . ?

(*Military command:*) Do you have a specialty.

BONFILA BEZHUKHOVNA BONCH-BRUEVICH: Pediatric oncology.

KATHERINA SERAFIMA GLEB: (*Sad:*) Kids with cancer.

IPPOLITE IPPOPOLITOVICH POPOLITIPOV: Moscow?

BONFILA BEZHUKHOVNA BONCH-BRUEVICH: I . . . Yes.

IPPOLITE IPPOPOLITOVICH POPOLITIPOV: (*Trying to keep it together but coming unglued:*) That's convenient for both of you. You are lucky. Moscow is an agreeable posting, for cosmopolitans such as you and I. Many doctors have to report to places more remote, Arctic outposts . . .

(*Little pause; becoming suddenly sad and weary:*)
Doctor, may I ask you a health-related question?

BONFILA BEZHUKHOVNA BONCH-BRUEVICH: Certainly.

IPPOLITE IPPOPOLITOVICH POPOLITIPOV: (*In confidence, in earnest:*) If a man were to shoot himself, against which of the various customary vulnerable points of the body would you advise he position the barrel of his gun?

BONFILA BEZHUKHOVNA BONCH-BRUEVICH: I . . .

IPPOLITE IPPOPOLITOVICH POPOLITIPOV: Temple? Soft palate? Heart?

KATHERINA SERAFIMA GLEB: I have a friend who died by shooting himself in the armpit. The bullet went through his shoulder and into his nose.

BONFILA BEZHUKHOVNA BONCH-BRUEVICH: I would advise him not to shoot himself, Comrade Commissar. I would advise him to live.

IPPOLITE IPPOPOLITOVICH POPOLITIPOV: Say his life had become unbearable.

BONFILA BEZHUKHOVNA BONCH-BRUEVICH: Life is almost never literally unbearable. We choose whether or not we bear up. We choose.

IPPOLITE IPPOPOLITOVICH POPOLITIPOV: Circumstances may dictate otherwise. History.

BONFILA BEZHUKHOVNA BONCH-BRUEVICH: People make their own history.

IPPOLITE IPPOPOLITOVICH POPOLITIPOV: Limits are set by the conditions of their social development.

KATHERINA SERAFIMA GLEB: (*By rote, a thing she learned in school:*) Those conditions are themselves affected by the state of their economic relations.
(*Pause. The others look at Katherina.*)
Which in turn are related to a particular stage of the mode of production.
(*She sits heavily, slumps over, falls asleep.*)

IPPOLITE IPPOPOLITOVICH POPOLITIPOV: Her head is stuffed full of pottery shards, rags, ash, and wind. She is the Revolution's Great-Granddaughter. She is . . . a barbarian.

BONFILA BEZHUKHOVNA BONCH-BRUEVICH: She's immature. And can't drink. And I think she doesn't like you very much.

IPPOLITE IPPOPOLITOVICH POPOLITIPOV: I must be going.

KATHERINA SERAFIMA GLEB: (*Still slumped over, drowsy:*) Try the armpit, Poppy.

IPPOLITE IPPOPOLITOVICH POPOLITIPOV: If I shoot myself, Katherina, will you miss me?

KATHERINA SERAFIMA GLEB: (*Looking up:*) Maybe. For a day or two. Maybe.

The cigarettes, definitely.

Not really. No.

Oh Poppy, I'm sorry, but you're a pig, you know, and I would like to be kind, but I can't. (*She sleeps.*)

IPPOLITE IPPOPOLITOVICH POPOLITIPOV: We have not made kind people. (*To Bonfila, not without menace:*) We have not made a world that makes people kind.

(*He leaves.*)

BONFILA BEZHUKHOVNA BONCH-BRUEVICH: Is he really going to shoot himself.

(*Katherina snores, loudly.*)

SCENE 2

The guardroom. Several hours later. Katherina and Bonfila sit at the table, both drunk, Katherina more drunk; the parcel, still wrapped, is on the table between them. Also on the table is a now-nearly empty bottle of vodka.

BONFILA BEZHUKHOVNA BONCH-BRUEVICH: My great-grandfather was Vladimir Dimitrievich Bonch-Bruevich. Do you know who that is? (*Katherina shakes her head "no."*)
First Secretary of the Sovnarkom.
The Council of People's Commissars. 1918. A founder of the Party.

KATHERINA SERAFIMA GLEB: Never heard of him.

BONFILA BEZHUKHOVNA BONCH-BRUEVICH: It's your history.

KATHERINA SERAFIMA GLEB: I have no history. What's in the package?

BONFILA BEZHUKHOVNA BONCH-BRUEVICH: My great-grandfather is the man who embalmed Lenin. He selected the design for the tomb.

KATHERINA SERAFIMA GLEB: You're angry with me because I'm drunk.

BONFILA BEZHUKHOVNA BONCH-BRUEVICH: Not as angry as I was when I was sober.

KATHERINA SERAFIMA GLEB: Promise we'll be lovers forever.

BONFILA BEZHUKHOVNA BONCH-BRUEVICH: No.

KATHERINA SERAFIMA GLEB: Promise we'll be lovers till I'm sober.

BONFILA BEZHUKHOVNA BONCH-BRUEVICH: Yes.

KATHERINA SERAFIMA GLEB: If you leave me I'll kill you.

BONFILA BEZHUKHOVNA BONCH-BRUEVICH: Oh bullshit.

KATHERINA SERAFIMA GLEB: Is Poppy dead yet, do you think?
You've been my lover for more than a month, and look, you still visit me late at night, you bring me mysterious packages . . .

BONFILA BEZHUKHOVNA BONCH-BRUEVICH: Three weeks, it's only been . . . It's still new to me, all this . . .

KATHERINA SERAFIMA GLEB: You won't leave me, will you?

BONFILA BEZHUKHOVNA BONCH-BRUEVICH: I love you.

KATHERINA SERAFIMA GLEB: That's not what I asked. Everyone loves me, but I'm unbearable. I need someone who will . . . stay, or . . . I'm sad again.

BONFILA BEZHUKHOVNA BONCH-BRUEVICH: My great-grandfather was also a great slavophile, a folklorist.

KATHERINA SERAFIMA GLEB: Sadness is the spiritual genius of the Slavic peoples.

BONFILA BEZHUKHOVNA BONCH-BRUEVICH: Uh huh.
He wrote that the revolts of the Old Believers against Peter the Great were early stirrings of the revolution among the peoples.

KATHERINA SERAFIMA GLEB: (*Overlap.*) Peter the Great, 1672-1725.

BONFILA BEZHUKHOVNA BONCH-BRUEVICH: (*Continuous from above, overlap:*) My great-grandfather also collected icons. And he planned the Lenin Cult.

KATHERINA SERAFIMA GLEB: Lenin: 1870-1923.

BONFILA BEZHUKHOVNA BONCH-BRUEVICH: 1924. When Lenin died, peasants from Tsarskoye Selo sent this to my great-grandpa, to put in the tomb.
(*She unwraps the package. It's an old icon, with a metal candleholder attached, in which is a red glass, inside of which is a candle.*)
See? It's Lenin. They painted his face over an icon of St. Sergius of Radonezh, who lived six hundred years ago . . .
(*Little pause. Katherina drinks most of the rest of the vodka, passes the last swallow to Bonfila, who drinks it.*)

BONFILA BEZHUKHOVNA BONCH-BRUEVICH: . . . And who is said to have been a great worker of miracles.

KATHERINA SERAFIMA GLEB: We need more vodka.

BONFILA BEZHUKHOVNA BONCH-BRUEVICH: There is no more vodka.

KATHERINA SERAFIMA GLEB: We must go out and get some more vodka.

BONFILA BEZHUKHOVNA BONCH-BRUEVICH: It's too late. It must be four AM. There won't be a store open.

KATHERINA SERAFIMA GLEB: Why won't you make love to me?

BONFILA BEZHUKHOVNA BONCH-BRUEVICH: *Here?*

KATHERINA SERAFIMA GLEB: Oh who gives a fuck where? Sure, here. If you love me what would it matter.

BONFILA BEZHUKHOVNA BONCH-BRUEVICH: Too creepy.

KATHERINA SERAFIMA GLEB: Do it, here. Put your hand down my coveralls, slip it deep inside me, blow hot fog-breath in my ears till my brains cook, let me lick your cunt till my whole face is wet, put my hair in your mouth, nip my buttocks, let me scream joyfully as if a hungry animal I want to feed is eating me up!

BONFILA BEZHUKHOVNA BONCH-BRUEVICH: You embarrass me.

KATHERINA SERAFIMA GLEB: You're afraid of sex with me.

BONFILA BEZHUKHOVNA BONCH-BRUEVICH: *Nonsense.*

(*Little pause.*)

I'm afraid of sex with you in front of a Deputy Secretary of . . .

KATHERINA SERAFIMA GLEB: He's off shooting himself.

We're alone. I still have all my clothes on. Something's wrong.

(*Little pause.*)

BONFILA BEZHUKHOVNA BONCH-BRUEVICH: He won't shoot himself, and tomorrow he'll have us both arrested. Ten years in an institution!

KATHERINA SERAFIMA GLEB: Under Gorbachev people will not be . . .

BONFILA BEZHUKHOVNA BONCH-BRUEVICH: (*Over.*) Or maybe he'll have me transferred, just me, alone, to some godforsaken town in Uzbekistan, it was very, very, very stupid of you to kiss me like that in the open like that, to . . .

KATHERINA SERAFIMA GLEB: He's probably dead by now, Poppy, and anyway he wouldn't . . .

BONFILA BEZHUKHOVNA BONCH-BRUEVICH: . . . to draw down attention like that, to deliberately . . . HOW THE HELL DO YOU KNOW WHAT HE'D . . .

You're ignorant. You don't know anything.

(*Pause.*)

KATHERINA SERAFIMA GLEB: St. Sergius of Radonezh. 1314-1392.

You're yelling because you're afraid of me.

BONFILA BEZHUKHOVNA BONCH-BRUEVICH: Yes.

(*They kiss. It gets hot, then hotter, then cold.*)

Sexual deviance is symptomatic of cultures of luxury, in which monied classes cultivate morbid fascinations with biological functions, especially sex, tending towards narcissistic, anti-social, unproductive behavior such as . . .

Anyway I don't believe in lesbians, I believe in the working class as the only repository for real historical agency.

You're right. I am afraid of you.

KATHERINA SERAFIMA GLEB: Why did you come?

BONFILA BEZHUKHOVNA BONCH-BRUEVICH: To show you this. (*The icon.*)

My great-grandmother is dying. She's 105 years old. Endurance is the spiritual genius of Slavic peoples.

She gave me this. She says it still works miracles.

KATHERINA SERAFIMA GLEB: Who do you pray to when you light the candle, Lenin or St. Sergius?

BONFILA BEZHUKHOVNA BONCH-BRUEVICH: She didn't say.

KATHERINA SERAFIMA GLEB: What miracles has it worked?

BONFILA BEZHUKHOVNA BONCH-BRUEVICH: She didn't say that either.

KATHERINA SERAFIMA GLEB: Let's pray for vodka.

BONFILA BEZHUKHOVNA BONCH-BRUEVICH: Shouldn't it be for something less frivolous?

KATHERINA SERAFIMA GLEB: I pray for you to love me enough to be true to your promise.

BONFILA BEZHUKHOVNA BONCH-BRUEVICH: What promise.

KATHERINA SERAFIMA GLEB: That you'll never leave me.

BONFILA BEZHUKHOVNA BONCH-BRUEVICH: Till you're sober.

KATHERINA SERAFIMA GLEB: (*Very serious:*) Then I must never be sober again.

Let's pray for vodka.

BONFILA BEZHUKHOVNA BONCH-BRUEVICH: Match.

(*Katherina gives her one. Bonfila lights the candle. The room darkens. Katherina kneels, bows her head.*)

KATHERINA SERAFIMA GLEB: St. Lenin or St. Sergius, whoever you are. Please hear the prayer of your little daughter. Look down on her from heaven, she's in the room of dead brains; send vodka. So that I may stay pathetically drunk so that she will never leave me, because I'm full of violence and self-pity and lies, but I do have decent feelings too, and dreams that are beautiful, that I'm not ashamed of having, and there was no earthly thing I could attach them to until I made her love me. Please help me little father. Please hear my prayer.

(*Pause. A big babushka enters, covered in snow.*)

BIG BABUSHKA: Kat, I'll tell you what, I was sweeping the snow off the steps up front and along comes this huge truckload of soldiers plowing down the street, sliding on the ice and bang it smacks into a telephone pole and goes over on its side and all the soldiers come tumbling out, and I rush over to see was anyone hurt, and someone was because a soldier's running up and down the street spattering blood in the snow and we can't get him to stop because naturally they're all drunken idiots from the sticks and he's screaming "I'm dying, I'm dying, mother, mother," and all the yelling frightens a dog who bites a cop who swings a club which smashes a big store window; dog, glass, blood, soldiers, and finally we got the boy calmed down and sent him off wrapped up in a bandage and the dog's run off and the cop sees it's a liquor store window he's smashed so he gives me a big bottle of this vodka to shut me up about it (because everyone knows my mouth) which I can't drink because my liver's already the size of my head and so here, I've brought it to you, you drunken slut, because I'm fond of you as if you were my own granddaughter, now I got to go finish sweeping the snow before more falls.

(*The big babushka slams a big bottle of vodka down on the table. She squints at the icon.*)

BIG BABUSHKA: St. Sergius of Radonezh with the face of Great Lenin.

(*She exits. Katherina and Bonfila look at the vodka, and each other, agape.*)

SCENE 3

Even later. Katherina is asleep with her head in Bonfila's lap. Bonfila strokes Katherina's hair and looks at the icon, before which the candle is still burning. The second bottle of vodka stands, almost empty, beside the first empty bottle.

BONFILA BEZHUKHOVNA BONCH-BRUEVICH: (*Very softly:*) Little father:

You left us alone and see the state we've fallen into? Shouldn't you come back to us now? We have suffered and suffered and Paradise has not arrived. Shouldn't you come back and tell us what went wrong?

She says your brain is in a jar next door: your body is across town. Pull yourself together, leave your tomb, come claim your brain, remember speech, and action, and once more, having surveyed the wreckage we have made, tell your children: What is to be done?

Shouldn't you come back now?

(*Little red candle lights blink on everywhere. Like on Christmas morning:*) Kat. Wake up. Kat. Wake up. Katherina.

KATHERINA SERAFIMA GLEB: What?

BONFILA BEZHUKHOVNA BONCH-BRUEVICH: (*Looking about at the lights, wonderingly:*) Do you . . .

KATHERINA SERAFIMA GLEB: (*Asleep:*) What is it?

BONFILA BEZHUKHOVNA BONCH-BRUEVICH: (*Standing:*) Do you see? Do you see? It's . . .

(*A little girl, dressed in a skirt and pullover sweater, enters, and silently looks at Bonfila.*
Bonfila screams.
Katherina stands up abruptly.)

KATHERINA SERAFIMA GLEB: (*Terrified, blind:*) I drank too much. Much too much. I've blinded myself. B.! B.! Don't leave me! Don't leave me!

The lights are going out.

(*The lights go out.*)

END OF ACT TWO

ACT THREE

"I'm hanging on to the tram strap of these
  terrible times,
and I don't know why I'm alive."

Osip Mandelstam's Notebooks
April, 1931

SCENE 1

Talmenka, Siberia: 1992. A white room in a medical facility. The little girl who appeared at the end of Act Two, Vodya Domik, is now sitting in a wooden chair. She is expressionless, and mostly very still, although she blinks and occasionally, though infrequently, scratches her arm or shifts in the chair. She sits alone for a few beats. Yegor Tremens Rodent enters, a hat, coat, mittens, muffler, umbrella, galoshes; he's carrying a cheap overstuffed briefcase. He is as always, timorous and deferential; but in the intervening years he's gotten nasty; he tries to hide this; as the scene progresses it emerges.
An old samovar stands in the corner, dead cold. Near it a kettle on a hot plate.
Rodent looks at Vodya, who stares ahead. Several beats pass.

YEGOR TREMENS RODENT: Hello little girl.
  (*Vodya has no reaction whatsoever, and has none throughout what follows. Rodent's tone is maddeningly unvaried: mild, cheerful, each attempt exactly the same as the one preceding, rather like a parrot.*)
  Hello little girl.
  Hello little girl.
  Hello.
  (*Little pause.*)
  Hello.
  Hello little girl.
  Hello little girl.
  Hello little girl.

Hello. Hello. Hello. Little girl.

Hello little girl.

Hello little girl.

Hello little girl.

Hello. Hello. Hello little girl. Little girl.

Little girl.

Little . . .

(*Pause. He looks at her.*)

Hello little girl.

(*While this is going on, Bonfila comes in, looking different (older, more tired) than in the previous act. Rodent doesn't hear her come in. She watches him.*)

Hello little girl.

Hello little girl.

Hello little girl.

BONFILA BEZHUKHOVNA BONCH-BRUEVICH: She doesn't …

(*Rodent, really, really startled, leaps an astonishing seven feet in the air.*)

YEGOR TREMENS RODENT: *OH!!*

BONFILA BEZHUKHOVNA BONCH-BRUEVICH: She doesn't speak. Deputy Counselor Rodent?

YEGOR TREMENS RODENT: (*Badly shaken; nervous:*) Assistant Deputy Counselor.

(*Little pause.*)

Rodent, um, yes.

(*Inclining his head towards Vodya.*)

She . . . is . . . Mute? Deaf-mute, or . . . ?

(*Bonfila shrugs.*)

BONFILA BEZHUKHOVNA BONCH-BRUEVICH: Welcome to Talmenka.

(*She exits. Rodent looks at the door through which she has exited, then turns back to Vodya, looks at her for a minute and then, exactly as before:*)

YEGOR TREMENS RODENT: Hello little girl.

Hello little girl.

Hello little girl.

Hello little girl.

Want a boiled sweet?

(*Mildly malicious.*) No, I don't have any boiled sweets.

Hello little girl.

Hello little girl.

Hello little . . .

(*Mrs. Shastlivyi Domik, Vodya's mother, enters abruptly; she is dressed pretty much like a young babushka. She isn't loud but every word she speaks is a bullet aimed at the person she's addressing. Rodent spins to face her.*)

MRS. SHASTLIVYI DOMIK: Her name is Vodya. Domik.

YEGOR TREMENS RODENT: Why doesn't she . . .

MRS. SHASTLIVYI DOMIK: She doesn't.

(*Mrs. Domik exits abruptly. Rodent looks at Vodya. A beat, then:*)

YEGOR TREMENS RODENT: Hello little girl.

Hello little . . .

(*Bonfila and Mrs. Domik enter together.*)

BONFILA BEZHUKHOVNA BONCH-BRUEVICH: Assistant Deputy Counselor Y.T. Rodent, this is Mrs. Shastlivyi Domik, the child's mother.

MRS. SHASTLIVYI DOMIK: Her name is Vodya.

BONFILA BEZHUKHOVNA BONCH-BRUEVICH: Assistant Deputy Counselor Rodent has come from Moscow. He's come to make a report to President Yeltsin.

YEGOR TREMENS RODENT: (*Nervous little laugh, then:*) Well, not *directly* to . . .

BONFILA BEZHUKHOVNA BONCH-BRUEVICH: (*Overlap.*) He's come to see what's going on here. About the children.

(*They all look at Vodya.*)

YEGOR TREMENS RODENT: (*Official, but still nervous:*) Can she hear what we say?

BONFILA BEZHUKHOVNA BONCH-BRUEVICH: Probably.

YEGOR TREMENS RODENT: But she doesn't speak.

BONFILA BEZHUKHOVNA BONCH-BRUEVICH: No.

YEGOR TREMENS RODENT: *Can* she, I mean is she . . .

BONFILA BEZHUKHOVNA BONCH-BRUEVICH: Theoretically, yes, I mean she's *able*, she has a larynx, a tongue, she . . . So theoretically, yes but . . .

MRS. SHASTLIVYI DOMIK: (*Overlapping on second "theoretically:"*) She doesn't speak. She never speaks.

YEGOR TREMENS RODENT: How old is she.

BONCH-BRUEVICH & DOMIK TOGETHER: Eight.

(*Pause.*)

YEGOR TREMENS RODENT: I . . .

(*Nervous laugh.*)

Well how horrible.

(*Pause.*)

BONFILA BEZHUKHOVNA BONCH-BRUEVICH: Several of the children have died before their sixth birthday. She's the oldest. She's our survivor.

YEGOR TREMENS RODENT: I thought . . . um, I was told she'd be, um, um, um, yellow.

BONFILA BEZHUKHOVNA BONCH-BRUEVICH: They're all yellow at birth, we have no idea why, really, but. That's why they're called Yellow Children. The jaundice fades by their first birthday.

The older they get the more we see it. Nervous system damage, renal malformation, liver, cataracts at three, bone marrow problems.

YEGOR TREMENS RODENT: See what?

BONFILA BEZHUKHOVNA BONCH-BRUEVICH: What?

YEGOR TREMENS RODENT: You said, "the more we see *it*." What is "it"?

BONFILA BEZHUKHOVNA BONCH-BRUEVICH: (*A beat, then a bit more assertive, confrontational:*) They mostly don't walk until . . . How old was Vodya?

MRS. SHASTLIVYI DOMIK: Four.

BONFILA BEZHUKHOVNA BONCH-BRUEVICH: And they don't speak. A few have words, minimal speech, she doesn't.

We've ruled out pretty much everything you'd normally look for: pesticides, industrial pollutants, something the parents are eating. They eat badly here but . . .

MRS. SHASTLIVYI DOMIK: We've always eaten badly.

(*Little pause.*)

YEGOR TREMENS RODENT: So it isn't the diet.

MRS. SHASTLIVYI DOMIK: We've always eaten badly.

BONFILA BEZHUKHOVNA BONCH-BRUEVICH: It's genetic. Inherited. Probably chromosome alteration due to her parents' exposure to ionizing radiation.

Or her parents' parents. In significantly high doses, wave, not particulate, not on the ground or on food, but from a . . .

In 1949, 250 miles from here, in Kazakhstan, in the Semipalatinsk area, the army detonated a nuclear warhead. They detonated the warhead to put out a minor oil fire. An experiment. No one of course was evacuated.

YEGOR TREMENS RODENT: (*Shrugs sadly.*) Stalin.

BONFILA BEZHUKHOVNA BONCH-BRUEVICH: (*Ever more aggressive:*) The place I worked in last year, Chelyabinsk, there's a cave, full of something in leaky barrels. Unmarked railway cars used to pass through the town late at night, smoking, on their way to the cave, you could smell the fumes everywhere. Not Stalin. Last year.

YEGOR TREMENS RODENT: It's a storage facility.

BONFILA BEZHUKHOVNA BONCH-BRUEVICH: So, basically, you ask what's wrong with her. Well, in my opinion and in the opinion of my colleagues, she's a mutation. A nuclear mutant. Third generation. She has a sister who's "healthy"; I wonder what *her* children will be like?

YEGOR TREMENS RODENT: (*To Mrs. Domik:*) I'm sorry.

(*Mrs. Domik walks out.*)

BONFILA BEZHUKHOVNA BONCH-BRUEVICH: In Altograd, which is where I was before I was in Chelyabinsk, there's twenty times the normal rate for thyroid cancer. There's a lake full of blind fish. Everyone has nosebleeds. Everyone's chronically fatigued. Leukemia is epidemic. The reactor plant near there has cracks in the casing, steam comes through several times a month, it's the same kind as at Chernobyl, it was supposed to be closed, it isn't, and the caves in Chelyabinsk? The stuff you have in there, probably cesium, strontium certainly bomb-grade plutonium, piled up since when? 1950? It's seeping into the aquifer; sixty feet per year. Do you know what that means? There's a river nearby. Millions drink from it. This is documented. The Dnieper's already shot from Chernobyl, and people still drink from that. Millions. The plutonium in that cave. Three hundred pounds of it could kill every person on the planet. You have thirty tons down there, in rusting drums. The people of Altograd voted for you to move it, a referendum, last year: Why? Why hasn't it been moved?

YEGOR TREMENS RODENT: To where?

BONFILA BEZHUKHOVNA BONCH-BRUEVICH: The whole country's a radioactive swamp, waste dumps, warheads, malfunctioning reactors, there are six hundred nuclear waste sites in Moscow, for God's sake. Hundreds upon hundreds of thousands of people have been exposed.

(*Little pause.*)

YEGOR TREMENS RODENT: The world has changed with an unimaginable rapidity. People grow impatient. Everything is new now, and everything is terrible. In the old days I would not have been forced to do this sort of work.

(*With a little menace:*)

In the old days you would not speak to me like this.

(*Little pause.*)

BONFILA BEZHUKHOVNA BONCH-BRUEVICH: All I ever see are the regional authorities, and they're just the same old party bosses who just . . .

YEGOR TREMENS RODENT: (*Official:*) But you see, doctor, there's nothing to be done.

We have no place to put it. We used to dump it into the sea, the . . . that's frowned on by the International Community, it's understandable, they'll take away our loans if we . . . We have no money. Trillions. It would cost trillions. And some of these places will simply never be inhabitable again. Regardless of the money. 20,000 years.

(*Mrs. Domik slams back into the room, stands glowering.*)

And anyway, we're broke.

BONFILA BEZHUKHOVNA BONCH-BRUEVICH: And now you're offering to process and store radioactive and toxic waste from the West.

YEGOR TREMENS RODENT: (*Overlap.*) They'll pay us.

BONFILA BEZHUKHOVNA BONCH-BRUEVICH: (*Overlap.*) But store it where?

YEGOR TREMENS RODENT: (*Overlap.*) We need the money. The Russian People need the . . .

BONFILA BEZHUKHOVNA BONCH-BRUEVICH: (*Overlap.*) You've conducted tests. On uninformed citizens. Whole populations, the Russian People . . .

YEGOR TREMENS RODENT: (*Overlap, snide:*) *I*, personally, never did that.

BONFILA BEZHUKHOVNA BONCH-BRUEVICH: (*Overlap.*) The West doesn't do that. Expose its citizens unknowingly to radiation, to . . . Even the United States would never do that.

YEGOR TREMENS RODENT: Oh don't be so certain . . .

BONFILA BEZHUKHOVNA BONCH-BRUEVICH: I am . . . certain, the Western democracies, even capitalist countries don't . . .

YEGOR TREMENS RODENT: (*Overlap.*) Then move to the West. Anyone can, now. If they'll let you in. Which of course they won't. What do you want from me?

BONFILA BEZHUKHOVNA BONCH-BRUEVICH: I want to know.

YEGOR TREMENS RODENT: What?

Bonfila Bezhukhovna Bonch-Bruevich: BECAUSE I AM . . . *STILL*, A SOCIALIST! Isn't that absurd! After all I've seen I still believe . . . And, and I want to know! And you, SOMEONE MUST TELL ME! How this . . . How this came to pass. How any of this came to pass. In a socialist country. In the world's first socialist country. (*Little pause.*)

Yegor Tremens Rodent: Naiveté.

(*Little pause.*)

Bonfila Bezhukhovna Bonch-Bruevich: It's the spiritual genius of Slavic peoples.

Yegor Tremens Rodent: (*Trying to figure her out, now he's got the upper hand:*) What are you doing in Siberia.

Bonfila Bezhukhovna Bonch-Bruevich: I was transferred by the Ministry of Health Services in 1985.

Yegor Tremens Rodent: You must have made someone angry.

Bonfila Bezhukhovna Bonch-Bruevich: As a matter of fact I did. Not angry, jealous. He had me transferred.

Yegor Tremens Rodent: But things are different now. You could go back.

Bonfila Bezhukhovna Bonch-Bruevich: Yes.

Yegor Tremens Rodent: In fact, you could have gone back in 1987. (*With mock enthusiasm:*) Perestroika!

Bonfila Bezhukhovna Bonch-Bruevich: I suppose so. I was afraid.

Yegor Tremens Rodent: Of the man who had you transferred?

Bonfila Bezhukhovna Bonch-Bruevich: No. Someone I disappointed. I disappointed a friend, I hurt her, badly, and I was afraid to face her again. So I stayed here. Why?

Yegor Tremens Rodent: (*Shrug, nasty smile:*) The steppes, the Taiga, it's an unhealthy place. Siberia, doctor, is making you shrill.

Mrs. Shastlivyi Domik: (*Suddenly, to Rodent, very upset.*) Compensation. Money. You're from Moscow, do you understand me?

Yegor Tremens Rodent: Yes, I understand what comp . . .

Mrs. Shastlivyi Domik: (*Continuous from above, and throughout this section she runs right over what Rodent says, taking only little breaths when he begins to speak.*) I want to be compensated. Look at her. Look. She'll never be anything.

Yegor Tremens Rodent: I'm truly sorry about your . . .

Mrs. Shastlivyi Domik: (*Overlap.*) I will need to be compensated.

Look. Look. What am I supposed to do with . . .

YEGOR TREMENS RODENT: I have forms for you to fill out and . . .

MRS. SHASTLIVYI DOMIK: (*Overlap.*) How am I supposed to feed her? You cut back on my assistance . . .

YEGOR TREMENS RODENT: It's very hard all over Russia, Mrs. . . .

MRS. SHASTLIVYI DOMIK: (*Overlap.*) I can't live without my assistance and you took most of it, it's a pittance, how am I supposed to feed her, she eats, and watch her, she has to be watched every second and you closed down the day hospital, you cut assistance so compensate me. And medicine, now I have to pay for medicine, more than half the money we have goes for . . .

YEGOR TREMENS RODENT: Austerity measures are necessary to . . . . Doctor, can you get her to . . .

MRS. SHASTLIVYI DOMIK: (*Overlap.*) . . . for medicine, and how do I pay for that, medicine is expensive, when I can't work because what work is there that *pays*, that really pays, and with *inflation* . . .

YEGOR TREMENS RODENT: The transition to a free market economy requires sacrifice.

MRS. SHASTLIVYI DOMIK: (*Overlap.*) . . . My God, inflation, money's worthless and who has what you need for the black market, it's impossible, I should be compensated and . . .

YEGOR TREMENS RODENT: The World Bank is promising . . .

BONFILA BEZHUKHOVNA BONCH-BRUEVICH: (*Simultaneous with Rodent:*) Mrs. Domik, I think you should maybe sit and I'll get some tea . . .

MRS. SHASTLIVYI DOMIK: (*Overlap.*) . . . and anyway who'll mind her if I work, (*To Bonfila:*) I DON'T WANT TEA, and what have you ever done for her, huh, except tests and tests and tests, you haven't helped any of the children, and she's not dying she's *growing*, and who's supposed to mind her if I have to work all day, she doesn't just sit now, she wanders, across roads, and . . . Well? WHAT ABOUT MY DAUGHTER? WHAT ABOUT MY DAUGHTER? WHAT ARE YOU GOING TO DO ABOUT MY DAUGHTER? WHO'LL PAY FOR THAT?

BONFILA BEZHUKHOVNA BONCH-BRUEVICH: Please, Mrs. Domik, there are other patients in the . . .

MRS. SHASTLIVYI DOMIK: Take her!

(*Mrs. Domik yanks Vodya out of the chair and drags her over to Rodent, who recoils with fear. Mrs. Domik shoves the child against*

Rodent.)

MRS. SHASTLIVYI DOMIK: She's not a, a, a person! NO! Take her to Yeltsin! Take her to Gorbachev! Take her to Gaidar! Take her to Clinton! *YOU* care for her! YOU did this! YOU did this! She's *YOURS.*

(*Mrs. Domik exits. Bonfila takes Vodya and leads her back to her chair.*)

YEGOR TREMENS RODENT: Um, um, um . . .

(*Bonfila goes out of the room.*
Rodent goes over to Vodya and pats her on the head.
Mrs. Domik comes back in, alone.)

MRS. SHASTLIVYI DOMIK: Get your filthy fucking hands off my child.

(*Rodent moves away from Vodya, sits. Mrs. Domik bundles Vodya up, preparing to leave.*)

YEGOR TREMENS RODENT: (*Quietly, carefully, furtively:*) Mrs. Domik, may I speak to you, not as a representative of the government but in confidence, as one Russian to another?

(*Little pause.*)

This nation is falling apart. It is in the hands of miscreants and fools. The government does not serve the people, but betrays the people to foreign interests. The tragedy of your daughter is but one instance, a tragic instance of the continuance of the crimes of the Communist era through to the present day. Chaos threatens. The land is poisoned. The United States is becoming our landlord. Dark-skinned people from the Caucasus regions, Moslems, asiatics, swarthy inferior races have flooded Moscow, and white Christian Russians such as you and I are expected to support them. There is no order and no strength; the army is bound hand and foot by foreign agents pretending to be our leaders, but they are not our leaders. They stand idly by as the United Nations imposes sanctions and threatens war against our brother Slavs in Serbia who are fighting to liberate Bosnia; the great Pan-Slavic empire has been stolen from us again by the International Jew. Not because we are weak: we have enormous bombs, chemicals, secret weapons. Because we lack a leader, a man of iron and will; but the leader is coming, Mrs. Domik, already he is here, already I and millions like us support him. We need more women. Motherland Mrs. Domik is the spiritual genius of Slavic people.

(*Reaching for his briefcase:*)
Would you like some literature?
(*Mrs. Domik takes the literature, looks it over as if examining a rotten piece of fruit; she fixes Rodent with a look, smiling in an ugly way; then crumples his pamphlets and drops it on the floor.*)

MRS. SHASTLIVYI DOMIK: (*Smiling:*) Listen, you fucking ferret, I'm not a fucking "Russian like you," I'm a Lithuanian, and I fucking hate Russians, and why am I here in Siberia, because fucking Stalin sent my grandma here fifty years ago. My grandpa and my great-uncles and great-aunts died tunneling through the Urals on chain-gangs. Their father and his brother were shot in Vilnius, their children were shot fighting Germans, my sister starved to death and my brother killed himself under fucking Brezhnev after fifteen years in a psychiatric hospital, I've tried twice to do the same – and my *daughter* . . . Fuck this century. Fuck your leader. Fuck the state. Fuck all governments, fuck the motherland, fuck your mother, your father and you.
(*Mrs. Domik takes Vodya's hand and exits. Rodent, ashen with terror, puts his literature back in his briefcase, stands, begins to put his coat and gear on. Bonfila enters.*)

BONFILA BEZHUKHOVNA BONCH-BRUEVICH: Leaving?

YEGOR TREMENS RODENT: Mm-hmm.

BONFILA BEZHUKHOVNA BONCH-BRUEVICH: Would you like to meet more of the children?

YEGOR TREMENS RODENT: Er, um, no, no, not necessary.

BONFILA BEZHUKHOVNA BONCH-BRUEVICH: We could go through files . . .

YEGOR TREMENS RODENT: Send them to my office, send them to Moscow.
(*Little pause.*)

BONFILA BEZHUKHOVNA BONCH-BRUEVICH: I also didn't go back to Moscow . . . You know when you asked me earlier? Why didn't I go back? Because I thought I could do some good here. In the face of all this impossibility, 20,000 years, that little girl who won't live five more years, I still believe that good can be done.

YEGOR TREMENS RODENT: (*A beat, then: making a gently ironic little toasting gesture:*) The spiritual genius of Slavic peoples.

BONFILA BEZHUKHOVNA BONCH-BRUEVICH: I still believe in good work, that there's work to be done. Good hard work.

YEGOR TREMENS RODENT: (*A little smile.*) To the Motherland. To the work ahead.

Goodbye.

(*He exits. Bonfila is alone for a beat. Little red candle lights appear. Katherina enters, dressed in a medical assistant's coat.*)

KATHERINA SERAFIMA GLEB: Done for the day. Are you ready for home?

BONFILA BEZHUKHOVNA BONCH-BRUEVICH: I'm ready.

END OF ACT THREE

EPILOGUE

"[Do] not rule off or rule out any
perspective except that which could lead to
things which bring no blessing."

The Principle Of Hope
– Ernst Bloch

"Necessity herself has finally submitted,
And has stepped pensively aside."

Ann Akhmatova's last poem
February 1966

S. E. Upgobkin and A. A. Prelapsarianov are in Heaven, a gloomy, derelict place like a city after an earthquake. They are dressed in high fur hats and greatcoats. Snow falls on them. They are seated on wooden crates. Between them is another crate they are using as a table. They are playing cards. A samovar stands on a fourth crate, brewing tea.

SERGE ESMERELDOVICH UPGOBKIN: I spent my many years on earth loud in proclaiming the faith that there is no God.

ALEKSII ANTEDILLUVIANOVICH PRELAPSARIANOV: Now you have been dead almost ten years. What do you think now?

SERGE ESMERELDOVICH UPGOBKIN: I am bewildered. I expected more from the Afterlife, in the way of conclusive proof, in some form or another . . .

ALEKSII ANTEDILLUVIANOVICH PRELAPSARIANOV: But the Ancient Of Days remains evasive, ineffable, in Heaven as on earth.

Heaven, I had been led to believe in my childhood, was not such a dark and gloomy place, which forces upon me the suspicion that my mother *lied* to me each night as I knelt by my bed, praying; a suspicion I cannot entertain.

Your deal.

SERGE ESMERELDOVICH UPGOBKIN: And I must admit I am tired of playing cards with you, Aleksii Antedilluvianovich.

ALEKSII ANTEDILLUVIANOVICH PRELAPSARIANOV: I believe I have improved my card game considerably, Serge Esmereldovich.

SERGE ESMERELDOVICH UPGOBKIN: After ten years of playing, Aleksii, it would actually be more interesting to me if your game had *not* improved.

Can we think of nothing else to do?

ALEKSII ANTEDILLUVIANOVICH PRELAPSARIANOV: We could look down on the earth, see how things are going for Russia.

(*Little pause.*)

SERGE ESMERELDOVICH UPGOBKIN: Let's not.

ALEKSII ANTEDILLUVIANOVICH PRELAPSARIANOV: Your deal.

SERGE ESMERELDOVICH UPGOBKIN: Tea?

(*Aleksii nods "yes," Serge gets the tea.*)

ALEKSII ANTEDILLUVIANOVICH PRELAPSARIANOV: We could look down on the earth and see how things are going elsewhere. America. North Korea. Cuba. Pakistan. Afghanistan.

SERGE ESMERELDOVICH UPGOBKIN: God forbid.

ALEKSII ANTEDILLUVIANOVICH PRELAPSARIANOV: Yes, perhaps not. It is depressing.

SERGE ESMERELDOVICH UPGOBKIN: It is very depressing.

ALEKSII ANTEDILLUVIANOVICH PRELAPSARIANOV: It is.

SERGE ESMERELDOVICH UPGOBKIN: (*Getting very frustrated:*) I had at least expected to see, if not the face of God or the face of Absolute Nothingness, then the Future, at least the Future: but ahead there is only a great cloud of turbulent midnight, and not even the dead can see what is to come.

(*Vodya Domik enters.*)

ALEKSII ANTEDILLUVIANOVICH PRELAPSARIANOV: Look, Serge, a child has come.

SERGE ESMERELDOVICH UPGOBKIN: Hello little girl.

VODYA DOMIK: Hello.

ALEKSII ANTEDILLUVIANOVICH PRELAPSARIANOV: How sad to see a little one wandering Night's Plutonian Shore.

VODYA DOMIK: Plutonium? Is there plutonium even here?

ALEKSII ANTEDILLUVIANOVICH PRELAPSARIANOV: No, no *plutonian-n-n-n,* not plutonium-m-m-m. I was quoting the great American poet, Edgar Allen Poe.

SERGE ESMERELDOVICH UPGOBKIN: I prefer Emerson. So dialectical! But moral and spiritual too, like Doestoevsky. If Doestoevsky had lived in America, and had had a sunnier disposition, he might have been Emerson! They were contemporaries. The world is fantastical. I miss it so.

ALEKSII ANTEDILLUVIANOVICH PRELAPSARIANOV: (*To Vodya:*) Welcome to Nevermore.

SERGE ESMERELDOVICH UPGOBKIN: How did you die, child?

VODYA DOMIK: Cancer, a wild profusion of cells; dark flowerings in my lungs, my brain, my blood, my bones; dandelion and morning glory vine seized and overwhelmed the field; life in my body ran riot. And here I am.

ALEKSII ANTEDILLUVIANOVICH PRELAPSARIANOV: I died from speaking too much.

SERGE ESMERELDOVICH UPGOBKIN: I died from leaping.

ALEKSII ANTEDILLUVIANOVICH PRELAPSARIANOV: He leapt, he died, and still he cannot see the New.

SERGE ESMERELDOVICH UPGOBKIN: It is bitter.

VODYA DOMIK: The socialist experiment in the Soviet Union has failed, grandfathers.

ALEKSII ANTEDILLUVIANOVICH PRELAPSARIANOV: It has.

VODYA DOMIK: And what sense are we to make of the wreckage?

Perhaps the principles were always wrong. Perhaps it is true that social justice, economic justice, equality, community, an end to master and slave, the withering away of the state: these are desirable but not realizable on earth.

(*Little pause.*)

Perhaps the failure of socialism in the East speaks only of the inadequacy and criminal folly of any attempt to organize more equitably and rationally the production and distribution of the wealth of nations. And chaos, market fluctuations, rich and poor, colonialism and war are all that we shall ever see.

(*Little pause.*)

Perhaps, even, the wreckage that became the Union of Soviet Socialist Republics is so dreadful to contemplate that the histories and legends of Red October, indeed of hundreds of years of communitarian, millennarian and socialist struggle, will come to seem mere prelude to Stalin, the gulags, the death of free thought, dignity, and human decency; and "socialist" become a foul epithet; and to the ravages of Capital there will be no conceivable alternative.

ALEKSII ANTEDILLUVIANOVICH PRELAPSARIANOV: It is bitter.

SERGE ESMERELDOVICH UPGOBKIN: It is very bitter.

VODYA DOMIK: I am inexpressibly sad, grandfathers. Tell me a story.
(*Little pause.*)

SERGE ESMERELDOVICH UPGOBKIN: I have this one story, a Russian story . . .

ALEKSII ANTEDILLUVIANOVICH PRELAPSARIANOV: Whatever they do, whatever the glory or ignominy, as we move through history, Russians make great stories.

SERGE ESMERELDOVICH UPGOBKIN: I have this one story, but I can say only that it happened, and not what it means: (*Vodya climbs up on his lap.*)

Vladimir Ilich Ulianov was very sad. He was seventeen years old, and the secret police had just hanged his brother Sasha, for having plotted to kill the Tsar. All this was long ago. Because he already missed his brother very much, Vladimir, who was to become Great Lenin, decided to read his brother's favorite book: a novel, by Chernyshevsky, the title and contents of which asked the immortal question; which Lenin asked and in asking stood the world on its head; the question which challenges us to both contemplation and, if we love the world, to action; the question which implies: something is terribly wrong with the world, and avers: human beings can change it; the question asked by the living and, apparently, by the fretful dead as well: What is to be done?
(*Little pause.*)

VODYA DOMIK: What *is* to be done?

ALEKSII ANTEDILLUVIANOVICH PRELAPSARIANOV: Yes. What is to be done?

END.

AFTERWORD

"What has capitalism accomplished in one year that
         communism couldn't accomplish in seventy years?"
"Making communism look good."

—Popular Moscow joke
as quoted in PBS's FRONTLINE 1994 documentary,
THE STRUGGLE FOR RUSSIA

Act One of Slavs! was originally written for PERESTROIKA, Part Two of ANGELS IN AMERICA. Each of the four scenes were curtain-raisers for the first four acts of PERESTROIKA. Because PERESTROIKA needed to be cut down to half its original length (seven hours!), the curtain-raisers were very quickly eliminated; only Prelapsarianov's big speech survived, in a shortened version, as prologue for the play.

After opening PERESTROIKA simultaneously at the National in London and on Broadway in the Fall of 1993, I was completely exhausted and didn't think I could write SLAVS!, which I'd been commissioned to do for the Humana Festival. I avoided Jon Jory's phone calls for as long as I could, until I finally worked up the nerve to call and tell him, mere weeks before the first rehearsal, that I was going to have to quit the project. Before I had gotten out a word of my resignation speech, Jon said to me, in a relaxed, pleasant voice, "Just tell me that everything is going to be fine." I was so surprised by his jolly demeanor and his disarming request that I said yes, of course it was going to be fine, and he said "Great!" and then got off the phone very quickly.

In the days following, each time I wanted to Give up in exasperation, I remembered that I had told Jon everything was going to be fine. I had somehow been made responsible for maintaining Jon Jory's well-being in the world, and under such compunction I finished the play. I had since then thought that, had Jon yelled at me and demanded I make good on my contract, I might well have gotten mulish and self-righteous and probably the play would not now exist. All of which goes to prove, perhaps, that trust and faith and recognizing mutual interdependence are more potent motivating forces than the exercising of raw power and coercion.

Principles like trust, faith, and mutual interdependence are part of the tradition and practice of socialism, in the sense that socialism, without the recognition of, and adherence to these principles is impossible. Without these principles you wind up with something else—Stalinism, perhaps, or fascism, or capitalism.

Socialism, loosely defined as Raymond Williams has done in the essay quoted at the top of Act One of SLAVS!, exists as the dialectical opposition to any social or economic order that does not proceed from an acknowledgment of the central fact of human existence, which is that human beings exist always as a "we" and never, ultimately, as an isolated "I".

The system created in Russia following the revolutions of 1918 needed badly to go. But it has taken with it belief in the viability of socialism as an idea. It seems to me, instead, that socialism is what has survived the wreck, in the sense that socialism may now develop independently, though not heedless of the ignominious history of Stalinism. Stalinism is one of the worst things that ever happened to a good idea (comparable maybe to what the Church of John Paul II had done with the excellent ideas expressed in the Sermon on the Mount).

SLAVS! doesn't address the role that the West played in the development of Stalinism, or the role it has played in the development of Brezhnevism, or the role it has played in Eastern Bloc environmental despoliation—or indeed the environmental despoliation of which the West is guilty. But I wanted in this play to get away from the Cold War model of analysis which mandates that, as an antidote to Western propaganda, every criticism of the Soviet system must be balanced with a criticism of the West. I rely on my audience's political sophistication in this regard, and my faith has so far been rewarded. Every crime of the Soviet system *can* of course be countered by crimes in the West; but I wanted to make a critique of the failure of the Soviet system from a socialist left standpoint, which does not seek to excuse the crimes of the Soviet system by contrasting them with the many crimes of the West.

And I assume that it is clear that SLAVS! is in every sense a play by an American, in part about America; it is as much about the territory Russia and the Soviet Union occupy in this American's imagination, as it is about anything historical and real. It aspires to literature, to theatre, not to documentary.

As long as the problems we face every day on the streets of New York City exist, people who believe that the world can be improved will ask questions that will lead us to alternatives to the systems which create such misery. Hope exists in the belief in change, and in workable alternatives; and life is impossible without such beliefs.

"Are the democracies that govern the world's richest countries capable of solving the problems that communism has failed to solve?" asks Norberto Bobbio in an essay, *The Upturned Utopia* (translated by Patrick Camiller):

"That is the question. Historical communism has failed, I don't deny it. But the problems remain—those same problems which the communist utopia pointed out and held to be solvable, and which now exist, or very soon will, on a world scale. That is why one would be foolish to rejoice at the defeat and to rub one's hands saying: 'We always said so.' Do people really think that the end of historical communism (I stress the word 'historical') has put an end to poverty and the thirst for justice? In our world the two-thirds society rules and prospers without having anything to fear from the third of the poor devils. But it would be good to bear in mind that in the rest of the world, the two-thirds (or four-fifths or nine-tenths) society is on the other side."

1969

or

Howie Takes a Trip

by Tina Landau

1969 was directed by Tina Landau with the following cast (in order of appearance):

ROYCE MARTINSON . . . . J. Ed Araiza
STEFANIE TELLER . . . . Sheila Daniels*
LESTER MOSKOWITZ . . . . Jesse Sinclair Lenat
HOWIE RASKIN . . . . Barney O'Hanlon
ROZ BERRINGER . . . . Dee Pelletier
ROBERT PERERRA . . . . Neil David Seibel*
CURTIS CALLENDER . . . . Timothy D. Stickney

* Members of ATL Apprentice/Intern Company

Scenic Designer . . . . Paul Owen
Costume Designer . . . . Laura Patterson
Lighting Designer . . . . Mary Louise Geiger
Sound Designer . . . . Darron L. West, Casey L. Warren
Props Master . . . . Mark Bissonnette
Stage Manager . . . . Craig Weindling
Assistant Stage Manager . . . . John David Flak
Dramaturg . . . . Michele Volansky
Casting . . . . Brett Goldstein

TINA LANDAU'S work, which she has both written directed, includes the musical pieces FLOYD COLLINS (with composer Adam Guettel) and STATES OF INDEPENDENCE (with composer Ricky Ian Gordon) at the American Music Theater Festival, AMERICAN VAUDEVILLE with director Anne Bogart at the Alley Theatre, IN TWILITE and MODERN FEARS at the American Repertory Theatre, and adaptations of Du Maurier's REBECCA and Dickens' A CHRISTMAS CAROL at Trinity Repertory Company and Ghelderode's THE BLIND MEN at Toronto Independent Dance Enterprise. Her recent directing credits include: Charles L. Mee Jr.'s ORESTES with En Garde Arts and José Rivera's MARISOL at the La Jolla Playhouse. Landau is a former NEA Artistic Associate, a TCG/NEA Director Fellow, and a recipient of grants from the W. Alton Jones, the Rockefeller, and the Princess Grace Foundations. After 1969, she will return to New York to write and direct STONEWALL for En Garde Arts, which will take place in the streets of Greenwich Village in June and July to celebrate the 25th anniversary of the Stonewall Riots.

Author's Note

When Jon Jory first approached me about creating a piece for the Humana Festival, he explained that he was interested in new ways of "writing." How else could material be generated and developed rather than by a lone individual in front of a computer? Jon had heard about several projects I had done by inviting a group of actors to come into a rehearsal room with me and create a piece from scratch. With this alternative way of "writing" in mind, he took the brave step of asking me to come to Louisville with nothing but a group of people and an idea.

1969 was created in four weeks of rehearsal at ATL. Everyone in the room—from the actors to the production assistants—contributed ideas, images, staging. We would spend each day either working on a section that was already on paper or we would generate raw material for a section I hadn't yet written. The process was exhilarating and surprising, and I think the quirkiness and fun of the piece comes a lot from the energy of those particular people in the room with me.

The written text of *1969* represents just one layer of several that actually make up the piece. There are two other "tracks" that are as important as the spoken one indicated here: the images (staging) and the sound score (music.) *1969* was scored like a piece of music—the aural world was continual and seamless and the physical choreography was complex. It's hard to imagine this piece merely by reading it. For me, the full meaning of the play can only become apparent when these additional "texts" of gesture, movement, sound, etc. are added to create resonance and clarity. What exists in the following pages is simply the blueprint for a piece which can only truly come to life in the form of a production.

I'd like to thank the cast and Craig and Michele and Darron for their contribution to the "text" as well as the various historical figures and writers whose words and/or ideas appear in *1969*.

—*Tina Landau*

FOR CAUTION NOTICE SEE PAGE OPPOSITE TABLE OF CONTENTS.

1969 by Tina Landau. © 1 March, 1994 by T. Landau. Reprinted by permission of the author. All inquiries should be addressed to Helen Merrill, at The Helen Merrill Agency, 435 W. 23rd St. Suite 1A, New York, NY 10011.

CHARACTERS

Howard J. Raskin (Howie)

Robert Parerra (Robbie)

Roz Berringer

Curtis Callender (Curt)

Stefanie Teller (Stef)

Lester Moskowitz (Logo)

Mr. Martinson (Royce)

TIME:

The action is Howie's memory of the final weeks of his senior year in high school, 1969.

1969

or

Howie Takes a Trip

*An empty space: a blank black-board, page of a yearbook, or
canvas. On the floor, there is a 1969 high school yearbook: Central
High.*
Howie Raskin stands frozen, staring at the yearbook.
It glows.
Howie begins to move slowly towards it, as:
Dick Cavett interviews Janis Joplin, ending with:

VOICEOVER JANIS: . . . They laughed me out of class, out of town, and
out of the state. So I'm goin' home.

(*As Howie picks up the yearbook, there is a buzzing sound. It
grows in intensity. Howie starts to open the yearbook with great
difficulty – as if it had a magnetic force keeping it closed. The
sound builds, suddenly Howie yanks it open, and we slam into:
Janis' PIECE OF MY HEART.*
*Around Howie, images of Central High swirl and disappear,
leaving him frozen with anxiety in the center.*
*Then, the Parade of Seniors begins. As each person's name is said,
the character crosses the space, introducing him/herself with a
gesture. "Name . . . Nickname . . . Activities . . . and Voted As
. . . " are said by a Voice and the answers are said by each
individual character.*)

VOICEOVERS:
Name: Robert Parerra
Nickname: Robbie Bobbie Baby
Activities: Varsity Football, Varsity Track, Yearbook Staff,
Photography Editor, Newspaper
Voted As: Most Well-Rounded

Name: Roz Berringer
Nickname: Little Betty
Activities: Oh there are so many, how could I list them, let's see, etc. –
Voted As: Class Commie, Most Likely to Get Arrested

Name: Curtis Callender
Nickname: Merc, for Mercury and Mercenary
Activities: Captain Varsity Football, Varsity Basketball, Varsity Track
Voted As: Most Athletic

Name: Stefanie Teller
Nickname: Pigeon
Activities: National Honor Society, Math Club, Spanish Club, Student Council
Voted As: Biggest Brain

Name: Lester Moskowitz
Nickname: Logo
Activities: (*Silence.*) Uh, excuse me, activities?
      Logo: Huh? Oh, yeah, man   Tugboat Club.
Voted As: Most Freaky

VOICE: Name?
HOWIE: Howard J. Raskin
VOICE: Nickname?
HOWIE: How- . . . How- . . .
VOICE: Activities?
HOWIE: JV Track, Chorus.
VOICE: Voted As?
HOWIE: Most . . . uh, most . . . um . . .
    (*Howie can't breathe. Logo plays the guitar. GUITAR SLAMS into: The guys are hanging out.*)

GROUP 1

ROBBIE: Hey man, what's up with Raskin?

LOGO: So I'm I'm I'm like, ya know, uh . . .

ROBBIE: Howie?

LOGO: Flashing – yeah, flashing, flashing, man, like . . .

ROBBIE: Curtis. Hey, Curt, man. Raskin's flipping out again. Hey –

CURT: Who? Pansie boy? What do you want with him?

LOGO: And so as I'm pullin' up to the fuckin' stop sign, ya know, it's goin' like ZZZ ZZZ ZZZ – stop stop STOP!

ROBBIE: Howie?

LOGO: (*Suddenly violent.*) Do you dig what I'm sayin'?!

CURT: Yo! Logo! – down boy . . .

ROBBIE: Come out of it, man –

CURT: What kind was it?

LOGO: Huh?

ROBBIE: (*Whispering.*) You're making a scene, Howie . . . just relax . . .

LOGO: Sunshine!

CURT: Oh man –

ROBBIE: Yeah –

CURT: No –

ROBBIE: That's right . . .

CURT: I meant the car, man. What kind of car?

LOGO: ZZZ ZZZ ZZZ – like that . . .

ROBBIE: You better get your shit together, Howie –

CURT: You're a big freak, Logo.

LOGO: (*To Howie.*) Hey, what's with you, Raskin? – here take this, here, where the fuck is it? – oh yeah here (*Drops it.*) oh fuck . . . yeah, yeah, here man, take this match box man it's good stuff, hey hey, hey Robbie, he's your little friend, tell him to take it man, ya know: wacky shit!

ROBBIE: Howie, ya don't want that shit, do you? Come on, Logo, lay off –

LOGO: Oh right, Papa's boy, good baby boy Raskin never in trouble kind of shit – (*Imitating Howie with his father.*) with Big Marine man: "But, Pa – yessir Captain Raskin sir! – no, sir! – you do NOT smell any marijuana on my breath, sir! – but, Pa, please – yessir, ay ay Captain Raskin sir! (*Gets slapped.*) Aaghh!" (*Suddenly to Curt, who is leaving.*) Hey Hey, where are you going, man?

CURT: The track.

LOGO: Wait up, man – (*To Howie.*) are you gonna try this shit or not?

CURT: Logo. (*Logo places the match box on Howie's shoulder. He and Curtis leave.*) You coming, Perarra?

ROBBIE: (*To Howie.*) You alright? I gotta go, man. Look, Howie I know I haven't been around a lot recently – (*Pause.*) I'm sorry, Howie . . .

HOWIE MONOLOGUE 1

MUSIC. THE IN CROWD. In the background, the other boys dance: á la girl group but laid back and cool.

HOWIE: I remember I remember the first day of high school and there we were and the morning was fine and there was no indication whatsoever that in a couple of hours a few people, one person in particular, Curtis Callender to be exact, would destroy my life. I mean why, I always wonder, I wasn't dressed funny I was kinda normal I think looking in fact so why was I immediately an outsider? Curtis, the leader, just stopped me in the hall, looked at me and grabbed me here by the collar and says "hey faggot, what are you doing in our school?" You see the funny thing about it like funny weird not funny ha-ha is that Curtis and I had, up to that point, no contact with each other whatsoever, I mean I may have seen him once in a while around town, but that was it. So that was the first time I heard the word "faggot" but I had to wait until I got to the safety spot of my own house before I could look it up, there's no place like home you know, and there it was, the truth right there in the dictionary: a bundle of twigs. I am a bundle of twigs, I am a bundle of twigs. Incomprehensible to me. Simply and irrevocably and always beyond meaning for me, I mean it was every day in the school year times four for each year of high school that I was called faggot and I mean, can you tell me please how could someone who barely knew me hate me so much? Well you know he's the most popular guy in the school, so you see he popularized this activity, I mean that of hating me, so everyone wanted to get into the act, you know, do the cool thing. That's how my horror began.

ISOLATION DANCE/THE RULES/THE IN CROWD

The others enter and do a unison dance to TIME HAS COME TODAY by the Chambers Brothers. It is a dance of conformity, excluding Howie. Inside the dance:

HEY!
HEY!
HEY!
HEY!

HOWIE: The Rules:

ROZ: Learn the lingo. Let it all hang out. Do your own thing.

CURTIS: Don't start a food fight unless you are sure everyone else will join in.

STEFANIE: Don't let people know your parents have complete and utter control over you.

LOGO: If you go to a concert, man, be sure to wear that tee-shirt next day – and reject all middle-class notions of cleanliness!

ROBBIE: Never admit you're a virgin.

HOWIE: Avoid all trouble spots: for instance, the bathroom, where you are a sitting duck. The hallway. The cafeteria. And above all, the locker room, the showers. Don't EVER take a shower in school because that's when guys can gather in cliques for more effective abuse of all losers and rejects. Strength in numbers, I suppose, E Pluribus Unum, well – WHAT KIND OF STUPID CONCEPT IS THIS COUNTRY FOUNDED ON ANYWAY?!

TIME!
TIME!
TIME!
TIME!

(The group exits, leaving Howie back in his panic mode, reaching for the yearbook. Royce enters and writes his name on a wall or locker or floor.)

ROYCE I

ROYCE: Hello. I'm Mr. Martinson. Royce. When I was in high school, Class of '61 – "Our life has just begun, we're the Class of '61" –

my nickname was Royce the Voice, because I always did Cousin Brucie imitations – "hey, baby, let's spin another platter and see what's the matter" . . . but my best buds called me The Raven, because I was crazy about Poe – is that redundant? is that redundant? Now in the faculty lounge they call me "Jack Kerouac" as in "who does he think he is?" My kids call me "Mr. Wizard," "Sid" as in Dartha, and Clark Kent, because they say when I get excited and take off my tie, I become Super-Teacher. I want to get the in-betweeners to consider college. I know the top of the class will definitely go and the bottom of the class will definitely not go – but there's that big middle group – and the bottom means Viet Nam. And the middle means Nam too. As for myself, I plan to go to finish grad school and . . . of course . . . my novel.

(*Sound of clock. As if testifying in a witness box:*)

STEFANIE: Royce? Oh, you mean Sid? Oh, nothing forget it. No, he's great, he's always saying.

ROYCE: Take your time, because it *is* your time.

LOGO: He plays guitar, man, whadda ya want? Bad guitar I must say. He's always saying:

ROYCE: I'm not your father, you're too ugly –

LOGO: To someone who's pretty, or –

ROYCE: Too pretty.

LOGO: To some ugly face.

ROZ: What he gets is!

ROYCE: Close your books and open your minds.

LOGO: And sometimes:

ROYCE: EEN LAH KEESH (*Sitar music.*) a Mayan saying from their POPUL VUH their Book of the Dead, or Life, it means:

ROYCE/HOWIE: I am your other you.

CURTIS: Super Teacher?

ROYCE: Bunuel! –

CURTIS: He says, you know when anything in class is especially strange or surreal, he goes:

ROYCE: Bunuel!

CURTIS: Whatever that means.

(*BUMP TO: Sound of rioting, chanting, protest. Royce at a microphone:*)

ROYCE: I'm afraid the Board will miss the point of history if you continue to see the present disruptions merely as aimless flailing around on the part of our kids. Look at history, folks: those who have power always try to blame whatever happens on those who do not have power. This is a deadly and immoral mistake. We all better start *listening* – listening with our full hearts and minds – to what is being said through this disruptive behavior. Learn to read the subtext of their behavior. Can't you see, gentlemen? – : nothing is what it seems to be here.

(*Plunge into Blackness. The last line repeats over and over.*)

HOWIE'S POEM

During the following we see a series of "snapshots" of Howie and Robbie as they grow from inseparable childhood friends into estranged young adults:
1.) They pose for a photograph as children.
2.) They do homework together; Howie helps Robbie.
3.) They wrestle.
4.) Robbie cheats from Howie on a test in school; he gets caught and points to Howie.
5.) Robbie and Curt walk past Howie in school.
6.) Robbie takes a photo of the group – excluding Howie.
Logo plays Hendrix's LITTLE WING.

HOWIE VOICEOVER:
Once upon a time
a long time ago
there were two friends who shared the world;
One was half child half animal
The other was so tall that to look in his eyes
You had to go star-gazing.
Like two parts of the same whole,
two hands entwined,
two blossoms on one stem.
In the beginning,
they played together,
shared secrets together
dreamed together

and grew together.
But time passed, as Time does.

LOGO: (*Singing.*) *Well she's walkin'*

HOWIE VOICEOVER: the children grew into adults,

LOGO: (*Singing.*) *Through the clouds*

HOWIE VOICEOVER: and one day another came

LOGO: (*Singing.*) *With a circus smile*

HOWIE VOICEOVER: to take one of the friends

LOGO: (*Singing.*) *That's runnin' wild*

HOWIE VOICEOVER: along another path.
And soon there were two paths
where once there had been only one.

LOGO: (*Singing.*) *Butterflies and zebras*
And moonbeams
And fairy tales

HOWIE VOICEOVER: Now he sits alone
half child half man
straining to see the stars
and thinks to himself:

LOGO: (*Singing.*) *When I'm sad*
She comes to me
With a thousand smiles
That she gives to me for free

HOWIE VOICEOVER: Still, the sound of your voice stays in my mind
that September appears in my dreams –
gives shape and color to these words, these sentences,
whatever theme I write, whatever thought flies by.

IN CLASS

Royce is grading Howie's poem.

ROYCE VOICEOVER: Howie – Emotional, quite romantic. I'm not sure
how this poem qualifies as your memoir but, hey – definitions
are meant to be stretched. B+
(*Royce is handing back papers. Logo is bent over his book, trying
to look as if he's reading, but actually sleeping.*)

ROYCE: Robbie . . . Stef . . . Curtis . . . Who wants to read aloud?

ROZ: I will.

ROYCE: Logo?

ROZ: Sid, I said –

ROYCE: Logo?

LOGO: Huh?

ROYCE: Close the book and open the mind.

LOGO: Hey, man, my mind's about as far open as the fuckin' Grand Canyon.

ROZ: Bleepin' Grand Canyon, Logo – really.

ROYCE: As open as the Grand Canyon, is a – what?

STEF: A simile.

ROYCE: Right. Now be like a patriot, and stand forth, Logo.

(He gets Logo up on his feet, standing before the class, to read.)

LOGO: (*Reading.*) From the Diary of a Far Out Freak or Subtitle: The Luny Legend of Lucky Logo Last Names are Bullshit Moskowitz. In the beginning, I was five years old and I already had long hair. I remember the days when I walked down public supermarket aisles shouting what sounded like "Buck! Buck! Buck" to everybody and everyone smiled at this little long haired girl and said How cute she is and my mother smiled in return thinking to herself if only they knew she was a he and is walking around and down the public aisles shouting "Fuck! Fuck! Fuck!" – (*To Roz.*) Bleep bleep bleep – at the top of his lungs, they would all be muttering under their breath: lunatic hippie freaks! We leave the supermarket, Mom smiling, and we get to the car, and I get a nice WHACK! right on my baby soft cheek. (*As in first scene.*) Aaagh . . .

ROZ: Excuse me, I don't mean to interrupt, but I really need to say something here.

(Chaos begins.)

ROYCE: Did I see a hand go up Miss Berringer?

ROZ: Ms. –

CURT: Oh man –

ROZ: I mean the problems are beginning in the home and that's where we have to look to start the real change – yes – the revolution, human rights, civil rights, women's rights – my mother my father my mother my father my mother my father and why couldn't they have worked it out? – and what do they expect of me anyway? – and Who's in charge here? – and Is there a God? –

CURT: She's off again –

LOGO: (Overlapping.) God who, man?

CURT: Can't we get through even one class without a speech? There's too many speeches going down 'round here –

LOGO: (Calling out, laughing.) God's not dead, man – he's just scoring some more acid!

ROYCE: Alright, alright! (Silence. Chaos over. Everyone goes back to their seats.) What about *your* home, Roz?

ROZ: Yeah, what? What about it?

ROYCE: You didn't write much about it in your assignment.

ROZ: (Silence.) So . . .

ROYCE: Why not? (After a beat, moving on.) What about home? The notion of "home"? What does it mean in *On Reflection?* Or in *Soul on Ice?* Or in *Manchild in the Promised Land?* Howie! – (*Howie lurches forward, dropping the yearbook. Sound of heavy breathing. Royce continues talking to where Howie "was.")* – what else does home represent in some of these autobiographics? How does it figure in "the Journey" as we've called it? And why are Odysseus and Dorothy trying so desperately to get home and why are all of us trying so desperately to leave it?

(Silence; then saving Howie:)

STEF: It represents the beginning. The place you start from . . . like childhood is for us . . . paradise.

(Chaos erupts in class again.)

ROZ: Oh get off it, come on, Pigeon! – it's where you have to get out from under before it traps you in its death clutches!

ROYCE: EEN LAH KESH! (Sitar music. All hang in suspension.) This is the account of how all was in suspense. All calm, in silence. All motionless, still and the expanse of the sky was empty. This is the first account. The first narrative.

(Restore to normal classroom.)

CURT: (A bit sarcastic.) Bunuel, man!

ROYCE: How so, man? How is that Bunuel?

CURTIS: I don't know what you're asking me for, man – it's *your* line.

(Curtis kicks over a chair and storms out. The bell rings. Class exits.)

ROYCE: (After them:) Curtis I – So this is what they call spring fever? Enjoy the weather. Take time to smell the flowers. Don't tear any ligaments. Pop quiz – tomorrow.

HOWIE AT HOME/TELEVISION

The television is on: images from Washington Square Park, New York City. Stefanie is doing homework. Howie stares at the television screen.

STEF: In the caf today . . . um . . . well I saw Robbie Parerra go up to Jean Gilman . . . ?

HOWIE: (*Paying no attention to her.*) Yeah?

STEF: Yeah. And . . . and he asked her to the Prom and then he turned all red.

HOWIE: Red, yeah . . .

STEF: I don't know why the Prom is such a significant thing for supposedly intelligent people . . . do you? I mean, either way, what's the point of getting so emotional about such . . . such a childish event . . . Robbie all red –

HOWIE: Red . . .

STEF: And Roz going on about boycotting it. What are you staring at like that?

HOWIE: Oz.

STEF: What? What are you talking about, Howie – hello?

HOWIE: Huh? Oh – uh – New York. Have you ever been there?

STEF: No. And I've never been to a Prom either. (*Pause.*) Howie?

HOWIE: Yeah.

STEF: Do you want to go to the Prom with me?

HOWIE: (*Suddenly turning.*) What?! Are you kidding?! –

STEF: My parents are making me go, I –

HOWIE: Stefanie, are you out of your mind?! Don't you understand?! – Unless you were to get asked by someone like Curtis and I was to go with Jean Gilman – the world's biggest impossibility ever – we're both still losers and two losers don't go to the Prom together because it's only more ammunition for them to get us with – No, I most certainly will NOT go to the Prom with you.

STEF: Well . . . I agree! (*Quietly.*) I mean, I . . . see your point.

THE SHOWERS/IN THE LOCKER ROOM

Howie is in the locker area; the other boys are in the showers. Steam. Music under: sexy blues. Howie undresses quickly and secretly: a routine he has practiced and mastered with great skill. As:

CURT: What about this William P. Williams cat? If he's so goddamn tough why doesn't he stop all this militant bullshit preaching stuff and get out there like a real guy on the field – (*Towel fight. In the voice of the Cowardly Lion:*) Ho Ho, watch it Logo! Shit man, put 'em up. Put 'em up. Which one of you is first? Ahhh – pulling a towel on me, eh? Oh, scared, eh? Come on, get up and fight ya' shivering junkyard. Come on you lopsided bag of hay.

(*The guys enter the locker area just as Howie manages to duck, unnoticed, into the showers. The guys get dressed.*)

ROBBIE: Don't you think he maybe has a point, man? He's only screaming about black rights – I mean, how can you disagree with him, you're black?

CURT: No?! I am?! Oh thanks Robbie man – gee, I hadn't noticed.

LOGO: Like just imagine me with black skin, man . . . yeah, like, fuckin' A, yeah, man I'd be out there fistin' it and speechifyin' shit all over like what's your hang up, man, what're you so afraid of! –

(*Curt suddenly slams Logo up and into Howie's locker, as he did to Howie in the Isolation Dance.*)

CURT: Afraid? Who's afraid, man? Who the fuck's afraid? You look like the little scairty cat 'round here, bro –

LOGO: (*Released.*) Whoa . . . Whoa . . . You're right, man, I'm the little scairty cat. Me – big ol' pussycat, meow – meow . . . (*He moves away.*) What's with Curtis?

ROBBIE: It's Willie P. Williams, man. They want him to join the Black Student Alliance . . . but he's, I don't know, he's playing it safe. Hey, Curt, man –

CURT: (*Suddenly whirling on them, laughing and making trouble.*) Hey hey hey hey, how do you seat four faggots in one chair comfortably?

ROBBIE: How?

CURT: You turn it upside down!

ROBBIE: (*Finishes dressing, starts to leave.*) See ya.

CURT: Yo, where're you going?

ROBBIE: I gotta finish the yearbook listings, man.

CURT: Pussy shit.

LOGO: Meow –

CURT: Hey, are you remembering that you're helping me out on Trig tonight or I'll break both your legs?

ROBBIE: Nine o'clock.

CURT: Nine o'clock – see ya, man. (*Robbie leaves. Curtis turns and stares at Logo.*)

LOGO: (*Uncomfortable but trying to be funny.*) Meow! Meow! (*Logo exits.*)

(*Curtis finishes dressing in silence. Howie comes out of the showers, thinking everyone has left. He watches Curtis for a moment as he pulls his shirt on over his bare, muscular body. Curtis senses someone and turns. Howie tries to dart away but doesn't make it.*)

HOWIE: Oh, sorry, I thought everyone left –

CURT: Hey hey hey . . . Raskin. Mellow out, boy. (*Slowly nears Howie.*) What're you so afraid of? No one's gonna bother you . . . Live and let live is my philosophy . . . (*touches him.*) Cool?

HOWIE: Yeah, cool . . . man.

(*Curtis leaves.*)

SONG OF THE FUTURE/YEARBOOK LISTINGS

Howie dresses. He looks up into the sky, as Logo sings:

LOGO: *Starlight, Starbright.*
First star I see tonight.
I wish I may, I wish I might.
Have the wish I wish tonight.
That always may your star be shining bright.
Just like that first star I see tonight.
(*MUSIC CONTINUES UNDER. Everyone is alone.*)

ROBBIE: Your goal?

STEF: To be a lawyer.

CURT: Pro ball player and the Big Bonus – ya know what I mean?

Roz: To become Miss America . . . just kidding. To effect progressive change. And I know this is just a dream. I want to be the First Woman President of the United States.

Howie: To become Janis, have Royce notice me, blow up the school, run away to New York City.

Robbie: Greatest fear?

Stef: Not having the guts to join the women's movement.

Curt: Blowing my chance for a football scholarship.

Roz: I'm afraid that all these thousands of ideas buzzing around in my head are the wrong ones.

Howie: (*Holding an envelope.*) This notice for my induction exam. Enlisting because my Dad wants me to.

All: *Starlight, Starbright.*
First star I see tonight.
I wish I may, I wish I might.
Have the wish I wish tonight.
That always may your star be shining bright.
Just like that first star I see tonight.

HOWIE AND LOGO 1

Howie: Logo?! Logo?! Where are you Lester Moskowitz?!

Logo: Psst – here here man. Up here. What's smokin', Raskin?

Howie: That, uh, that thing you had before, that match book –

Logo: *Box.* Match *box.* Help me down, will ya?

Howie: That match box.

Logo: (*Like the Scarecrow.*) Shit, it's tedious being stuck up here all day long.

Howie: I mean, well, um – What's it like?
(*Music: Intro to Trip.*)

Logo: Hoo Hoo – Raskin's warmin' to the groove! –

Howie: I mean, what . . . what will happen to me?

Logo: You'll turn into Superman. You'll fly, man – blow your mind – you'll you'll you'll open up to so much shit, and beauty, man – God in you and you in God and God on the TV, man (*Laughs.*) the white light, the you are home feeling, one and holy holy – hey, you got a match?

Howie: How much do I pay you?

LOGO: Hey, do I look like a capitalist, man – it's on me. Free Free –
that's the way it should be!

HOWIE: Well, uh . . . can I have some . . . I mean, where is it?

LOGO: Where is it? Where is it? Right there, man (*Points to the match
box.*) – it's been there all along. You dig?
(*TRIP MUSIC BEGINS. Howie walks slowly towards the box.*)
(*Full of glee.*) Go ahead, Howie, open the box.
(*Howie opens the box.*)

TRIP 1 – THE HAPPY TRIP

GROOVIN'. Colors all over. Howie whirls.

HOWIE: We must be over the rainbow.

LOGO: Here we go!!!!
(*IN A GADDA DA VIDA: a red rubber ball rolls across the stage.
Howie and Logo dance. Howie takes off his shirt. The girls appear
from inside the lockers, dressed in green and holding green
tambourines.*
*FEELIN' GROOVY: a red rubber ball rolls across the stage. Curtis
and Robbie enter, wearing bright red jogging suits and exercising.*
RED RUBBER BALL: all dance.)

LOGO: Holy holy holy!
(*GREEN TAMBOURINE: they all do Yoga. Royce enters, blows
smoke from his mouth and ears. Exits.*
RED RUBBER BALL: more balls roll across.
*IT'S GETTING BETTER. Stefanie plays Mama Cass and sings to
Howie. Howie looks up into a cascade of red poppies which fall on
him. He twirls in space.*
RED RUBBER BALL: more balls rolling around.)

ALL: (*They all sing and dance: RED RUBBER BALL.*)

Howie: Are you my friend now, Logo?

LOGO: Yeah, man . . . I'm the Candyman . . . I'm your friend, Raskin
. . . I *am* . . . your friend.

WILLIAM P. WILLIAMS

On a platform, giving a speech, wearing "panther"-like garb, is Willie P. Williams. Music under: THE REVOLUTION WILL NOT BE TELEVISED loop. Howie around Willie's shadow, huge and ominous on one of the walls.

WILLIAMS: It's alright to keep your white friends, but you better THINK black, baby. ACT black. BE black. Black Power, brothers and sisters – black power! The System is trying to force you to aspire to the middle-class, to alienate you, to make you ashamed of your heritage, to usurp your inherited blackness to become half-white members of the negro middle-class. They do this by pretending that you can get good grades, or play by the rules, or get a football scholarship, brother Curtis, and move ahead – AHEAD where?! Into THEIR system. The WHITE MAN's system! Our school has no program for us except to melt us down and recast us in the mold of the white man. Say No! Say HELL NO to this processing! Say until we have Black pride, a Black place, a Black power, on our teams, in our plays, in our studies, we're gonna say NO! – Join me my Black brothers and sisters – walk out on the newspaper, walk out on band practice, walk out on the track team If violent action is the only effective way to take what is ours, then – you got it right, baby – violent action is what we gotta use here! We want Black Power! Black Power! Black Power!
(Time freezes on Williams – fist up and fighting . . . Howie looks at him, then at:)

INTO CLASS 2

ROYCE: In 1959 *My Weekly Reader* did an article about a highway that would stretch across the nation with no traffic lights, and they'd be working on it through the 60's. *(The class enters and sets up, as if hypnotized. Music: Psychedelic guitar.)*
The same vision, a dream, really, of limitless exploration, no stop lights, no rules, of something brand new that could speed

Americans across the new frontier, has occurred in different ways at different times to many people. (*Music: TWILIGHT ZONE.*) Submitted for your approval. Aldous Huxley. *The Door of Perception.* The theory that the brain is a screening mechanism, that it transmits only a tiny fraction of "the Mind-at-Large," lets in only information necessary for everyday survival. If this screening mechanism was temporarily suspended, if the doors of perception were suddenly thrust open by, oh let's say, a chemical such as . . .

LOGO: Mescaline . . .

ROYCE: . . . or LSD (*Some look at Howie.*) – then the world would appear in an entirely new light. From ancient times, humankind has experimented with drugs. Today it might be drugs again, or technology as McCluhan says, or or . . . space . . . or psychoanalysis . . . it really doesn't matter. The impulse toward expansion is the same. Always the same. To break out, to change the rules.

(*BUMP TO: in the classroom.*)

Which brings me to the matter of Willie Williams' suspension –

CURTIS: What?

ROYCE: Why didn't our administrators see his actions as something necessary and human, the affirmation of man's most precious dream?

ROZ: And woman's –

ROYCE: And woman's. (*He starts ripping off his tie, jacket, etc.*) All of us chafe under oppression, restriction – all of us cherish freedom, right? – and all of us are capable of participating in the collective direction of our own destiny?

(*Sits defiantly on the floor.*)

CURTIS: What are you, man, a preacher or a teacher?

ROZ: (*To Curtis.*) I'd consider it an honor to be suspended under such circumstances. I think the Black Students Alliance did exactly the right thing –

ROBBIE: Except for screwing up their chances for graduation –

STEFANIE: And college.

ROYCE: What do you think, Curtis?

(*Silence.*)

CURTIS: Why are you asking me, man? Why me? Because my skin is the same color . . . so I dress and act and think just like him? Is that it? That's *your* prejudice, man. No. Not me. I'll be seeing you on the football field, not in jail.

ROZ: Oh come off it, Curtis – don't you see how you're just giving in to the Establishment –

CURTIS: When you go up there on the podium and talk, talk, talk, they just sit there and laugh, laugh, laugh. When you go out there on the field and move, move, move, *then* they get up and pay attention. All the best athletes in this school are black, Roz. If we all walked out, there'd be no track team. Is that what you want?
(*Roz exits. The bell rings. Curtis exits. Everyone starts to go during:*)

ROYCE: Hey, Curtis, man – I just – (*Curtis is gone.*)
Enjoy the weather everyone. Think outer space. Expansion.
By the way, Friday night at the NuArt they're screening a new Japanese film. This is not an assignment but I thought it might just – I thought it might.

HOWIE AND CURTIS

Howie is at home, staring into the television: Janis Joplin is being interviewed at her high school reunion.
In another place, Curtis stares into his locker, from which light comes out.

CURTIS: Out of the corner of my eye, I saw this small delegation from the Black Students Alliance outside the gate of the track field. I felt this . . . this affinity for them . . . I did. I had an image of myself slogging through the field, dragging my ass, going through all the paces, but having this . . . this secret desire to join them. For better or worse, I am part of the American experience and hey, I don't know, maybe there's no way I can bridge the gap. What if I'm not . . . accepted . . . What if I'm like . . . a whole different species?

INTERVIEWER: How were you different from your schoolmates when you were in TJ?

JANIS JOPLIN: I don't know, why don't you ask them?

INTERVIEWER: It was they who made you different?

JANIS: No, I've –

INTERVIEWER: In other words, you were different in comparison to them? Or were you?

JANIS: I felt apart from them, I think is what –

INTERVIEWER: Did you go to football games?

JANIS: I think (*Pause.*) not. I didn't go to the high school prom . . .
(*Loop.*) I didn't go to the high school prom . . .
I didn't go to the high school prom . . .
(*Howie falls asleep and begins to dream:*)

DREAM OF THE PROM

MUSIC: Janis' MAYBE, Mirror ball, etc.

ROBBIE: (*Into microphone.*) Welcome to Central High Senior Prom – Class of 1969 – Somewhere There's a Place for Us Over the Rainbow!
(*Everyone is at the Prom: Robbie dances with Stef. Logo dances with Roz. Howie is searching for a date but can't find anyone.*)
Introducing this year's Prom King – Curtis Callender.
(*Curtis arrives as the Cowardly Lion and sings IF I WERE KING OF THE FOREST. Robbie turns into the Tinman, Logo into the Scarecrow. They join with the Lion and the three turn to Howie to say:*)

LION, TINMAN, SCARECROW: Dorothy – are you coming with us?

HOWIE: Huh no you're in my dream this is a dream –
(*They put Howie in Dorothy's dress.*
They split off again and dance in couples, leaving Howie looking for his date. Royce enters, wearing a tuxedo and ball mask.
He and Howie slow dance together. Romance.)

WAKING 1

Howie bolts upright, from his sleep. THE WIZARD OF OZ has come on television. He stares at the screen.

INTO ASSEMBLY – STEF AND HOWIE

STEF: Howie, psst – come on – it's time for assembly –

HOWIE: Assembly, no no, not assembly, not now, I can't –

STEF: It's important. Roz is giving her speech.

HOWIE: I've heard her speech – about a quillion times.

STEF: Not this one. She's going to . . . to . . . um . . . deviate.

HOWIE: What? How do you know anything about "deviate"?

STEF: I – I was at the Union.

HOWIE: You were at the Union?

STEF: I mean, in the back . . . kind of, you know . . . eavesdropping.

THE ASSEMBLY

Applause. The students are in the auditorium. Roz stands at the microphone, wearing a black armband as a protest against the Vietnam War.

ROZ: Dear school administrators, faculty and fellow students. Our protest today concerns two grievous conditions in our school – one is racial discrimination, as waged against Willie Williams, the other is discrimination levelled against all students, black and white equally. In both categories students are being denied the basic human rights and freedoms which the Constitution supposedly guarantees everyone, even those of us under twenty-one years of age, (*Applause.*) thank you. We want to know why we must pledge allegiance to a bleepin' flag who's symbolism is not respected by school officials towards the student body. We want to know why we must wear our hair a certain length. (*Logo reacts.*) Why we cannot wear certain clothes we like (*Drumbeat starts – all stare at Stef's skirt.*) As if keeping our bangs a quarter of an inch above our eyebrows and our skirts a half inch below our knees is related in any way to our willingness to learn and our teachers' ability to teach. We want to know WHY. We want explanations for these absurd rules. Not the student handbook thrust in our faces. We want to know why in a language we can understand.

We demand the abolition of the present "tracking" system. We demand an end to all politically initiated suspensions and expulsions. We demand an end to giving students' names to the draft boards, an end to ROTC, to military recruiters on campus, an end to all police and narcotics agents on school grounds. (*One by one, all students join this Unison Robot Dance of the High School Students.*)

LOGO: We look at these rows of desks, the other bored students, our unfinished homework, and some of our culturally mechanized teachers and say, "Fuck it."

ROZ: One of the weapons the school uses in directing our course is humiliation which starts the moment we learn as kids that we must raise our hand – an absurd ritual!

STEF: Hundreds of orderly lines we all form to move 'round the school –

ROBBIE: The disgrace we suffer when we give a wrong answer –

ROZ: The pattern which continues all day, every day, until within weeks from beginning of school, the student body is demoralized, disinterested, and finally programmed.

HOWIE: Imagine spending your entire life attending classes which are planned by someone thirty years older –

HOWIE/ROZ/LOGO: Having your daily schedule worked out by someone who has probably never seen you –

WITH OTHERS: Sitting down in assigned desks at the signal of a bell and standing up again in fifty minutes at another signal, only to move to another preplanned class, all day, every day, all day, every day, the same routine, the dreary gray!

(*BUMP TO: Back in the reality of assembly, Roz is being pulled off stage.*)

ROZ: No, let me finish – Most of us, in our different ways, have perceived the meaninglessness of this, the the hypocrisy that lies behind our parents' culture, don't you see: life becomes purposeless! Let me finish – a a a web of patterns, beaten paths, that that that we follow blindly! Let go of me – no, no – screw you!

(*Roz gives the finger, and Time freezes her. Stillness. Electric guitar under:*)

ASSEMBLY TRANSITION

Light up on Howie, walking slowly towards his yearbook, as at the beginning.

LOGO: Some of us acid-crawlbacks want to stand and be counted, too. Now if only I could find my feet. Ha-ha, man. One way to change life is to just live it differently, instead of trying to change the the structures, you know, in a direct confrontational way . . . you just drop out and live it the way you think it ought to be.

THE MOVIES/LOGO

Royce, Howie and Stef are on the street. Streets sounds.)

ROYCE: I guess it'll just be the three of us then for the film.
HOWIE: So, can we go?
  (Roz enters.)
ROZ: Hey.
ROYCE: Hey, Roz. Are you joining us?
ROZ: This is a school activity, isn't it? I mean, technically . . , you know, I was bleepin' . . . suspended.
ROYCE: No reason your education has to stop. Come on. *(They begin walking off.)* Nice speech! *(Howie passes Logo, who gives him the matchbox. They do the drugs, as:.)*
LOGO: The world is divided into two types of people, man – straight and hip. Turn on to the scene, tune in to what's happening, and drop out, man. Grow your hair long, makes your soul strong, but you catch shit everyday. I mean, does society hang by a hair? Beethoven with a crewcut? Hey, it's 1969, not 1984!
  (Royce, Howie, Stef and Roz watch LIFE, the Japanese movie. The image is projected on their faces. Howie is focused on Royce, who sits next to him, close. In the course of the film, Howie begins tripping.
  Learn the hippie smile – wide eyed, big grin, chock full of wonder – and just a hint of brain damage. Use it on the cops, it drives them crazy. But when you smile at another, you get the same back. As for me, last year I stopped wearing underwear,

started smoking dope and dropping acid. And – as everyone knows – once you stop wearing underwear . . . the sky's the limit.

(*On the street.*)

ROZ: This is us.

ROYCE: Goodnight, ladies.

STEF: Thanks, Sid. It was . . . um . . . (*The girls laugh.*) interesting.

ROYCE: I – I didn't know it would be so –

ROZ: (*Still laughing.*) Yeah, nite. (*Pause. She goes close to him.*) Hey, thanks . . . I mean, you know . . .

ROYCE: Sshh. No need for words . . . Little Betty.

(*The two girls take off in an opposite direction. Royce and Howie walk home. City street sounds change to a quiet spring night: crickets, breeze, etc.*)

THE WALK HOME

ROYCE: Well . . . looks like it's just us men . . .   (*Silence.*) It's a beautiful night. (*Silence.*) What are you thinking?

HOWIE: Uh . . . I . . . (*He scoots away, finding it hard to breathe.*)

ROYCE: Howie, are you all right?

HOWIE: Lo . . . Logo . . . Lo . . . Logo . . .

ROYCE: Logo? (*Howie nods.*) Breathe. Relax. It's alright. I'm not surprised. I'm not angry. I'm not shocked. It's cool, man. I won't get you busted. Breathe. Relax. Don't be afraid. I'll take care of you. That's right . . . I'll be here for you . . . your guide . . .

(*Royce has calmed Howie down, and now takes him by the hand . .*)

ROYCE VOICEOVER: "Come, follow me, and leave the world to its babblings." Dante, PURGATORIO V. What was the sense in doing external journeying when obviously what he had been looking for was inside his head . . .

ROYCE/ROYCE VOICEOVER: Whatever it is . . . you are here now . . . and everything is okay.

HOWIE: The world . . . I want to see . . . see the world, Royce!

(*They take a step together. GUN SHOT. Then color.*)

TRIP #2 – THE POLITICAL TRIP – SEEING THE WORLD

MUSIC: HELLO HELLO by Sopwith Camel. They dance.

ROYCE: Here we are, kid!
Stick with me!
That's right, let your mind go free!
A magical mystery tour!
Places to go,
People to see –
Say hello!
(*Political figures enter. GUN SHOT. Underscore: EVE OF DESTRUCTION. The following speeches are on tape, with characters lip-synching.*)

BELLA ABZUG: And we are here, to search out the substance and structure to build a practical, realistic, political movement with the strength of millions of women behind it, to win our objectives.

LBJ: Accordingly, I shall not seek, and I will not accept, the nomination of my party for another term as your president.

AGNEW: The name of Spiro Agnew is not a household name. I certainly hope that it will become one within the next couple of months.

NIXON: We find ourselves rich in goods but ragged in spirit, reaching with magnificent precision for the moon, the moon, the moon, but falling into raucous discord on earth, earth, earth.

ROYCE AS COUSIN BRUCIE: 95% of all homes have TV sets in the United States. I'll never forget the very first color TV show I ever saw . . . and I remember Arthur Godfrey. And I remember watching –
(*Ed Sullivan is announced and enters to great applause and fanfare.*)

ED SULLIVAN: Thank you very much ladies and gentlemen! And here, especially for you youngsters, is one of the hottest rock groups in the entire country.
(*Logo as Jim Morrison sings BREAK ON THROUGH.*)

JIM MORRISON: *You know the day destroys the night;*
night divides the day:
try to run; try to hide;
break on thru to the other side;

break on thru to the other side;
break on thru to the other side;

We chased our pleasures here;
dug up treasures there –
(GUN SHOT. Everyone falls. Opera music.)

ROYCE: The world. Don't worry Howie – I'll be with you . . .
(He touches Howie. Suddenly, AND SUDDENLY. Howie spins.)
Oh Howie, if your friends could see you now!
(MUSIC: IF THEY COULD SEE ME NOW. Howie dances with the characters of the world.
Suddenly, GUN SHOT. Everyone falls.
Opera Music. Everyone keeps falling. Like a battlefield.
GUN SHOT. Howie turns and finds that there are bodies everywhere. Back to EVE OF DESTRUCTION. Howie wanders through the landscape; he comes across JFK. Although JFK's body moves slowly and lifelessly, like a mannequin, his eyes are alive and filled with his vision.)

JFK: I believe this nation should commit itself should commit itself should commit itself to achieving the goal, before this decade is out, of landing a man on the moon on the moon on the moon and returning him safely to the earth the earth the earth—
(GUN SHOT. JFK slowly falls as Malcolm X rises.)

MALCOLM X: They're gonna find out that this little Negro that they thought was passive has become a roaring, uncontrollable lion right in, right at their door. Not at their doorstep, inside their house, in their bed, in their kitchen, in their attic, in their basement—
(GUN SHOT. Malcolm slowly falls as Martin Luther King rises.)

MARTIN LUTHER KING: Like anybody, I would like to live a long life, longevity has its place. But I'm not concerned about that now. I just want to do God's will. And He's allowed me to go up to the mountain. And I've looked over and I've seen the promised land. I may not get there with you. But I want you to know tonight, that we as a people will get to the promised land. So I'm happy tonight, I'm not worried about anything. I'm not fearing any man –
(GUN SHOT. Martin Luther King slowly falls as Robert Kennedy rises.)

RFK: I run to seek new policies. Policies to end the bloodshed in Vietnam and in our cities. Policies to close the gaps that now exist between black and white, between rich and poor, between young and old, in this country and around the rest of the world. I run for the presidency because I want the Democratic Party and the United States of America to stand for hope instead of despair –

(GUN SHOT. RFK closes his eyes.

Royce walks Howie through 'the world' as he sings Barry McGuire's EVE OF DESTRUCTION to him.

All around them, people light candles and hold them up.

Royce gestures to where the matchbox once was. Now there is a gun sitting on the floor.

Howie walks slowly to it and picks it up.

He has a flower in his hand.

He lifts the gun high in the air and very slowly places the flower in the mouth of the gun.

Candles blow out, to BLACK – and:)

ROYCE VOICEOVER: Nothing is what it seems to be here.

Nothing is what it seems to be here.

Nothing is what it seems to be here.

Nothing is what it seems to be here.

(On his electric guitar, Logo plays Jimi Hendrix's ANGEL.)

LOGO: *Angel came down from heaven yesterday*

She stayed long enough to rescue me . . . etc.

THE LETTER 1 – HOWIE AND ROBBIE

Howie writes to Royce.

HOWIE VOICEOVER: Still, Royce, the sound of your voice stays in my mind

that night appears in my dreams –

gives shape and color to these words, these sentences,

whatever theme I write, whatever thought flies by.

With all love and respect . . . Howie.

(Howie seals his letter to Royce. Robbie enters, holding a sealed envelope.)

ROBBIE: Hey, man. Did you get another copy?

HOWIE: Huh?

ROBBIE: That letter. Did they send you a second notice?

HOWIE: What?

ROBBIE: Your notice, man . . . I got it here. You left it in the newsroom. It's been sitting there for two weeks. (*Silence.*) Hey, man . . . you better open it . . . you know . . . it's from –

HOWIE: The draft board. Yeah, I know, Robbie.

ROBBIE: So you better open it. It's probably just your card, man.

HOWIE: No, it's not . . . I don't think it's just my card. (*Pause.*) It might be . . . um . . . my date . . . for an induction exam.

ROBBIE: What? That's not possible, man – you just registered, you're going to college, you –

HOWIE: My father, Robbie. My father. "Go. You'll learn something. You'll grow up to be a man. Go." What does a man do, Dad? "A man stands alone against impossible odds, meets the Apache chief in single combat to protect the manifest destiny of the wagon train, plays guitar and gets the girl, leaps tall buildings in a single bound, plants the flag on Iwo Jima, falls on a grenade to save his foxhole buddies and then takes a bow to thundering applause." Sometimes I fantasize about what it would be like if I go . . .

ROBBIE: You can't fuckin' enlist, Howie!

HOWIE: I'll decide whatever I want –

(*Howie walks away.*)

ROBBIE: Howie!?

(*In another space:*)

HOWIE: Logo?!

ROBBIE: Howie?! (*He runs off.*)

HOWIE: Logo?! Where are you Lester Moskowitz?!

HOWIE AND LOGO 2

LOGO: Psst – here, man. What's groovin'?

HOWIE: The matchbox, the matchbox, where is it?

LOGO: Whoa, whoa, slow down, man . . .

You know, man, you shouldn't take this shit in the state you're in . . .

HOWIE: But but . . . my exam . . . I have to go for . . . please, please . . .

LOGO: Alright, man . . . (*Points to the matchbox.*) Have a nice trip. (*Howie goes to the matchbox and picks it up.*)

TRIP 3 – THE BAD TRIP – BOOT CAMP HALLUCINATION

MUSIC: Drums.
Everything in this trip is distorted, aggressive, frightening.
Logo, Curtis, Robbie and Howie enlist in the army. Their Captain is Royce.
On an airplane: Excruciating sound.
Howie gets thrown out, free falls.
Howie can't keep up with the others in training.
Howie is called "faggot."
The locker room scenes repeats its action – but in a nightmare version of the memory.
The lockers are on the floor. The men are showering; Curtis turns and spies Howie. He approaches him and slowly puts his hand on his shoulder. Howie is thrown between the lockers and the men harass him.
The men slowly transform into just Stef, trying to comfort Howie as he writhes on the floor.)

WAKING 2

STEF: Howie . . . Howie . . . I'm here. It's alright now . . . that's right . . . sshh . . .

HOWIE: Stef? . . . I . . . I don't know . . . where is . . . ? Don't cry. Why are you crying . . . ?

STEF: You've been freaking out, Howie . . . really freaking out . . . I couldn't find anyone . . . I didn't want to get anyone, I mean to tell anyone . . .

HOWIE: Where . . . how . . . there was a man . . . in a uniform . . .

STEF: (*Hitting him.*) You idiot! You went in for your exam. (*Silence.*) You . . . goddamn idiot – (*She struggles with him; they hold each other.*)

HOWIE: Sshh. That's right . . . we're . . . we're . . . we're . . . here . . .
   (*A long silence.*) I'll go, Stef . . . I'll go . . .
STEF: To Vietnam?
HOWIE: (*Laughs.*) No, to . . . I'll . . . go to the Prom with you, Stef.
   Okay? Okay? Fuck 'em . . .
   (*They hug, crying. Silence.*)
STEF: Howie . . . have you heard about Royce?

THE LETTER 2/ROYCE'S DISMISSAL

*Curtis and Robbie find the letter Howie had written for Royce
earlier. They open and read it, while:*

ROYCE: I'm afraid the Board will miss the point of history if you
   continue to see the present disruptions merely as aimless flailing
   around on the part of our kids.
   (*Robbie and Curtis stand before the Principal/School Board as the
   students each did earlier in Royce's introduction. Sound of clock.*)
CURTIS: No sir, I am not a black panther. In fact, I've never even
   attended a political rally sir. Well you see, I want to graduate sir –
   I'll be be playing ball for Penn State next year. We just found the
   letter and thought that it would be best to turn it in.
ROBBIE: Huh, me? No, no political affiliations, sir. (*Pause.*) Well . . .
   I . . .
CURTIS: Part of our responsibility to Central . . .   Yes sir,
   homosexuality is a sickness . . .
ROBBIE: Yes, sir. Well no, I don't think he has that kind of thing going
   on with his students –
CURTIS: No, I absolutely know nothing about drugs in this school with
   Super Teacher. No, he's a good guy. I didn't mean to –
   (*Howie walks through an eerie, distorted version of his school:
   scenes and memories and characters merge and separate . . .*)
ROYCE: Look at history, folks: those who have power always try to
   blame whatever happens on those who do not have the power.
CURTIS: But, wait a minute –
STEF: Royce? Oh, you mean Sid? Oh, nothing, forget it. No – he's
   great.
CURTIS: No, listen, I think there's been a mistake here –

ROYCE: This is a deadly and immoral mistake.

LOGO: He plays guitar, man, what do you want?

ROYCE: Nothing is what it seems to be here.

CURTIS: I mean, I don't think Mr. Martinson should be dismissed.

ROYCE: The point is that a school where so many students *do* get high to face – and then sometimes not face – class, has to be . . . well, to put it bluntly, a very bad school. We continually scuttle the goals of good education in the name of of . . . dead, dry scholarship.

CURTIS: Well, yes, I said that, but –

ROYCE: In the arrogance of power at our disposal –

CURTIS: I – I don't know –

ROYCE: We have shielded the whites –

CURTIS: You're confusing –

ROYCE: From the blacks –

CURTIS: The issues –

ROYCE: And psychologically destroyed the latter.

CURTIS: The issues . . . I don't know . . .

ROYCE: Yes, gentlemen, I *do* support these students – and hope they, and I, continue taking dead aim at reforming this type of education.

CURTIS: I'm confused, man . . . alright?

ROYCE: I bid them Godspeed in their endeavor. (*Pause.*) Yes sir, I'll hand in my resignation effective as of tomorrow. (*Walking off.*) Yes . . . yes . . . I heard you . . . loud and clear . . .

SONG – IS THERE ANYBODY HERE? by Phil Ochs

LOGO: *Is there anybody here who'd like to change his clothes into a uniform?*
Is there anybody here who thinks they're only serving on a raging storm?
Is there anybody here with glory in his eye, loyal to the end, whose duty is to die?
I wanna see him, I wanna wish him luck!
I wanna shake his hand, wanna call his name, put a medal on the man!

LOGO/ROZ: *Is there anybody here who'd like to wrap the flag around an early grave?*

LOGO/ROZ/ROBBIE: *Is there anybody here who thinks they're standin'
taller on a battle wave?*

LOGO/ROZ/ROBBIE/CURTIS: *Is there anybody here who'd like to do his
part, soldier of the world, a hero to his heart?*

I wanna see him, I wanna wish him luck!

*I wanna shake his hand, wanna call his name, put a medal on
the man!*

*Is there anybody here, proud of the parade, who'd like to give a
cheer, and show they're not afraid!*

I'd like to ask him what he's trying to defend.

I'd like to ask him what he thinks he's gonna win!

LOGO: *Is there anybody here who thinks, that followin' the orders takes
away the blame?*

CURTIS: *Is there anybody here who wouldn't mind a murder by another
name?*

LOGO/ROZ/ROBBIE/CURTIS: I*s there anybody here whose pride is on the
line, with the honor of the brave, and the courage of the blind?*

I wanna see him, I wanna wish him luck!

*I wanna shake his hand, wanna call his name, put a medal on
the man!*

*Put a medal on the man! Put a medal on the man! Put a medal
on the man!*

(*During song, word travels about Royce's dismissal. At the end,
Howie rings a doorbell.*)

VOICE: Who rang that bell? Can't you read? Bell out of order. Please
knock.

HOWIE: Is Royce there? Where did he go? Royce? Royce Martinson –
where are you?

HOWIE AND ROZ

Roz enters, "in flames."

ROZ: New York. He's gone. They fucking fired him. I can't fucking
believe it. This is it – they have no imagination, no innovation,
just BAM! WHACK! SQUASH! – repression. Key, zipper, lock,
throw away. Fucking scapegoats, that's all they want. I'm not

staying, I'm not staying here, I gotta get out of here –

HOWIE: I'm going too, I wanna go too, Roz –

ROZ: (*Stops suddenly.*) What? What are you talking about? Go where?

HOWIE: To New York. I mean, can't we . . . let's just . . . you know . . . get the fuck out of here. I mean . . . you know . . .

ROZ: Like . . . what? . . . You mean, run away . . . like that?

HOWIE: Yeah, together . . . like Peter Fonda and um, Dennis Dennis Dennis Dennis Dennis Dennis –

ROZ: Hopper Hopper –

HOWIE: Dennis Hopper, Dennis Hopper, yeah, right. On the road. But to New York. There's all this stuff happening there. I mean, like, like, like I've seen on TV. Roz, Roz, listen: there's a place called Washington Square Park, in a place called Greenwich Village –

ROZ: I know what Greenwich Village is, Howie.

HOWIE: It's the polar opposite of this place. I mean, a huge place, where you can get lost – where people talk fast, walk fast, act cool –

(*Howie begins building a tower on the floor, out of the lockers.*)

ROZ: But how would we get there? How would we pay for it, on what? And, I mean, I'm sure my parents would call the cops out instantly, and we'd be running, like two . . . two hunted . . .

HOWIE: I don't know, I don't care, . . . we'll find a way – I'll dodge . . . I don't care, I'll burn my draft card, I'll . . . I'll change my name, anything, I don't care, I don't care, Roz I just want to get out of here . . . this unreal suburban landscape . . . this vast map of "normalcy" – let's get out of here!!!

(*Howie and Roz have finished building a tower/barricade of lockers. They stand on top, triumphant. After several beats of silence, of waiting for something magical to happen, Roz comes back to reality, wilts.*)

ROZ: We can't get out of this place . . .

HOWIE: Yes . . . we can. It's simple, Roz. Close your eyes, tap your heels together three times and just think to yourself . . .

(*Roz mouths "There's no place like home" as Stef begins singing the Mamas and the Papas' DREAM A LITTLE DREAM.*)

STEF: *Star shining bright above you*
Night breezes seem to whisper "I love you"
Birds singing in the sycamore tree
Dream a Little Dream of me.

Say nightie-night and kiss me
Just hold me tight and
Tell me you'll miss me
While I'm alone and as blue as can be
Dream a Little Dream of me.
(Music continues under:)

HOWIE SAYS GOODBYE TO ROBBIE

ROBBIE: Are you okay, man?

HOWIE: I'm leaving town, Robbie. I'm going to New York.

ROBBIE: Hey, breathe, man . . . just relax, Howie –

HOWIE: I'm relaxed, I'm breathing, I'm fine, Robbie. I've come to say goodbye.

ROBBIE: What about the Marines, they could throw you in jail –

HOWIE: Not if they can't find me. *(Pause.)* Besides, jail, marines, high school, prison . . . you know . . . for a "faggot" like me . . .
(A long silence.)

ROBBIE: Remember how, when we were kids, we used to watch The Wizard of Oz each year, man . . . ? Remember how I always wanted to be the Tinman . . . ?

HOWIE: Yeah, and I wanted to be –

BOTH: Dorothy.

ROBBIE: Well you see, I guess I kind of, you know . . . related to him or something freaky like that . . . I mean, like I remember when I heard about having butterflies in the stomach and I spent weeks looking in there, trying to see them . . . I thought there were really butterflies flying around in there . . . well, when I heard that the tinsmith forgot to give him a heart . . . I, you know . . . I got scared and I spent all this time alone, banging on my chest . . . trying to see if it was in there or not . . .

HOWIE: "Hearts will never be practical until they are unbreakable . . . "

ROBBIE: "We all love you, Dorothy. We don't want you to go . . . "

HOWIE: Hey, "don't cry . . . you'll rust."

ROBBIE: "Now I know I got a heart, because it's breaking . . . "
(Howie leaves.)

STEF: *Sweet dreams till sunbeams find you*

Sweet dreams that leave all worries far behind you
But in your dreams whatever they be
Dream a Little Dream of me.
(Stefanie is dressed for the Prom. She walks slowly towards the
door and rings the bell.)

STEF: Howie? It's seven thirty. Howie . . . ?

VOICE: Who rang the bell? Can't you read? Bell out of order. Please knock.

STEF: Howie? Are you there? Howie?! (*Stef runs off as we SLAM INTO:)*

ON THE ROAD

MUSIC: JOHNNIE WAS A GOOD BOY BY THE MYSTERY TREND.
Howie and Roz are on the road, hitching.
Cars pass them by. They decide to walk.
They walk.
Time passes: speeds up, slows down, etc.
They take drugs.
Howie burns his draft card.
Sirens, lights, a car.)

HOWIE: Oh, shit . . . the cops! Come on, Roz. We have to get to Emerald City!
(*They run.*
Time passes.
Rain.
Roz falls.
They run more.
Roz lags behind and finally stops.
Rain, music, etc. continue under.)
What are you doing, Roz? Come on!

ROZ: I'm frightened, Howie. I want to go home. I want to graduate.

HOWIE: So, we came all this way for nothing. I was so happy, Roz. I thought I was on my way home.

ROZ: You were, Howie. You are. But my home is back there.

HOWIE: (*Starting to panic.*) Where . . . where's mine?!
(*Images mix and blur: Strains of OVER THE RAINBOW mix with*
JOHNNIE, rain, and the beginning of POMP AND

CIRCUMSTANCE. Stef is there, in cap and gown.)

STEFANIE: That my yellow brick road meanders through twisted corridors of the mind, or the Big Bad Apple, or through Fields of Poisoned Poppies is at times terrifying to me –

HOWIE: Where's mine?!

ROZ: You'll find it, Howie – I know you will! –

STEFANIE: I am at times a child. A child stuck in a dream from which I am too frightened to awaken –

VOICEOVER: Parents, teachers, friends and administrators of Central High –

ROZ: Have a good trip, Howie – God bless.

(She throws a kiss and leaves.)

VOICEOVER: We present to you the graduating class of 1969!

(Graduation. Stef is giving the graduation speech. The Senior Class enters, one at a time, as at the beginning, except that this time, they are wearing cap and gown. MUSIC: POMP AND CIRCUMSTANCE.)

STEF: But I feel my world changing – I feel our country changing (*VOICEOVER – Robert Parerra.*) because the minds of those people destined to inherit the nation are changing. This change is reflected in the integrity and convictions of so many of the students I have known here at Central. (*VOICEOVER – Curtis Callender.*) They will not compromise their basic precepts: liberty, equality, and freedom in education. They understand that education is an organic part of life (*VOICEOVER – Roz Berringer.*) and the key to the liberation and unleashing of human potential. Twenty-five years from now, we might be paying dearly for our naiveté, but for a time (*VOICEOVER – Lester J. Moskowitz.*), for this time, it really seems as if the old order can crumble and each of us can expand to fill the void.

V.O.: Howard J. Raskin.

STEF: We are finally at the beginning.

V.O.: Howard J. Raskin.

STEF: We are finally free to invent ourselves.

V.O.: Howard J. Raskin!

STEF: We are finally free to invent ourselves . . .

(This line repeats over and over, becoming increasingly distorted. Howie runs and runs. Finally he stops, out of breath. He looks up and finds that he is in New York City.)

NEW YORK

Images: Washington Square. The lockers as City. Sounds of the City. Flashes.
MUSIC: NEON RAINBOW by the Box Tops.
Howie discovers the city. He travels closer and closer to the heart of Greenwich Village, passing a colorful array of characters.)

City lights, pretty lights
They can warm the coldest nights
All the people going places
Smiling with electric faces
What they find the snow erases
And what they lose the glow replaces
and life is love

In a neon rainbow, a neon rainbow.

Moving lines, flashing signs
Blinking faster than the mind
Leaving people with suggestions
Leaving no unanswered questions
You can live without direction
And you don't have to be perfection
And life is love

In a neon rainbow, a neon rainbow . . .

(Howie arrives in Greenwich Village. He watches a group of gay people – couples marching, kissing, raising peace signs . . . A glimpse of the first gay pride parade. He joins them. PO MO HOMO SLO MO.)

A neon rainbow, a neon rainbow . . .

(Things swirl and disappear around Howie.)

CODA/TRANSITION TO STONEWALL

Sudden quiet.

HOWIE: Where . . . where am I?
  (*A voice from the shadows.*)
DRAG QUEEN: Hudson Street.
  (*Howie looks up and sees a Drag Queen.*)
HOWIE: Where?
DRAG QUEEN: The Village of Odds . . .
HOWIE: Oz . . . ?
DRAG QUEEN: Odds, honey, odds. O-D-D-S.
HOWIE: Who . . . who are you?
DRAG QUEEN: Glinda the Good Witch. What's your name?
HOWIE: Uh . . . it's . . . Tim . . . Timothy . . .
DRAG QUEEN: Well, I'm the Queen of Puerto Rico, honey. But everyone is welcome here, you know, in the Land of E Pluribus Unum.
  "Bring me your tired old queens, your poor drags,
  Your horny masses yearning to be free,
  The diesel dykes of this teeming land,
  Send all these tempest-toss'd homos to me,
  And I will lift my skirts and take them in."
HOWIE: You're . . . you're in my dream . . .
DRAG QUEEN: No, honey, you're in my trip and you're bringing me down so go home why don't you!
  (*She walks away. Howie remains on stage, lost. To herself:*)
  Ah, Glinda, you're such a sucker for a good looking blonde.
  (*Back to Howie.*) You looking for a place to crash, sweetie?
  (*In the background, Janis Joplin's version of SUMMERTIME begins.*)
HOWIE: It's not a dream . . . ? It's a place . . . a real . . . truly live place . . .
DRAG QUEEN: Are you looking for your dreamboat, sweetie . . . ?
  (*The Drag Queen approaches Howie, gently. In the background, Janis/Howie are being interviewed. The Drag Queen leads Howie offstage.*)
DICK CAVETT VOICEOVER: And do you think you'll have a lot to say to

your old high school classmates?

HOWIE: I'm gonna laugh a lot.

DICK CAVETT: Were you not surrounded by friends in high school?

HOWIE: They laughed me out of class, out of town, out of the state.

DICK CAVETT VOICEOVER: Hmmm –

HOWIE: That's why I'm goin' home . . .

(*Howie leaves the stage. Janis sings. The 1969 yearbook remains glowing as the lights go down.*)

END.

Shotgun

by Romulus Linney

SHOTGUN was directed by Tom Bullard with the following cast (in order of appearance) :

JOHN	Tom Stechschulte
FRED	Michael Kevin
BETH	Jeanne Paulsen
WILLIAM	Bob Burrus
SARAH	Gloria Cromwell

Scenic Designer	Paul Owen
Costume Designer	Laura Patterson
Lighting Designer	Kenneth Posner
Sound Designer	Casey L. Warren
Props Master	Ron Riall
Production Stage Manager	Debra Acquavella
Assistant Stage Manager	Susan R. Fenty
Dramaturg	Marcia Dixcy
Casting	Jay Binder

ROMULUS LINNEY has written three novels and 13 long and 22 short plays which have been seen throughout the U.S. and Europe. They include: THE SORROWS OF FREDERICK, HOLY GHOSTS, CHILDE BYRON, APRIL SNOW and THREE POETS. Six of Mr. Linney's one acts have appeared in *Best Short Plays*, and *Time* magazine picked LAUGHING STOCK as one of the ten best plays of 1984. Linney's adaptation and direction of his 1962 novel HEATHEN VALLEY won the National Critics Award, as did his play *2* which premiered in the 1990 Humana Festival and subsequently appeared in *Best Plays of the Year, 1987-88*. Mr. Linney has received two Obie Awards, three Drama-Logue Awards, the Mishima Prize for Fiction, and the 1984 Award in Literature from the American Academy and Institute of Arts and Letters. He has directed his plays for Milwaukee Repertory Theater, Alley Theatre, and the Signature Theatre Company, and he is a member of the Council of the Dramatists Guild, Inc. and the Fellowship of Southern Writers. A graduate of Oberlin College and the Yale School of Drama, he is Professor of the Arts at Columbia University and Adjunct Professor of English at the University of Pennsylvania.

Author's Note

SHOTGUN is a one act version of the play produced at Louisville.

I am indebted as often before to Jon Jory and the Actors Theatre of Louisville for producing it. The Humana Festival is beyond description as a creator of these oppportunities, which have brought into being so many new American Plays.

My gratitude goes as well to the fine cast: Gloria Cromwell, Jeanne Paulsen, Bob Burrus, Michael Kevin, Tom Stechschulte, to Marcia Dixcy, the dramaturg, and to Tom Bullard, who directed.

—*Romulus Linney*

FOR CAUTION NOTICE SEE PAGE OPPOSITE TABLE OF CONTENTS.

SHOTGUN by Romulus Linney. ©1993 by Romulus Linney. Reprinted by permission of the author.

Inquiries concerning all rights should be addressed to Peter Hagen, Writers and Artists Agency, 119 W. 44th St., Suite 1000, New York, NY 10036.

CHARACTERS

John
Beth
Fred
William
Sarah

TIME:

Summer, 1993

LOCATION:

An old vacation home on a lake.

Shotgun

The living room of a vacation home by a lake is abstractly represented by a back wall of aged wood. Three door openings: one to outside, kitchen, back of house, lake, etc.; one to steps going upstairs to bedrooms, one slightly larger at center and with a door, to a spare room. The floor is the same aged dark wood. Furniture is also of bare wood: a bench like sofa with few pillows, chairs with crates beside them, old chest. No rugs, lamps, etc. Maybe one nice leather footstool. It is rustic and stark because it is kept that way. Light discovers John, sitting in a rocking chair. He rocks and thinks. Fred comes down the stairs. He gives John a large book.

FRED: Beth says please keep this.
JOHN: Thanks.
FRED: I saw the inscription.
    (John opens the flyleaf, reads the inscription.)
JOHN: "To my husband. A book I know he loved as a child."
FRED: You should keep it.
JOHN: I will.
FRED: Anything else from up there?
JOHN: Nope.
    (John looks at pages in the book.)
    Everything's done.
FRED: I guess so.
JOHN: We managed.
FRED: Sure did.
    (Enter Beth.)
BETH: Where's your Mom and Dad?
JOHN: Out by the lake. *(Holds up the book.)* Thanks for this.
BETH: Welcome. When shall we tell them?
JOHN: Anytime.
BETH: You're sure?
JOHN: Of course.

BETH: They only just got here.

FRED: Maybe you should let them settle in.

JOHN: I don't think so.

(*He sets the book aside. Enter William.*)

WILLIAM: Talking about us?

BETH: Yes, sir, we were. Now?

JOHN: OK.

BETH: You? Me?

JOHN: I'll do it. Dad, would you call Mother inside. We have something to tell you both.

WILLIAM: Something's happened, since dinner?

JOHN: No, we just didn't talk about it then.

BETH: We've been waiting.

JOHN: It's important.

WILLIAM: OK.

(*Exit William.*)

FRED: Are you sure this is the right time to do this?

JOHN: Positive.

BETH: Why not, Fred?

FRED: I just worry.

JOHN: What about?

BETH: Losing your nerve?

FRED: Never.

BETH: Good!

(*Enter William and Sarah.*)

SARAH: So what's all this?

JOHN: We have something to tell you, Mother.

SARAH: Sounds very dramatic.

JOHN: Well, it is.

SARAH: My goodness.

WILLIAM: All right.

SARAH: I'm ready.

WILLIAM: Shoot.

JOHN: Beth and I have separated. We'll be getting a divorce.

(*Pause.*)

SARAH: Really?

WILLIAM: I declare.

JOHN: We haven't told you before because we wanted it to just go along without any fuss. As you can see, it's entirely amicable.

SARAH: But you're still living together.

WILLIAM: So why are you getting divorced?

JOHN: Because Beth is going to marry Fred.

(*Pause.*)

WILLIAM: What?

SARAH: (*Simultaneous:*) Really?

JOHN: Yes.

SARAH: Fred?

FRED: Yes.

WILLIAM: I declare.

SARAH: Bill thought there was something.

BETH: Well, here it is.

WILLIAM: I just don't understand why you're still living together.

SARAH: With Fred. Is it a threesome?

JOHN: No!

BETH & FRED: No!

SARAH: That I could understand.

JOHN: We went to a mediator. The divorce will take awhile but it's coming.

BETH: In the meantime, we've just stayed put.

SARAH: With Fred.

BETH: Coming and going.

SARAH: I'll be blunt. Who sleeps where?

JOHN: Fred sleeps in the spare room. Beth in the children's room, upstairs.

WILLIAM: Where do you sleep?

JOHN: Upstairs, back.

SARAH: Where do we sleep?

JOHN: Upstairs front, where I put your bags. It's the biggest room, twin beds, but you'll have to be together. All right?

SARAH: Perfectly.

FRED: If this is uncomfortable for you, I'll leave.

WILLIAM: Oh, no.

FRED: I wouldn't mind.

SARAH: Dear Fred. You know we love you, too. Like one of the family. Which you will now be now. Sort of.

SARAH: What about the children?

BETH: They know already. They're grown up.

JOHN: They weren't happy, either.

WILLIAM: It's not so much the divorce, as you and Fred getting married.

SARAH: You're getting married as soon as you can?

BETH: The day the divorce comes.

SARAH: Oh, well.

WILLIAM: Could you – tell us how it happened?

SARAH: If you want to, that is!

WILLIAM: If you want to, of course!

JOHN: We do.

BETH: You or me?

JOHN: Let Fred do it.

BETH: Fred?

JOHN: Why not?

BETH: Fred?

FRED: All right. I'm in love with my best friend's wife. We know each other for thirty-one years. I never marry. I bring my dates to dinner with John and with Beth. Then I suppose something caught up with me, and I just lived alone. I thought I would always live alone. Then it happened.

BETH: John bought the place!

JOHN: I saw this lake and I turned into the little road that circled it and looked at the houses and saw this one with its FOR SALE sign. The owners were home. They asked me in. It was old. It was sturdy! I went to the broker and bought it!

BETH: Without a word to me!

(*Pause.*)

SARAH: For you and Beth?

WILLIAM: To keep her?

JOHN: I don't know. I just wanted the place.

BETH: So out we came.

JOHN: Every weekend.

WILLIAM: While you and Fred . . .

BETH: Were beginning.

FRED: And John began building the extra room.

WILLIAM: (*To Sarah.*) Have you seen it?

SARAH: Not yet.

WILLIAM: It looks like it was part of the house from the beginning.

BETH: Then, one day, while John was working on it, we invited Fred to come sleep in it.

FRED: I had a great time.

JOHN: So we asked him back.

FRED: And I came again and again until it was every weekend and whenever else I could.

JOHN: It wasn't very dramatic. Fred said he had to tell me he loved Beth. I said I loved her, too. We said, let her choose.

WILLIAM: Life is life.

JOHN: Are you all right with this?

SARAH: Give us a minute.

WILLIAM: Of course we are.

SARAH: But give us a minute.

WILLIAM: It's just that it's unexpected.

BETH: It was unexpected for us, too.

WILLIAM: When did it really begin?

BETH: John was working on the spare room. He'd been sawing and planing and running a drill, so Fred and I went for a swim. When we came back, John was quiet and said he'd be working for the rest of the afternoon, measuring things.

JOHN: I'd made some mistakes.

BETH: So we relaxed in here and put on some Bach. And I guess the blood circulating like that after our swim and our minds elevated by the music and it happened.

FRED: Not here!

BETH: There's a motel. We went there for the afternoon.

JOHN: I want Beth to be happy. Fred, too.

SARAH: What about you?

JOHN: A little sad. That's normal.

BETH: We did so well, for a long time.

JOHN: People used to live short lives. Marry at twenty. Children. You get old and it's over. Now, we take care of ourselves and, God willing, live for ninety years. That means being married to the same person for seventy years.

BETH: Not for everybody.

JOHN: Not for us.

(*Pause.*)

BETH: Well.

SARAH: Well.

JOHN: That's the story.

BETH: Plain and simple.

WILLIAM: Not quite!

SARAH: No.

WILLIAM: Shall we?

SARAH: I can't think of a better time.

WILLIAM: We have something to tell you, too.

JOHN: Really?

BETH: Good.

FRED: Shoot.

WILLIAM: You or me?

SARAH: You first.

WILLIAM: (*To John:*) Your mother and father are getting married again.
(*Pause.*)

JOHN: Ah.

BETH: *Are* you?

FRED: Congratulations.

WILLIAM: Didn't you suspect anything?

JOHN: I did think it odd that you were both coming here at the same
time.

FRED: How did *this* happen?

WILLIAM: Our divorce wasn't as easy as John's will be. It was bitter.

SARAH: We weren't civilized about it.

WILLIAM: We were angry and we were mean.

SARAH: We had lived for our family. We forgot to live for ourselves.

FRED: Well, congratulations.

JOHN: When are you getting married again?

WILLIAM: Soon!

SARAH: We're in no rush, but soon.

JOHN: Make it a double feature. Sarah and William, my mother and
father. Beth and Fred, my wife and my chum.

BETH: John.

JOHN: No, it's just funny. Excuse me.
(*Exit John.*)

FRED: John?

BETH: It's all right.

SARAH: Is it?

JOHN: (*Off stage.*) Heinekens, anybody?

BETH: You see?

WILLIAM: That's for me!

FRED: Me, too.

JOHN: OK. Come on.

(*Exit John, followed by William and Fred. Sarah and Beth smile at each other.*)

BETH: I think we can both say, that went off all right.

SARAH: Like a happy ending.

BETH: Yes.

SARAH: Tell me the truth. How is he?

BETH: Honestly, he's fine.

(*The doorbell rings.*)

Excuse me.

(*Exit Beth. Sarah sits, thinking. She begins to sing.*)

SARAH: (*Singing:*) Beautiful Dreamer, Wake unto me,
> Starlight and dew drops are waiting for thee.
> Sounds of the rude world, heard in the day.
> Lulled by the moonlight have all passed away.

(*Sarah gets up and goes to the spare room. She turns on a light, which spills into the darkened empty room. She is heard singing offstage.*)

> Beautiful Dreamer, Queen of my song,
> List while I woo thee with soft melody,
> Gone are the cares of life's busy throng,
> Beautiful Dreamer, awake unto me.

(*Sarah re-enters. She closes the door.*)

> Beautiful Dreamer, awake unto me.

(*Enter Beth, with a package. She puts it down.*)

BETH: Package for John.

(*Beth goes to the kitchen door. Calls.*)

Package for you, John!

JOHN: (*Off stage:*) Thank you!

SARAH: John bought this house before the separation?

BETH: Yes.

SARAH: So who gets it?

BETH: We're going to share it.

SARAH: What?

BETH: Time share.

(*Enter John.*)

JOHN: Package?

BETH: Over there.

JOHN: Thanks.

(*John picks up the pa 'kage.*)

BETH: What is it?

JOHN: Something I ordered.

BETH: It wasn't from a store. Just a man.

JOHN: From a pawnshop. Do you want to know what this is?

BETH: Your business is your business.

JOHN: As yours is yours.

BETH: Right. I'm going to get some air.

SARAH: Can I come?

BETH: Oh, please do.

 (*Beth and Sarah start out.*)

JOHN: Ask Dad to come in, will you?

BETH: Right. (*As they go out.*) We'll get Fred.

 (*They go out. John takes a brown paper wrapping off the package. There is a leather case. He opens it. He looks at its contents a moment. He takes a small bottle and a set of swabs from it. A wire brush. He sets them down. He opens the bottle, sniffs its contents. He takes a stock and trigger from the bag, looks at it carefully. William enters, stays at door, watching him.*
 Then the barrel, which John fits onto the stock, then the undercarriage, which he locks into place. He hefts the shotgun this way and that. Then he takes a handkerchief and wipes the moisture off the barrel. He puts the gun to his shoulder.)

WILLIAM: Hi.

JOHN: Look.

WILLIAM: Shotgun.

JOHN: I was walking by a pawnshop. There it was, in a window. I never asked you why you sold them. The rods and reels and fly tying machines. All the dogs and every gun you ever had. Even the cabinets you built to keep them in.

WILLIAM: I wanted to live a different life.

JOHN: I was twelve.

WILLIAM: And a half.

JOHN: So twenty-five years later I buy this very old lake house. Then I stop to look at a shotgun in a pawnshop window.

 (*He breaks it open, holds the barrels up and looks through them.*)

Barrels are pitted. It'll fire, but wild.

 (*John suddenly tosses the shotgun to his father.*)

See?

(*William looks through the barrels.*)

WILLIAM: Pitted, all right.

(*John snatches it back from him, snaps it shut.*)

JOHN: So I got some swabs and brushes and Hoppe's Number Nine Gun Oil. Remember that smell?

WILLIAM: Of course.

JOHN: To a twelve-year-old boy, the sweetest in the world. Magic. Won't change the neglect, of course, but it won't get any worse, either.

WILLIAM: Good.

JOHN: Yeah.

(*John hefts the shotgun, throws it up and points, as if following a bird. It gets pointed close to William, who ducks.*)

Sorry.

WILLIAM: OK.

JOHN: Jimmy Sharps felt sorry for me when you left us. He took me hunting one day. Substitute Dad, helping a little boy. Dog got a covey but when the quail flushed, I lead them too far. I swung the gun toward him. Bang. He felt buckshot burn by his cheek. I almost killed him. "Sorry," I said. He didn't take me hunting any more.

(*Enter Fred.*)

FRED: What's up?

(*He sees the shotgun.*)

What's that?

JOHN: Old gun.

(*John quickly puts it back in its case.*)

Politically incorrect symbol of things past. Pitted, out of date, lost and gone thing a little boy loved. That's all.

(*John takes it and the book and exits.*)

FRED: I thought we should have taken more time with this.

WILLIAM: I think you were right.

FRED: Beth thinks it's fine. John says it's fine. I'm the one who came in here and broke up this home –

WILLIAM: No, you haven't –

FRED: – well, yes I have –

WILLIAM: When he looked at me over two shotgun barrels his eyes were the saddest things I have ever seen. My new life is happy and healthy. But my son is hurt.

(*Enter Sarah and Beth.*)

SARAH: What's the matter with John?

BETH: He went by us without saying a word.

SARAH: Carrying a big leather case.

FRED: Did he tell you what was in it?

BETH: No, he wouldn't.

SARAH: What is in it?

WILLIAM: A shotgun.

BETH: A what?

FRED: A double-barrelled shotgun, Beth. Now tell me he's perfectly all right.

BETH: A shotgun? John? He hated all that.

(*Enter John, smiling.*)

JOHN: Hello.

(*Pause.*)

What's all this?

(*Pause.*)

You're staring at me.

BETH: You bought a shotgun?

JOHN: (*Smiling.*) Uh, yeah.

BETH: What are you going to do with it?

JOHN: I'm going to hunt with it. Maybe shoot some skeet.

BETH: You told me you never wanted to do any of that again as long as you lived.

JOHN: Well, everybody else changed their minds. Why can't I? There's a skeet shoot at the club every other Saturday in the summer. I can drive fifty miles south and hunt quail in the fall.

(*The doorbell rings.*)

Excuse me.

(*Exit John. Pause.*)

FRED: I don't like this.

BETH: Neither do I.

SARAH: He loved those guns, when he was a boy.

WILLIAM: But did he? I taught him to, and he did his best to please me, but did he really want to go hunting with me? Fishing, either? He had no choice. I leaned on him.

SARAH: Bill, you didn't.

WILLIAM: Of course I did.

(*Enter John, with a package and a long cardboard tube.*)

JOHN: You'll be wondering. In here is a Thompson fly-tying vise. With plenty of gut and duck feathers and great things like that. In here is a set of H.L. Leonard split-cane fly rods, with a Hardy reel on the way.

(*He looks from one to the other.*)

Trout streams. They glittered in the sunshine, but the rocks were sharp. They were dangerous to get lost in after dark. Fishing rods I thought elegant. A beautiful shotgun. They are coming back to me now. I am glad to see them again. I missed them.

BETH: I'd like to talk to John alone, please.

FRED: Beth –

BETH: Alone, please! Thank you.

(*Exit Fred, Sarah and William.*)

You're acting crazy!

JOHN: How? I buy something that reminds me of my childhood, bring it home, clean it up and this fall I'm going to hunt quail with it.

BETH: You've been saying one thing and thinking something else.

JOHN: Clear it up for me.

BETH: We don't love each other any more!

JOHN: Meaning what?

BETH: Meaning there was a death between us and not all the care and consideration and listening to each other makes any difference. Our marriage died. It was a perfectly good marriage and it lasted a long time.

JOHN: Then it just fell over dead, right?

BETH: Then you bought this house!

(*Sarah and William stand at the outside door listening.*)

JOHN: Yes, I did that. Then we invited Fred.

BETH: You invited Fred!

JOHN: Wull, I invited him. But you slept with him!

(*Beth goes, turns and comes back.*)

BETH: What do you think we've been doing?

JOHN: Wull, what I was taught. Do unto others, you know.

BETH: I don't think you know what you're doing, at all. I think you are playing crazy games, and I'm leaving you. Not gracefully and not tomorrow. Now.

(*Exit Beth, upstairs.*)

JOHN: Wull. Goodbye.

(*Enter Fred, past Sarah and William.*)

FRED: What's with Beth?

JOHN: She's packing.

FRED: What for?

JOHN: She'll want you with her.

FRED: Why is she doing that?

JOHN: Packing, or leaving me? Will you just go?

> (*Enter Sarah and William.*)

SARAH: Wait. I'll talk to her.

> (*Exit Sarah.*)

JOHN: Refreshments? Lemonade? Tea?

FRED: There's a bottle of scotch, I think.

JOHN: Let's do that, then. Dad?

WILLIAM: I guess a little won't hurt.

FRED: I'll get it.

> (*Exit Fred.*)

WILLIAM: Son.

JOHN: Daddy?

WILLIAM: Son, what's the matter?

JOHN: I need a Rolaid!

WILLIAM: I've never seen you like this!

JOHN: Aw, sure you have! (*In William's voice.*) You just weren't looking!!

WILLIAM: Don't mock me!

JOHN: Why not? "Better late than never. Truer words were never spoken. What is the matter with you? I've never seen you like this. Stop it!" Clichés, all true, all coming home to roost.

> (*Enter Fred, with a bottle of scotch and three small glasses, hands them around.*)

FRED: Water or anything?

WILLIAM: Not for me.

JOHN: Naw.

FRED: Here we go.

WILLIAM: Just a little now.

> (*Fred pours a little scotch for each.*)

FRED: Cheers.

WILLIAM: Cheers.

> (*Re-enter Sarah and Beth.*)

SARAH: We finished our talk.

JOHN: So soon?

BETH: (*Cold:*) Yes.

SARAH: The point I tried to make was that this complication is hard but not fatal.

WILLIAM: It just happened.

BETH: Like you.

SARAH: Me?

BETH: You two. Together again after all these years.

SARAH: Oh.

WILLIAM: Life is life. You can't say no to it.

(*John looks at Beth.*)

JOHN: Some people do.

FRED: Don't start.

JOHN: I will.

BETH: I did.

JOHN: You sure did.

BETH: When we first came to the house, I got pregnant again. We'd be older parents and raise another baby. I refused, and went to the hospital. I'm forty years old and I've raised two children and that's it. But I think John can rightly wonder who is saying no to life and who isn't.

SARAH: (*To John:*) So that's why you built a spare room.

JOHN: Yes.

SARAH: Then the spare room –

BETH: Would have been the nursery.

JOHN: In the coarse way of brutal sexism, yes. Difficult wife? Another baby!

BETH: You are not coarse and you are not brutal. You are a good man. We worked so hard so long. All the stages. Love marriage fun struggle achievement children. But it stopped! It stopped right here, in this house you bought! John, we wish you the joy we have found! We wish you the joy your mother and father have found! What we hope the children will find! But we are no longer prisoners of life, of custom!

JOHN: Custom?

FRED: We have the right to change our lives!

BETH: This is all good, John! Do what we are doing!

FRED: It's your life.

BETH: I'm sorry I said anything about your shotgun. It was important to your childhood and your relationship to your father. Any gun is foreign and threatening to me but it was stupid to think you would ever hurt anybody with one. I hope you will forget that, let me change my mind and not leave our house in anger. Fred?

FRED: Whatever he wants.

BETH: John?

SARAH: John?

WILLIAM: John?

FRED: John?

JOHN: Good people do right. Good. People. Do. Right.

WILLIAM: What?

JOHN: I am taking up a train of thought begun by my wife who asked me to stop being a prisoner of custom.

WILLIAM: Just go ahead.

JOHN: Good people do right. But good, right people turn into bad, wrong people and do wrong to some other good right people. All over the world, headlines everyday at home and abroad, week, month, year, decade, century, say it isn't so. EVERYTHING, it seems, is CUSTOM!

(*Pause. They just stare at him.*)

No answer. Incomprehension. Well, it's a hard life. It's all Darwin.

FRED: What do you know about Darwin?

JOHN: I can read.

FRED: Because animals eat each other doesn't mean people do!

JOHN: Sure they do!

BETH: John, you're hurt and saying anything.

JOHN: War. That's what I think.

FRED: Now stop it.

JOHN: Eternal, universal and everywhere! It reaches through battlefields and executions, into the living room, the bedroom, and the BABY'S ROOM!

FRED: Stop insulting Beth.

JOHN: Getting walked out on *twice* in one day, I'll insult anybody I want to.

SARAH: What do you mean, twice?

JOHN: Wife, that's one. You two, that's two!

WILLIAM: How have we walked out on you?

JOHN: By cancelling out everything I lived with, for twenty-eight years! Everything I felt, making up for you!

FRED: What does that have to do with war?

JOHN: Everything!

FRED: What leads to war isn't what happens to you!

JOHN: What is it, then?

FRED: Lay off this, John!

JOHN: Take terrorism.

WILLIAM: Take what?

FRED: You're jumping from one thing to another!

JOHN: New ways to kill people! What else do you think the world is interested in?

FRED: Now you're just raving!

JOHN: What makes a good man's heart beat faster: other men's bones blown up in explosions! Ask any boy and his movie producer! (*To William.*) You taught me how to use a gun. Then you sold it.

WILLIAM: So what?

JOHN: So everything!

BETH: Stop shouting.

JOHN: Sorry!

SARAH: Let him finish!

JOHN: Mother, we all say one thing and do another. We look east and row the boat west. And we end up doing everything all over again. Understand that?

SARAH: No, I do not.

JOHN: I wish you happiness but I don't think you'll find it. Understand THAT?

SARAH: As bitterness, but nothing else.

JOHN: I'll keep it simple.

(*To Beth.*)

You don't love your husband any more. OK. He gave you your freedom. In the house he bought to try to keep you.

BETH: With a baby.

JOHN: Horrible, sinful enslavement of women, right. So he gave you your freedom, and you were glad to get it, right?

BETH: Yes and no.

JOHN: Got to be one or the other!

BETH: All right, yes! I'm glad!

JOHN: And I'm glad you're glad! But more of my blood couldn't have been shed with a bomb!

FRED: Or hers?

BETH: Fred!!

FRED: We did do it in there!

BETH: Fred!!

JOHN: Who's surprised?

BETH: You think I wanted to go to that hospital? That's when I said yes! And made love to Fred.

(*Points to the spare room.*)

In there!

FRED: Did you know that?

JOHN: Of course.

FRED: Then why didn't you say so?

BETH: You said we'd work it out!

JOHN: And we did!

WILLIAM: I can't follow this, John.

JOHN: Fred can! He knew what he wanted! What's complicated?

FRED: What did I want?

SARAH: Beth.

JOHN: In passing!

FRED: What else?

JOHN: I have already told you.

FRED: Tell me again.

JOHN: Do I have to?

FRED: War?

JOHN: Absolutely.

FRED: Fundamental, eternal?

JOHN: Absolutely.

FRED: That's your great idea?

JOHN: Yes.

FRED: That's it?

JOHN: That's it.

FRED: Has to be?

JOHN: Has to be.

FRED: I know who you sound like now.

JOHN: Who?

FRED: You sound like Hitler.

BETH: Fred.

(*Pause.*)

JOHN: You have a lot of nerve saying that to me. I give you the woman I treasure, mother of my children. And you call me Hitler. You get yourself and my slut wife out of my house and never let

me set eyes on either one of you again.
(*Exit John, slamming the front door.*
They sit for a moment.
Silence.
Then, explosively, they all begin to talk at once.)

BETH: I have to go after him!

FRED: I'm sorry but I meant it!

BETH: Oh, John!

FRED: And I'll say it again!

SARAH: No, you won't!

BETH: I have to go after him!

FRED: We're finished with him!

BETH: You may be, but I'm not!

FRED: My bag's packed and I'm leaving.

(*Exit Fred, into the spare room.*)

SARAH: Beth?

(*Pause.*)

BETH: Leave me alone!

WILLIAM: Sarah.

SARAH: What?

WILLIAM: Hush.

(*Enter Fred, with his bag.*)

FRED: Beth?

BETH: Go ahead! I'll come with you.

(*Exit Fred and then Beth.*)

WILLIAM: Sarah?

SARAH: We can't leave him like this.

WILLIAM: Could you get me a beer?

SARAH: I want one, too.

(*Exit Sarah. William sees the large book Beth sent down to John by Fred at the beginning of the play. He opens it, looks at an inscription. Sarah enters, with two bottles of Heinekens.*)

WILLIAM: Did you see this?

SARAH: No.

WILLIAM: LAST OF THE MOHICANS. There's an inscription. "To my husband. A book I know he loved as a boy. From his wife, Beth."

(*Sarah takes the book and puts it down.*)

SARAH: It will be all right now. Drink your beer.

(*She sits next to William. They drink.*)

WILLIAM: I need to hold you.

SARAH: Please.

> (*William puts his arm around her. They drink. Pause.*)
> "Lean on my heart."

WILLIAM: (*Singing:*) Beautiful Dreamer, Lean on my heart
> E'en as the morn on the streamlet and sea,

WILLIAM & SARAH: (*Singing.*) Then will the clouds of sorrow depart,
> Beautiful Dreamer awake unto me,
> Beautiful Dreamer, Awake unto me.

SARAH: Fred's gone.

WILLIAM: All right.

> (*William and Sarah go into the spare room.*
> *Pause.*
> *Lights change, dimmer and colder.*
> *Time passes.*
> *Enter John, wearing an old hunting jacket.*
> *He looks at his house, with pleasure. He adjusts something.*
> *He picks up the book.*
> *He looks at the inscription.*
> *John shuts the book. He takes up the shotgun in its case. Carrying*
> *it with the book, he leaves, going past the door to the spare room.*
> *John stops there, listening.*
> *He hears sounds in the spare room. Sexual sounds.*
> *John is astounded and enraged.*
> *John opens the gun case and begins to assemble the shotgun.*
> (*Lights fade.*)

END.

The Survivor:
A Cambodian Odyssey

by Jon Lipsky

Based on A CAMBODIAN ODYSSEY by Haing Ngor with Roger Warner.
Originally commissioned for Professional World Premiere Production by the Merrimack Repertory
Theatre, David G. Kent, Artistic Director, Lowell, Massachusetts, March 22, 1993.

THE SURVIVOR: A CAMBODIAN ODYSSEY was directed by Vincent Murphy
with the following cast (in order of appearance):

HAING NGOR .... Peter Kwong
HUOY MY CHANG... Yunjin Kim
PEN TIP .... Mark W. Conklin
NAGA MAN .... Eric Steinberg
NAGA WOMAN.. Midori Nakamura
THE GIRL .... Nicole Scherzinger
CAMBODIAN DANCER .... Sokhanarith Moeur

Choreographer .... Eva Lee
Scenic Designer .... Paul Owen
Costume Designer .... Esther Marquis
Lighting Designer .... Kenneth Posner
Sound Designer .... Darron L. West
Props Master .... Ron Riall
Stage Manager .... Gregg Fletcher
Assistant Stage Manager .... Susan R. Fenty
Dramaturg .... Elizabeth Wong
Cambodian Cultural Advisor .... Samnang Wilson
Casting .... Mary & Karen Margiotta, Sonia Nikore

The original cast of that production included: Ernest Abuba, Francois Chau, Somaly Hay, Sopia Im,
Eva Lee, Chris Odo, Dawn Akemi Saito.

Jon Lipsky makes his ATL debut with THE SURVIVOR: A CAMBODIAN ODYSSEY, which was first staged by the Merrimack Repertory Theatre in Lowell, Massachusetts. He is also the author of BEGINNER'S LUCK, the story of King Saul in the Bible, LIVING IN EXILE, a retelling of the *Illiad*, DREAMING WITH AN AIDS PATIENT, MASTER OF ECSTACY, THEY ALL WANT TO PLAY HAMLET and most recently, MAGGIE'S RIFF, a play based on Jack Kerouac's coming-of-age novel *Maggie Cassidy*. His plays have been seen in the Guest Series at American Repertory Theatre, at Missouri Repertory Theatre, Merrimack Repertory Theatre, Atlanta's Theater Emory and Amsterdam's Melkweg Theater, among others. At Boston's TheaterWorks, he was playwright-in-residence and developed scripts in collaboration with artistic directors Vincent Murphy and Tim McDonough. Mr. Lipsky is in the process of developing a cabaret theatre of dreams called THE DREAM CAFE. He lives with his wife, Kanta, and sons, Adam and Jonah, in Boston where he teaches acting and playwriting at Boston University's School for the Arts.

Author's Note

THE SURVIVOR: A CAMBODIAN ODYSSEY was commissioned by the Merrimack Repertory Theatre as part of a series of plays intended to serve the communities of Lowell, Massachusetts. Lowell has one of the largest Cambodian populations in the United States, and we wanted to present a story that touched on their experiences. Dr. Ngor's autobiography not only served this purpose, but went beyond it; after all, the most common and striking images of Cambodia in the minds of most Americans comes from his role in *The Killing Fields*. It is, so to speak, common ground for all of us.

Common ground is important because it is very difficult for any people to really share the experience of another people, especially when it concerns an unimaginable holocaust. On some level, there is no way most Americans, safe in our homes, with plenty to eat, can begin to comprehend, no less empathize with, the devastation imposed on the Cambodian people by the Pol Pot regime. Still we have to try.

Haing Ngor, in his autobiography, makes it clear that there is not such a great distinction between good guys and bad guys when survival is at stake. Everyone becomes morally compromised. In this respect, I hope this play conveys the notion that we all have the capacity for the violence of the Khmer Rouge. At the same time, I also hope it conveys the sense that love—the kind of love that helped Haing Ngor survive—is a jewel which we should all cherish.

One last thing: as I write, the Khmer Rouge is on the march again; Cambodians are once again killing one another in this endless civil war; the United States is considering whether or not to bolster the legitimate Cambodian government. This story is not over.

—Jon Lipsky

FOR CAUTION NOTICE SEE PAGE OPPOSITE TABLE OF CONTENTS.

THE SURVIVOR: A CAMBODIAN ODYSSEY by Jon Lipsky. ©1993 by Jon Lipsky. Reprinted by permission of the author. All inquiries should be addressed to Bruce Ostler, c/o Fifi Oscard Agency 24 West 40th St., New York, NY 10018. (212) 764.1100.

This play is dedicated to my father, Eleazar Lipsky, an eloquent man,
who died on the day it was completed,
and to the Cambodian people and their own eloquent dead.

CHARACTERS

Haing Ngor – A Cambodian doctor.

Huoy My Chang – His fiancée.

Pen Tip – A radiology lab worker.

Naga Man & Naga Woman – Two transformational figures who perform traditional movement and play many parts.

Teenage Girl – Another transformational figure who plays a Khmer Rouge spy and other children.

SETTING:

Act I – Cambodia (1974-79).

Act II – The scene shifts back and forth between Cambodia in the late 1970s and the making of "The Killing Fields" in the 1980s.

The play is performed on a set which suggests rural Cambodia, watched over by a huge, silent Buddha. Watchtowers with large loudspeakers stand on either side of the stage. In the background there are elements of a movie sound stage, like camera lights and boom mikes, which will become more prominent in Act II. Also onstage there is a screen onto which slides, flickering images, and/or shadow plays can be projected. As part of the design it is suggested that a Classical Cambodian Dancer participate in the show, representing, among other things, the spirit of the rich Cambodian culture that was almost destroyed.

The Survivor:
A Cambodian Odyssey

ACT ONE

Lights up on the Classical Cambodian Dancer.
Naga Man & Woman stand head to head with the Classical Dancer, the rest of the Ensemble behind. This is the image of the mythological Naga, the many-headed King Cobra.
The King Cobra breaks apart into its component parts, revealing Ngor behind, sitting in a movie chair in a white tux.
Over the loudspeakers, we hear a voice:

LOUDSPEAKER: (*V.O.*) And the third nominee for best feature film is "The Killing Fields," David Putnam, producer.
(*Music: "The Killing Fields" theme. Ngor, in flickering light, watches a film clip.*)
"For godsake Sydney, why didn't you get him out while you had the chance?"
"Tell my wife I love her, Sydney, and look out for my children."
"She doesn't speak any English, Sydney. Please, don't let anyone be bad to my wife." (*Blackout.*)

BONJOUR

Lights up on Phnom Penh before 1975.
We hear a Cambodian child's song: "Sareka Kai-oi." Teenage Girl appears skipping.
Naga Man & Woman dance images of Phnom Penh before the Khmer Rouge takeover: a vendor, for instance, calls in Cambodian, "Oranges, oranges"; a taxi driver calls, "Taxi! Taxi!"
Then: French pop music, "Et pourtant."
Naga Man & Woman dance images of sophisticated post-colonial

life, for instance waiters and diners in fancy restaurants.
A sign appears on a screen in English and Cambodian. It says,
"Bonjour."
Pen Tip enters.

PEN TIP: Bonjour, bonjour. Bonjour, mes amis. Bonjour, and welcome to our play. We welcome you just as we might welcome you to the city of Phnom Penh in 1975: Bonjour! Bonjour! To the city of Bonjour! Yes, the city of Bonjour because the French – those clever Longnoses – taught Cambodia all about bonjour.
"Bonjour" said monsieur as he pocketed your payoff.
"Bonjour" said the bureaucrat as he took your bribe.
"Bonjour" said the judge as he exchanged your payment for a light jail sentence.
Bonjour bonjour bonjour! Until bonjour was the only way anyone knew how to do any business in the city of Phnom Penh.
Now there are two other French words we would like you to learn before we begin our story: "Bonnheur," and "honneur."
Just as "bon appetite" is "good appetite," "bonnheur" is good feeling – a good feeling between people, a bond between people, the bond that ties us together. And as for "honneur," it means simply, honor, whatever that means.
Our bond and our honor. As our story begins both are about to be destroyed in Cambodia forever.
Our story – and it's a true story, like "The Killing Fields," this really happened – our story begins with this word, "Bonjour!" and it ends:

NGOR: I will never be forgiven by my memories.

PEN TIP: – "I will never be forgiven by my memories."
(Lights up on the young Ngor and Huoy.)

NGOR: So if you put carbon, hydrogen and oxygen together to make sugar, how will they combine?

HUOY: It would be C12 H22 and O11, luk teacher, for sugars like glucose and sucrose.

NGOR: Correct, Miss Chang.

PEN TIP: *(To the audience.)* But first let us introduce you to our three main characters.

NGOR: Though those three elements also combine with others to form an entire class of organic compounds, the carbohydrates. Can you write the formula, Miss Chang?

HUOY: Yes, luk teacher.

(*She writes.*)

PEN TIP: This actor plays Haing Ngor, a raw young medical student who is supporting himself by teaching chemistry on the side.

HUOY: Did I get it right, luk teacher?

NGOR: Yes, Miss Chang. And where do we find carbohydrates in nature?

HUOY: Most edible plants, like yams.

NGOR: And if you burn yams, Miss Chang?

(*She writes long formula for burning carbohydrates.*)

PEN TIP: (*To the audience.*) And this character plays his student, Chang My Huoy. Chang is her family name. My means beautiful and Huoy means petals of a flower.

(*She finishes writing the formula.*)

HUOY: If you burn yams, you drive off the oxygen and hydrogen and what is left is carbon.

NGOR: Thank you, Miss Sugar. I . . . um . . . Mademoiselle, time for tea.

HUOY: (*Giggling.*) Yes, luk teacher.

(*She hands him a bowl of oranges.*

She eats. He eats.

They remain very aware of each other.)

PEN TIP: And here is the third main character in our play, a character who is all-powerful, a character who is incredibly seductive, a character whose presence is felt most in absentia.

(*Pause.*)

I'm speaking, of course, about . . .

(*Picks up an orange.*)

. . . food.

(*French romantic music, "Qui en arrivera." Naga Man & Woman set up the restaurant. Ngor seats Huoy and presents dinner.*)

HUOY: (*To Ngor.*) Steamed milk fish!

NGOR: Steamed milk fish with garlic lemon sauce.

HUOY: Garlic lemon sauce!

NGOR: And for dessert . . . (*He uncovers it.*)

HUOY: Pralines!

NGOR: Pralines!

HUOY: My favorite!

NGOR: We must have done something right in some past life.

(*They toast each other.*)

Bonheur!

HUOY: Bonheur!

(*She drinks. He hands her a bolt of silk.*)

Oh. Oh, sweet! Such fine silk . . .

NGOR: When your mother sews the dress, she can set the date. Happy?

HUOY: I will be happy if my husband is happy. My husband will be happy if our families are happy. If our families are happy, the village is happy. If the village is happy, the Gods are happy.

NGOR: Yes, let's be happy. They're dancing the romvong tonight at "La Paiyott."

(*He eats. She does not.*)

HUOY: You know, Sweet, my mother worries for you.

NGOR: Because I spend too much money?

HUOY: Because of the war. Ma thinks maybe you should leave the country. Go to Paris. Voulez a Paree, voulez a Paree!

NGOR: Tell Ma not to be silly. (*Sarcastically.*) "Voulez a Paree."

HUOY: But if Phnom Penh falls . . .

NGOR: (*Annoyed.*) I said: don't be silly! Phnom Penh isn't going to fall. Let's enjoy the evening.

HUOY: Yes, Sweet.

NGOR: It's a beautiful evening.

HUOY: Yes, Sweet.

NGOR: And you're my apsara, my angel.

(*Pause.*)

HUOY: But if the communists . . .

NGOR: Forget about the communists. I'm a doctor, an obstetrician, a specialist in childbirth. Even the Khmer Rouge has babies.

(*The Ensemble dances the romvong to romantic French music.*)

PEN TIP: Ah, l'amour, l'amour, l'amour en la guerre. While the bombs go off in the countryside, all the young lovers huddle in the ritzy cafes over cognac. Phnom Penh becomes a little island of peace and their puppy love becomes its bubble.

(*Sound of explosions in the distance.*)

Then late at night you see them promenade along the river towards the Royal Palace. His hand around her waist, the wind in her hair. The moon reflects off the dancing ripples as dark shapes slip through the oily flow.

(*Loud explosion; Ngor enters surgery wearing a mask. Naga man transforms into an Assistant Doctor. Naga woman transforms into a wounded patient.*)

NGOR: What the hell happened here!

ASSISTANT DOCTOR: Khmer Rouge ambush. Inside the city.

NGOR: Where's radiology!

(*Looks at the patient's belly.*)

Oooo, messy.

(*Shouting off-stage.*)

X-rays, goddammit!

(*Pen Tip runs in with X-rays.*)

PEN TIP: Coming, coming . . .

NGOR: On the screen! On the screen!

(*Ngor tosses them at Pen Tip impatiently. Pen Tip picks them up and obediently hangs them up on a screen.*

More explosions. Lights flicker. Pen Tip holds a flashlight. Doctors joke as they work furiously to save the patient.)

There's shrapnel lodged behind the pancreas.

ASSISTANT DOCTOR: – son of a bitch Lon Nol, why doesn't he just step down?

NGOR: Because if he steps down he'll fall over.

ASSISTANT DOCTOR: And why will Lon Nol fall over?

NGOR: Tertiary syphilis. From fucking the Americans.

ASSISTANT DOCTOR: You mean his "corruption" has spread from his cock to his brain.

NGOR: His cock *is* his brain. There! Let's sew this up quick.

ASSISTANT DOCTOR: Look! Out there! White flags!

NGOR: Bleeder! Clamps!

(*He works to stop the bleeding.*)

Let the bastards take over. The Khmer Rouge can't be any dirtier than this government. Sutures!

ASSISTANT DOCTOR: What if they come here?

NGOR: Just relax. They'll probably just liberate our pretty nurses.

(*Sound of automatic rifle fire. Teenage Girl enters as Khmer Rouge with an AK-47.*)

KHMER ROUGE: Don't move!

LOUDSPEAKERS: (*V.O. Overlapping.*) Don't move!

KHMER ROUGE: Don't move!

LOUDSPEAKERS: (*V.O. Overlapping.*) Don't move!

KHMER ROUGE: You the Captain Doctor?

LOUDSPEAKERS: (*V.O. Overlapping.*) You the Captain Doctor?

KHMER ROUGE: You the Captain Doctor?

LOUDSPEAKERS: (*V.O. Overlapping.*) You the Captain Doctor?
   (*Pause.*)

NGOR: No, the Captain Doctor left when he heard you coming.

KHMER ROUGE: Liar!

LOUDSPEAKERS: (*V.O. Overlapping.*) Liar!

KHMER ROUGE: Liar!

LOUDSPEAKERS: (*V.O. Overlapping.*) Liar!

KHMER ROUGE: If we don't find the Captain Doctor!

LOUDSPEAKERS: (*V.O. Overlapping.*) If we don't find the Captain Doctor!

KHMER ROUGE: You are all going to sleep!

LOUDSPEAKERS: (*V.O. Overlapping.*) You are all going to sleep!
   (*Khmer Rouge Girl backs off.*)

NGOR: Okay, everyone – leave right now.

ASSISTANT DOCTOR: B-But . . . The patient!

NGOR: Leave her.

ASSISTANT DOCTOR: But we have to finish . . .

NGOR: She's finished.

ASSISTANT DOCTOR: You son-of-a-bitch, we haven't sewn her up yet.

NGOR: No time! It's all over! It's done!
   (*Pause.*)
   Move!
   (*As Ngor exits he turns to look at the wounded patient. Suddenly she twitches on the table. He freezes.*
   BLACKOUT.
   Lights up on Huoy, Ngor and Pen Tip as they narrate the evacuation of Phnom Penh.
   Naga Man & Woman dance images of the evacuation. Teenage Girl as Khmer Rouge stands over them all with an AK-47.
   Everyone is looking for members of their families.
   Throughout the scene the actors speak as if trying to call to loved ones over unbearable Chinese marching music.)

KHMER ROUGE GIRL/LOUDSPEAKERS: (*Overlapping.*) Long live Angka!

KHMER ROUGE GIRL/LOUDSPEAKERS: (*Overlapping.*) Long live the Glorious Revolution!

PEN TIP: They tell us we will only be gone three hours.

HUOY: Sweet, where are you?

NGOR: The soldiers block the way.

PEN TIP: Then they say three days.

HUOY: Why don't you come?

NGOR: I can't get through the roadblocks.

PEN TIP: I can't even wait for my wife.

KHMER ROUGE & LOUDSPEAKERS: (*Overlapping.*) The wheel of history is turning! The wheel of history rolls on!

HUOY: All I can take is a pot of rice, my wedding silk, and a picture of you.

NGOR: Papa and I join a train of doctors pushing their Mercedes.

HUOY: I never got to say goodbye to Mama.

NGOR: A train of Mercedes packed with TVs and air conditioners.

HUOY: Mama . . . Mama . . .

PEN TIP: I walk in circles through the crowd, circling slowly through the crowd looking for my wife.

KHMER ROUGE & LOUDSPEAKERS: Don't move!

PEN TIP: – then I see her sneaking back against the flow of traffic, and a twelve year old with an AK-47 puts a bullet through her head.

KHMER ROUGE & LOUDSPEAKERS: Don't move!

HUOY: Don't think about it.

NGOR: Hide the cry.

PEN TIP: After that I do what I am told.

KHMER ROUGE & LOUDSPEAKERS: (*Overlapping.*) Let Angka eliminate the hidden enemies. Let Angka provide you with everything you need.

HUOY: I leave notes for you on all the trees knowing you will never find them.

NGOR: I show them your picture at every check point knowing they will only laugh.

KHMER ROUGE & LOUDSPEAKERS: Move!

PEN TIP: Everywhere I see in surging crowds through streaming rain my wife's face. But it always turns out to be a shimmering mirage.

NGOR: They offer rewards for skilled workers and one of the doctors volunteers.

KHMER ROUGE & LOUDSPEAKERS: Move!

NGOR: A soldier puts a plastic bag over the doctor's head until his body stops twitching.

KHMER ROUGE & LOUDSPEAKERS: Don't move!

HUOY: Make yourself invisible.

PEN TIP: Things disappear.

NGOR: I tell them I am a taxi driver and they let me go.

KHMER ROUGE & LOUDSPEAKERS: (*Overlapping.*) If your hands try to stop
    the wheel, they will be slashed by the spokes.

NGOR: (*Gesture: driving.*) Taxi . . . Taxi . . .

KHMER ROUGE & LOUDSPEAKERS: If your feet try to stop the wheel they
    will be crushed by the weight.

PEN TIP: At the roadblock, I begin directing traffic.

KHMER ROUGE & LOUDSPEAKERS: Move!

PEN TIP: And people obey.

KHMER ROUGE & LOUDSPEAKERS: Move!

PEN TIP: Some even offer me bribes of rice, the new bonjour.

KHMER ROUGE & LOUDSPEAKERS: Don't move!

NGOR: At the river, I ditch my glasses and tear clothes off the corpses
    to blend in with the crowd.

PEN TIP: Bonjour . . . bonjour . . .

HUOY: Then I see a white Peugot smash the barricades, leap the river
    bank . . .

NGOR: Floating . . .

PEN TIP: Floating . . .

HUOY: Floating on the river right before my eyes. People inside.
    Inside the car. A man and woman. All dressed up.

NGOR: All dressed in fine polyesters.

HUOY: And children with their noses up against the back window.

NGOR: Children . . .

PEN TIP: Clutching their Hong Kong toys.

HUOY: The water rises.

NGOR: The car sinks.

HUOY: Down . . .

NGOR: Down . . .

    (*Pause.*)

PEN TIP: Another rich guy buys the easy way out.

    (*Pen Tip turns away; Ngor sees Huoy.*)

HUOY: (*Softly to herself.*) Oh, mama, mama, mama. . . . (*Etc.*)

NGOR: Is it you? Don't move!

KHMER ROUGE & LOUDSPEAKERS: This is the start of the New Year.

NGOR: If it's you! Don't move!

KHMER ROUGE & LOUDSPEAKERS: This is Year Zero!

NGOR: It's me.

KHMER ROUGE & LOUDSPEAKERS: Year Zero!

NGOR: I'm here.

KHMER ROUGE & LOUDSPEAKERS: YEAR ZERO!

NGOR: DON'T MOVE!

> (*Whispering right into her ear.*)
> Things disappear. Don't think about it. Make yourself invisible.
> Sweet, sweet . . . Hide the cry.
> (*They embrace: hands, foreheads touching. Pen Tip, Naga Man &
> Woman watch them.*)

PEN TIP: In the middle of the road, you two embrace. She won't let
go. She just holds on, leaning up against your chest. In front of
your father. In front of your brothers. A crowd forms, drawn by
this indelicate public display. Still you stay locked in your own
private world. You look familiar to me, but I can't place the face.
Then you hear someone in the crowd murmur: "Samnang nas!
Samnang nas!" – "How lucky! How lucky! How lucky to have
each other."

That was me, Pen Tip, that was I, Pen Tip. Pen Tip, your humble
servant. You didn't notice me – you were too busy with your
indecent touches. But I know you heard me through your bliss.
"Samnang nas! Samnang nas!" 'Cause that's the nickname you
take for yourself: "Samnang" – your nom de guerre. "Samnang" –
to hide your true identity. "Samnang" – that's what you call
yourself, "Lucky."

YEAR ZERO

> *BELLS BELLS BELLS. A sign on a screen: "Year Zero."*

PEN TIP: Bells wake us up before daylight.

> (*BELLS BELLS BELLS.*)
> Bells send us off to the rice fields in the dark.
> (*BELLS BELLS BELLS.*
> *Lights come up slowly on Ensemble dressing in black pajamas,
> Khmer Rouge uniforms.*)

The trick is to work steadily without working hard.

(*They take bamboo poles into the fields. They work. Sad Cambodian music: "Neang Kang Rey."*

Teenage Girl enters as Khmer Rouge Girl with an AK-47. The work speeds up in her presence, until:

BELLS BELLS BELLS.)

KHMER ROUGE GIRL/LOUDSPEAKERS: We will claim victory over the elements.

ENSEMBLE: (*By rote.*) Victory over the elements.

KHMER ROUGE GIRL/LOUDSPEAKERS: We are masters of the rice paddies.

ENSEMBLE: (*By rote.*) Masters of the rice paddies.

KHMER ROUGE GIRL/LOUDSPEAKERS: Masters over all the earth.

ENSEMBLE: (*By rote.*) Masters over all the earth.

KHMER ROUGE GIRL/LOUDSPEAKERS: You will now give me a big round of applause.

ENSEMBLE: (*By rote, fists in air.*) Chey yuo! Chey yuo! Chey yuo!

(*Ngor does not complete the last "Chey yuo!" He sees something on the ground and bends to get it. Khmer Rouge Girl points her finger at him.*

Naga Man & Woman place a yoke around Ngor. He pulls a plow.

Everyone goes back to work. Work music. Huoy can't work, though. She watches Ngor.)

PEN TIP: (*To the audience.*) So, I'm working in the rice fields and I see them yoke you to a plow.

(*Sound of the whip.*)

They make you pull the plow beside an ox. And whip you when you fall behind.

(*Sound of the whip.*)

You push with all your might but that plodding beast goes on and on.

(*Sound of the whip.*)

The plow veers left; you can't keep up. And – there! – up on the dyke I see your sweetheart –

(*Sound of the whip.*)

Looking down on you, her body twitching with each whip lash!

(*Sound of the whip; Huoy cries out. Pen Tip stops work to look at her.*)

Better hide the cry, mon cherie. Hide the cry.

(*Khmer Rouge Girl points at Pen Tip. He runs and takes his place beside Ngor.)*

Pull harder, Lucky, Samnang, whatever your name is, you better pull harder. If your Sweetie makes a scene up there, she's gonna disappear.

(*Ngor looks up. Sees Huoy, puts his shoulder to the yoke. Pen Tip and Ngor push the plow hard.*

BELLS, BELLS, BELLS.

Lights change. Huoy and Ngor are alone in their hut.)

NGOR: (*Furious.*) Don't ever, ever stop your work!

HUOY: I know!

NGOR: Don't ever, ever watch me!

HUOY: I know!

NGOR: You have no complaints, no questions, no intelligence at all! Don't you see who's disappearing: businessmen, bureaucrats, teachers. Doctors!! We're "new" people, "new" people, never forget it. The "old" people are watching, watching every step we take. You have to make yourself invisible.

HUOY: (*Hysterically.*) I'm trying, sweet. I'm trying. I've lost twenty pounds. My hair's falling out. My feet are bleeding. I'm becoming invisible. I want to be invisible. I want to be with my mother. I want my mother. Mama, mama.

NGOR: Okay, Okay . . .

(*She struggles against him.*)

HUOY: Let go of me! Let go! I want my mama!

(*He holds her close.*)

NGOR: Stop it! I'm your mama, now. I'm your mama. I'm your mama.

(*She calms down.*)

Here!

(*He holds out two snails.*)

HUOY: (*With distaste.*) Snails?

NGOR: Escargot.

(*Pause.*)

HUOY: Oh, Sweet, what is this hunger?

NGOR: Hunger is your own body eating itself.

HUOY: (*Considering this.*) My own body eating itself. (*Pause.*) Like a cannibal.

NGOR: Like a cannibal.

(*He sucks the snail out of its shell. She sucks the other snail out of its shell.*

Lights change. Pen Tip addresses the audience.)

PEN TIP: After a few weeks on the plow, Samnang and I got revenge on that fucking ox. Just before dawn, when the guards were napping, I stood watch while Lucky whacked its tail off.

(*Demonstrating.*)

Shht. Shht. What a feast! Ox tail soup. That dumb beast hardly felt a thing. Oh, my Lucky – what a guy – he cut off the tail with the precision – shht! shht! – of a surgeon.

A surgeon. But: "Dam doum kor," that's my motto. Plant a kor tree. See that's a pun. In Cambodian kor is both a tree and the word for mute, closed mouthed. So: dam doum kor. Plant a kor tree. Shut your mouth. Get it?

How come everyone's lost their sense of humor?

(*Lights change. Ngor and Huoy have reversed positions; she is now cradling him.*)

HUOY: I just looked at your mess in the latrine.

NGOR: Yes.

HUOY: There's blood.

NGOR: Yes.

HUOY: There's pus.

NGOR: Yes.

(*Looking at his skin.*)

I'm all yellow.

(*Groans holding his belly, curls up in a fetal position.*)

Scrape the bark off the guava trees.

HUOY: I did.

NGOR: Pick the leaves off the tips of the branches.

HUOY: I did.

NGOR: Then where's my tea?

HUOY: (*Tiredly, resentfully.*) I made the tea!

NGOR: Did I drink it?

HUOY: You drank it. Here!

NGOR: What . . . ?

HUOY: Tetracycline. I told you I could get some.

NGOR: How many?

HUOY: Four.

NGOR: Not enough.

HUOY: That's all I could . . .

NGOR: Not enough! You're a crab. You got the shell of a crab. If you don't toughen up . . .

HUOY: I'll try again.

(*She starts to leave.*)

NGOR: Wait! There's one thing you haven't tried.

HUOY: I've tried everything.

NGOR: Burn some food over the fire. Burn it to charcoal. The charcoal sometimes traps the gases, sometimes even traps the disease.

HUOY: Burn food?

NGOR: Yes.

HUOY: What food?

NGOR: Food. Just food.

HUOY: Sweet, you can have whatever food there is. You can have whatever I can find. You can have my share. But I'm not gonna burn it. I won't do it! I won't!

(*Pause.*)

NGOR: Call my father.

HUOY: I'm not calling my father.

NGOR: It's time.

HUOY: Be strong.

NGOR: My heart . . .

HUOY: Be strong in your mind.

NGOR: Over my grave, release a dove.

HUOY: There are no doves. They've all been eaten.

(*Prayer music. Naga Man & Woman perform a prayer dance.*)

NAGA MAN & WOMAN: Preah put, preah thor, preach sang.
Preah put, preah thor, preach sang.
Spin the wheel of the dharma, spin the wheel of the law.
Spin the wheel of the law, spin the wheel . . . (*Etc.*)

NGOR: (*Simultaneously.*) Father, father – treat my sweet like your own daughter.

HUOY: (*Simultaneously.*) Mother, mother – care for my sweet in paradise.

NGOR: Let life be good to her in her next life.

HUOY: Always watch over him.

NGOR: Always protect her.

HUOY: May he be reborn where there's food.

NGOR: (*Overlapping.*) May she be reborn where there's food.

(*Pause.*)

PEN TIP: Yams! Yams! Get your yams!

HUOY: Yams?

PEN TIP: Angka has one for every family. Rations from Angka: get your yams!

HUOY: A yam. (*To Ngor.*) A sweet yam.

(*Pen Tip looks at Ngor.*)

PEN TIP: Take my advice, cherie. He's too far gone.

(*He hands her the yam.*)

Bon appetite.

(*Long pause. She looks at the yam hungrily. Then, drops it in the fire.*)

HUOY: (*To the audience.*) I burned the yam to black, a charcoal cake, speckled with yellow streaks. I fed him the ashes flake by flake. And then he slept. And the next day the gases in his bowel stopped gurgling and his trips to the latrine slowed down.

(*Naga woman appears as Midwife.*)

And after a week, I draped him over my shoulder and took him for a walk by the railroad tracks and by chance we met an old woman, a midwife, who reached into her baby sack and gave my sweet a poison fruit to complete his healing. She said, "The medicine is in the poison, the poison is in the medicine."

NAGA WOMAN: The medicine is in the poison, the poison is in the medicine.

HUOY: And then she reached into her baby sack again and handed us an ear of corn. And we watched this miraculous person disappear down the tracks and that night my sweet ate the poison fruit, but he made me eat the corn myself – every last kernel – to repay me, he said, in some small way for my share of that yam.

(*Naga Man & Woman are sleeping in hammocks. Huoy and Ngor are outside their hut. She washes one foot with the other, brushes her hair, pretending not to notice Ngor is watching.*)

PEN TIP: (*To the audience.*) Samnang, Lucky, what a guy – always likes to flaunt his wife. He's supposed to be on the back lines recovering from his sickness, safe! But he's lop-lop. Every night he risks his fool neck to sneak up here on the front lines just to cuddle with his darling.

NGOR: I love the way you comb your hair. As if we were about to promenade the night along the river to the Royal Palace. I love the way you smell. The soap you cook from the "kor" fruit makes you smell so sweet.

(*Pen Tip approaches them.*)

PEN TIP: I love the way you cuddle. Hey, Lucky, some of us aren't as lucky as you. Do you have to make such a show of it?

NGOR: Of course. Angka says we must share everything. So I share with you my love.

PEN TIP: How about sharing your love with Angka?

(*Huoy leaves, goes to her hammock, but listens in.*)

NGOR: I give ninety-nine percent of myself to Angka. Can't I keep one percent for myself?

PEN TIP: Aeeeeee, I hope your "one percent" is big and long enough for her. What a lover. I haven't seen such loving since I left my old job in Phnom Penh.

NGOR: What was your old job?

PEN TIP: Oh, I was the prince of Phnom Penh, but I quit to become a garbage inspector.

NGOR: Oh yes, me, too. I used to be the King of Phnom Penh but I quit to be a toilet engineer.

PEN TIP: Oh, no. You used to be something higher than that.

(*Pause.*)

NGOR: Don't talk like that, comrade.

PEN TIP: We're just joking. Dam doum kor. See, to survive the Khmer Rouge, you have to keep a sense of humor. I tell the cadre in the kitchen, "you're not communist. You're "kum-monuss."

It's another pun. Communist. Kum-monuss. Kum is revenge. Monuss is people. Kum-monuss. Revenge-people. Get it?

NGOR: I got it.

PEN TIP: Well, at least Uncle Mao likes my jokes. Gave him a good laugh. Gave me some extra rice.

(*He gives Ngor some rice. He hides it quickly.*)

NGOR: How do you get away with it, Pen Tip?

PEN TIP: Oh, after all those years of bombing by the B-52s the "old" people love to be called "kum-monuss." They take it as a compliment.

NGOR: No, I mean, how do you get the "old" people to trust you?

PEN TIP: They should trust me. I just married one of them.

NGOR: You just married?

PEN TIP: Oh, yes. The "kum-monuss" want lots of little baby "kum-monusses" so I let Uncle Mao pick me a wife. From among the "old" people.

(*Beckons for him to follow.*)

Come. I'll show you how to get some extra rice. It's easy. Come.
(*They leave Huoy and cross to a hut.*)

NGOR: That's Uncle Mao's hut.

PEN TIP: Uncle Mao can help us a lot.
(*Hands him some more rice.*)
Are you interested, Samnang . . . Lucky . . . Whoever you are?

NGOR: (*Suddenly suspicious.*) What do you want from me?
(*Naga Man appears in silhouette as "dying baby." Naga Woman appears in silhouette as Khmer Rouge nurse holding a syringe. We hear "poison" music.*)

PEN TIP: Uncle Mao has a very sick son in there. Angka sent a Khmer Rouge nurse but he doesn't trust her. She'll inject the baby with whatever she's got. She can't even read the labels.

NGOR: What can I do?

PEN TIP: I told him I would find a real doctor.

NGOR: I'm not a real doctor.

PEN TIP: If we save his son, he'll be most grateful.

NGOR: I'm a taxi driver.

PEN TIP: Even if you're a taxi driver he'll be most grateful. Come on, Lucky. I've helped you. You help me.

NGOR: Too risky.

PEN TIP: You're not afraid of risks, Lucky. You take risks every time you sneak up to the front lines just to cuddle.
(*Ngor freezes; Pen Tip hands him a bottle.*)
Look! The Khmer Rouge Nurse is planning to inject the kid with this. Just tell me what it is.

NGOR: I don't know. (*Reluctantly.*) Maybe Vitamin B.

PEN TIP: Oh. Well, at least it won't hurt the baby.

NGOR: A full syringe. It'll kill him.
(*Naga Woman does stylized gesture, filling a syringe.*)

PEN TIP: Well, go in there. Tell her.

NGOR: You tell her.

PEN TIP: Oh, sure, she'd listen to me. Hey, I just pushed a button on an X-ray machine.

NGOR: I am not a doctor.

PEN TIP: What? Are you just gonna watch?! Stop her!!
(*Naga Man does "dying baby" movements.*)
Look! It's quivering . . .
(*Pause.*)

It's twitching . . .

(*Pause.*)

It's dead.

(*Poison music ends.*)

Thanks a lot, Lucky. You have cost me a lot of merit. That dead baby could have done us a lot of good. We would have had Uncle Mao in our armpit!

NGOR: I'm a taxi driver!

PEN TIP: Hey, don't think about it. Things disappear. Ah, honneur: one moment it's here. Next moment it's gone!

(*Pen Tip points an accusing finger at Ngor. Khmer Rouge Girl enters with an AK-47.*)

KING OF DEATH

Sound of a motorcycle. A sign appears on a screen: KING OF DEATH. Naga Man enters wearing the mask of the King of Death. Pen Tip narrates to Ngor as King of Death mirrors the action.

PEN TIP: Hear that? On a Honda motorcycle, comes the King of Death. That's what the prisoners call him, the King of Death. He speaks to you softly, calmly, with a smile on his face. He says, "If you live there is no gain. If you die there is no loss."

KING OF DEATH: If you live there is no gain. If you die there is no loss.

PEN TIP: He asks, "Were you a Captain Doctor?" If you were a Captain Doctor, he says, "Angka will forgive you. Angka needs Doctors." You say, "Taxi! Taxi!"

NGOR: Taxi! Taxi!

PEN TIP: He says, "Okay. If you live there is no gain."

KING OF DEATH: (*Overlapping.*) If you live there is no gain.

PEN TIP: "If you die there is no loss."

KING OF DEATH: (*Overlapping.*) If you die there is no loss.

(*Sound of motorcycle revving.*)

PEN TIP: He leads you out to a field of crosses. Tied to these crosses are bodies, limp and floppy, dangling from ropes. Beneath these bodies are mounds of rice husks, and the rice husks are burning, burning very slowly.

NGOR: (*Overlapping.*) Taxi! Taxi!

(*King of Death flicks a cigarette lighter. The sound is amplified by the Loudspeakers: Flick.*)

PEN TIP: The King of Death hoists your body up on a cross and flicks his cigarette lighter at the mound of rice husks beneath your feet. Flick. To your right hangs a pregnant woman begging for her mother. Flick. To your left hangs an old man who has soiled himself. Flick. The fire ignites. Thick smoke swirls about you. The flames lick your feet. Flick. If you live there is no gain. If you die there is no loss.

KING OF DEATH: (*Whispering.*) If you live there is no gain. If you die there is no loss.

PEN TIP: After four days, he takes you down, opens your eyes a crack. Beside you is the pregnant woman lying on her full, round belly. He kicks her over. Rips her blouse. Still, she lies there, very still. He picks up a bayonet and slashes her belly. He pulls out her baby and breaks its neck. Around its neck, he ties a string. Suddenly you know what you saw hanging from the prison parapets, those black shrivelled things. He digs down again and pulls out her liver.

(*He forces Ngor to look at the liver.*)

Hungry?

(*Pen Tip and King of Death exit.*)

Khmer Rouge Girl enters with Huoy and watches over them from a distance. They talk in whispers hardly moving, hardly looking at one another.

HUOY: I'm here.

NGOR: Yes.

HUOY: Don't talk.

NGOR: Yes. Who else . . . ?

HUOY: Shhh . . .

NGOR: Who!

HUOY: (*Whispering.*) Shhh. . . . A big purge. Anyone who speaks French. Anyone with light skin.

NGOR: My brothers?

(*Huoy is silent.*)

My father?

(*Huoy is silent.*)

HUOY: Your father wanted very much to tell you something. (*Pause.*) Are you well enough to listen?

(*Ngor nods.*)

Your father's last request.

(*Pause.*)

Give up this revenge.

NGOR: What revenge?

HUOY: The revenge you are plotting against Pen Tip. Forget the poison.

NGOR: What poison?

HUOY: The poison your father taught you to make out of bark and sugar to kill the wolves, the chkai chor-chork.

(*Pause.*)

NGOR: I would know where to get the bark. I'm not sure about the sugar.

HUOY: Don't do it, Sweet. Pen Tip is an ignorant person. You're an educated man.

NGOR: Yes, you're right – I want him to know who did it. Maybe I should use my hatchet.

HUOY: Then you're no different from Khmer Rouge.

NGOR: Oh, yes. I've thought about it: I'm just like them.

HUOY: No. Listen to your father! You'll get us both killed!

NGOR: Shhh, Sweet, don't worry. I won't do anything stupid. Pen Tip has done me a great favor. Because of him I now have all I need to stay alive.

HUOY: What?

NGOR: Someone to love. And someone to kill.

(*Pen Tip enters with two hatchets. Huoy exits.*)

PEN TIP: (*To the audience.*) Revenge. We Cambodians have our own peculiar concept of revenge. We call it "kum." "Kum" is really a grudge, a long-standing grudge, that you keep bottled up inside and then when the time is ripe you strike back with much worse than you ever received. If I slap you in public and a year later you put a bullet through my head, that's kum. That's kum. It's particularly delicious if you break my face first.

(*Ngor and Pen Tip take tools and walk together.*)

We're almost there, Lucky. Isn't it great to be off the front lines?

NGOR: Don't volunteer me for things, Pen Tip. I'm trying to disappear.

PEN TIP: Oh, no one's watching us. Uncle Mao trusts me. We can go at our own pace, take a nap, hunt for lizards, mmm, tasty! Just you and me. Doesn't that excite you?

NGOR: More than you can know.

PEN TIP: Good. Then all we have to do is bring back a few loads of lumber. Uncle Mao wants to build a bridge.

NGOR: What lumber?

PEN TIP: Here!

(*Lights up on the Buddhist temple. Buddhist music. Naga Man & Woman do a "Naga" snake dance. The Classical Dancer presides over the temple.*)

NAGA MAN & WOMAN: (*To the audience.*) Our temple grounds lay in ruins. The Khmer Rouge had stripped the wood off the doors, the door frames, the roof. Even the snake railings, the Holy Nagas, the King Cobras, on whose body the gods sleep between the destruction of the world and its recreation.

(*Music fades.*)

PEN TIP: Well?

NGOR: I'm not taking this temple apart.

PEN TIP: Hey, you're not going to get precious with me, now. I'm giving you a chance to rehabilitate yourself.

NGOR: Don't! Don't think about it. I don't exist to you. I have no name to you. I have no birth.

PEN TIP: Then do it for your sweetie.

NGOR: Worry about your own sweetie.

PEN TIP: What sweetie?

NGOR: What happened?

PEN TIP: My Angka bride? We had a falling out. Things disappear.
(*Pause. He hands Ngor a hatchet.*)
Lucky, you live in a little bubble with your sweetie. Haven't you learned, it's not enough any more to sit around sipping cognac. You have to bend a little.

NGOR: Kiss the feet of Uncle Mao.

PEN TIP: Show appreciation for your friends. Earn merit. Didn't prison teach you anything?
(*Pause. Ngor stares hard at Pen Tip.*)
Ah, Lucky, don't you see we're like two brothers. Practically twins. You try to control your fate by doing nothing. I try to control my fate by doing something. But this is Year Zero. You have to *do* something to improve your kama.

NGOR: And just what are you doing to improve your kama, Pen Tip?

PEN TIP: I'm scratching out a little worm hole on the carcass of the Khmer Rouge. Just as Lon Nol scratched out a worm hole on the carcass of the C.I.A. Just as you scratched out a worm hole on the carcass of Phnom Penh.

(*Pause.*)

So, Lucky. Grab your hatchet.

NGOR: No.

PEN TIP: "Let's launch an offensive to conquer the elements and master our glorious destiny!"

NGOR: I won't do it.

PEN TIP: (*Laughing.*) Yes, you will, Lucky. I know you. Yes, you will.

(*Ngor grabs his hatchet and is about to attack Pen Tip who faces him with his own hatchet.*)

If not for yourself, then for your sweetie.

(*They climb the ladders to the top of the temple. Buddhist music. Pen Tip addresses the audience.*)

He climbed to the roof and started prying rafters loose with his hatchet under the eyes of Lord Buddha, the eyes of the Nagas, the eyes of Angka and the eyes of Pen Tip.

(*Music fades.*

In silhouette, we see a figure raise a bucket on a long pole.

Houy enters.)

Bonjour, cherie, bonjour. Oh, pardon my French.

HUOY: I don't speak French.

PEN TIP: No one speaks French any more, isn't that funny? So, greetings, comrade sister. How do you sleep?

HUOY: Well, thank you, comrade brother. And you?

PEN TIP: Like a baby. I've brought you some soap.

HUOY: We're not dirty. (*She refuses the soap.*)

PEN TIP: Your husband's dirty. Working on the shit brigade. Mixing fertilizer in his bucket. Don't you mind the smell?

HUOY: I'm used to it. It smells sweet to me now.

PEN TIP: Aren't you afraid it will rub off on you? I can help you stay clean.

(*Holds out the soap again.*)

HUOY: I make my own soap, thank you.

PEN TIP: Well, you never know when you'll need some soap. If you ever run out, you know who to come to. I've tried my best to rehabilitate your husband but – he's so lop-lop – he continues to break the rules.

HUOY: What rules?

PEN TIP: I think he's stealing food and hiding it under the night soil.

HUOY: No.

PEN TIP: No? I'll take your word for it. But then maybe you can help me get your husband to be more cooperative.

HUOY: He obeys Uncle Mao in everything.

PEN TIP: Not everything. Uncle Mao told him to put salt in the shit.

HUOY: My husband says fertilizer doesn't need salt.

PEN TIP: Uncle Mao says the shit needs salt. So the shit needs salt. Don't you agree?

(*Pause.*)

HUOY: Tell Uncle Mao he is welcome to taste it. You may taste it too if you like. We would value your opinion.

PEN TIP: Thank you, no. I'll just pass your message along.

HUOY: Yes, write it down in your big black book.

(*Ngor sits upstage and speaks to the audience. Pen Tip stands off to the side holding wood blocks. Huoy kneels downstage peeling an orange, listening.*)

NGOR: To be tortured once is one thing; to be tortured twice is unthinkable. Your mind invents the pain before it happens. You imagine it over and over again. You become your own torturer.

(*Sound of wood blocks: BAM! BAM!*)

They beat me with a bamboo pole . . .

(*Sound of wood blocks: BAM! BAM!*) . . .

– and leave me on a mound of ants.

(*Sound of wood blocks: BAM! BAM!*)

They throw me in a suffocating oven on a floor of human waste.

(*Sound of wood blocks: BAM! BAM!*)

That night I hear the prowling wolves, the chkai chor-chork, gnawing on corpses. The next morning they lock my wrists and ankles into brackets on the ground. The King of Death appears before me holding a vise. The vise is studded with spikes. He clamps my skull in this vise of spikes. And hangs above my head a pail of water.

(*Naga Man, the figure in silhouette, holds the bucket on a pole high above Ngor's head. He wears the mask of the King of Death.*)

Now I know my torture.

PEN TIP: Drop.

   (*Loudspeaker amplifies the sound: DROP.*)

NGOR: A drop.

PEN TIP: Drop.

   (*Sound of water: DROP.*)

NGOR: A drop of water leaks from a pinhole in the pail.

PEN TIP: Drop.

   (*Sound of water: DROP.*)

NGOR: Drops onto a soft spot in the middle of my forehead.

PEN TIP: Drop.

   (*Sound of water: DROP.*)

NGOR: Drops fall like pebbles. Like needles. Like nails. After a while I
   close my eyes. I feel a weight on the soft spot in the middle of
   my forehead, a weight on my eyes, pressing down on my eyes,
   pressing down through my eyes to a hole in my brain.

   (*Sound: DROP DROP DROP.*)

   Yes, I'm a Captain Doctor.

   (*Sound: DROP.*)

   Yes, kill the Captain Doctor.

   (*Sound: DROP.*)

   Kill me, please.

   (*Sound: DROP.*)

   Kill me now.

PEN TIP: Drop. Drop. Drop.

   (*Sound: DROP DROP DROP.*)

NGOR: But – no, no, no, I say nothing, nothing – some small part of
   my brain reminds me: first they kill the Captain Doctor, then they
   kill the Doctor's wife. I see my sweet thrown on the ant hill, food
   for wolves, and I keep my lips shut tight.

PEN TIP: Drop.

   (*Sound: DROP.*)

NGOR: I go numb.

   (*Sound: DROP.*)

PEN TIP: Drop.

   (*Sound: DROP.*)

NGOR: Brain – numb.

PEN TIP: Drop.

   (*Sound: DROP.*)

NGOR: Body – numb.

PEN TIP: Drop. Drop. Drop.

(*Sound: DROP DROP DROP.*)

NGOR: I send a message on the wind saying goodbye to my sweet. I sink down inside myself to await the King of Death. I pray he comes quickly. I welcome him in. In that deep place, safe inside, I see . . . I see a face. At last, a face. The face of . . .

(*Pause.*)

. . . sweet? Her face. I see her face. She's looking at me, she's studying me, with her big round eyes.

(*Pause.*)

She's holding something in her lap. Cradling something in her lap, cupped in her soft hands. She wants me to have it, wants me to take it, holds it out to me . . .

(*Huoy holds it out to him.*)

. . . an orange.

(*We continue to hear the sound of dropping water.*)

HUOY: When we go back . . .

NGOR: Yes.

HUOY: Go back home . . .

NGOR; Yes.

HUOY: I'm going to get revenge.

NGOR: Yes.

HUOY: Do you know how I'm going to get revenge?

(*Pause.*)

I'm going to get you into bed.

NGOR: Good.

HUOY: And I'm going to make love to you day and night.

NGOR: Good.

HUOY: Until you can't make love any more. And do you know what I'm going to do after we make love.

(*Pause.*)

I'm going to make babies.

NGOR: Babies?

HUOY: Lots of babies. And those babies are going to grow up and I am going to tell them who did this to you and they'll remember. They'll know – all of your sons and daughters – they'll never forget what you've been through.

(*She rolls the orange towards him and exits.*

The King of Death throws the bucket of water on him and exits with Pen Tip.)

NGOR: The next thing I know, I open my eyes. The sun is a fireball on the horizon and the sky is blazing with flames of orange, beautiful beyond belief.

CROSSING THE WATERS

The sound of drops transforms into rain. A sign appears on a screen: "Crossing the Waters." Naga Woman and the Classical Dancer perform a "kama" ceremony. Huoy does a "kama" ritual, too.

HUOY: (*To the audience.*) The rains came. The sky turned dark and the cool wind shook the trees.

NAGA WOMAN: Take refuge in the dharma.
Take refuge in the law.

HUOY: Buds sprouted, the rice turned green, and fish and crabs swam in the pools.

NAGA WOMAN: Preah put, preah thor, preah sang.

HUOY: Preah put, preah thor, preah sang.

NAGA WOMAN: Spin the wheel of the dharma. Spin the wheel of the law.

HUOY: (*To Ngor.*) When I first saw you I wept for joy, then I saw your wounds and wept for pity, and then I started grieving for your soul.

NAGA WOMAN: The law of kama is very simple. Cause and effect . . .

HUOY: (*Overlapping.*) Cause and effect.

NAGA WOMAN: If you do bad you will suffer for it in this life or another.

HUOY: (*Overlapping.*) – in this life or another.

NAGA WOMAN: If you do good you will gain merit in this life or another.

HUOY: (*Overlapping.*) – in this life or another. Spin the wheel of the dharma. Spin the wheel of the law.
(*Naga Woman continues to recite:*
"Preah put, preah sang, preah thor.
"Spin the wheel, spin the wheel, spin the wheel . . . "
Pen Tip enters.)

PEN TIP: You sent for me, comrade sister?

HUOY: Yes, comrade brother. I want to serve Angka.

PEN TIP: I'm sure Angka welcomes your services.

HUOY: But I cannot serve Angka if I must care for my husband. And my husband cannot serve Angka in his weak condition.

PEN TIP: What can I do? I'm no doctor.

HUOY: You could talk to Uncle Mao on our behalf. Perhaps he would transfer us to the back lines. On the back lines, I could nurse my sweet back to health. Then we could work for Angka.

PEN TIP: Why would I do that?

HUOY: To gain merit.

PEN TIP: With you?

HUOY: With the Lord of the Universe.

(*Pause.*)

PEN TIP: Does my influence extend that high?

(*Pen Tip claps his hands. Naga Man appears carrying bamboo.*
"House" music. Naga Man & Woman do a "house building" dance with the bamboo. The Classical Dancer presides over the spirit of the house.
Pen Tip presides over the building of the house. He addresses the audience.)

They built their house of thatch and it was strong. They built it on a hill to keep it dry. Water, sprinkled on the dirt floor, kept it cool. Windows in the roof let in the air. Banana trees along the south side gave them shade. The thatch protected them from sun and rain.

(*Pause. Naga Man & Woman exit.*)

And I joined them on the back lines. Safe on the back lines. And watched her – everyday I watched her – plant her garden.

HUOY: (*To the audience.*) Yams, taro, arrowroot. Onions, pumpkins, beans and corn.

(*She chases chickens around laughing.*)

Ducks and chickens. Chickens and ducks. The ducks had ducklings, the chickens had chicks. I love to carry them to the termite mounds and hear them peck and squeak.

(*Ngor throws a net over Huoy's face.*)

NGOR: Close your eyes. Sweet, close your eyes.

HUOY: What?

NGOR: I have something for you. Smell it.

HUOY: What? (*Pause.*) A milk fish! A milk fish! How . . . ?
NGOR: I caught it with our mosquito net.
(*She keeps hugging him while he is awkwardly holding the fish.*)
Sweet, we can't just stand here with this fish. Hide it! If a chhlop should see . . . Why are you crying?
HUOY: I'm happy, sweet. I'm happy.
NGOR: I have an idea.
HUOY: What idea, sweet?
NGOR: Let's go to America.
HUOY: America?
NGOR: The dogs eat out of cans in America.
HUOY: But we can't . . .
NGOR: But someday . . .
HUOY: Someday.
NGOR: Soon. The cracks are showing. Everyone is stealing food now. There's talk of Vietnam invading from the north. Saigon they say has fallen. I tell you, Angka cannot last.
HUOY: Can *we?*
NGOR: If we keep our minds strong.
HUOY: I don't have much mind left.
NGOR: I know. So I traded a fish . . . for this.
(*Pulls out a book; she pulls away in fear.*)
HUOY: Hide it! Hide it!
NGOR: Just look.
HUOY: What is it?
NGOR: English. We'll study English.
(*He hides the book.*)
HUOY: Study English?
(*Perking up, making the connections.*)
Ah, we learn English, and go to America.
NGOR: Exactly.
(*Handing her the book.*)
Want to hear English?
HUOY: You know English?
NGOR: Listen!
HUOY: (*To the audience.*) And he started speaking words that sounded so enchanting, like magic incantations, like ancient prayers.
(*Ngor and Huoy recite the lesson with stylized formality, like an*

ancient prayer.
Prayer music.)

NGOR: Have you tea? Have you any tea?

HUOY: Of course, madam, how much you want?

NGOR: Two pounds, sir, and box of biscuit.

HUOY: You want butter?

NGOR: No, thanks. Got plenty home.

HUOY: Pay you, please, one pound twenty.

NGOR: Oh, dear. Got only one pound.

(*To the audience.*) I like that: "Oh dear! Got only one pound!"

HUOY: Don't you worry, madam. Pay next time.

NGOR: Thanks much, sir. You are so kind.

HUOY: You are so kind.

NGOR: You are so kind.

(*They laugh.*)

HUOY: America!

NGOR: America!

HUOY: I'll wear my silk in America.

NGOR: Of course, of course.

HUOY: You know, I have been thinking of going on a journey, too.

NGOR: What journey?

HUOY: Oh, some place nice.

NGOR: Like America.

HUOY: Better than America.

NGOR: What could be better than America?

HUOY: Crossing the waters.

NGOR: Crossing the waters?

(*Pause, realizing what she is saying.*)

Oh, crossing the waters? A baby! A baby!

HUOY: Do you want a boy or a girl?

NGOR: I want a little version of you. A little apsara. A little angel.

(*Fiercely, to her belly.*) Do you hear? An angel! An angel!

HUOY: (*Laughing.*) Don't scare her. Gently, gently.

(*She opens his fists and places his hands on her belly.
The Classical Dancer gestures, bringing on the vision of the
Teenage Girl who appears singing her song: "Sareka Kai-oi."*)

END OF ACT ONE

ACT TWO

THE AUDITION

Rock & Roll like the Eagles' HOTEL CALIFORNIA. A sign on a screen says, "The Audition."
Naga Man & Woman confused, disoriented, do a stylized "transit" dance with suitcases wearing transit numbers: "T#62147," "T#62148" etc.
Ngor enters wearing a sports coat, American dress. Naga Man & Woman transform into Refugee Man & Woman. Ngor sits them down, talks to them forcefully.

NGOR: This is welfare check. This is food stamp.
REFUGEE MAN: (*Trying to understand.*) Check . . . ?
REFUGEE WOMAN: Stamp . . . ?
NGOR: Take food stamp to Supermarket.
REFUGEE MAN: Super . . . ? Super . . . ?
NGOR: Market. Take welfare check to Trust Bank. (*French pronunciation.*) Banque.
REFUGEE WOMAN: Ah, banque.
REFUGEE MAN: Luk, som meta, please you show me?
NGOR: Te! Te! You do yourself.
REFUGEE WOMAN: Too much, luk, it is too much.
NGOR: (*Forcefully, but not unkindly.*) No, eat your pride. Lose face. But do for yourself. Think like me: "I am not bigshot American. I am not helpless refugee. I am animal from jungle. I have just escaped my cage."
   (*Ngor hands them checks and stamps. Refugees exit.*
   Pen Tip enters.)
PEN TIP: He lives in a little apartment outside LA. He drives a little Volkswagen to work. His Volkswagen has a leaky valve. His apartment has a leaky faucet.
   (*Sound of water drops.*)
   Drop. Drop. Drop.
   (*Sound of water drops.*)
   He drives home. He drives to work. He does his work. He drives home.
   (*Sound of water drops.*)

Drop. Drop. Drop. He doesn't think about it. He makes himself invisible.

(*Sound of water drops.*)

Dam doum kor.

(*More rock music like HOTEL CALIFORNIA.*)

But then one day he goes to a wedding party. A Cambodian wedding. All the refugees are there.

(*Naga Woman steps out in a "longnose" mask, the mask of a western woman. She transforms to Longnose Woman, with a Polaroid flash camera.*)

LONGNOSE WOMAN: Excuse me. Can I take your picture?

NGOR: Why?

LONGNOSE WOMAN: It's for a movie.

NGOR: What movie?

LONGNOSE WOMAN: A Cambodian movie.

NGOR: Thank you. I only go to American movie.

LONGNOSE WOMAN: We're *making* a Cambodian movie.

NGOR: No. "Ghost Busters" – what I like.

LONGNOSE WOMAN: Please, I'm auditioning practically everyone here.

NGOR: I don't want. I am not your Hollywood guy.

(*Suddenly, music changes to traditional rom vong dance. Backlit, as shadow figures, Naga Man is seen dancing with Huoy in her wedding dress.*)

LONGNOSE WOMAN: There are no forms to fill out. It'll just take . . .

NGOR: Look. They dance the "rom vong." Long time now since I dance the rom vong.

LONGNOSE WOMAN: Here's my phone number . . .

(*Pause.*)

In case you change your mind.

(*Naga Man and Huoy continue to dance.*)

PEN TIP: And that night he lies in bed listening to his leaky faucet and dreaming of the bride dancing in her wedding dress.

(*Lights up for an instant on Huoy dancing with the Naga Man who wears the mask of the King of Death.*)

(*Lights up on audition room.*)

LONGNOSE WOMAN: Okay, Haing, imagine you are a Cambodian doctor.

NGOR: Yes.

LONGNOSE MAN: And imagine you are in love with an American nurse.

(*Speaking of Longnose Woman.*) A beautiful American nurse. (*They laugh.*)

NGOR: Yes.

LONGNOSE MAN: And imagine the Khmer Rouge is about to overrun the city. What do you say to your lover?
(*Pause.*)

NGOR: You haf to leave right now. You haf to listen me. You – you are American. You are longnose. Khmer Rouge don't like you. Khmer Rouge break you. For me no problem. I am Cambodian. I am doctor. Khmer Rouge does not hurt Cambodian doctor.

LONGNOSE WOMAN: Okay, let's change the set up. I'm your Cambodian wife. I have to get on a helicopter with the children because the Khmer Rouge is coming. How do you break the news to me?

NGOR: Now.

LONGNOSE MAN: Whenever you're ready.
(*Pause.*)

NGOR: Sweet, sweet, my mother worries for you. She says maybe you must go away now – go to Paris. Voulez a Paree! Voulez a Paree! Voulez a Paree! (*Pause. He has surprised himself by his own urgency.*)
I sorry. You want English, I think.

LONGNOSE MAN: No. No. You're doing fine. We'll just do one more. This one won't be such a downer.

NGOR: A downer?

LONGNOSE WOMAN: Not so sad, okay?

NGOR: Okay.

LONGNOSE WOMAN: Suppose you have a patient on the operating table . . .
(*She lays down for an operation, like the woman in the Operating Room Scene, Act I.*)
And it's a very difficult operation – you don't expect her to pull through – but then, against all odds, you save her. You save her! What is your reaction?
(*Pause. Ngor looks into his memories and can't take it. He exits.*)
Haing? Haing?
(*Sound of an airplane.*)

PEN TIP: On the airplane to Thailand you still don't know what part you are supposed to play.
(*Sound of explosion.*)

But then at first rehearsal, the director, Roland Joffe, tells you that you will play Dith Pran. The main role! The lead! The star!

(*Sound of explosion.*)

LOUDSPEAKER: Please fasten your seatbelts and prepare for landing.

PEN TIP: Thousands audition and you get the part! You must have done something right, Lucky, in some past life.

(*Sound of explosion.*)

LOUDSPEAKER: Welcome to Bangkok.

PEN TIP: Welcome home.

(*Awful Chinese marching music from the Evacuation of Phnom Penh Scene. Images repeat from Act I.*)

KHMER ROUGE GIRL/LOUDSPEAKER: The wheel of history is turning. The wheel of history rolls on. This is the start of the New Year! This is Year Zero! This is Year Zero! This is Year Zero!

(*Ngor enters dressed in black pajamas of a war slave.*)

LONGNOSE MAN: Cut!

(*Music stops. We are on the set of "The Killing Fields:" bright lights, boom mikes; Longnose Woman holds a clipboard, Longnose Man holds a script and coaches Ngor.*)

So you are standing in the mud on the front lines in the pouring rain. And you see a lizard. And you grab that lizard. And you think…?

NGOR: Lizard. Tasty!

(*Longnose Man nods to Longnose Woman.*)

LONGNOSE WOMAN: Lizard Scene. Take one.

(*Sound of the clapboard.*)

LONGNOSE MAN: So while the guards are napping in the heat of the day, you sneak up on an ox to drink its blood. Fake blood, of course. So, you cut a vein open in the ox's neck. And you think…?

NGOR: Maybe I chop off the tail of this fucking ox.

(*Longnose Man nods to Longnose Woman.*)

LONGNOSE WOMAN: Ox Scene. Take Three.

(*Sound of the clapboard.*)

LONGNOSE MAN: So. You sneak away on your belly in the flooded rice fields and just as you think you have made your escape, you slip into a swamp of skulls and bones. Skulls and bones as far as the eye can see. And you think…?

(*Pause.*)

NGOR: (*Whispering.*) "Birth is suffering, old age is suffering, sickness is suffering, death is suffering . . . " (*Etc.*)

(*Longnose Man nods to Longnose Woman.*)

LONGNOSE WOMAN: (*Overlapping.*) Bones Scene. Take two.

(*Lights change. We are back in Cambodia. A sign on a screen says: "The Noble Truths." The Classical Dancer appears in a prayer dance. Huoy's voice is heard overlapping with Ngor's.*)

THE NOBLE TRUTHS

HUOY: "Birth is suffering . . .
   Old age is suffering . . .
   Sickness is suffering . . .
   Death is suffering . . . "

NGOR: (*Whispering.*) What are you doing?

HUOY: I'm teaching the Noble Truths to baby.
   (*Continues praying.*)
   "Sorrow is suffering . . .
   Pain is suffering . . .
   Grief is suffering . . .
   Despair is suffering . . . "

NGOR: (*Whispering.*) Baby isn't born yet.

HUOY: She can learn inside. She has to learn inside.

NGOR: Why?
   (*Pause. She looks at Ngor and, then, answers:*)

HUOY: "Being with those you hate is suffering.
   Separation from those you love is suffering."

NGOR: Go to bed! I'll find you some food.

HUOY: There is no food. We've eaten the flowers off the pumpkins, all the buds off the yams.

NGOR: It's like a plague of locust out there. Everybody's foraging.

HUOY: They've eaten the chicks. There won't be chickens. They've eaten the ducklings. There won't be ducks. The baby will be a monster.

NGOR: She won't be a . . .

HUOY: A monster! A monster! At least let me die on the road so someone can eat me. People eat people now like chkai chor-chork, like cannibals.

NGOR: You're not going to die. The Khmer Rouge is falling apart.

They're purging each other. They're destroying themselves.

HUOY: Too late. If there is no food, the baby will be retarded.

NGOR: I've examined you. The baby will be fine.

HUOY: Even if the baby's fine, there will be no milk.

NGOR: Your breasts will make milk automatically. Believe me, I'm your doctor.

HUOY: But not enough milk. If there's not enough food, there's not enough milk. Isn't that right, Doctor? Isn't that right?

(*Pause.*)

Doctor?

(*Ngor hesitates. Lights change and we are back on the set of "The Killing Fields".*)

NGOR: I-I . . .

(*He breaks out of the scene.*)

LONGNOSE MAN: Cut!

NGOR: I can't do. I am no good.

LONGNOSE MAN: But you're doing fine.

NGOR: No good. No good. I don't know what to do.

LONGNOSE WOMAN: Haing, just do what comes naturally.

NGOR: But I am no actor. I don't know nothing how to act.

LONGNOSE WOMAN: Don't worry. Don't think about it. You were there.

NGOR: Yes, that is trouble. I was there. But Dith Pran is hero. How do Dith Pran talk? How do Dith Pran act? I do better if I do Dith Pran.

LONGNOSE WOMAN: Haing, don't worry about Dith Pran. As far as we're concerned, you are Dith Pran.

NGOR: I am Dith Pran?

LONGNOSE WOMAN: Dith Pran is you.

(*Pause.*)

So . . . Don't act, just . . . Be yourself.

NGOR: (*Despairingly.*) Myself.

LONGNOSE MAN: This is a story of love and friendship . . .

(*From the shadows we hear Huoy's voice, a distant echo.*)

HUOY: (*Overlapping.*) This is a story of love and friendship.

LONGNOSE MAN: – of the bond between two human beings.

HUOY: – of the bond between two human beings.

LONGNOSE MAN: An unbreakable bond.

HUOY: An unbreakable bond.

(*Pause.*)

LONGNOSE MAN: Do you know that bond?

(*Pause.*)

NGOR: I know. I know.

LONGNOSE WOMAN: Then you can play this role.

PEN TIP: (*To the audience.*) And so to strengthen that bond and to make you Dith Pran, the director sends you and your co-star, Sam Waterston, to a refugee camp on the Thai border to interview real refugees.

(*Naga Man & Woman transform into refugees and stand beside Pen Tip in a refugee "camp." Ngor approaches them acting as an interpreter with a notebook.*)

NGOR: (*To Pen Tip.*) Do you have enough to eat?

PEN TIP: (*To the audience.*) You translate to Sam Waterston, the movie star, just like Dith Pran translated for his boss, Sydney Schanberg, a reporter for the New York Times.

NGOR: (*To Pen Tip.*) Do you have enough medicine?

PEN TIP: (*To the audience.*) The acting exercise goes along smoothly until:

(*Pen Tip faces Ngor.*)

– you come across a Khmer Rouge collaborator.

NGOR: Do you have enough weapons?

(*Pause. They stare at each other.*)

PEN TIP: And he stares at you. And you stare at him. And you both get very . . . very . . . quiet.

(*Pause.*)

"Frere Jacques, Frere Jacques . . ." (*Etc.*)

(*Pen Tip walks out of the scene in the refugee camp. We are back in Cambodia.*)

(*Singing.*) "Frere Jacques, Frere Jacques,

Dormais vous, Dormais vous . . ." (*Etc.*)

(*Pen Tip watches Huoy sleeping, speaks softly in her ear.*)

Sleep baby sleep. Sleep while you can. Make yourself invisible. It's too hot to do anything else.

Out here it's the hot season, perfect weather for purges. Everything withers. Dust chokes your lungs. The pools dry up. The lizards shrivel. Creatures even eat each other when they mate.

HUOY: Get out of here!

PEN TIP: Ah, you're awake . . .

HUOY: Get out!

PEN TIP: Shhhh!

HUOY: GET OUT!

PEN TIP: Here!

(*He holds out a pile of palm sugar wrapped in a broad leaf.*)

Sugar. For the baby.

(*Huoy reaches for it. Takes her hand away.*)

HUOY: My husband will kill you if he finds you here.

PEN TIP: Ah, but he'll be out all night. A thief in the night. With no food to steal. All the food disappears in box cars heading north to (*Chanting.*) "Fight the imperialist Vietnamese invaders!" What will become of baby?

HUOY: What do you care?

PEN TIP: I care for your good health. And baby's.

(*Pause.*)

Uncle Mao wants me to bury sugar outside the huts of his enemies. Your husband is one of his enemies. I thought I should warn you.

HUOY: Please – I have no birth to you. I have no name.

PEN TIP: But then who will be your friend when your husband's dead and gone?

HUOY: My husband is already dead. He's died three times. Haven't you heard? He's the King of Death. You can't kill him, no one can.

PEN TIP: Oh, that's not true. All he has to do is deliver your baby. Then they'll know for certain he's a Captain Doctor. And then he'll disappear. (*Pause.*) And then you'll disappear. (*Pause.*) And then your baby.

HUOY: He's a taxi driver. Someone else will deliver my baby.

PEN TIP: There! Already I have contributed to your health. And baby's.

HUOY: Go!!

PEN TIP: Don't you understand? I just want . . .

(*He steps toward her.*)

HUOY: Never!

PEN TIP: (*Whispering urgently.*) Never say never. In this graveyard, you never know what small act of tenderness, of generosity, perhaps even of love . . . Can be the difference between life and death.

HUOY: Get away from me, you awful, evil man!

PEN TIP: Careful, comrade sister, or I'll "get angry."

(*He approaches her. She steps back.*)

See, that's just another little pun. When a man "gets angry" with a woman it means he also gets . . .

HUOY: I know what he gets.

(*She kneels to pray.*)

Spin the wheel of the dharma, spin the wheel of the law,

Spin the wheel of the dharma, spin the wheel of the law . . . (*Etc.*)

(*Pen Tip backs off.*)

PEN TIP: (*Overlapping the prayer.*) I'll leave the sugar for baby anyway. If you eat it, they can't use it against your husband . . .

(*Huoy stops praying.*)

. . . and at least I'll know you're thinking of me. That alone is some comfort.

(*Pen Tip starts to exit.*)

The greatest gift in the whole wide world is a full belly.

(*Huoy, alone, looks at the sugar. She hesitates, then speaks to the audience.*)

HUOY: Sugar. I love sugar. I love to suck on something sweet. I'm so sick in the mornings – sweets are the only thing I can keep down.

But I won't eat it right away. First I pray. For its soul, as if it had a soul, as if it were a living thing. I offer it up to Lord Buddha. Then I offer it up to my mother. And then I offer it up to my baby. And then I eat.

(*Eats the sugar.*)

It begins as a tingling on the tip of my tongue. Not a taste, but a tingling. That shivers the hairs on the back of my neck. Then the sweet shock washes over the sides of my mouth, and water floods up from under my cheeks. My heart begins to pound and I feel giddy, weak. Like something's tickling me. Something out of reach.

And . . . I swallow. Swallow it. A soothing flame penetrates my throat, opens my throat, spreads like a wound in my breast. Like a blood wound. Like a stain.

For a moment I feel I'm dying but then this . . . this noise comes up from my belly, from my bowels and I have to breathe, have to catch my breath. I want to growl. I want to roar.

I hold my belly. Hold my baby. The walls of my womb quiver. Inside I think I feel my baby twitch and shake from all this sugar.

I laugh. She laughs. We laugh and laugh, sucking on sugar, me and my dancing baby.
(*Lights fade.*)

Lights up on Khmer Rouge Girl, the spy, the chhlop.
She points at Ngor who puts his hands behind his head. She points at Pen Tip who puts his hands behind his head.
She signals them to stand together.

PEN TIP: What's happening? What's this all about?

NGOR: You made a big mistake this time, Pen Tip. I never stole any sugar. You set me up.

PEN TIP: I didn't set you up.

NGOR: You buried sugar in my garden.

PEN TIP: I brought sugar to your wife. For your baby.

NGOR: Oh, sure. This purge is going to backfire. I reported you to the King of Death. I told him all about you and your lies.

PEN TIP: But I saved you. I spared you. Your wife ate the sugar!

NGOR: Good joke. Tell it to Angka. They're going to get *you* this time.

PEN TIP: You think they'll listen to you? Against me?

NGOR: Oh, yes. Angka's scared to death of phoney accusations. They set one another up all the time. They know your kind will turn on them one day.

PEN TIP: Samnang, this is lop-lop.

NGOR: No. It's time you met the King of Death. He knows me. He knows I would never come before him unless I was a virgin.
(*Sound of a motorcycle. King of Death appears.*)

PEN TIP: Samnang, listen to me.

NGOR: Beg for your life, comrade.

PEN TIP: He will kill us both.

NGOR: Beg.
(*They both fall to their knees, heads bowed.*
The King of Death hovers over them. Then he takes off his mask, and becomes Longnose Man.)

LONGNOSE MAN: Torture Scene. Take one.
(*Sound of clapboard.*)

NGOR: W-what scene are we in?
(*A sign appears on a screen: "Torture Scene. Take One."*)

TORTURE SCENE: TAKE ONE.

Ngor is tied back-to-back with Pen Tip, and hung up as in Act I.

LONGNOSE MAN: (*To Ngor.*) Dith Pran is caught stealing food and so the Khmer Rouge tie him to a tree and beat him. Of course, there's padding in your costume and, don't worry, the actors are going to beat you with just a very light bamboo pole.
(*Sound of clapboard.*)

TORTURE SCENE: TAKE TWO

PEN TIP: (*Whispering to Ngor.*) But then the bamboo breaks and is replaced by mistake by a heavy, wooden bat. And the bat misses the padding . . .
(*Sound of clapboard.*)

TORTURE SCENE: TAKE THREE

PEN TIP: (*Cont.*) Misses the padding in your costume. And . . .
(*Sound of clapboard. Ngor's body twitches as in Act I.*)

TORTURE SCENE: TAKE FOUR

Sound of clapboard. Ngor's body twitches.

TORTURE SCENE: TAKE FIVE

Sound of clapboard. Ngor's body twitches.

NGOR: Taxi! Taxi!
LONGNOSE MAN: Cut! Are you okay? Haing? Haing?
PEN TIP: Then someone on the set offers you a cigarette and . . .
(*Pen Tip gestures; flick of a lighter.*)
Flick.
(*Ngor and Pen Tip, still back-to-back as if tied together, sink to the ground.*
Rock music like HOTEL CALIFORNIA.)
NGOR: (*To Pen Tip.*) Yes, it made me think of you, Pen Tip, my twin.

But – dam doum kor – that night at the hotel I went to a party with the cast and crew as if nothing had happened. What a feast!

PEN TIP: A feast?

NGOR: Milk fish in garlic lemon sauce. Fried chicken. Corn on the cob. And what a scene.

PEN TIP: What a scene!

NGOR: Men and women of both races who had been in the Killing Fields just this morning, now laughing and dancing to that mean Western music. The kind you would've liked. I wish you could've been there.

PEN TIP: So, did you eat? Did you dance?

NGOR: No, I just went to my room and lay there. Thinking of you. Of you and me. In our jail cell. Pleading for our lives over a cup of sugar. Until late at night, in the prison of my mind, a thought came stalking, stalking like the chkai chor-chork. A thought you would have understood. The thought was "kum."

PEN TIP: (*In the dark.*) Ah, kum.

NGOR: Yes, "kum." This movie will be my revenge.

(*A flickering "fire" light begins to glow as they sit back-to-back talking and we are back in Cambodia.*)

PEN TIP: Shhhh. Voices.

NGOR: What voices?

PEN TIP: Voices! Outside the prison.

NGOR: The dead.

PEN TIP: What?

NGOR: The dead. Whispering your name (*Like a ghost.*) "Pen Tip . . . "

PEN TIP: Shut up.

NGOR: "Pen Tip . . . Pen Tip . . . "

PEN TIP: Don't talk like that, Lucky.

NGOR: What's the matter, comrade. Nervous, waiting for the King of Death?

PEN TIP: Stop it! Stop it! We can still get out of this. Say we made a mistake about the sugar. Support each other's stories.

(*Ngor laughs.*)

We have to stop this or we'll both disappear.

NGOR: But I'm invisible already.

PEN TIP: You like this?

NGOR: Yes, it makes me feel alive. Alive and . . .

PEN TIP: There it is again. Voices . . .

(*Ngor is suddenly on the alert.*)

NGOR: On the roof.

PEN TIP: On the thatch.

NGOR: (*Softly.*) Fire.

PEN TIP: Fire.

    (*Roar of fire. Naga Man & Woman do a "torch" dance. Ngor and Pen Tip pull each other up looking through the "flames."*)

NGOR: The roof!

PEN TIP: Burning!

NGOR: Torches!

PEN TIP: Screaming!

NGOR: Look out!

PEN TIP: (*Crying out.*) Fallllllling . . .

NGOR: Quick. The door.

PEN TIP: I can't.

NGOR: The flames!

PEN TIP: I can't.

NGOR: Get up.

PEN TIP: My leg.

NGOR: Stand up.

PEN TIP: I can't! I can't!

    (*Ngor puts Pen Tip on his back.*)

NGOR: Now!

    (*They cry out and break through the "torch" dance.*
    Looking back, Pen Tip tells what is happening in the prison as the fires die down.)

PEN TIP: Look! The prison. See! The torches. It's the guards. The guards! The guards are throwing the torches. They're setting fire to their own prison. They're burning their own prison down! Look, Lucky, look! It's the beginning of the end.

NGOR: Yes. Yes, Pen Tip, for you – for *you* – the beginning of the end.

    (*Naga Man & Woman loom ominously over Ngor and Pen Tip and with the "torches" cut their bonds. Pen Tip exits.*
    Naga Man & Woman transform into Longnose Man and Woman.)

LONGNOSE WOMAN: Break's over.

LONGNOSE MAN: Ready on the set.

    (*Ngor is lost in memory.*)
    Ready?

NGOR: Oh . . . Oh, thank you.

LONGNOSE MAN: Haing, are you okay? We're really sorry about the torture scene.

NGOR: No, that is okay. That is good for me?

LONGNOSE MAN: Good? How come?

NGOR: We have the saying, "the medicine is in the poison, the poison is in the medicine."

LONGNOSE MAN: Well, look, if you want to take it easy today . . . ?

NGOR: No. I can do this. I have very good training.

LONGNOSE MAN: What training?

NGOR: The Khmer Rouge School of Acting.

(*Huoy enters. We are back in Cambodia.*)

HUOY: (*Excitedly.*) You won. You won.

NGOR: Nobody won. No one even lost face.

HUOY: Did Angka hurt you?

NGOR: No. No, I'm just. Disappointed it's not over. I-I was ready for it to be over. I'm not ready to be back.

HUOY: Pen Tip?

NGOR: He's back too. But not for long.

HUOY: Oh, sweet . . .

(*She gets the sugar that Pen Tip left.*)

Here. Eat. You'll feel better.

NGOR: What is this? What is it?

HUOY: Sugar. I-I saved half of it for you.

NGOR: *His* sugar? You took *his* sugar?!

HUOY: Y-yes. No.

NGOR: You just flash it in the open. After all I've been through.

HUOY: I-I didn't think . . .

NGOR: No you didn't think! This could mean my life.

HUOY: I-I . . .

NGOR: If the spies saw this . . .

HUOY: But there's no one.

NGOR: Always someone. Their chhlops are everywhere. But you don't care. You don't care. You just care about your belly.

HUOY: I didn't mean . . .

NGOR: What do you think they'll feed me this time?

HUOY: Oh, Sweet.

NGOR: Fire?

HUOY: No.

NGOR: Water?

HUOY: No.

NGOR: Or something more delicious?

HUOY: I'm sorry. I'm sorry.

NGOR: Sorry? Sorry? Is that what I should say to them: I'm sorry!

HUOY: Please . . .

NGOR: Don't talk to me. Don't talk! You have no birth to me. You have no name.

HUOY: No.

NGOR: If you say anything to me, I'll never speak to you again. I'll rip you out of my heart.

HUOY: Nooo . . .

NGOR: Do you hear me?

HUOY: Please . . .

NGOR: Not one word. DO YOU HEAR ME!

(*He stops her from talking.*)

Not one word.

(*Lights change. Huoy exits. We are back on the set of "The Killing Fields."*

Ngor, angry and upset, talks out to the audience as if addressing the assistant director.)

Tell Mr. Joffe: I think his movie is not enough cruel. He must make her more cruel if he want to be true.

(*Holding up whip.*)

Take whip. You must whip the war-slave at the plow to show Khmer Rouge working.

(*Holding up plastic bag.*)

Take bag. You must put bag over head of war-slave to show Khmer Rouge killing.

(*Holding up bamboo stick that beat him.*)

Stick is nothing! Stick is toy! Take fire. Take water. This is torture! This is torture!

(*Longnose Woman enters.*)

LONGNOSE WOMAN: He says he'll use the plastic bag but most of the other stuff is too much. He says there's a limit to how much cruelty Western audiences can watch.

NGOR: Yes. Maybe so. (*To the audience.*) We cannot show you everything. Too much. Too much.

LONGNOSE WOMAN: Still, he wants the picture to be authentic. Here . . .

(*Longnose Man appears with Teenage Girl who walks over to Longnose Woman and stands behind her.*)
Maybe you can help.

NGOR: What?

LONGNOSE MAN: We want to cast her as a village spy, as a "chhlop" you would call her.

NGOR: Chhlop?

LONGNOSE MAN: Yes, but she's too shy. She just hides behind her mother's skirt.

NGOR: What can I do?

LONGNOSE WOMAN: Coach her.

NGOR: Coach her? To be chhlop?

LONGNOSE WOMAN: Someone's got to. You were there.

(*Ngor signals for Teenage Girl to step forward. She does this reluctantly.*)

NGOR: Tuck your hair behind ears. Look like boy.

(*Teenage Girl tucks the hair.*

He beckons her in Khmer, "mok ne, mok ne . . . ")

You are suppose to pick people for torture. Okay, pick me for torture. (*Beckoning.*) Mok ne! Mok ne! Don't be shy.

(*She goes up to him, pokes him shyly with finger.*)

That is tickling.

(*She laughs.*)

Do you want to be Khmer Rouge?

(*She nods.*)

Then look at me with power.

(*She tries.*)

No, look right at me. Tilt your head back. Stare down on me. Yes. Let your lower lip and jaw stick out. Yes. Yes. No. Stop.

(*To Longnose Man and Woman.*)

She doesn't have the eyes right. To be Khmer Rouge, she has to get the eyes right.

(*She tries again.*)

Don't blink. Just stare at me. Hard. Hard. Like you hate me. Like you want to hit me. Hit me. HIT ME!

(*She stares at him with power. Ngor backs off with fear and hatred.*)

Eyes. Eyes. Look, look at her eyes! Her eyes. Her eyes.

(*In Khmer.*) Look! Look! Her eyes, her eyes. (*Etc.*)

(*Longnose Man and Woman restrain him.*)

LONGNOSE MAN: What's the matter with you?

NGOR: She's Khmer Rouge! Khmer Rouge! Khmer Rouge!

LONGNOSE MAN: What? She's one of them? What do you mean?

NGOR: I mean . . .

(*Pause.*)

I-I don't know what I mean.

(*Pause.*)

LONGNOSE WOMAN: Half hour everyone!

TALK TO ME

We are back in Cambodia. On a screen: "Talk to Me." The Classical Dancer watches over the household.
Ngor sits with his back to Huoy ignoring her.

HUOY: Sweet . . . ?

(*A chhlop walks by. Ngor stiffens. She stands nearby outside and smokes.*)

Chhlop.

(*Pause. He does not respond.*)

Food is hidden.

(*Pause.*)

One can left.

(*Pause.*)

When she leaves, want to eat?

(*Pause.*)

"Have you any tea?" "Yes, please." "You are so kind."

(*Pause.*)

"You are so kind."

(*She looks at Ngor. He ignores her. She looks away. Ngor looks at her. Then looks away.*)

I won't talk to you. But I have to talk.

(*Pause.*)

You don't have to listen. But I have to talk.

(*Pause.*)

I've been thinking about baby. If something happens to me, someone has to teach her how to sompeah. The children have forgotten how to sompeah.

(*She demonstrates sompeah.*)

Also, they don't know how to feed the monks. There are no monks any more. Someone has to teach her how to honor the monks.

(*She demonstrates, bowing with offerings to the monks.*)

Also, the children don't know their king. Even if he wasn't always a very good king, our baby should know that she has a king. Someone has to teach her that we have a king! There is a king!

(*She turns to him.*)

Where is the king, Sweet!? Where is the king?

(*She kneels before him.*)

Sweet! Talk to me. I was bad. I know I was bad. But please . . . Please . . . Say something.

(*Pause.*)

Anything! Beat me if you want. Beat me. Beat me. But talk to me. Talk to me. Talk, talk, talk, talk, . . . (*Etc.*)

(*She starts to beat herself, hurt herself.*)

NGOR: I'll talk. See! I'm talking! I'm talking. Sweet, I'm talking.

(*He lifts her up, holds her.*)

I'm the bad one sweet. I'm the one who's bad. I don't know why but my heart . . . My heart is . . . Bad. You're my food. You're my drink. You're my body. You're my blood.

(*He kneels before her.*)

I'm going to talk to you and talk to you and talk to you till you grow old.

(*Touching her sampot.*)

What's this?

HUOY: I'm wet.

NGOR: Water?

HUOY: Blood.

NGOR: Lie down, Sweet. Lie down.

(*Longnose Man and Woman enter; Ngor stays with Huoy. We are still in Cambodia, but the filming of "The Killing Fields" goes on behind them like a dream.*

Pen Tip and the chhlop watch from a distance.)

LONGNOSE MAN: "For godsake, Sydney, why didn't you get him out while you had the chance?" That's your cue, Haing. From the top. It's the central scene of the movie. The Embassy Scene. Dith Pran has to leave the French Embassy and say goodbye to Sydney Schanberg.

HUOY: What is it? Tell me? Tell me what it is?

NGOR: Labor. Early labor.

HUOY: Noooo! It's not time. Oh, mama, help me. Help me. It's not time!

LONGNOSE MAN: He knows he's got to go. And he knows he's going to die. And he knows he'll never see his best friend again.

LONGNOSE WOMAN: Rolling. Speed.

NGOR: Tell my wife I love her, Sydney. Tell my wife I love her.

(*Sound of clapboard.*)

HUOY: Water! Water! Where's it all coming from?

NGOR: Your water's breaking. The baby's coming.

(*Holding up two spoons.*)

Here. Let me look. It'll be alright. I promise.

PEN TIP: (*To the audience.*) Alright! Really? A month premature?

(*Ngor examines Huoy.*)

HUOY: Sweet, I had an awful thought. All those bodies on the road – no legs, no heads – when those souls get born again, they won't be born with all their parts.

NGOR: You're only three centimeters.

HUOY: Three centimeters.

NGOR: Contractions getting further apart.

HUOY: Oh, God.

(*Praying.*)

Eyes, ears, mouth, nose. Hands, fingers, feet, toes.

LONGNOSE MAN: (*Softly.*) Take two.

LONGNOSE WOMAN: (*Softly.*) Rolling. Speed.

HUOY: (*Praying.*) Preah put. Preah thor. Preah sang.

Preah put. Preah thor. Preah sang.

NGOR: She doesn't speak any English, Sydney. She doesn't speak any English.

(*Sound of clapboard.*

Huoy feels a pain, grabs Ngor suddenly.)

What? What?

HUOY: (*Whispering.*) The baby! Save the baby!

NGOR: No scalpel. No sutures. No morphine.

HUOY: Please. Please.

NGOR: Listen to me sweet. *You* have to get this baby out. There's a chhlop outside. I can't cut you open. Before I finish the second cut, they'll take me away.

LONGNOSE MAN: Take three.

LONGNOSE WOMAN: Rolling. Speed.

NGOR: Sydney, please, look after my children.

HUOY: Eyesearsmouthnose. Handsfingersfeettoes.
Preahput. Preahthor. Preah . . .

NGOR: Here. Sweet. Sugar. There's still some sugar.

PEN TIP: (*To the audience.*) Ah, the sugar.

NGOR: Gather your strength.
(*He feeds her sugar, bit by bit.*)

HUOY: Talk.

NGOR: About what?

HUOY: Just . . . talk.
(*Pause. Ngor feeds her the last of the sugar.*)

NGOR: Pralines, Sweet. Remember our pralines. Here, eat your
pralines. (*Pause.*) Now I have to press on your belly.

HUOY: No, no . . .

NGOR: I have to, Sweet. I have to.
(*He presses down. She cries out.*)

LONGNOSE MAN: Take four.

LONGNOSE WOMAN: Rolling. Speed.
(*Sound of clapboard.*)

NGOR: Please, don't let anyone be bad to my wife!
(*Presses down. She cries out. Sound of clapboard.*)
Please, don't let anyone be bad to my wife!
(*Presses down. She cries out. Sound of clapboard.*)
Please, don't let anyone be bad to my wife!
(*Presses down. She cries out. Sound of clapboard.*
Blackout. Lights up on Pen Tip. Ngor is seen in silhouette kneeling
before him.)

PEN TIP: He came to me in the middle of the night. He bowed to me
and went down on his knees. He begged me – begged *me* – to
ask Uncle Mao for permission to go to the district hospital to get
a Caesarean section.
(*Pause.*)
And I did it. Yes I did. I went to Uncle Mao. I bowed, bowed
down, down on my knees, pleading for my Lucky. My brother,
Lucky. My twin.
(*To Ngor.*)

I'm sorry. He says the district hospital is out of the question. You're a war-slave. You have no merit. A Caesarean section? He just laughed. Lucky, he doesn't even know what it is!

(*Lights up on Ngor and Huoy.*)

HUOY: (*Weakly.*) Sweet? Sweet?

NGOR: I'm here. I'm . . . (*Presents her wedding silk.*) Here.

HUOY: (*Hugging the silk.*) Good. Hate black.

NGOR: Hate black. Hate black!

HUOY: Shhhh. Shhhh. Gently.

(*She whispers, pulling him down to her.*)

Touch me.

(*He touches her face.*)

Touch you.

(*She touches his face.*)

There.

(*She dies.*)

NGOR: Tell my wife I love her, Sydney. And look after my children. She doesn't speak any English. Please, I don't want anyone to be bad to my wife.

(*Sound of the clapboard.*

Lots of activity, breaking down the set.

Overlapping voices are heard as if from a distance.)

LONGNOSE MAN: It's a keeper.

LONGNOSE WOMAN: That's a wrap.

(*Sound of explosion.*)

LONGNOSE MAN: Okay, let's break it down.

LONGNOSE WOMAN: Nine o'clock tomorrow's call.

(*Sound of explosion.*

The Classical Dancer exits.

Pen Tip looks down on Ngor from a distance.)

PEN TIP: Lucky . . . (*Pause.*) Lucky, it's time to go.

(*Sound of explosion, automatic rifle fire.*)

The Vietnamese army is almost here.

(*Sound of explosion, automatic rifle fire.*)

Angka is moving everyone south.

(*Sound of explosion, automatic weapon fire.*)

Lucky. Do you hear me?

(*They stare at one another.*)

It's over.

(*Pause.*)

It's done.

(*Naga Woman appears as a War-Slave. Naga Man appears as Khmer Rouge Man.*

They do stylized movement with a bamboo pole: War-Slave beating up the Khmer Rouge Man.)

NGOR: (*To the audience.*) On the road I see a man. I see a man in an angry crowd. A well-fed man in a hungry crowd. Dressed in black pajama. His face is swollen, his body bruised. Every time he stumbles, the crowd hauls him up again and shoves him down the road shouting: "Say it. Say it."

WAR-SLAVE/LOUDSPEAKER: Say it! Say it!

NGOR: Say, "I'm Khmer Rouge."

WAR-SLAVE/LOUDSPEAKER: "I'm Khmer Rouge."

NGOR: Louder! Louder!

WAR-SLAVE/LOUDSPEAKER: Louder! Louder!

NGOR: "I'm Khmer Rouge."

WAR-SLAVE/LOUDSPEAKER: "I'm Khmer Rouge."

NGOR: One hit each, they shout. Only one hit each.

WAR-SLAVE/LOUDSPEAKER: One hit each. Only one hit each.

NGOR: You must take turns.

WAR-SLAVE/LOUDSPEAKER: You must take turns.

NGOR: Like an ant to blood I'm drawn to them.

WAR-SLAVE/LOUDSPEAKER: Say it! Say it!

NGOR: Then it's my turn.

WAR-SLAVE/LOUDSPEAKER: "I'm Khmer Rouge."

NGOR: I aim a kick between his legs.

WAR-SLAVE/LOUDSPEAKER: One at a time –

NGOR: And kick him hard.

WAR-SLAVE/LOUDSPEAKER: You must take turns.

NGOR: And kick –

WAR-SLAVE/LOUDSPEAKER: (*Simultaneously.*) Say it!

NGOR: And kick –

WAR-SLAVE/LOUDSPEAKER: (*Simultaneously.*) Say it!

NGOR: Louder!

WAR-SLAVE/LOUDSPEAKER (*Simultaneously.*) Louder!

NGOR & WAR-SLAVE/LOUDSPEAKER: LOUDER!!

(*Pause.*)

NGOR: I don't know what stopped me. Maybe I just wanted to give someone else a turn.

(Pause.)

Later down the road, I saw his severed head stuck on a pike beside his severed limbs. Nailed to the pike was a charcoal sign. The sign had one word scrawled across it. The word was "Kum."

WRAP PARTY

On a screen: "Wrap Party."
Ngor sits with Pen Tip, Naga Man & Woman to watch the movie in the flickering light.

NGOR: I never get to see the whole movie until the London opening. I'm dressed in a tuxedo sitting across the aisle from the Duchess of Kent.

And when the lights go down I watch myself, larger than life, in this . . . this story. And the audience is very quiet. They're watching this story too.

And there I am saying goodbye to my wife in the helicopter.

PEN TIP & NAGA MAN & WOMAN: *(Overlapping.)* There I am saying goodbye to my wife in the helicopter.

NGOR: And there I am saying goodbye to my friends in the French Embassy.

PEN TIP & NAGA MAN & WOMAN: *(Overlapping.)* And there I am saying goodbye to my friends in the French Embassy.

NGOR: And there I am falling into a mass grave of bones.

PEN TIP & NAGA MAN & WOMAN: *(Overlapping.)* And there I am falling into a mass grave of bones.

NGOR: And suddenly I hear muffled noises in the flickering dark. These strangers – these longnoses – they're hiding the cry. Someone hands me a tissue across the aisle. She's crying too. It's the Duchess of Kent.

(Theme music from "The Killing Fields.")

PEN TIP: And when it's all over and the film is "in the can" you go to the party for the cast and crew dressed in a Khmer Rouge uniform.

NGOR: Yes. I guess I shocked a few people with my black pajamas.
(In a mock salute:) Chey yo! Chey yo! Chey yo!

PEN TIP: You make a little speech wearing the uniform of the Khmer

Rouge to remind everyone about "kum."

NGOR: Yes, "kum."

PEN TIP: "If we hold onto our revenge," you say . . .

NGOR: (*To the audience.*) If we hold onto our revenge . . .

PEN TIP: "This will never be over."

NGOR: (*To the audience.*) This will never end.

(*To Pen Tip.*)

That's what I said. But you got one thing wrong.

PEN TIP: What's that?

NGOR: I didn't come dressed as Khmer Rouge.

(*Pause.*)

I came dressed as you.

NAGA WOMAN: (*As Stewardess.*) Fasten your seat belts.

PEN TIP: So you're flying back in first class sipping champagne –

NGOR: – sipping champagne – and thinking about kama.

PEN TIP: Ah, kama.

NGOR: And the twists of fate.

PEN TIP: The twists of fate.

(*Pen Tip helps Ngor on with a tuxedo jacket.*)

NAGA WOMAN: (*As Stewardess.*) Prepare for landing.

NGOR: (*To Pen Tip.*) You're back in Phnom Penh now working for the new government – as a doctor, no less. Think of that.

NAGA WOMAN: (*As Stewardess.*) We hope you've had a pleasant flight.

PEN TIP: And you're flying low over the orange groves, the grape arbors, the avocado fields of Southern California on your way to becoming the most recognizable Cambodian in the world. Think of that.

NAGA MAN: (*As M.C.*) And the winner for Best Supporting Actor in a Feature Film is: Dr. Haing S. Ngor. Dr. Haing S. Ngor for "The Killing Fields."

(*Sound of applause.*)

PEN TIP: Congratulations. Lucky.

NGOR: I-I wish to thank all members of Motion Picture Academy for this great honor. I thank David Puttnam, producer, and Roland Joffe, director, for giving me this chance and I share this award also to my friend Sam Waterston, Dith Pran, and Sydney Schanberg.

(*Pause.*)

And I thank Warner Brothers for helping me tell my story to the world, what happened to my country.

(*Pause.*)

And I thank . . .

(*Pause. Huoy enters in her wedding dress and walks around Ngor.*)

I thank God Buddha that I am even here.

(*Ngor steps away from the podium and takes Huoy's hand.*)

I-I didn't say your name.

HUOY: I understand.

NGOR: I'm sorry. The little red light was flashing and I couldn't . . .

HUOY: Shhh. It doesn't matter.

NGOR: But . . . What I wanted to say . . . What I wanted to say is:

(*Takes off his tux. Addresses the audience.*)

I'm no hero. I'm no Hollywood guy. I'm a survivor of the Khmer Rouge. That's who I am. That's all I am. I'm a survivor.

(*To Huoy.*)

And – God help me – you're not.

HUOY: Remember how we used to walk along the riverfront in Phnom Penh in the evening?

NGOR: The lights reflecting off the surface of the water.

HUOY: The wind –

NGOR: (*Laughing.*) The wind –

HUOY: The wind in my hair.

NGOR: I remember. And someday, Sweet, when Cambodia is free, I'll rebuild the Buddhist temple and ask the monks to perform a ceremony at your grave.

(*The Ensemble performs the closing ceremony suggesting a release of birds. The Teenage Girl sings a classical Cambodian love song. A prayer is presented. All this is presided over by the Classical Dancer.*)

PEN TIP: Citram Titthatu Saddhammo . . .

NAGA MAN & WOMAN: Citram Titthatu Saddhammo . . .

HUOY: (*Overlapping.*) May the true dharma flourish.

NGOR: And I'll release a hundred birds to set your spirit free and remind you of my vows.

(*Sound of birds in flight.*)

PEN TIP: Sabbe Satta Avera Hontu . . .

NAGA MAN & WOMAN: Sabbe Satta Avera Hontu . . .

HUOY: (*Overlapping.*) May all of God's creatures be free from hate.

NGOR: These are my vows.

PEN TIP: Sukhita Hontu Panino . . .

NAGA MAN & WOMAN: Sukhita Hontu Panino . . .

HUOY: (*Overlapping.*) May all of God's creatures be happy.

NGOR: I will always love you; I will never forget you; and I will never be forgiven by my memories.

(*Curtain.*)

END.

Stones and Bones

by Marion McClinton

*Mr. McClinton dedicates all his work to
the memory of his mother, Lenora McClinton.*

STONES AND BONES was directed by Marion McClinton with the following cast (in order of appearance):

MISTER BONES. . . . . Timothy D. Stickney
SISTUH STONES . . . . Stacy Highsmith
BONE . . . . Terry E. Bellamy
STONY. . . . . Fanni Green

Scenic Designer . . . . Paul Owen
Costume Designer . . . . Kevin R. McLeod
Lighting Designer . . . . Matthew Reinert
Sound Designer . . . . Casey L. Warren
Props Master . . . . Mark Bissonnette
Dramaturg . . . . Michele Volansky

MARION McCLINTON is a company member of Penumbra Theatre, a member playwright of New Dramatists, an alumni Advisee of the Playwrights Center, and an artistic associate of Baltimore's Center Stage. He has received a TCG/Pew Charitable Trust National Theatre Artists Residency Grant, a Bush Fellowship, two Jerome Fellowships, a McKnight Advancement Grant, Charles H. Revson Fellowship Commission from Playwrights Horizons, and the 1992 Kesselring Prize for his play POLICE BOYS.

His plays have been produced at such theaters as Center Stage, Penumbra Theatre, Seattle group Theatre, and the Hudson Guild Theatre, and he has directed at those theaters, as well as the New York Shakespeare Festival/Joseph Papp Public Theatre, the Goodman Theatre, Hartford Stage, the Young Playwrights Festival at Playwrights Horizons, Portland Stage Company, among others.

Author's Note

In explaining why I wrote STONES AND BONES, and not wanting to sound too pretentious or self-important, I will say just this simply: it is about our need to be loved, to love someone else, and to love ourselves, and how little we understand the whole damn thing intellectually, and how deep we understand it in the center of our heart. And how much that scares the living shit out of us, knowing that we cannot live by our ego alone. Especially when the lights go out at night. The characters, as I, are black. That does not make the play about race. It makes it about human beings fighting to keep their humanity above water, breathing God's air for as long as we can, holding onto each other for dear life. Which makes it about us all.

Peace, love, and hope.

—*Marion McClinton*

FOR CAUTION NOTICE SEE PAGE OPPOSITE TABLE OF CONTENTS.

STONES AND BONES by Marion McClinton. © 1993 by Marion McClinton. Reprinted by permission of the author. All inquiries should be addressed to Tracy Weinstein, Don Buchwald & Associates, 10 E 44th St., New York, NY 10017.

CHARACTERS

Mister Bones – a young Black man

Sistuh Stones – a young Black woman

Bone – a Black man

Stony – a Black woman

SETTING:

Very minimal. Should be all done with light and sound. No furniture, no props, nothing save the imagination of the artists is necessary. This will make the piece very stylized, but that is the way it should be. Mister Bones and Sistuh Stones are dressed in the primary colors of the hip-hop fashion. Stony and Bone are buppies to the max. Both groups of couples are on stage the entire play. It should not be played for the psychological subtext, but rather the effect they have on each other. They can notice each other as seems fit.

Stones and Bones

There will be no other stage direction until the end of the play except for this: Music starts. Lights up.

MISTER BONES: Yo, baby.

SISTUH STONES: Hello.

MISTER BONES: Yo baby, yo baby, yo baby, yo.

SISTUH STONES: (Shit.)

MISTER BONES: What's up, you fine cutie, honeybear-looking thing you.

SISTUH STONES: Uh huh.

MISTER BONES: What you got going on this fine motherfucking day, and shit? Man, fine as this motherfucking day is with all that sunshine and shit, the bitch ain't no kind of ways finer than your sweet motherfucking ass, I know that. What I don't know is if you're wearing the sunshine, or if that sunshine is wearing you. You know what I'm saying?

SISTUH STONES: Yeah.

MISTER BONES: So fuck all the dumb shit, you know what I'm saying?

SISTUH STONES: I wish we would.

MISTER BONES: Yeah, move over and let me sit next to your fine motherfucking ass. I'm the number one nigger, ain't a motherfucker bigger, who make your body all a quiver, and find your soul's motherfucking trigger. I'm the true for real dope motherfucker on time with all the hype rhymes, you know what I'm saying?

SISTUH STONES: Look . . . I just changed my seat, okay?

MISTER BONES: Yeah . . . so?

SISTUH STONES: I would rather not have to move again. There's too much ignorance perpetrating itself on this bus, and not enough seats to go around . . . you hear what I'm saying?

(*Pause.*)

MISTER BONES: You saying I'm a counterfeit motherfucker? Is that what you saying?

SISTUH STONES: As a three dollar bill with Whoopi Goldberg's picture on it . . . my brother.

MISTER BONES: Oh, it's like that now, huh? You just gonna front my manhood all off and shit like I'm some kind of bust out punk, and shit?

SISTUH STONES: Yeah, well, you know what they say?

MISTER BONES: No, what do they say?

SISTUH STONES: If your shit is to the curb, you gonna wind up in the gutter.

MISTER BONES: Yeah? Well, fuck you, bitch!

SISTUH STONES: Not in this life, junior.

(*Mister Bones leaves. A moment. Mister Bones returns.*)

MISTER BONES: So, you busy tonight or what?

SISTUH STONES: I can't believe you . . .

MISTER BONES: Believe it, baby, I'm for real.

SISTUH STONES: This goes beyond all the normal boundaries of stupidity into something truly weird.

MISTER BONES: Whatever . . . so you busy tonight?

SISTUH STONES: Nigger, drop dead.

MISTER BONES: So what about tomorrow?

SISTUH STONES: Nigger, I wouldn't accept a glass of ice water from you if I was on a roasting pit in hell for a thousand motherfucking years! A thousand years, you hear me!

MISTER BONES: That's all right, baby. I'm a nineties nigger. I'll just wait for the next millennium to make its way by here. You worth waiting a thousand years for. Shit, the devil will quench his motherfucking thirst before I'm done waiting on you. Shit, baby, I'm a nineties nigger. I ain't got nothing promised me but time. You know what I'm saying?

BONE: Something wrong?

STONY: You tell me?

BONE: What?

STONY: Can't you talk?

BONE: I don't know what you're talking about.

STONY: You are a lie and a half. I can smell the truth stinking all over your tongue. Tell me the truth, and get your taste back.

(*Pause.*)

BONE: How do you know? I thought I was . . . I don't know . . .

STONY: Careful? (God, I hope you were careful.) I have danced with you inside of my heart with my soul, Bone. Who did you think I was? Come on . . . speak. You were always such a good talker. So good with words. Tell me something true, Bone.

MISTER BONES: Miss me much, baby?

SISTUH STONES: You . . . shit.

MISTER BONES: Where you been?

SISTUH STONES: I'm mourning my life.

MISTER BONES: I knew your ass missed me. You missed me, didn't you?

SISTUH STONES: I'm sorry, brother . . .

MISTER BONES: Mister Bones.

SISTUH STONES: Whatever . . . you put too much pressure on somebody. Hard to remain a lady if I listen to you, do what you want me to do. Understand? You need to chill down. You too psychotic about it.

MISTER BONES: Why I gotta be all of that? I just think you and me could be fantastic together. I see you, and I see my whole life stretched out before me, and I get excited. I don't usually get excited about my future, so I gotta grab that motherfucking ring when it swings on by, you know what I'm saying? I talk shit, but I ain't a not about shit motherfucker . . . shit . . . I want the motherfucking finer things in life my own damn self, and you, sweet honey in the rock, is one of them kinds of things.

SISTUH STONES: That's exactly what I feel like when I talk to brothers like you, Mister Bones. Some kind of thing for some coonshow nigger who thinks he got some kind of rap that got something to say to me. All you roughneck gangstuh brothers been hitting on me so hard I'm a serious TKO behind all that mess you talk. You all done hit on me until your words got tired, and your mouth got sore. I ain't here anymore.

MISTER BONES: Look, I walk through the world like I got some kind of right of way in it. I'm loud because nobody gives enough of a shit about nothing to do with me to pay attention to whatever I'm saying. I ain't like y'all sistuhs. Y'all done bought that white girl chickenshit about being victims so long lately you become addicted to victimization. I don't tear you down. You do a good enough job of that your own damn self. To tell you the truth, I hate to look at it. Breaks my motherfucking heart.

SISTUH STONES: You might not be trying to tear me down, but you sure as shit ain't trying to help build me up. Ask me what's on my mind outside of do I want to do the nasty with you. You hate to look at it? Good. I wish you would quit looking here, and take your twenty-twenty somewhere's else. I need a mate, not a date . . . you know?

BONE: So you wanna know anything else?

STONY: No.

BONE: About whether they married, or have children, or anything?

STONY: No.

BONE: Their age, weight, height, the color of their eyes, whether they remind me of you or not?

STONY: If they got children, and are married, and unsatisfied with their life, then I already know what about them reminds you of me.

BONE: I still want us to be together.

STONY: I don't believe this chickenshit bullshit.

BONE: Look, I don't take them out, I never fucked them through the night, and ignore you in our own bed, I don't buy them things, I don't call them every chance I get in the day free and clear, I never said anything about them being better lovers, or finer women than you, or that being unhappy with you was the reason I was with them, you know what I'm saying? I didn't, don't, and won't love them period.

It's me! Okay? I'm just wrong! I'm all of everything you was afraid I was gonna be! I'm wrong, down and dirty, no good to the motherfucking bone! Okay! I don't know why! What else you want me to say? How many more ways can I say it?

STONY: There is one thing you could tell me. Something you neglected to mention.

BONE: What, Stony, damn?

STONY: Whether or not these bitches are white. You can talk about that.

MISTER BONES: Well . . . this is where I hang. The motherfucking crib in all its glory.

SISTUH STONES: Yeah. Charming, or something.

MISTER BONES: So you like?

SISTUH STONES: It's all right.

MISTER BONES: I tried calling you, you know, all afternoon and shit, and like you weren't never around, or nothing.

SISTUH STONES: Yeah? So?

MISTER BONES: Look, this shit ain't easy for me either, you know what I'm saying? It's hard to get next to somebody on the real tip. This shit hurts my gut it's so bugging, you know what I'm saying? I'm trying to touch another like motherfucking human being and shit. I mean, like fuck the dumb shit, you picked up on me, and I want to deliver. Not just that physical thing, but I mean I want to thaw out your soul, raise you up, I mean, I don't even know why you even are up here with my black ass this minute, you know . . .

SISTUH STONES: Just be all right with me being here, that's all you gotta do, and I'll be cool with it.

MISTER BONES: No, fuck that, I gotta know! Why here, why with me, why . . . any of it, why?

SISTUH STONES: You need something? All right . . . because you brush your teeth three times a day, put some deodorant under those funky armpits, and every other word out of your mouth ain't "bitch" or "ho".

(*Pause.*)

Because you said I was beautiful, and meant it. Said it sweetly, and smiled with a smile looked like it was full of French champagne when you said it.

MISTER BONES: I ain't that kind of motherfucker. I wish I was, but I truly . . .

SISTUH STONES: I don't need to hear it from your lips, baby. I know all of that already. Besides I didn't come up in here to talk to you anyway. You promised me something else, some other kind of time. I'm here for that. I don't want to talk about it anymore. I want to taste all that sweet champagne you got behind your lips. I want to drink my full.

(*Pause.*)

MISTER BONES: You better go home, honeybaby. You know too much, and you too thirsty.

SISTUH STONES: What . . . you kidding me right? A round-the-way fellow with the funky fuck of the ages up inside of your pants? I thought . . .

MISTER BONES: I ain't got that much champagne in me. I'll call you tomorrow.

SISTUH STONES: Jesus will have come back, and gone by then. I can't wait that long.

MISTER BONES: I'm scared, Sistuh Stones.

SISTUH STONES: I know the feeling, Mister Bones. We sitting chin deep in some blackfaced, shit stomping, low down blues, baby, and we can't get up out of it without each other.

(*Pause.*)

This shit is supposed to be scary.

STONY: You know . . .

BONE: No, what?

STONY: When I'm breathing, when my heart is flying all around up in my mouth screaming, all I can do is think about it . . .

BONE: Think about what?

STONY: You touching them with your smile all wide open, slipping all of that champagne that be all mine by right of birth, all turned around, turned out, and your smile.

BONE: Enough, baby. You gonna lose your mind behind all of this. I just better go.

STONY: Yeah, well enough is never enough . . . I ain't thinking about that. That – what is stealing my sleep away from me all through the night. Something else.

BONE: What, Stony?

STONY: If I could take my nose, and cut it, pull my flesh from off my bones and put on a skin made of peaches like it was a new winter coat, if I could look at you like you were a criminal all the time, cross to the other side of the street every time I see you coming my way, never wait on you first when it's your turn in line, never sit next to you on the bus even if it's the only seat, make you forget you had a mama that always looked old, and a daddy that always seemed broken, if I could make you forget the manhood that supposed to be in between your legs, make you dream in black and white, and turn the black to gray, if it were true that I had more fun, and knew what Clairol knows, and could make you feel it's all right and cool with me if you take every last bit of black that was passed down to you from every African hanging from your family tree, and trash it like it wasn't never there, wasn't never anything worth keeping no how. If I can get you to change how you talk, if I can refine all the loudness from out of your soul . . . if I didn't know nothing about nothing worth knowing about you . . . if I was white would I stop intimidating you so you could hold me through the night

clutched to your chest? Would you be scared of me then? Would you stop being scared of yourself then?
(*Silence.*)

BONE: I don't know. I don't know. (*Beat.*)

STONY: Oh.

SISTUH STONES: God dammit . . . that was the best . . . I hoped you was something special . . .

STONY: Okay.

MISTER BONES: Shit, baby, I knew I could rock your world.

BONE: I do know it wouldn't change anything. I been trying to fuck myself into a new life. I ain't got that much juice in me.

SISTUH STONES: This shit is frightening, ain't it?

STONY: Well.

BONE: I don't recognize my own voice anymore.

MISTER BONES: Seem like I know myself so well when I'm inside of you.

STONY: I know you . . .

SISTUH STONES: I know.

MISTER BONES: Just gonna get better and better.

BONE: I don't know.

SISTUH STONES: Ain't nobody else supposed to make me feel like you do. Maybe that's it.

STONY: Maybe you just plain can't . . .

BONE: Love you? Maybe I never did.

MISTER BONES: Shit, baby, you with the jam master blaster of ceremonies hisself.

STONY: You love me. Probably always will. It'll be the only thing that will keep you alive in the end. But until you can love yourself and we can take each other in hand, neither of us will ever live.

MISTER BONES: We gonna be getting busy, and swapping spit full of Dom Perignon, and being happy forever and a day. Forever and ever and ever and ever . . .

MISTER BONES AND SISTUH STONES: . . . and ever, forever, and ever, and ever, and ever . . . until death do us part . . . amen.

(*Lights go down to black as Mister Bones and Sistuh Stones are in an embrace, and Stony and Bone are far apart, as we hear the sounds of lovemaking, mingled with the sounds of crying tears.*)

END.

My Left Breast

by Susan Miller

For the ones who have kept me aloft
My Father. My Mother. My Son.

MY LEFT BREAST was directed by Nela Wagman and performed by Susan Miller.

Scenic Designer	Paul Owen
Costume Designer	Hollis Jenkins-Evans
Lighting Designer	Matthew Reinert
Sound Designer	Darron L. West
Props Master	Mark Bissonnette
Stage Manager	Julie a. Richardson
Assistant Stage Manager	John David Flak
Dramaturg	Marcia Dixcy

Running Time: 1 hr., 10 min.
Performed without an intermission.

SUSAN MILLER is an Obie Award-winning playwright whose works NASTY RUMORS AND FINAL REMARKS, FOR DEAR LIFE and FLUX were produced by Joseph Papp and the New York Shakespeare Festival. Her plays CROSS COUNTRY and CONFESSIONS OF A FEMALE DISORDER were staged by the Mark Taper Forum in Los Angeles. She has also been produced by Second Stage and Naked Angels, among others. Miller has participated in the National Playwrights Conference at the Eugene O'Neill Center, received grants from the NEA, as well as a Rockefeller Grant, and has twice been a finalist for the Susan Smith Blackburn Prize in Playwriting. Miller's films include LADY BEWARE and for television she has written for THIRTYSOMETHING, TRIALS OF ROSIE O'NEILL and L.A. LAW. among others. She has been a fellow at the Yaddo Arts Colony and is a part-time faculty member of NYU's Dramatic Writing Program. Her work is published in *The Best American Short Plays 1992-93; Avon's Gay Plays, Volume I*; the forthcoming anthology *Facing Forward* edited by Leah Frank for Broadway Play Publishing; and *One On One, The Best Women's Monologues for the Nineties*, Applause Books; and *Monologues for Women by Women*, edited by Tori Haring-Smith for Heinemann.

FOR CAUTION NOTICE SEE PAGE OPPOSITE TABLE OF CONTENTS.

MY LEFT BREAST by Susan Miller. © 1993 by Susan Miller. Reprinted by permission of the author.

All inquiries should be addressed to Joyce Ketay, The Joyce Ketay Agency, 1501 Broadway Suite 1910, New York, NY 10036.

My Left Breast

LIGHTS UP:
I come out dancing. Then, after a moment:

The night before I went to the hospital, that's what I did. I danced.
(*Indicates breasts.*)
One of these is not real.
Can you tell which?
(*Beat.*)
I was fourteen the first time a boy touched my breast. My left breast, in fact. I felt so guilty with pleasure I could hardly face my parents that night. It was exquisite. Well, you remember.
(*Beat.*)
I always wonder in the movies when the female star has to appear topless in a love scene and the male star is caressing her nipples, how the actress is supposed to remain professional. See, I don't think this would be expected of a man whose penis was being fondled.
(*Beat.*)
Anyhow, breast cancer.

The year it happened my son was eight. He looked at my chest, the day I told him. We had these matching Pep Boys tee shirts. You know – Manny, Mo, and Jack. He looked at my chest and said, "Which one was it? Manny or Jack?"

"Jack," I tell him.

"What did they do with it?"

"I don't know."

He starts to cry. "Well, I'm going to get it back for you!"

Now he is twenty and I am still his mother. I am still here. We are still arguing. He is twenty and I wear his oversized boxer shorts with a belt and he borrows my jackets and we wear white tee shirts and torn jeans and he says, 'Why don't you get a tattoo."

"A tattoo?"

"Over your scar. It'd be cool."

* * *

Here's what I wear under my clothes.
(*Show breast prosthesis to audience.*)
Don't worry. It's a spare. When you go for a fitting, you can hear the women in the other booths. Some of them have lost their hair and shop for wigs. Some are very young and their mothers are thinking: Why didn't this happen to me, instead? And there's the feeling you had when you got your first bra, and the saleswoman cupped you to fit. Cupped you and yanked at the straps. Fastened you into the rest of your life.
(*Beat.*)
I miss it but it's not a hand. I miss it but it's not my mind. I miss it but it's not the roof over my head. I miss it but it's not a word I need. It's not a sentence I can't live without. I miss it, but it's not a conversation with my son. It's not my courage or my lack of faith.
(*Beat.*)
I miss it – but it's not HER.

* * *

Skinnied on the left side like a girl, I summon my breast and you there where it was with your mouth sucking a phantom flutter from my viny scar.

* * *

We met at an artists' colony. One night at Charades, (*That's what people do there.*) when an outstanding short story writer was on all fours, being a horse, I sat on the floor and leaned against the sofa. I rubbed my back against what I thought was the hard edge of it. And realized after a minute that I was rubbing against Franny's knee.

"God, I'm sorry."

"Don't be."

"I thought you were the couch."

"It's the nicest thing that's happened to me all day," she said.

In town, one afternoon, we run into each other in the bookstore. It might as well be a hotel room. We might as well be pulling the bedspread off in a fever. We are in a heap. We are thinking the things you think when you are going to run away together. It is only a matter of time.
(*Beat.*)
"You don't finish your sentences," she said.

"I've been told."

"I'm starting to get the drift, however. I know where you're headed."

I was headed toward tumult, headed toward breakage, headed toward her.
(*Beat.*)
It's been a year since she left me and how do I tell someone new? Even though it will probably be a woman. See, a woman might be threatened. A woman might see her own odds. She might not want the reminder.

* * *

I threw on my ripped jeans and a pair of – I pulled on my black tights under a short black shirt – I threw on a white tee shirt and an oversized Armani Jacket – my hair was, well, this was not a bad hair day.

"I guess it's a date," I said to my therapist. "Two single gay women who don't know each other except through a mutual friend. I guess you'd call it a date."

"Do you realize you called yourself a gay woman? I've never heard you refer to yourself that way before."

"Well, it just doesn't seem to matter anymore. What I'm called."

"You mean, since Franny left. Interesting."

"You sound like a shrink."

"Why do you think it doesn't matter anymore," she says.

Because, I want to say, when you're a hurt and leaky thing, all definitions are off. What you were, who you told everyone you might be had a sheen, the spit of artifice. There was always something covert. But now, you've come apart. Like an accident victim in shock, you don't see who sees you and you don't care how you are seen. You are a creature, simply. You move or stop or lurch from side to side as you are able. You make a sound without will. Your former self, the husk of you, hovering near, looks on startled and concerned. But you are not. You are shorn of image. You are waiting to eat again and to speak in a language with meaning. You are not gay. You are not a woman. You are not. And by this, you are everything your former self defended against, apologized for, explained away, took pride in. You are all of it. None of it. You want only to breathe in and out. And know what your limbs will do. You are at the beginning.

* * *

Hey want to meet for a cappuccino at Café Franny? Gotta run, I'm off to the latest Franny film. Meet you at the corner of 83rd and Franny? How about Concerto in Franny at Carnegie Franny? Was

anything ever called by any other name?
(*Beat.*)
Oh, you play the piano? Franny plays the piano. You say words in English. Well, see so did Franny. Uh, huh, you have hair. That's interesting because you know, she also had hair.
(*Beat.*)
Maybe I'm paying for the moment when I looked at her and thought I don't know if I love her anymore. Maybe she saw me look at her this way and believed what she saw, even though it was no more true than the first day when you looked at someone and thought, "She's the One." Thought, "I'm saved."

But, nothing can save you. Not your friends, not the best Fred Astaire musical you've ever seen – the grace of it, not your mother's beauty, not a line from a letter you find at the bottom of a drawer, not a magazine or the next day. Nothing can save you. And you stand in the moonlight and a sweetness comes off the top of the trees, and the fence around the yard seals you off from the dark·and you can't breathe. It is all so familiar and possible. It is too simple that there is this much good and you don't know how to have it. And it makes you wonder when it was you lost your place. Then you catch a breeze, so warm and ripe, it makes you hope that someone will come who also cannot save you, but who will think you are worth saving.

* * *

A man I know said to me, "Lesbians are the Chosen people these days. No AIDS." I said, "Lesbians are women. Women get AIDS. Women get ovarian cancer. Women get breast cancer. Women die. In great numbers. In the silent epidemic." He said, "I see what you mean."
(*Beat.*)
I miss it but maybe I wouldn't have to if anyone paid attention to women's health care.

* * *

The surgeon in Los Angeles said it was a fibroadenoma.

"Someday you might want to have it removed," he said. "But no rush. It's benign." I watched it grow. Then in New York, I saw another surgeon.

He said, "What have you been told?"

"Fibroadenoma," I say.

"Well, I'm concerned," he said. "I want to biopsy it."

You know how when everything is going right, you figure it's only a matter of time until that bus swerves on to the sidewalk or you finally make it to the post office to buy stamps and that's the day a crazed postal worker fires his Uzi into the crowd.

Everything was going right for me. I had just won an Obie for a play at the Public Theatre. I had a contract for my first novel – I was in the beginning chapters. And a new relationship.

It was Jane who found the lump. The gynecologist said it was a gland. When it didn't go away, she sent me to the surgeon who said it was something it wasn't.

All of this happened at the beginning of a new decade. When we would all lose our innocence. It was 1980. In New York. I heard the Fourth of July fireworks from my hospital bed. I was 36. I was too young. People were celebrating. And they were too young for the plague that was coming.

* * *

There were two positive nodes. I went through 11 months of chemotherapy and I had only one more month to go. But at my next to the last treatment, after they removed the IV, the oncologist and his nurse looked at me with what I distinctly recognized as menace. I thought, they're trying to kill me. If I come back again, they'll kill me. I never went back.

* * *

There are those who insist that certain types of people get cancer. So I wonder, are there certain types of people who get raped and tortured? Are there certain types who die young? Are there certain types of Bosnians, Somalians, Jews? Are there certain types of Gay men? Are there certain types of children who are abused and caught in the crossfire? Is there a type of African American who is denied, excluded, lynched? Were the victims of the Killing Fields people who couldn't express themselves? Are one out of eight women – count 'em folks – just holding on to their goddamned anger?

This is my body – where the past and the future collide. This is my body. All at once, timely. All at once, chic. My deviations. My battle scars. My idiosyncratic response to the physical realm. The past deprivations and the future howl.

I am a One Breasted, Menopausal, Jewish, Bisexual, Lesbian Mom and I am the topic of our times. I am the hot issue. I am the cover of Newsweek, the editorial in the paper. I am a best seller. And I am coming soon to a theatre near you. I am a One Breasted, Menopausal, Jewish, Bisexual, Lesbian Mom and I am in.

* * *

My son is having symptoms. His stomach hurts. He feels a tumor in his neck. He injures his toes in a game of basketball and suspects gangrene. He says, "My organs are failing." He stands in front of the refrigerator opening and closing the door. "Can I make you some breakfast?" I want to do something for him. I haven't done anything for him, it seems, in awhile. I mean like my mother would do for me. But he isn't hungry. It's just a reflex, this refrigerator door thing. Some small comfort.

He walks into the living room and throws his leg over the arm of our formerly white chair. Sitting across from me, disheveled, morning dazed, he says, accusingly, "I think I'm dying."

"You're not dying."

"Maybe it won't happen right away, but I'm dying."

"Honey, you're talking yourself into it. Why are you so worried about everything?"

"What if I have AIDS?"

That's something I didn't have to think about when I was 20.

"Everybody's going to die. You'll see. All my friends. It's going to happen."

"Talk to me."

He's a dark thing. His eyes match my own. He'll see a child, overweight, wearing glasses maybe – he'll notice a child like this somewhere, trying to make his way against the odds and it will seem to Jeremy heroic. "Stud," he says. And means it.

"Maybe I have spinal meningitis."

I try not to laugh.

"I'm serious."

"I'm sorry."

Things are breaking down.

* * *

He is twirling a strand of hair around his finger. We're in the Brandeis parking area, waiting to take our children to their dorms. It's an oppressive August day. Everyone has gotten out of his car, but Jeremy won't move. He's in the back seat, regretting his decision. There are no pretty girls. The guys are losers. This was a big mistake.

Suddenly I'm in another August day. I've just put my eight year old on a bus to day camp. He looks out at me from the window. A pale reed, he is twirling his hair around his finger. I watch him do this until the bus pulls away. What have I done? I go home and fall onto my bed. I lie there and mourn all the lost Jeremys. My three year old, my infant boy. I lie on my bed and have grim notions. What if something happened to me and he came home from camp and I wasn't there to pick him up? What if I had an accident? Who would take care of him? What happens to the child of a single parent who is kidnapped by a madman? Then I imagine him lost. I see him twirling his hair as it grows dark in some abandoned warehouse. He walks the streets of a strange neighborhood. I know that he is crying in the woods. He has gotten himself into an old refrigerator. He falls into a well. He is in the danger zone. He has wandered too far from me. I have cancer and what if I never see him grown. "I'll go and get it back for you, Mom."

By the time I have to pick him up from camp, I'm frantic. Somehow, we survived. Until now.

We get to his dorm and unload. His room is in the basement. It is moldy and I feel homesick. This isn't right. Parents move toward their cars dazed and fighting every urge to run back and save their young from this new danger – independence. (*Beat.*) When I get home, the sound of Jeremy not in his room is deafening.

* * *

THE PHONE CALLS:

Mom, I'm all right. Don't get upset. Just listen, okay. I got arrested last night.

Mom, I'm all right. Don't get upset. Just listen, okay. I'm in the infirmary. The Doctor says it's pneumonia.

Mom, I'm all right. Don't get upset. I was playing rugby and I broke my nose. (That beautiful nose!)

"Mom," He calls from Los Angeles, where he is visiting his girlfriend, on the day there is an earthquake that measures 6.6. "Mom, I'm all right, but I think L.A. is gone."

He transfers to NYU and calls to tell me a car has driven into a crowd of people in Washington Square Park, but he's all right. He calls to say that the boy who was his catcher on the high school baseball team has jumped from a building. "I was walking down his street, Mom. I saw the ambulance. I saw his feet coming out from under a blanket. I can't stop seeing his feet."

* * *

Once after Franny and I had a fight, Jeremy and I were out to dinner. He was 13. I must've looked particularly hopeless. Maybe it was my inattention. Whatever shadowed my face, it was enough for him to say, "Are you going to die?" Did he worry himself orphaned every day since I had cancer?

"No, honey, no," I say, shocked into responsibility. "I'm sorry. Franny and I just had a fight. It's nothing. I'm fine. I'm not going to die."

"You looked so sad," he said.

I want to report myself to the nearest authorities. Take me now. I'm busted.

He was two-and-a-half days old the day he came to us. My parents drove my husband and me to the lawyer's office. We handed over a sweater and cap we had brought with us and a blanket my sister made. And we waited. We waited for every known thing to change. Jeremy says he remembers the ride back. The Pennsylvania mountains. And how it was to be held in my arms. How it was to be carried home.

* * *

A woman is ironing her son's shirt. The palm tree shivers outside the window. Gardenia wafts through. Althought she can't smell it.

It's 4 A.M.. She has laid out his button down Oxford cloth shirt along with two lines of cocaine on the ironing board. She does them. After his sleeves.

Mothers have no business doing cocaine. Mothers have no business being tired all the time and sick from chemotherapy.

The surgeon said, "Don't join a cancer support group. It'll only depress you."

The drug of choice for most people undergoing chemo is marijuana. It's supposed to help the nausea. But, marijuana didn't work for me. I wanted something to keep me awake, to keep me going. Something I associated with good times, former times, something that assured me there was time.

Sleep, rest, these things were too close to the end of it all. I couldn't give in. If I stopped, the whole thing might stop.

The woman ironing her son's shirt was testing everyone. Who would stay after she'd pushed them away?

There were powerful drugs in her body. But the one she took through the nose kept her from knowing what she knew. Kept her from the ache of caring. In her dreams she could smell the truth. Cocaine — sharp, thrilling. The cancer drugs, acrid and sere. Terrifying. They were Proust's asparagus in her urine. A toxic taste in her mouth.

She had control over cocaine. She administered this to herself. In a breath. There were no needles, no invasion. It was a ritual of pleasure and retreat. It blotted out the anxiety of the waiting room.

And finally, it destroyed what was healthy and cured nothing at all.

The woman ironing her son's shirt felt ashamed. She was not the cancer heroine she'd hoped to be.

Some people would say, this woman is doing the best she can. And that's all anyone can do. But, I think that's just another moral loophole. She can do better. She will do better.

Morning broke. Her son came running down the hall. Her lover called to sing her show tunes.

"I might lose them, "the woman thought. "But not while I can still have them." She vowed to stop. "This will be my last time." And it was. Her son was very pleased with his shirt.

* * *

I didn't lose my hair, I lost my period. Chemo knocks out your estrogen, which knocks out your period, which puts you, ready or not, into menopause. So, at 37 I was having hot flashes and panic in the left hand turn lane.
(*Beat.*)
It's like this. I'm driving and I'm in the left hand lane and the light turns red before I can make the turn. This isn't good. This for me is a life threatening situation. My heart races. My hands and feet tingle. I hyperventilate. I'm a lot of laughs.

Sometimes this happens if I walk too far from my house.

A lot of women take estrogen replacement therapy. But, you can't take estrogen if you've had breast cancer which is estrogen positive, and for most women under 40, that's the case. So years later, when the hot flashes are over and I can finally manage to sit in the left hand turn lane without calling the paramedics, Franny and I are visiting my parents and I take a swing at a golf ball. Oh, don't misinterpret. This is my parents' golf course. Their idea. But it's a beautiful day. And I tee off quite nicely. I'm feeling proud of myself, so I take my second swing and I get this sudden, searing pain accompanied by a kind of pop in my side. I've fractured a rib. A year later. Same swing. Same thing.

Then, another time, I reach out my side of the car to remove a twig from the windshield. Pop. My friend Brock runs up behind me, lifts me into the air with his arms around my chest. Pop. I sit the wrong way on a theatre seat. I bend and reach awkwardly for something I've dropped. My trainer pushes my knees into my chest. Pop. Pop. Pop.

The bone scan is negative, but the bone densitometry shows a significant demineralization – or bone loss. Is the structure of everything dissolving? I can't count on whatever it was that held me up, supported my notions, my exertions. Osteoporosis. It's hard to say the word. It's an old person's disease. It's the antifeminine. It's the crone.

I go to see the doctor in Gerontology. The waiting room is full of old people. Naturally. They've come with their husbands. Or their grandchildren. With each other.

A few days after coming home from the hospital, after my mastectomy, I go to the movies in the middle of the afternoon. I notice two older women, arm in arm, walking to their seats. And I know what I want. I want to get old and walk arm and arm with my old friend to a movie in the middle of the afternoon.

What movies are you seeing, Franny? Do you still walk out in the middle? On the street, do you take someone's arm? Will you grow old with her?

The gerontologist consults with my internist who consults with an oncologist, who probably consults with somebody else. The rib fractures seem consistent with chemotherapy and the resulting loss of estrogen. But she'd like to run more blood tests. I especially love the one they call a tumor marker. And why are these things always given on a Friday?

Excuse me, I need to scream now.
(*Opens mouth wide and screams.*)
That was good. But what I really want to do is break a chair.

(*Beat.*)
I have destroyed so much property in my mind. I have smashed so many plates against the wall, ripped so many books from cover to cover. In my mind, I have trashed apartments, taken all the guilty parties to court. Done damage for damage done. But, I'm the accommodating patient. I move on. Get over it. Exercise restraint. I am appropriate.
(*Beat.*)
Except for the day the doorman ate my pizza.

I was coming home from Chemotherapy. With a pizza. Jane was trying to get me to eat right. Well, trying to get me to eat. So we had this pizza and then I got an urge for LiLac Chocolate which was right down the block from where we lived. I gave the doorman my pizza and asked him to hold it for a couple minutes. When I got back with my chocolate I asked him for my pizza. And he said, "I ate it."

You ate it? You fucking ate my pizza. You fucking murdered my child, you fucking destroyed my career, you fucking robbed me of my youth, you fucking betrayed me, you fucking know that? You fucking fucking idiot!

He offered to pay me for the pizza.

* * *

I walk home from Mt. Sinai, after the Gerontologist, down Madison across the park. Trembling. The possibility that there is something else…

I walk around the reservoir. And I see a doorknob from my old house, hanging on the fence. Then a remnant of a child's blanket worn down to a sad shred. My wedding band. And messages no one has picked up. "Come home. All is forgiven." Gifts that came too late. The opal ring I gave Franny at Christmas. A page torn from Chekhov.

There's a black and white photograph. It's a group of friends.

When everything was fine. Before the bad news. I walk farther and I see people testifying. Telling their stories. Here at the wailing wall. And then I see my pink suitcase.

I have this pink suitcase. I don't know how I ended up with it really. It belonged to my sister. I was given the powder blue set for high school graduation. And she got the pink. Well, anyway, it's mine now.

My agent said, "I'm sorry. There's nothing more I can do. Maybe if you spoke to the publisher yourself." I had gotten a year's extension on my novel. It was up now. I called the publisher. I said, "Look, I just need a little more time. I've had this thing happen to me and – "

"I know," she said. "That's unfortunate."

"I've been writing, though. I have about 100 pages."

"I'm sure it's a wonderful book," she said, "Although I haven't read any of it, but we just can't give you any more time."

She asked for the return of my advance. The Author's League gave me half the money. I paid the rest, put my novel in the pink suitcase, and turned the lock.

It is all that is incomplete in me. The waste. My fraud.

* * *

While I'm waiting for the results of this tumor marker, I go with an old college chum to a gay bar. We had gone to the Expo in Montreal together with our young husbands. We deposited our children at the same camp. She's divorced and seeing a woman now.

The first time it ever occurred to me that I might make love with a woman, I was in bed with my husband and I thought, I wonder what it feels like making love to me.

I don't understand the concept of this place. Everyone is cruising, but no one makes a move. All around me women are whispering, "Go on. Talk to her. Now's your chance." It ripples through the narrow, smoky, room. "Go on. Talk to her. Now's your chance."

Two women kiss nearby. I halt. I cave. To see this.

* * *

The gay bar in Paris, it was Franny's first. The women were fresh and attractive and we danced to a French hit. The lyrics, translated, meant the death of love, but we were far from dying. We were expressing ourselves in Paris.

A slave to love when she spoke French. A goner to her version of the Frenchman in America. The accent, the pout, the hands – she had them down. I was seduced. Sometimes after a rough patch, I'd say, all you have to do is speak in French and I'm yours. In the middle of a fight, switch to it, take me.

I had four years of college French, but I could say only, "Have you any stamps" and order grapefruit juice. "Vous avez jus de pamplemousse?"

She required me to say pamplemousse back in the United States, in our bed.

When will a French family struggling with directions on the subway fail to remind me?

* * *

We are mothers. We know the same thing. And sometimes it is too much to know. It drew me to her and it is the thing that would come between us.

She's a mother. I trusted she would take better care of things. A mother is a safe bet. A mother would never leave her children for someone else's children. A mother shows up. Stays put. She installs a light in the hall. Franny's a mother, I thought. She won't harm me.

* * *

It keeps coming back. What she said. The way she looked saying it. "We're not in the same place." WHAT DO YOU MEAN? "I don't think we'll ever live together." WAIT. DON'T. PLEASE WAIT. "This is so hard." she says. OH MY GOD. HAVE YOU MET SOMEONE?

I can be standing in line for bagels. I can be punching in my secret code at the bank machine. It returns to me. A howl goes up.

* * *

"Well, Susan, you look fabulous."

"I'm a wreck."

"You'll see. People find that very attractive."

* * *

Every room. Every way the light fell. Every room we walked. Every way we combined there. Every room you moved into and out of. Every absence. Every room of our inclining. Every tender routine. Every room and way I learned you. Clings.

* * *

Just two and half months before Jeremy was born, my first baby died, and the doctor injected me with something so the milk in my breasts would dry up. My breasts became engorged. Hard and full to bursting. It's painful, this swelling of something that wants to come.

When I was pregnant, I took something called Provera. Later it was shown to cause birth defects.

So, when I got breast cancer I wondered, was it the time someone sprayed my apartment for roaches? Or too much fat in my diet? Was it the deodorant with aluminum, or my birth control pills? Or was it genetic?

"Here are your choices," the bone specialist in L.A. said. "Pick one. A shot every day of Calcitonin which costs a fortune. I wouldn't do it. Etidronate which can cause softening of the bones. Or Tamoxifan, an anitestrogen that acts like an estrogen."

I really hate this arrogant, out-of-touch, son-of-a-bitch specialist, you know? But my internist concurs, and him I love. So, I take the Tamoxifan.

Side effects: increase in blood clots, endometrial cancer, liver changes.

Something interesting happens. My ovaries ache. I'm . . . well, how do I say this . . . the juices are flowing. But I'm in L.A. working on a television show and Franny's in New York. When I come home for good at Christmas, she tells me it's over. And I'm left to stew in my own juices.

* * *

I didn't call her the day I had a cold. I didn't call her on Friday because I wanted to talk to her so badly my throat closed up. I didn't call her the day before that around 15 times because I was trying to make it until Friday. I didn't call her one day because I was at the bookstore waiting and hoping. I didn't call her on Wednesday because it would have been a failure, so I swallowed the history of it down. I didn't call just now to save my life, because the instrument of rescue was already in my hands.

* * *

I go back to Mt. Sinai to see the gerontologist. All my tests are normal. "There's really nothing to do. Increase the calcium in your diet. Maintain a consistent exercise program. Especially weight lifting."

Well, hey, I belong to a health club. With TV sets. And I was starting to see some nice rips in my shoulders. But, then over a period of 5 months, I had three separate rib fractures. They take 4 to 6 weeks to heal, so how do I maintain a consistent exercise program?

The doctor is a gracious woman and she sees my frustration and, frankly, is tired of hearing me whine. "All right, look, I know this sounds like I'm waffling, but I think I want to put you on Etidronate."

I don't think the names of these drugs are very friendly, do you?

"We'll follow you closely for a year," she says and gives me a prescription.

I haven't filled it yet.

* * *

When my baby died, I felt I had no right to talk about childbirth or being pregnant. I had a baby. I was pregnant. I had morning sickness. I bought clothes and furniture. I had a son. He lived three hours. He was born to me. I finally understood what women were. And I wanted to talk about this, but it made people uncomfortable. In some ways losing Franny is like that.

I want to remember a Scrabble game where we made up words and meanings and laughed until we were in pain. I want to express my affection for her Miro bag, which held my glasses, a half stick of gum. I want to tell about the vegetable stand at the side of the road where we left our money in a bucket and the invisible proprietor trusted us to love his tomatoes and his sweet corn and his zucchini and we did.

I want to talk about these things but I feel I don't have the right to tell the love story because it ended badly.

* * *

Okay, I'm in her kitchen and I grab wild for a knife and plunge it into my belly. She can't believe it. She says, "But I had to cut your bagels for you." I say, "Well that stopped, didn't it?" And I die. Better, I huddle against a wall outside of her apartment. All night long. In the morning when she leaves for work, she sees me there. Cold. Unattended. The drift that I am. Her detritus. She drops her books and bends to me. "Susan? Susan?" Who, I strain is that. And the call. The call to say, oh this is from my friends, they call her. "Susan's dead." And they hang up.

* * *

My friends, these women with wild hair and good eyes, these women friends who engage my light and do not refuse me, dark as I am these days. These friends make room for disturbance. They have the wit to see it coming. This is who they are, these people who school themselves and event the city and construe fresh arguments and listen to the heart beat its woe. These friends are my history. What they know about me is in the record. Errors. Shifts. Defeats. Occasions of grace. They were there when I looked up from my hospital bed. They were there when I looked up after Franny left and couldn't see a thing. And these people, my friends, are taking out an ad. In the personals. "She's adorable. She's smart. And would you please take her off our hands? We can't stand it anymore!"

* * *

Maybe we're only given a certain amount of time with anyone. Or we can have the whole time if we remember on the days it is not going well that these are not the days to measure by. The moment we marry is often so minor, so quotidian, that later we forget we've taken vows. When Franny walked to her study to write, I took my vows. When she asked me before sleep, if I wanted some magic cream on my cuticles and rubbed it into my fingers, I took vows. When I weeded her mother's garden, cleaned under her son's bed.

(*Beat.*)

Is it there in the beginning? The thing that finishes us?

* * *

Out in the country with my friends, I wake in the morning to the sound of a wasp in its death throes. A screen door shuts and the dog's paws sound like a hot drummer's brush across the floor. I walk outside to the buzz and the click and the hum. Suddenly, I feel bereft.

My favorite book in the Golden Book series was "The Happy Family." Imagine. Well, here's the picture. Beautiful clean-cut boy and girl. Mother and Father. Crates arrive. Brand new bikes. They all go on a picnic. It was my touchstone.

* * *

He was dark and thin. She was dark and beautiful and not as thin. He introduced himself to her as Frank Lamonica. And she was Judy Grey, a singer with her own show on the radio. "I'll never smile again, until I smile at you." He said, "We're going to come back here next year, married."

Isaac Figlin and Thelma Freifelder. My model for romance.

There was a war. He went. She was a bride. They wrote letters. She sent him a lock of my hair.

Now she is 74 and he is 83. My father says, "I've never been more in love with your mother than I am right now." On the night before my father has surgery to remove a kidney, my mother climbs up next to him in his hospital bed. We, my brother and sister and I, turn our heads. Were they really ours? Who might we have become without these two people who said yes one mad summer in the Poconos and taught us how to dance and spell and drive a car. Taught us what was good. They were good.

After I lost my baby, I was taken back to my room. And I saw my parents standing there, in the doorway, waiting for me.
(*Beat.*)
So, I told them a funny story and made them laugh.

After my mastectomy, my father rubs my feet. My mother sings me a song. They do this for me and I let them.

* * *

House. It's a concept that cries out deconstruct. There is the universal notion of house and there is Susan's house. The house that longing built.

There was something important about Franny and me. I don't know. Maybe it was only that we tried.

We have children and we had to bring them up. We had to be their mothers. We would cry when we saw orphans arrive from Korea on television. But we had ours and they were still becoming and they had something to say about it. Now they are grown into that beauty of starting up.

The first time I went to Franny's house, I recognized the familiar aroma of boy's feet. Simon's sneakers were lurking under the coffee table. It reminded me of home.

Jody sings commercials and tells me silly jokes. She is lovely, Franny's daughter. She is lovely and strong and difficult. She is Franny's daughter. Simon sits at the piano. "Hey Susan, do you like this?" I do. I like what he plays. I like him. And so when I walk into the living room at the end, at Christmas, and see him, I come apart.

They were 10, 12, and 14, when we started out. Nearly 8 years later, we'd lived through puberty and three sets of college applications.

* * *

"You bitch."
"You're such a bitch."
Our teenagers were not having a good day.

My son punches his fist through a wall. Her daughter stops eating. The oldest weeps his lost structure. How much of this has to do with us, I can't say, but we blame ourselves, each other, and sometimes who we are.

"I can't do this," Franny would say. "I don't know how to be a mother and a lover. Can't we just wait until the children are grown and find each other again?"

A family is the faces you see and know you will see whenever you look up. When Franny is on the phone and Simon is reading a book, when Jody's watching her soaps, and Jeremy is in the kitchen complaining there isn't anything to eat. When a person says, as casual as heartbreak, "Do you want a cup of coffee, honey?"

* * *

Here's what I did. I really did this. I rented a car and drove to the Howard Johnson's Motor Lodge outside of Woodstock. It was OUR place. We stayed there when we visited her parents. It seemed like every time we stayed at a cheap motel, there was child abuse going on in the next room. Perhaps it was only a haunting. Our own children tormenting us for the time we abandoned them at camp or wouldn't let them stay up late to watch some TV show or maybe they were just pissed off at us for having the bed to ourselves.

The motel is its orange self. Why do I weep? The air in the

parking lot is hot and familiar. Somewhere close. Somewhere in the trees, around the bend, over the hill, she is. I can't breathe. It was in one of these rooms she asked me to make love to her. Her father had just died. And she needed this from me. I knew how to marry love with death. I knew if you kissed someone who needed you to live, you would live.

The day after I came home from the hospital, still bandaged, half crazy from residual drugs and fear, Jane and I made love. I didn't care if my stiches came free. Let them rip. I shouldn't have been able to move in the ways I moved to her, but I was powerful. The possibility of death nearly broke our bed. In a few days I would start chemo, but that night I was not in possession of the facts. I was a body in disrepair and someone was healing me.

I wanted to heal Franny. I wanted to swoop her up, take her in my jaws, protect this love. She kissed me with her teeth. I swallowed her loss down whole. Everything was streaked with us. "My love." "Don't stop." "Darling." I placed myself at the source. So lovely. So known to me. Then she took me in her mouth. I shivered. We jammed our stuff against the bed. And for awhile at the Howard Johnson's outside of Woodstock, we kept chaos at bay.

I went to the town square. I didn't know where to walk exactly or where to set my sights. I wondered if people could see me, or was I invisible because I didn't belong anymore? And if Franny actually came to town on this day, would she walk right past me? Turning a few feet away to look back as if there were something, a sensation she couldn't name, my scent more powerful than my substance, wafting through to catch her up short. I steadied myself against a store window and wished for a prop.
(*Beat.*)
There she was. On the other side of the street, her hands in her pockets, singing Rodgers and Hart. Or thinking about semiotics. Going on about her life.
(*Beat.*)
Just like I needed to go on about my own.
(*Beat.*)

Goodbye Franny. Goodbye my friend. Goodbye my left breast. Goodbye my infant son. Goodbye my period. Goodbye 35. Goodbye old neighborhood.

Your doctor says "It's positive." Your lover says, "It's over." And you say goodbye to the person you thought you were.

* * *

I'm going to show you my scar. In a minute.

When you have a brush with death, you think, if I pull through this, I'm going to do it all differently. I'm going to say exactly what I think. I'll be a kind and generous citizen. I won't be impatient with my son. I won't shut down to my lover. I'll learn to play the trumpet. I'll never waste another minute.
(*Beat.*)
Then you don't die. And it's God, I hate my hair! Would you please pick up your clothes! How long do we have to stand in this fucking line?

One day I'm sitting in a cafe and a man with ordinary difficulties is complaining. Our water heater is on the fritz. Just like that he says it. OUR something isn't working and WE are worrying about it.

I want to say – cherish the day your car broke down, the water pump soured, the new bed didn't arrive on time. Celebrate the time you got lost and maps failed. On your knees to this domestic snafu, you blessed pair. While you can still feel the other's skin in the night, her foot caressing your calf, preoccupations catching on the damp sheets. You twist, haul an arm over. Remote kisses motor your dreams.

* * *

The people who made love to me, afterwards – there have been three. Jane, of course who slept with me in my hospital bed, pretending to be my sister. David. And Franny. It's the way David said, "It's wildly sexy this body of yours that has given birth and given up a part." It's the way Franny loved me more for my lack of it, this symmetry that other women have.

How do I tell someone new? Okay, help me out here. Say I've finally met someone I like. Do I tell her over the salad? Wait until dessert? Do I tell her when we're getting undressed? Does it matter? Would it matter to you?
(*Beat.*)
I miss it but there is something growing in its place. And it is not a tougher skin.
(*Beat.*)
The doctor says my heart is more exposed now. Closer to the air. You don't have any protective tissue, she says. I hardly need a stethoscope to hear it beat.

* * *

I cherish this scar. It's a mark of experience. It's the history of me. A permanent fix on the impermanence of it all. A line that suggests I take it seriously. Which I do. A line that suggests my beginning and my end. I have no other like it. I have no visible reminder of the baby I lost. Or the friend. No constant monument to the passing of my relationship. There is no other sign on my body that repeats the incongruity and dislocation, the alarm. A scar is a challenge to see ourselves as survivors, after all. Here is the evidence. The body repairs. And the human heart, even after it has broken into a million pieces, will make itself large again.

* * *

My son did get it back for me. In a way. Not the year it happened. But the year after that and the year and the year and the year after that.
(*Beat.*)
It was little league that saved me. It was Jeremy up to the plate. It was Gabe Goldstein at second. It was Chris Chandler catching a pop fly. It was Jeremy stealing home. It was providing refreshments and washing his uniform. It was trying to get him to

wear a jock strap. It was screaming, "Batter. Batter. Batter." It was Jeremy pitching the last out with the bases loaded. It was the Moms. The Moms and Dads and the coolers. It was the hats we wore and the blankets. It was driving him home from practice. It was his bloody knees. It was the sun going down on us, watching our sons and daughters play and be well.
(*Beat.*)
This was the cure for cancer.

* * *

I miss it, but I want to tell all the women in the changing booths, that we are still beautiful, we are still powerful, we are still sexy, we are still here.

(*I unbutton my shirt to reveal my scar as the LIGHTS FADE.*)

END.

Trip's Cinch

by Phyllis Nagy

For Mel.

TRIP'S CINCH was directed by Lisa Peterson with the following cast (in order of appearance):

BENJAMIN TRIP	Steven Culp
VAL GRECO	Barbara eda-Young
LUCY PARKS	Mary Schultz

Scenic Designer	Paul Owen
Costume Designer	Esther Marquis
Lighting Designer	Mary Louise Geiger
Sound Designer	Casey L. Warren
Props Master	Mark Bissonnette
Stage Manager	Paul Mills Holmes
Assistant Stage Manager	John David Flak
Dramaturg	Michele Volansky
Casting	Jay Binder

PHYLLIS NAGY was born in New York City and now lives in London. Her works include BUTTERFLY KISS (Almeida Theatre, London); WELDON RISING (Royal Court Theatre, London; Liverpool Playhouse, German and Israeli productions); TRIP'S CINCH, commissioned and produced by the Actors Theatre of Louisville; an adaptation of Nathaniel Hawthorne's THE SCARLET LETTER, commissioned and produced by the Denver Center Theatre; and the Mobil prize-winning DISAPPEARED, which will tour the United Kingdom in early 1995. She is currently under commission to the Hampstead Theatre, Radio 4, BBC television and the Royal Court Theatre, where she is the Arts Council Writer-in-Residence. Phyllis has received two playwriting fellowships from the National Endowment for the Arts, and has been awarded playwriting fellowships from the McKnight Foundation and the New York Foundation for the Arts. She is a member of New Dramatists, New York.

CHARACTERS

Benjamin Trip – Mid 30s. He is quite handsome, utterly charming and groomed in a manner that suggests great old wealth.

Lucy Parks – Early-to-mid 30s. Strong, good looking and very sure of herself. Her barbed wit is dry and measured rather than overtly hostile.

Val Greco – Mid-to late 40s. Opinionated, charismatic, formidable academic.

THE SETTING:

A non-naturalistic landscape which is covered almost entirely by sand. It is as if there has been a blizzard of sand: high sand banks, drifts, etc. Beyond the sand, there is a clear, black night sky, stretching as far as the eye can see. In scene one an executive desk and two office chairs should be placed in this landscape as if they've always been there. In scene two, the desk and chairs are replaced with a simple kitchen table and two straight-back chairs which are placed in exactly the same position as the desk and chairs in scene one. In scene three, the table and chairs are replaced by the kind of small, round bar table and chairs that are found at outdoor clubs.

THE TIME:

The present.

Trip's Cinch

SCENE 1

> *Val is bent over the desk. Trip stands behind her.*

TRIP: Stand on your left leg.
> (*Val lifts her right leg, bending it at the knee.*)

VAL: Like this?

TRIP: Hold it straight out. Like this.
> (*Trip extends Val's leg out as straight as it will go. He holds on to her leg. Pause.*)

VAL: What are you doing now?

TRIP: I'm checking for runs in your stocking.

VAL: Do you find any?

TRIP: No. But I check for a long time. Like this.
> (*Trip runs his hand up and down Val's leg. He takes his time.*)
> You may relax your leg now.
> (*Val does.*)

VAL: Thank you.

TRIP: You have lovely legs.

VAL: I don't. But thanks anyway. (*A beat.*) Is that right?

TRIP: Yes. Ask me to come closer.

VAL: Now?

TRIP: Yes.

VAL: Without further *prelude?*

TRIP: Yes.

VAL: Just: come closer?

TRIP: Yes. Please say it.

VAL: Come closer.

TRIP: I'm there.
> (*Trip is pressed against Val.*)

VAL: Can anyone see us? Are we being watched?

TRIP: It's past closing time.

VAL: The staff?

TRIP: They're discreet.

VAL: So we can't be seen.

TRIP: Ask me again: come closer.

VAL: You can't come *much* closer. You can't *move*.

TRIP: I can move. Ask me.

VAL: Move. (*A beat.*) Please.

   (*A pause.*)

   What are you doing now?

TRIP: I'm listening to you cry.

VAL: I'm crying? I'm *upset?*

TRIP: You're relieved. Happy. Grateful. Tell me you're grateful.

VAL: Are you sure? I mean, are you really *sure* about this?

TRIP: Yes.

VAL: All right, then. (*A beat.*) I'm grateful.

TRIP: You have lovely legs.

VAL: I'm so....so....fucking *grateful.*

TRIP: No.

VAL: I'm *not* grateful?

TRIP: You don't swear.

VAL: Ah. Of course. I'm sorry.

TRIP: I'm slipping my hand beneath your skirt.

VAL: Do I resist?

TRIP: You cry.

VAL: More gratefulness.

TRIP: You're wet.

VAL: I'm *hot?*

TRIP: I'm *touching* you. I generate great heat.

VAL: So. I'm crying. I'm wet. I'm hot. What else?

TRIP: Tell me how hard I am.

VAL: How hard *are* you?

TRIP: I'm the hardest you've felt. Tell me.

VAL: (*Flatly.*) Okay. You're the hardest.

TRIP: You have lovely legs.

VAL: Is that *all?*

TRIP: Pardon?

VAL: You tell me I have lovely legs three times. Am I unlovely everywhere else?

TRIP: (*After a beat.*) It's the heat of the moment. I say whatever comes to mind.

VAL: Oh.

TRIP: I'm overcome.

VAL: And am I still crying?

TRIP: Yes. It excites me.

VAL: You're already the hardest I've ever felt. You can't get more excited than that.

TRIP: Don't talk. Cry.

VAL: Okay.

(*A pause.*)

What next?

TRIP: I wait.

VAL: For what?

TRIP: You ask me to make love to you.

VAL: *I* ask *you?*

TRIP: You have to invite me inside.

VAL: Like a vampire. Right.

TRIP: Ask me.

VAL: What do I say? *Enter* me? Is that what I say?

TRIP: Yes.

VAL: Fine. (*A beat.*) Enter me.

TRIP: I'm there.

(*A pause. Trip backs away from Val.*)

I'm done.

(*Val rises and turns to Trip. She begins to laugh.*)

TRIP: You don't laugh.

VAL: (*But she can't help herself.*) No, no, I – of *course* I don't laugh – of *course*. I mean, well, I find this all a bit difficult to –

TRIP: You don't *laugh*.

VAL: Yes, yes, but it's difficult to believe, if not *impossible* to to –

TRIP: Nonetheless. (*A beat.*) There is no laughter.

(*Val stops laughing.*)

VAL: I'm terribly sorry.

(*A pause. Trip removes a handkerchief from his breast pocket and begins to methodically wipe his hands clean.*)

VAL: Is there something . . . wrong is there, I don't know, did you dirty yourself?

TRIP: Yes.

VAL: Then? That night? You you . . .*came* . . . in your hands?

TRIP: No.

VAL: What? What then?

(*A pause. Trip folds his handkerchief neatly and replaces it in his breast pocket.*)

TRIP: Miss Parks did not laugh when we made love.

VAL: So the trial transcripts –

TRIP: The trial is completed. I am telling you –

VAL: Yes yes but the trial is a matter of –

TRIP: You mustn't rely on transcripts. Human error contributes –

VAL: – a matter of public *record*.

(*A pause.*)

The trial transcript is a matter of public record, Mr. Trip. It is an invaluable research tool.

TRIP: It might be wrong. The transcriber might have made errors. Don't believe everything you read.

VAL: Are you telling me that the transcript is incorrect? That that it's, I don't – is it *flawed*?

TRIP: There could be mistakes.

VAL: So you're saying the transcriber possibly, what? Fucked up? She fucked up the transcript?

TRIP: (*After a beat.*) Greco. That's an Italian name.

VAL: Yes. Sicilian.

TRIP: Sicily. Cows. Volcanoes. Poverty.

VAL: (*After a beat.*) *I* wasn't born there.

TRIP: What is the saying? You can take a girl out of Sicily . . .

(*A pause.*)

VAL: She was bent over a . . . what was it? A small sand dune?

TRIP: Your train of thought is very scattered, Ms. Greco. It *is* Ms. Greco, no?

VAL: Lucy Parks. That night. A couple of G and T's at the Club Fortune. You walked along the beach. Listened to the waves. It was clear. The sky was full of stars. She bent over a small sand dune to show you the runs in her stocking. (*A beat.*) I am unmarried. Yes.

(*A pause.*)

TRIP: Do you research all your books in this manner?

VAL: I research. I inquire.

TRIP: But I don't suppose you've researched them in quite this way.

VAL: No. No, it's not – ordinarily, I'm speaking of my usual methods here – *ordinarily*, I write about the dead.

TRIP: Byron. Shelley. Elvis Presley.

VAL: Among others. I've done others.

TRIP: So *ordinarily* your subjects are unavailable to you. To speak to, that is.

VAL: I couldn't re-enact Shelley's drowning with him. If that's what you mean.

(*A pause. Trip takes a brand new deck of cards, still in its box and cellophane wrapper, from his inside jacket pocket and places it on the table.*)

TRIP: Where was it you said you teach? Bakersfield? Cleveland?

VAL: Minneapolis.

TRIP: How delightful, I'm sure.

VAL: The home of Prince. There's plenty of booze and bingo halls. What more could I ask?

TRIP: The Ivy League.

VAL: Been there. Seen that, Mr. Trip. (*A beat.*) What's with the cards?

TRIP: My secretary has read me your essays on popular culture.

VAL: I hadn't thought of them as bedtime stories.

TRIP: They're appalling.

VAL: Does your secretary tuck you in as well as read to you?

TRIP: Though, I must admit your theories on – and I can't recall your precise phrase– the supremacy of the male libido and the necessity for its its –

VAL: Unfettered appetite.

TRIP: Thank you – its unfettered appetite – is crucial to the optimal development of western civilization. (*A beat; Trip unwraps the cellophane wrapper from the deck of cards, puts the box back on the table and puts the wrapper in his jacket pocket.*) Or perhaps it was all civilization.

(*A pause.*)

VAL: No no. Western civilization. That's right.

TRIP: Interesting. If a bit laughable.

VAL: I beg your pardon but –

TRIP: I am merely expressing my opinion. You understand I have the greatest respect for your intellect and of course I can't can't really say what –

VAL: – but if you would articulate your position more clearly, Mr. Trip. If you could –

TRIP: I am incapable of *articulating*. I leave that to those of you who write books. I act on impulse.

(*Trip removes the cards from their box and begins to shuffle them slowly and deliberately.*)

VAL: Fair enough.

TRIP: I see a beautiful car: I buy it. I see a beggar in the street and I cross to avoid him.

VAL: No no, fair enough. All right.

TRIP: Most people, Ms. Greco, the *majority* of people are not even self aware enough to realize that they act on impulse. They actually believe they think out their decisions rationally and with great care. This, they believe, is civilized behavior. (*A beat; Trip stops shuffling the cards and places them on the table.*) You're a bit long in tooth to be single.

VAL: I always make rational decisions, Mr. Trip. (*A beat.*) I like men. I'm not partial to marriage.

TRIP: The jury, for instance, acted on impulse. They acquitted because their hunch was – and I am speaking off the record you understand – that I was correct. They looked at me and they looked at her and –

VAL: I'm on your side. Don't misunderstand –

TRIP: No no no let me finish – the jury did not need the trial *transcript* to come to their conclusion. They understood the nature of the beast without the need for –

VAL: Although, I find this line of theorizing highly dubious –

TRIP: – without the need for analysis, without the need for for *articulation.*

VAL: Well. That blows trials by jury, I guess.

TRIP: There you go. There you *go*. People like you make a mockery of the system.

VAL: Which system?

TRIP: The whole the the – *all* systems, for chrissake.

(*A pause.*)

VAL: It was a joke. I made a *joke.*

TRIP: If you always act rationally, why were you bent over a desk re-enacting a rape?

VAL: There was no rape, Mr. Trip. There was only a beach. Stars. The thrill of it all.

TRIP: It was a figure of speech.

VAL: I'm aware of that. I am *aware* – I don't appreciate, Mr. Trip – please understand that I am not being antagonistic here, really I am not – however, I do *not* appreciate what I perceive to be condescension –

(*Trip begins to deal out a hand of Solitaire.*)

TRIP: You know Ms. Greco, you are rather attractive when –

VAL: – I have come here with good intentions. I support your position and I am not I am not willing –

TRIP: – when you're slightly angry. Yes. Your eyes take on a positively, yes, a positively brilliant aspect and I must say –

VAL: – I am not willing to put up with – especially when there are so many, yes, I have to say it, so many inconsistencies in your account – I will not put up with this shit. (*A beat.*) Anger becoming women is a cliché, Mr. Trip.

TRIP: Nonetheless, it is a much admired cliché, Ms. Greco. I felt you might appreciate it as part of the *lore* of popular culture. Which, as you remind me, you so respect. You so so . . . *elevate.*

VAL: I observe trends. I investigate their validity.

TRIP: Am I a trend?

VAL: Well. You're certainly *popular.*

TRIP: I *am* popular culture.

VAL: Hold on now just – surely you can't believe –

TRIP: No, but I am, Ms. Greco. The tide of popular opinion and support rushes my way. It *rushes*. It it – (*He studies his Solitaire hand for a moment.*) red ten on red jack. (*He corrects his mistake.*)

VAL: There are those who say you are a criminal. That your position and your wealth and –

TRIP: My *position?* What what – what is that? *Position?*

VAL: Look look. How can I convince you, Mr. Trip – my sincerity my my total belief in your – but my investigative skills would would be lacking –

TRIP: I am not some some criminal some poor – I am not jobless and and poor and black like that that *animal* – that what's his name –

VAL: The the integrity of my scholarship would be sorely doubted if I did not ask – look I trust you absolutely. There is, believe me, no uncertainty but please tell me why – look look what are you *doing* with those cards–

TRIP: *He's* the criminal and what do you *mean* by my position? Am I penalized somehow because –

VAL: You're making me very nervous. I am very uncomfortable and if you insist on that card game I will I will –

TRIP: Why? Because I have *money?* Because – well I don't know – because I am handsome? Healthy? Because *any* woman would be beside herself – in a manner of speaking, you understand – not *every* woman, but perhaps quite a few would be thrilled – oh for God's sake what's his *name?*

(*Trip slams what's left of the deck of cards onto the table. Val looks at Trip's Solitaire hand.*)

VAL: Myself, I like poker. (*A beat.*) I don't recall his name. But I know he's doing time.

TRIP: (*Resumes playing his hand.*) That's as it should be.

VAL: His defense was your defense

TRIP: That that defenseless woman – the abuse, the gall of that man – black seven on red eight – the unmitigated *gall* –

VAL: Is there something wrong with your hands, Mr. Trip? Is there some kind of – I ask because earlier you, your *handkerchief,* well, I –

TRIP: I love women – no no don't interrupt – I love women and I cannot support their continued brutalization at the hands of –

VAL: You're shorter than you appear to be in photographs. (*A beat.*) I don't know why that's occurred to me.

TRIP: (*After a beat.*) Do you believe I raped Lucy Parks?

VAL: No.

TRIP: Why not?

VAL: Did you? I mean, if what you're saying is –

TRIP: (*His attempt at a joke.*) Answer mine and I'll answer yours.

VAL: Listen I will not engage in semantic games I don't have the –

TRIP: Lucy Parks and I met by chance. We drank gin and tonics. I taught her to play Solitaire. We flirted in the usual manner. And though I did not find her to be physically – what shall we call it, *compelling* –

VAL: I've never understood the Solitaire. I've never, I mean, why? Why in the midst of –

TRIP: – I looked at Lucy Parks and saw on her tired face the years of loneliness spread out like a map of despair, Ms. Greco, and I could not refuse, I could not *allow* her –

VAL: Why why – of course, women are illogical, I appreciate that, even I am susceptible and Mr. Trip, I can't tell you how I despise the weakness of illogical action – but why Lucy Parks would bend over a sand dune to have you check her –

TRIP: I could not allow her to leave without some – and I remind you that I acted with her consent – I I I was full of of compassion, a deep compassion – she deserved some, and naturally so did I –

VAL: Her stockings I just, I really just don't know what to make of – and the Solitaire, I mean you were in a bar for fuck sake *drinking* – and *hard* booze, mind you–

TRIP: There is always a moment of doubt in a sexual encounter, Ms. Greco, a a a millisecond when consent might be withdrawn or or or – well, the idea is to get beyond that moment to to surpass that natural doubt and move on to the even more natural state of desire that that lurks everywhere, it it –

VAL: You understand that I never *never* allow a sexual encounter to progress beyond a stage where I cannot control its outcome and I find it incomprehensible that Lucy Parks could not could not –
(*Trip quite suddenly places his fingertips over Val's lips. This should appear to be a gentle, rather than an aggressive, action.*)

TRIP: Exactly.
(*A pause. Trip removes the handkerchief from his breast pocket and once again methodically wipes his hands clean.*)
Do you play Solitaire, Ms. Greco? Oh, I know you prefer a rousing hand of five card stud, but given your your *background* I find it entirely predictable and so –

VAL: Don't touch me. Don't you touch me. (*A beat.*) I am not Lucy Parks, Mr. Trip.

TRIP: Pity.
(*Trip folds up the handkerchief and replaces it in his breast pocket. A pause.*)

VAL: Is something, is there – why in the *fuck* do you keep wiping your hands, Mr. Trip?

TRIP: When do you expect your book to be published, Ms. Greco?

VAL: Some would say you're being – and I'm not necessarily one of them I want you to know that – some might say you're being, well, evasive, Mr. Trip. (*A beat.*) I don't know when the book will be – of course it really *should* be published in time for tenure review –

TRIP: Do you need photographs?

VAL: You have, what *pictures* of the the –

TRIP: Portraits, Ms. Greco. Of me.

VAL: What?

TRIP: Black and white eight by tens. Posed, candids. I'm exceptionally photogenic. My secretary would be happy to –

VAL: No no it's really – thank you, Mr. Trip. That's very kind of you, but I don't need –

TRIP: My secretary is quite good about about you know, *personal* errands. She wrote a lovely note to Lucy Parks when I sent – and I don't mean to be immodest – the check.

VAL: What's this? What are you – you sent her *money?* Is this what you're – no no I feel you must explain –

TRIP: Lucy Parks lost her job. Her *livelihood,* Ms. Greco. I am surprised you're not aware, because you are so on *top* of things that I naturally –

VAL: I am aware of her difficulty. I am just taken aback by by your –

TRIP: Generosity?

VAL: Something like that. Yes.

TRIP: My secretary wept when she saw the amount of the check.

VAL: Does your secretary have a name?

TRIP: Yes.

(*A pause. Trip removes the handkerchief from his pocket and begins to wipe his hands clean.*)

Sweaty palms. (*A beat.*) You won't tell anyone, will you?
Blackout.

SCENE 2

Val visits with Lucy. The desk and office chairs have been replaced with a kitchen table and two straight-back chairs. There are several neat stacks of mail-order catalogues on the table.

LUCY: I've never met a reporter who didn't take notes.

VAL: I'm not a reporter. I'm a professor.

LUCY: You don't look like a teacher.

VAL: I'm a professor of English literature. Actually.

LUCY: Like I said. You don't look like a teacher. Still, you ought to take notes.

VAL: This is an informal interview, Lucy.

LUCY: Do I *know* you?

VAL: Pardon?

LUCY: See. You can't even follow my *questions* without notes. How are you supposed to remember my answers? (*A beat.*) I'm tired of familiarity. I'd like a little *formality.*

VAL: You've been through an ordeal, Lucy, and I'd like to make this as –

LUCY: Miss Parks.

VAL: Okay, okay, I only thought – the two of us, we –

LUCY: I see. You want girl talk.

VAL: I had assumed you might be comfortable, *amenable* even to to –

LUCY: Amenable?

VAL: (*She's searching for synonyms.*) Receptive, willing, uhm –

LUCY: I know what it means.

VAL: (*Trying to lighten the atmosphere a bit.*) So. If I don't look like a teacher, what *do* I look like?

LUCY: An asshole.

VAL: Fine fine. The level of your hostility is perfectly understandable after what you've been through, but the use of obscenity is is –

LUCY: I know who you are and why you've come here and and – what do you mean, after what I've *been* through? What do you think I've been *through?*

VAL: Well. The trial. For one thing. And the the –

LUCY: You can't even say it, can you? (*A beat.*) I'm aware of your *brief,* professor. And anyway, you read the papers: it never happened.

VAL: I believe in the efficacy of our legal system, Miss Parks.

LUCY: So do I.

VAL: You do?

LUCY: Uh-huh.

VAL: Good. *Good.* I'm impressed by your ability to accept –

LUCY: I said I believed in its efficacy. I don't accept its infallibility.

VAL: (*After a beat.*) If I could just get a few details, Miss Parks, you know – a little background on your your – you're a grade-school crossing guard with ten years –

LUCY: I was. (*A beat.*) Val. Val Greco. Val *Val* – short for . . .?

VAL: – with ten years service and and I understand you are single? Never been married? Is that correct?

LUCY: Free. For the moment. Too bad, huh, because I'm kind of *past* it, right? Kind of like you, professor. (*A beat.*) What *is* Val short for?

VAL: (*A beat.*) Valentina. After my grandmother.

LUCY: A real *whopper* of a name. Phew. Hey, listen, I don't blame you for hiding behind a diminutive. So do I. Me, now, I was named after a Little Richard song.

VAL: This is, this is – please, Lucy, I'd really like to talk, to to really *talk* –

LUCY: Gal to gal? (*A beat.*) Miss Parks. I insist.

VAL: I'm sorry. I've been traveling too much. Aeroplanes make me – look look, aren't you going to offer me a cup of coffee?

LUCY: No.

(*A pause.*)

VAL: Tea, then. I'll take tea.

LUCY: How much you getting to write this book? More or less than you can stuff into a breadbox?

(*A pause. Lucy begins flipping through a catalogue.*)

VAL: I'm very thirsty.

LUCY: I'm a really bad hostess.

VAL: Look look Lu – Miss Parks – without your cooperation I will be unable to present a balanced portrait of the complexities of of –

LUCY: Complexities? You're talking to me about *complexities?* Listen to *me*, Valentina. Have you any idea – have you any *notion* of what it means to be under public scrutiny – oh oh, well, I guess you *do*, professor, you've got –

VAL: My celebrity is a different matter altogether and I resent –

LUCY: Oh yes yes yes you've got, let's see, you've got *rock* stars and and shit kicking academics from Yale and politicians arguing –

VAL: I have earned my spotlight in a a decent and time-honoured manner –

LUCY: Pimply boy-prodigy novelists and wanna-be *poetesses* ripping each other's eyes out over your your half-assed ramblings on the virtue of *dicks* –

VAL: No no you mustn't – hold on hold on I have earned public recognition through difficult – and yes, it must be said, ball-breaking scholarship into the –

LUCY: So have *I* earned public recognition, professor. And look where it's got me. (*A beat; she flips through a catalogue.*) What do you think? A Whirlpool or an Amana fridge-freezer?

VAL: All right. Let's think this through rationally and with – wait wait. Why *shouldn't* I take advantage of the spotlight cast on me? Why not?

LUCY: Because it makes me look ridiculous. (*A beat.*) The spotlight cast upon me. What a turn of phrase.

VAL: I'd really like something to drink.

LUCY: Nope. All out of drinks. Will you remember to write about my bad table manners in your book? And don't forget to mention my bad haircut which the press – bless their little olive pit hearts – evidently took as an indication of my latent lesbianism.

VAL: (*After a beat.*) Are you a lesbian? Because, if you are – and I place no judgment on this at all, none whatsoever – I would understand the complications of –

LUCY: Wait wait wait wait – you want to know if I'm –

VAL: The probable emotional difficulties involved in discussing your sexuality after such a traumatic several –

LUCY: You want to know if I'm *gay?*

VAL: (*A beat.*) You can tell me.

LUCY: You really want to know this? This would be, what? *Helpful* to your research?

VAL: It has its value. Yes.

LUCY: Uh-huh. Well. No. I'm not.

VAL: You're not. Okay. I don't mind if you don't want –

LUCY: I'm not gay. Sorry. Another theory bites –

VAL: *I* used to be. For a couple of years. Therefore, I really *do* understand the complex nature of –

LUCY: No no no you will not, you will *not* confess. This is not a church, Valentina. (*A beat.*) Though with your your – how should I put this – with your *views* on us girls I'm not surprised none of us would have you after a couple of years.

VAL: I didn't say *that*.

LUCY: No. You didn't. I did.

VAL: (*After a beat.*) If you would talk about your plans for the future –

LUCY: I'm gonna buy a lot of appliances.

VAL: Fine fine. Appliances. Uhm. What? Kitchen appli –

LUCY: Do not patronize me. (*A beat.*) Your essays on the romantic poets are very entertaining, Valentina.

VAL: I I – thank you. I'm flattered you read them – and given your hostility towards me I'm surprised you –

LUCY: You ought to stick to the romantics. You're a little loopy on the real beasts, though. Like him.

VAL: I don't know who you're –

LUCY: Yes you do.

(*A pause. Lucy re-arranges her catalogue piles on the table.*)

Now. I keep separate piles for electronics, clothing, household goods and and – oh what have we *here* – my newest category: luxury goods.

VAL: Luxury goods?

LUCY: I've gone beyond J. C. Penney and Sears, professor. Way beyond. Look. Look at this: a combination fax, laptop computer and paper shredder. What do you think?

VAL: Why did you lose your job? I mean, one reads all sorts –

LUCY: Why do *you* think I lost my job?

VAL: I really couldn't say.

LUCY: Then keep reading.

VAL: (*After a beat.*) While I don't necessarily condone the actions taken by your school board you must understand – and I am being completely objective in my analysis of the of the –

LUCY: Objective? What what – is it really, do you you – objectivity isn't *relative*, professor, it isn't –

VAL: My analysis of the situation is oh – and look look you cannot fault their concern for the welfare of their students, many of whom are –

LUCY: My financial situation wasn't *objective* – how how the *fuck* could you even –

VAL: Many of whom are young *girls*. Miss Parks: they are very young girls and perhaps the school board's action was a pre-emptive – a a *precaution* against what possibly –

LUCY: Oh. Yeah. I forgot about that. Sure sure. Stupid me.

VAL: I don't mean to suggest I *believe* –

LUCY: Well I guess I better be on the horn to *your* school board to tell them about *your* dip in the waters of –

VAL: They know. (*A beat.*) And of course, my position isn't controlled by a school board. Higher education has its own governing body, Miss Parks, and there is not anything wrong –

LUCY: Anyway, it's trendy now. Right?

VAL: There is some, there is a marked trend – yes – in that direction.

LUCY: Can you think of any practical use for a paper shredder? In the home, I mean? (*A beat.*) The spotlight, professor, is his. And yours. Me, I'm collecting junk mail and contemplating a better haircut.

VAL: It's good, really *admirable* that you've kept your sense of humor.

LUCY: Must be my working class upbringing.

VAL: Have *you* noticed that, too? I mean, the way the working class responds to adversity is is is well I can't *begin* to –

LUCY: You really know how to shovel the shit.

(*A pause. Val takes a catalogue and begins to leaf through it.*)

VAL: So. What will you do now, Miss Parks?

LUCY: Fuck all.

(*Lucy takes the catalogue away from Val. Her action is not overtly aggressive.*)

VAL: Surely that's not healthy, it's not conducive to the process of –

LUCY: I've *earned* fuck-all status. (*A beat.*) You shouldn't touch what's not yours, Valentina.

VAL: Fair enough. (*A beat.*) I was not *born* into privilege, Miss Parks. I was not handed my opportunities. I took I learned I *strove* for the excellence that was lacking in my environment and my actions entitled me –

LUCY: Yeah yeah I've heard this this – pull-yourself-up-from-your-bootstrap stories are passé, professor. Listen listen I bet you –

VAL: No no you don't you can't compare –

LUCY: I bet you all your *entitlement* that I have more cash tucked away for a rainy day – but wait I'm not being fair because well – wink wink – I haven't really *earned* my recent income, have I? I haven't sweated over over literary *trivia* and –

VAL: Don't you dare compare our our – you foolish –

LUCY: I haven't been peering up my own asshole looking for people to to *insult* and and –

VAL: You lying little – you you *coarse* –

LUCY: Lying? *Lying?* I've got half a million bucks stashed away in a dozen bank accounts. How about you?

VAL: You cashed – wait wait you didn't actually *accept* –

LUCY: You go out for what you think is a quiet drink on the beach, you know, just you and your inconsequential thoughts out there in the night air, with your *bad* haircut –

VAL: I hadn't – I must admit I hadn't thought, well of course Mr. Trip told me he sent he he *mentioned* that he –

LUCY: *So*. You go out for a couple of gin and tonics and you wind up with a stack of junk mail and half a million in the bank. Who knew? (*A beat.*) Mr. Trip? *Mister* Trip?

(*A pause. Val picks up the catalogue she'd leafed through earlier. She leafs through it again, finds what she's looking for and places the open catalogue on the table.*)

VAL: I prefer Whirlpool fridge-freezers. Always have.

LUCY: (*Looks at the catalogue.*) That's a nice one. Do you want it?

VAL: I have – mine is perfectly adequate –

LUCY: I can buy you one. I can buy you *ten*.

VAL: No no no that's not necessary though it's it's really very *good* of you to –

LUCY: What do you think happened to me on that beach? What do you do you –

VAL: Lucy I don't – listen I don't really – I don't believe that anybody can ever *precisely* know –

LUCY: Fuck you. All right? Call me *Miss* Parks. Fuck you.

VAL: (*After a beat.*) I was going to say I was was –

LUCY: I know. And believe me, I will not bite the hand that's *fed* me, professor. I know my place. Do you?

VAL: (*After a beat.*) If we could set up another appointment another, a a time when we could –

LUCY: I've got plenty of mail-order to slosh through. I'm in no hurry. Why are *you* in such a hurry?

VAL: Actually I have – I really must catch a flight to to – but I would like to *discuss* with you the the –

LUCY: What *what* – the finer points of your just-say-no theory? The the *reasons* why I drank gin that night instead of beer, which – and I've got to say this is my favorite press hunch – which somehow made it clear to him that I was *ready* for –

VAL: Look look I'm running late. I'm late. For a television appearance. Really.

LUCY: An *appearance?* Is this some kind of a I don't know some kind of a joke or or maybe –

VAL: No no I mean I am sincerely running late for a *discussion* –

LUCY: Hey hey I'm so *late* I don't know where time went and what the *fuck* are you talking about on *television?*

VAL: Well. I'm – it's on the political implications of gender. Actually.
LUCY: That old chestnut.
>   (*A pause. Lucy picks up the open catalogue.*)
>   Listen, *Valentina*. You write down the model number of that
>   Whirlpool and it'll pop up on your doorstep before you know it.
>   Me, I'm gonna make myself a nice hot cup of coffee. You want
>   some?
>   (*Val touches Lucy's arm. Several beats before Lucy pulls her arm
>   away.*)
LUCY: (*After a beat.*) I bet you're the cream and sugar type.
Blackout.

SCENE 3

> *Trip and Lucy at the beach. The kitchen table and straight-back
> chairs have been replaced with a cocktail table and a couple of
> nondescript outdoor chairs. A pitcher of gin and tonics and two
> glasses are on the table. One glass, Trip's, is full. The other hasn't
> been used. Lucy wears a bright yellow school-crossing guard's
> raincoat.*

LUCY: It could rain at any moment.
TRIP: All right I – did I say anything about it? Did I?
LUCY: Okay okay so it's the only – what are you gonna do, *sue* me? I
>   *like* yellow. I can be seen in the dark. (*A beat.*) You know, there
>   are plenty of tables out here that you could easily – I don't see
>   why you –
TRIP: Could be Paris. Could be Rome.
LUCY: Really I am sure the waiter would be happy to – what? What
>   about – what are you talking about?
TRIP: Here. Tonight. Could be Paris. Could be Rome.
LUCY: Well if you're a *jerk* maybe but –
TRIP: People sit like this. Together. In Europe.
LUCY: We sit like this here too. Only we tend to *know* the people we
>   sit with.
TRIP: No no you don't see what I'm –
LUCY: I see it. (*A beat.*) This is not my idea of a vacation paradise.
TRIP: I'm sorry. You're not feeling well. I should have been more

sensitive, I know, but the exuberance of –

LUCY: I feel fine. My travel agent, however, *isn't* going to feel so hot when I get back home.

TRIP: You don't – you're not a –

LUCY: Local. No. Neither are you.

TRIP: As a matter of fact, I'm not. How did you –

LUCY: Do I look – what's wrong with me? Do I look stupid or something? Do I look *European?*

TRIP: Maybe I should take this from the – I merely sought to point out that were we in *Paris*, were we two two –

LUCY: Ships passing in the night?

TRIP: Yes. Yes, I see you're a romantic at –

LUCY: Yeah, well, I've seen all those ships-passing-in-the-night movies and you know what? They all end badly.

TRIP: Do they?

LUCY: Oh yeah. Real badly. (*A beat.*) Do they end badly in Europe, too?

(*A pause. Trip finishes off his drink and pours himself another.*)

TRIP: I wasn't – look, I *like* your coat.

LUCY: I don't. But it's part of the job.

TRIP: I wasn't looking at it. I wasn't looking at you – of course, I *was* looking. At you. But but that is only natural as I am *sitting* – and what is your job, Mrs. Mrs. . .

LUCY: I don't talk shop on vacation. (*A beat.*) Why do you assume I'm married?

TRIP: I didn't, I don't, I –

LUCY: Yes. You do. You *did.*

TRIP: I wish you'd share a drink with me. We could be the only two people –

LUCY: Oh oh oh now don't, just don't lay that kind of line –

TRIP: No no please, you must – I speak *metaphorically.*

LUCY: The insane speak metaphorically. Are you insane?

(*A pause. Trip pours her a drink.*)

TRIP: So. I take it you've never been to Europe Miss, Miss –

LUCY: Listen. This, however pathetic it may be, is my *holiday.* My fucking two weeks of fun in the sun. And all right, okay, I can't tell you *why* I've chosen to drag along part of my goddamned uniform except, well, you know it *is* a very fine raincoat–

TRIP: Your name. Please. I'm just trying to be – listen listen it's common courtesy and I –

LUCY: Oh *please* mister I'm so tired and I should have flown here but I can't stand – I can't *afford* – oh fuck I actually *like* Greyhounds and –

(*Trip suddenly touches his fingertips to Lucy's lips. A beat. He withdraws his hand.*)

TRIP: I'm Benjamin Trip.

(*A pause. Lucy downs her drink.*)

LUCY: Touch me again and I'll tear off your face. (*A beat.*) Jesus. I hate gin and tonic.

TRIP: I'm Benjamin Trip.

LUCY: Do you think maybe a waiter will come by some time this *century* so I can order a beer because, really, I have to tell you, this stuff is –

TRIP: Did you hear what I said?

LUCY: Yes. And I repeat: Touch me again and I'll tear off your face. (*A beat.*) Now, I'd like a beer.

TRIP: I have just told you that I am –

LUCY: Oh and by the way, Mr. Trip, I'm Michelle Pfeiffer. Oh sure, I'm looking a bit rough between films, but, hey, on my good days you could –

TRIP: What do I have to do to convince you that – to make you *understand* that – wait wait – here –

(*Trip removes his wallet from his inside jacket pocket and holds out his driver's license for her to see. She tries to take it, as one would naturally. Trip pulls it slightly back.*)

Please – I really – please don't touch it.

LUCY: (*Taking a good look at the license.*) Fine. I – no *kidding.* You're that that *guy* with the–

TRIP: Yes. I am.

LUCY: The guy with real estate? The *casinos?*

TRIP: No no not him.

LUCY: Oh sure, not *him.* You're the one with the –

TRIP: Yes. Yes. I am he.

LUCY: God, the insurance companies – You could knock me *down* – God I can't *believe* –

TRIP: No no no no – airlines.

LUCY: What?

TRIP: I'm in *airlines.*

LUCY: Oh, right. Airlines, casinos. Yeah.

    (*A beat. Lucy pours herself another drink.*)

    So. You're *that* guy.

TRIP: Interesting, no?

LUCY: No. It's not interesting.

TRIP: A happy coincidence, then.

LUCY: Well. It certainly is a coincidence. (*A beat; she downs her drink.*) So what's the situation? Some over-eager tour operator sell you a bad *trip?*

    (*Lucy laughs at her own bad joke. Trip doesn't. A beat.*)

TRIP: You're very funny.

LUCY: No. I'm very tired. And pissed off at this crummy *resort.*

TRIP: I like it here. (*A beat.*) Pour me a drink?

LUCY: They have waiters for that.

TRIP: The waiters are not present.

LUCY: And I am?

TRIP: Yes.

LUCY: Oh oh now you can, you can just go and –

TRIP: I do not mean to – it was – I simply asked you to –

LUCY: You want a drink you want a – is *that* what you want?

TRIP: Yes. That's all.

LUCY: Okay I'll give you a – *here* – here it *is.*

    (*Lucy pours gin and tonic into Trip's glass. She overpours, and liquid falls into Trip's lap.*)

TRIP: What the – that's that's come on, that's –

    (*Lucy stops pouring.*)

LUCY: I failed home economics.

    (*A pause. Trip ignores the spilled drink in his lap. He calmly sips at his gin and tonic. Lucy laughs.*)

LUCY: I'm sorry I shouldn't be laughing but this is this is – oh *God* this is just a really bad day I'm such an *idiot.*

    (*A beat, and Trip joins in the laughter.*)

TRIP: You're having a bad day. So? What the hell – we all have bad –

LUCY: Yes we all *do* have – oh my *God* what did I do to your suit it's it's – the material *alone* would cost what I–

TRIP: Never mind. Never mind. I deserved it.

LUCY: No no you didn't deserve some *harridan* with a yellow school-crossing guard coat –

TRIP: Yes but sometimes I do overstep my – of course, it's a natural extension of – well, a man in my position can sometimes be a tad insensitive to to to –

LUCY: My mistake, really – people tell me all the time what a–

TRIP: Is *that* what you do?

LUCY: I – sorry, I don't know –

TRIP: A school-crossing guard. Is *that* what you are?

LUCY: Yes, but how –

TRIP: The coat. The yellow coat. Of *course*.

LUCY: Whoops. Me and my big mouth.

TRIP: It must be quite an interesting –

LUCY: It's not.

   (*A beat. Lucy pours herself another drink.*)

TRIP: Surely, it's quite a responsible –

LUCY: How exactly did you get into the airline business?

TRIP: From the ground up.

   (*A beat. Lucy laughs.*)

LUCY: Oh man, this is my lucky day, I'll tell you –

TRIP: What? Did I say something funny?

LUCY: (*She breaks up again.*) Did you – did you – oh forget it. (*A beat.*) Do you think you could maybe *fly* a waiter in to bring me a beer?

TRIP: I'm sorry. I seem to be making a dreadful impression.

LUCY: Forget it.

TRIP: I'd hate to think that *I'm* contributing to your nightmare holiday.

LUCY: Listen, it's – oh well you know – it's not important it's not – what are *you* doing here, anyway?

TRIP: I'm having a drink with you.

LUCY: Me, now, it makes sense that *me* with my *responsible* little salary and my –

TRIP: My first business was based here. Electrical cabling. Sprockets.

LUCY: *Sprockets?*

TRIP: Ten man shop. Three-story warehouse. Simple. Neat. Sometimes I really miss –

LUCY: Oh oh oh here it comes: sentimentality alert. Please. Spare me the, you know, the –

TRIP: I don't miss the business. I miss the place. The *location*. (*A beat.*) I'm never recognized here. There's not a fax machine in sight.

LUCY: I'm never recognized here, either.

   (*A pause. Trip pours them both another drink.*)

TRIP: Isn't it a bit warm for you? In the coat, I mean.

LUCY: This? Warm? Nah. It's really kind of – (*She pats it down as she speaks.*) substantial, and like I said it could rain at just about – (*She finds something in her pocket and removes it. It's a wrapped deck of cards.*) Oh. Found these in the toilet.

TRIP: Pardon?

LUCY: Yeah. They were right there in the Greyhound toilet. I thought I – thought I remembered it was – I don't know – bad luck or something to pass up a wrapped deck of cards.

TRIP: Bad luck?

LUCY: Maybe it's something I picked up in catechism, just one of those –

TRIP: Do you play?

LUCY: I don't know. Do I?

TRIP: Shall we open them?

LUCY: I don't know. Sure.

TRIP: You're making me warm.

LUCY: All right all right –

TRIP: No no – the coat – it's making me sweat.

LUCY: (*After a beat.*) Go on. Open the deck.

TRIP: What shall we play?

LUCY: I don't know. Whatever.

TRIP: Bridge? Well, of course, we need four to –

LUCY: *Bridge?* It's a little fancy for –

TRIP: Okay okay I know– *baccarat* – no no that's really –

LUCY: Maybe it's not a good – maybe I ought to go

TRIP: Old maid. (*A beat.*) Do you know that one?

(*A pause.*)

LUCY: Now that you mention it, I'm really – maybe I *am* a little warm with the coat but I had this accident –

TRIP: You had a – you're *hurt?*

LUCY: No no I had this – I was in the toilet, on the bus, and you know how sometimes you see things, well, you really don't *see* them fully but perhaps out of the corner of your eye –

TRIP: Quite. Quite. I sometimes–

LUCY: And I saw this, I don't – who *knows* what I thought it was but I thought it was moving like some – it could have been an animal a rodent or or –

TRIP: I *hate* when that happens.

LUCY: Or who knows but – well I didn't *want* to know so I whipped around and caught my leg, I caught my *stocking* on the edge –

TRIP: Oh how horrible –

LUCY: The edge of the metal what do you call – the *waste* bin and well, it's torn all the way up to –

TRIP: I understand. Yes.

LUCY: And it's a funny thing but I really feel somehow exposed or –

TRIP: Naked.

LUCY: Yes with the – without stockings. (*A beat.*) I'm kind of old fashioned. So. So that's why – that's why I'm wearing –

TRIP: The coat.

LUCY: Precisely. (*A beat.*) I've always wanted to learn how to play Solitaire. Sounds like a good one to know for a, you know –

TRIP: A rainy day?

LUCY: Yeah. That's right.

TRIP: Can I see?

LUCY: Can you –

TRIP: The stocking. I might be able to repair –

LUCY: I doubt it.

TRIP: (*After a beat.*) I know all the Solitaire variations.

LUCY: You're a versatile guy. Sprockets. Card games. Stockings. (*A beat.*) I wish I had a camera. Right now.

TRIP: Why?

LUCY: Don't know really.

TRIP: (*Reaching for the pitcher of G and Ts.*) Perhaps you'd like – you'd maybe consider – oh I don't know *what* I'm –
(*Trip knocks over the pitcher. A beat. He begins to sob.*)

LUCY: Hey hey now what the – come on, now – we could get some –

TRIP: I've made such a such a goddamned *fool* of myself out here.

LUCY: No no no don't even think – listen I'm really a terrible bitch but it's –

TRIP: It's just – I'm so *isolated*, you see, and striking up a conversation with a perfectly *ordinary* – oh God you think I'm some kind of a –

LUCY: But it's only my self-preservation *instinct* kicking in – don't take any notice –

TRIP: I should go I should pay the – oh why do I bother –
(*Trip begins to shiver.*)

LUCY: Hey hey wait a min – where the *hell* are the waiters when you need them – are you okay are you gonna be – oh here here –

(*Lucy removes her coat and puts it over Trip's shoulders.*)
Is that better? Is that – oh come on – yes yes breathe deeply breathe – yeah that's right that's – you're fine fine.
(*A pause. Trip stops crying.*)
TRIP: You have lovely legs.
LUCY: (*After a beat.*) I've never seen a man like – listen, you're just too *rich* or something to cry. Okay? (*A beat.*) I don't have lovely legs. But thanks anyway.
TRIP: I meant no –
LUCY: None taken. I better – will you be all right to get – I don't know – wherever you're going?
TRIP: My car is over –
LUCY: Is that yours? The big black what? BMW?
TRIP: Mercedes convertible.
LUCY: Over there – on the beach, that one?
TRIP: Yes. I like driving on sand. Makes me feel young.
LUCY: You're not so old.
TRIP: I'm old enough.
LUCY: Aren't we all.
TRIP: I'm sorry to be such a bother. I usually am much more able –
LUCY: No no no, it's too late in the evening for apologies and – are you okay – you still got the shakes?
TRIP. It's been a long day.
LUCY: Yeah. It's been long.
(*Lucy walks towards the endless horizon. Trip watches her. A pause as she looks out towards the beach.*)
I'll never understand why I talked myself into a beach vacation. I *hate* sand.
(*She turns towards Trip. He sits comfortably, Lucy's coat wrapped around him. He watches her.*)
What are you waiting for? Come on. On your feet.
TRIP: (*Regarding the coat.*) The shoulders are perfect.
LUCY: Up and at 'em. Well. Come on. Come closer.
(*Lucy gestures to Trip. A beat, then: Blackout.*)

END.

Smith and Kraus *Books For Actors*
THE MONOLOGUE SERIES
The Best Men's/Women's Stage Monologues of 1993
The Best Men's/Women's Stage Monologues of 1992
The Best Men's/Women's Stage Monologues of 1991
The Best Men's/Women's Stage Monologues of 1990
One Hundred Men's/Women's Stage Monologues from the 1980's
2 Minutes and Under: Character Monologues for Actors
Street Talk: Character Monologues for Actors
Uptown: Character Monologues for Actors
Monologues from Contemporary Literature: Volume I
Monologues from Classic Plays 468 B.C. to 1960 A.D.
FESTIVAL MONOLOGUE SERIES
The Great Monologues from the Humana Festival
The Great Monologues from the EST Marathon
The Great Monologues from the Women's Project
The Great Monologues from the Mark Taper Forum
YOUNG ACTORS SERIES
Great Scenes and Monologues for Children
New Plays from A.C.T.'s Young Conservatory
Great Scenes for Young Actors from the Stage
Great Monologues for Young Actors
Multicultural Monologues for Young Actors
Multicultural Scenes for Young Actors
SCENE STUDY SERIES
Scenes From Classic Plays 468 B.C. to 1970 A.D.
The Best Stage Scenes of 1993
The Best Stage Scenes of 1992
The Best Stage Scenes for Women from the 1980's
The Best Stage Scenes for Men from the 1980's
CONTEMPORARY PLAYWRIGHTS
Romulus Linney: 17 Short Plays
Eric Overmyer: Collected Plays
Lanford Wilson: 21 Short Plays
William Mastrosimone: Collected Plays
Horton Foote: 4 New Plays
Israel Horovitz: 16 Short Plays
Terrence McNally: 15 Short Plays
Women Playwrights: The Best Plays of 1993
Women Playwrights: The Best Plays of 1992
Humana Festival '93: The Complete Plays
GREAT TRANSLATION FOR ACTORS SERIES
The Wood Demon: Anton Chekhov *translated by N. Saunders & F. Dwyer*
The Seagull: Anton Chekhov *translated by N. Saunders & F. Dwyer*
OTHER BOOKS IN OUR COLLECTION
The Actor's Chekhov
Kiss and Tell: Restoration Scenes, Monologues, & History
Cold Readings: Some Do's and Don'ts for Actors at Auditions

If you require pre-publication information about upcoming Smith and Kraus monologues collections, scene collections, play anthologies, advanced acting books, and books for young actors, you may receive our semi-annual catalogue, free of charge, by sending your name and address to *Smith and Kraus Catalogue, One Main Street, PO Box 127 Lyme, NH 03768. Telephone 603.795.4331 Fax 603.795.4427.*